W9-CIB-342

ISSUES IN EDUCATIONAL RESEARCH

Titles of related interest

KEEVES
Educational Research, Methodology, and Measurement: An International Handbook
(2nd edn)

MASTERS & KEEVES
Advances in Measurement in Educational Research and Assessment

ROBINSON
Problem-Based Methodology: Research for the Improvement of Practice

SCHEERENS & BOSKER
The Foundations of Educational Effectiveness

Related journals – sample copies available on request

Learning and Instruction
International Journal of Educational Research
Studies in Educational Evaluation
Evaluation and Program Planning

Issues in Educational Research

Edited by

John P. Keeves

and

Gabriele Lakomski

1999

PERGAMON
An imprint of Elsevier Science
Amsterdam · Lausanne · New York · Oxford · Shannon · Singapore · Tokyo

ELSEVIER SCIENCE Ltd
The Boulevard, Langford Lane, Kidlington, Oxford OX5 1GB, UK

First edition 1999

Library of Congress Cataloging-in-Publication Data
Issues in educational research
    edited by John P. Keeves and Gabriele Lakomski. — 1st ed.
        p.   cm.
    Includes bibliographical references.
    ISBN 0–08–043349–9
    1. Education—Research. 2. Education-Research-Methodology.
    I. Keeves, John P.   II. Lakomski, Gabriele.
    LB1028.I84   1999
370'.7'2—dc21   98–32190
                                                                                   CIP

British Library Cataloguing in Publication Data
A catalogue record from the British Library has been applied for.

ISBN: 0-08-043349-9

⊚ The paper used in this publication meets the requirements of ANSI/NISO Z39.48-1992 (Permanence of Paper).

Printed in The Netherlands.

Contents

v

The Contributors

Contributors are listed in alphabetical order together with their affiliations. Titles of articles which they have authored follow in alphabetical order, along with the respective page numbers. Where articles are coauthored, this has been indicated by an asterisk preceding the article title.

CLANDININ, D. J. (University of Alberta, Edmonton, Alberta, Canada)
* Narrative Inquiry, 132–140.

CONNELLY, F. M. (Ontario Institute for Studies in Education, University of Toronto, Toronto, Ontario Canada)
* Narrative Inquiry, 132–140.

de LANDSHEERE, G. (Université de Liège, Belgium)
History of Educational Research, 15–30.

DENZIN, N. K. (University of Illinois at Urbana-Champaign, Urbana, Illinois, United States of America)
Biographical Research Methods, 92–102.

EVERS, C. W. (University of Hong Kong, Hong Kong)
* Research in Education: Epistemological Issues, 40–56,
From Foundations to Coherence in Educational Research, 264–279.

GUBA, E. G. (Indiana Univerity, Bloomington, Indiana, United States of America)
* Naturalistic and Rationalistic Enquiry, 141–149.

HAIG, B. D. (University of Canterbury, Christchurch, Canterbury, New Zealand)
Feminist Research Methodology, 222–231.

HOLLINGSWORTH, S. (Michigan State University, East Lansing Michigan, United States of America)
Teachers as Researchers, 57–63.

HOWE, K. R. (University of Colorado, Boulder, Colorado, United States of America)
Equality of Educational Opportunity: Philosophical Issues, 215–221.

HUSÉN, T. (University of Stockholm, Stockholm, Sweden)
Research Paradigms in Education, 31–39.

KAESTLE, C. F. (University of Wisconsin - Madison, Madison, Wisconsin, United States of America)
Historical Methods in Educational Research, 121–131.

KAPLAN, A. (University of Haifa, Haifa, Israel)
Scientific Methods in Educational Research, 79–91.

KEEVES, J. P. (The Flinders University of South Australia, Adelaide, South Australia, Australia)
Overview of Issues in Educational Research, 3–14, * Research in Education: Nature, Needs, and Priorities, 201–214, Measurement in Educational Research, 232–241.

KEMMIS, S. (University of Ballarat, Ballarat, Victoria, Australia)
Action Research, 150–160.

KERDEMAN, D. (University of Washington, Seattle, Washington, United States of America)
* Hermeneutics, 184–197.

LAKOMSKI, G. (University of Melbourne, Melbourne, Victoria Australia)
Critical Theory and Education, 174–183, Symbol Processing, Situated Action, and Social Cognition: Implications for Educational Research and Methodology, 280–301.

LINCOLN, Y. S. (Texas, A & M University, College Station, Texas, United States of America)
* Naturalistic and Rationalistic Enquiry, 141–149.

LUKE, A. (University of Queensland, Brisbane, Queensland, Australia)
Critical Discourse Analysis, 161–173.

MARSHALL, J. (University of Auckland, Auckland, New Zealand)
* Postmodernism, 242–248.

MCKENZIE, P. A. (Australian Council for Educational Research, Melbourne, Victoria, Australia)
* Research in Education: Nature, Needs, and Priorities, 201–214.

NISBET, J. (University of Aberdeen, Aberdeen, Scotland, United Kingdom)
Policy-Oriented Research, 64–75.

ÖDMAN, P. J. (University of Stockholm, Stockholm, Sweden)
    * Hermeneutics, 184–197.

PETERS, M. (University of Auckland, Auckland, New Zealand)
    * Postmodernism, 242–248.

PHILLIPS, D. C. (Stanford University, Stanford, California, United States of America)
    Positivism, Antipositivism, and Empiricism, 249–255.

SMALL, R. (Monash University, Clayton, Victoria, Australia)
    Phenomenology and Existentialism, 256–263.

STURMAN, A. (University of Southern Queensland, Toowoomba, Queensland, Australia)
    Case Study Methods, 103–112.

TAFT, R. (Monash University, Clayton, Victoria, Australia)
    Ethnographic Research Methods, 113–119.

WALKER, J. C. (University of Western Sydney, Nepean, New South Wales, Australia)
    * Research in Education: Epistemological Issues, 40–56.

Preface

This volume on *Issues in Educational Research* has been prepared to provide an overview of the many controversial questions that arise in conferences, symposia, seminars, class discussions in graduate education courses, and in argument, wherever educational research workers meet to talk over a meal or cups of coffee. The issues concerned with the nature of inquiry in the field have been widely debated in terms of the existence of paradigms and the division between decision-oriented and conclusion-oriented strategies of research. In recent years, on the one hand, research that may be described as participatory action research and that leads to the empowerment of individuals and groups, has advanced in popularity and gained in acceptance. On the other hand, there have been important developments in the techniques of measurement and in the statistical analysis of data which have arisen from the increasing power and access to desk-top computers.

The customary distinction advanced by the physical and biological sciences between pure and applied research, or that proposed by social scientists between policy and discipline-oriented research are generally unhelpful when extended to the field of educational research. These distinctions not only fail to take into account the multidisciplinary nature of educational research, but they also ignore the fact that education itself is at the core of the change processes which apply in human affairs.

Furthermore, the distinctions that are commonly drawn between quantitative and qualitative approaches, or between the causal and the interpretative paradigms would not seem to portray accurately the manner in which educational research is conducted. In general, the methods employed to investigate a particular problem situation depend on the nature of the problem, and the extent to which previous research has been undertaken into the problem.

As a consequence, it is of value to assemble into one volume the many different faces of educational research that are advanced by different scholars, each from their own particular orientation. These different perspectives are presented in juxtaposition so that graduate students and research scholars can examine the different views being advanced and debate their meaning with respect to a particular time and research situation.

This volume is presented in three parts. In the first part, general questions are addressed. In the second, those procedures relating to the many different approaches to research are considered. The closing part of the volume considers several important issues facing educational research in the latter years of the twentieth century and that will almost certainly carry over into the early decades of the next.

The editors of this volume accept the challenge provided by the publication to present the view that educational research possesses a unity which extends across different disciplinary perspectives and their methods of inquiry, that rejects the existence of the quantitative and qualitative divide, and that discards the superficial dichotomies of basic and applied, or conclusion-oriented and decision-oriented, or disciplinary and policy research. This unity of the educational research enterprise is presented as having sound epistemological foundations. Positivism is rejected in its various forms, as well as the idea of multiple realities. The purpose of inquiry in educational research is the building of a coherent body of knowledge that has been examined against evidence from the real world, and that is available for transforming the real world through human agency and social action. This view of the unity of educational research permeates many of the articles presented in this volume. However, the articles in this volume are written by a large number of different authors, each of whom has an individual view of the nature of educational research. The volume seeks to present these different views and does not deliberately restrict itself to a single perspective. The debate that must inevitably occur is supported and strengthened by the alternative views. Nevertheless, the editors have sought to present their stand on the unity of educational research as well as a clear international perspective, in the hope that a rich and coherent consensus will be formed worldwide about the nature of the endless quest into the aspects of human activity covered by the processes of education.

The purpose of this Preface is to answer four specific questions in order to explain the principles that have guided the selection of articles for this volume.

1. What are the key issues that the volume seeks to address and that are considered to be central to debate about educational research at the turn of the millennium?
2. What are the relationships between the three parts into which the volume is divided?
3. What are the links between this volume and the first and second editions of the *International Encyclopedia of Education*, and what principles guided the preparation of this present volume?
4. How can this volume and the various sources of information incorporated within it best be used?

Key issues

There are many issues that arise directly and indirectly from the articles presented in this volume and it is necessary to restrict this listing of key issues to those that are considered to be central to the research enterprise in education. As a consequence, the ten issues enumerated are perhaps best seen as a personal list provided by the editors for the purposes of debate and discussion rather than as a definitive statement.

1. Are there two main paradigms associated with educational research, that can be seen to be complementary, or is there an essential unity of educational research?
2. Has educational research advanced a body of knowledge about educational processes, or do the findings of educational research merely serve as guidance for policy and practice?
3. What are the relationships between theory and practice and why have schools and universities been so successful in enabling learning during the twentieth century?
4. Is the distinction between quantitative and qualitative research methods meaningful, and does it lead to incompatible approaches to research?
5. Do the many different disciplines that contribute to educational research each bring its own distinct methods of inquiry to the examination of education and educational processes, so that it is **not** meaningful to view educational research as a unity?
6. Is there a difference between an analytic approach to educational research as contrasted with a systemic or holistic approach that prevents research activity into educational processes being viewed as coherent and unified?
7. Does critical theory draw on a body of knowledge about educational processes and does it contribute to the advancement of a body of knowledge?
8. Does social action necessarily involve the perspectives of critical theory, and does education involve training in the use of social action?
9. Do the perspectives of postmodernism and the existence of multiple realities deny the meaningfulness of inquiry into educational problems?
10. Can recently acquired knowledge about how human minds or brains work contribute to an understanding of the processes of inquiry and the methods used in educational research?

These and many other issues are addressed either directly or indirectly in this volume. In general terms the ten issues listed above have been advanced by identifying issues from each of the three parts of the volume in order of presentation. There is, however, considerable overlap both between issues and between parts. Moreover, the views and perspectives of the editors intrude into both the issues listed, into the choice of articles, and into the statements made within the articles for which they are directly responsible. Nevertheless, these qualifications should not serve to close debate and controversy but should, hopefully, extend the discussion which it is intended that this volume would serve to support as well as assist in the resolution of some of these issues.

In order to clarify presentation, and as mentioned earlier this volume has been divided into three parts.

Part I   Introduction

In Part I the opening article provides a view of the nature of systematic inquiry and, in particular, in the field of education (see *Overview of Issues in Educational Research*). It is followed by an article on the *History of Educational Research* from its beginnings about 100 years ago. The articles that follow consider the problem of paradigms in educational research (see *Research Paradigms in Education*) and the epistemological foundations of educational inquiry (see *Research in Education: Epistemological Issues*). Likewise, it can be asked whether educational research is an activity for highly trained research workers or whether it is an activity in which classroom teachers can also engage to improve their day-to-day work in schools (see *Teachers as Researchers*). There are, however, larger problems associated with policy making in education to which educational research can contribute (see *Policy-Oriented Research*).

Part II   The range of approaches

An increasing number of alternative and different approaches to research are being employed in the investigation of educational problems. No longer is there a simple dichotomy between the scientific and the humanistic approaches, although in some English-speaking countries such a split is commonly forced upon scholars during their secondary school years by specialization and what Snow has referred to as the two cultures (Snow, 1964). The articles in this part present the growing number of approaches that are currently being used in educational research. Not all of the diverse approaches can be expected to survive through the twenty-first century as further new methods of investigation are added. However, at the close of the twentieth century, each of the approaches listed has a following among educational researchers.

This part is introduced by an article on the conduct of inquiry within the empirical research tradition. A series of articles follow which are derived, in the main, from the methods employed as different disciplinary strategies are used to investigate educational problems.

Further articles in the part consider those approaches being employed in educational research from the perspectives of critical theory, and with concern for the context within which the research is conducted.

Part III   Issues

The concluding part opens with an article on *Research in Education, Nature, Needs and Priorities*, which warns of the dangers of establishing rigid priorities for the funding of research, and considers which issues and which studies should be supported. Consideration of issues in two areas of current interest in educational research in the quest for greater social equity follow (see *Equality of Educational Opportunity: Philosophical Issues*; and *Feminist Research Methodology*). These issues have given rise to fields of priority for research and social action during the latter half of the twentieth century in many parts of the world.

An article on more technical matters is presented next. It is concerned with *Measurement in Educational Research*. Three rather more general articles follow that would seem to have their origins in a challenge to empirical research and the examination of data by statistical analysis. These articles are concerned with *Postmodernism; Positivism, Antipositivism, and Empiricism*; and *Phenomenology and Existentialism*. The impact of the debate on the issues considered in these articles has profound consequences for educational and social research, since they address attempts being made to question the feasibility and meaningfulness of building a coherent body of knowledge about education and educational processes.

The concluding articles in the volume address directly the issue of the unity of educational research (see *From Foundations to Coherence in Educational Research*; and *Symbol Processing, Situated Action and Social Cognition: Implications for Educational Research and Methodology*) and present the editors' views of a way forward that is coherent and likely to be fruitful.

The preparation of this volume

This volume has been developed from the first and second editions of the *International Encyclopedia of Education* which were edited by Torsten Husén and Neville Postlethwaite with the assistance of an editorial board and which were published in 1985 and 1994 respectively. Both editions of the Encyclopedia were organized around areas of scholarly specialization related to education. One area was concerned with educational research, methodology and measurement, and another with the philosophy of education, and this volume draws largely on articles from these two areas. After the second edition of the Encyclopedia was published, it was recognized that there was a need for a series of shorter collections of articles for university teachers and graduate students, who were reading and studying in different spheres of educational inquiry. Thus it was proposed that a volume should be prepared that was concerned with issues in educational research. Between the time of publication of the first and second editions of the Encyclopedia and this volume, developments in educational research methods proceeded apace and some new entries were commissioned for publication in this volume. In addition, some authors have revised their entries before publication. Thus, every effort has been made to ensure that the material presented in this volume is as up to date and as relevant as possible.

How to use this volume

Educational research draws on diverse disciplines that have a bearing on problems in the field of education. In addition, over recent decades educational research has built up a body of theoretical knowledge concerned with the processes of education and has developed a battery of methodological strategies, as well as a range of analytical procedures that are particularly suited to the problems encountered in educational research. While it is the editors' contention that there is a coherence running through this volume that is consistent with the unity that exists in the domain of educational research, this volume must be seen as a compendium of entries, written by different scholars with different research traditions and drawn from different countries of the world. Thus, the volume is intended as a reference or a source book for university and college teachers to use in the preparation of lectures; for graduate students to use as a first introduction to issues in educational research; and for practising research workers to obtain information on the research approaches associated with their work. As a consequence of the inclusion of articles on so many topics in a single volume, it is clear that no individual entry can be complete in itself. Therefore, each entry seeks not only to be relevant and up-to-date, but also to provide guidance, through a concise set of references and a bibliography to key articles or publications likely to be readily available, from which the scholar, student, teacher or research worker could obtain further information. Furthermore, in order to facilitate the search for information, references are provided within each entry to other entries in the volume where related information has been presented.

In addition, both a detailed Name Index and a Subject Index based on key words or phrases have been compiled to assist the reader in the search for information. As a consequence, the user of this volume who wants information on a specific topic could begin by looking up appropriate words in the Subject Index in order to locate either an entry related to the topic or to identify entries where the topic as referenced by the key words is considered. In a similar way, the Name Index can be used to locate references to the writings of a particular author who is known to have made a substantial contribution to a sphere of research related to the issue on which information is sought. In order to facilitate this task, page numbers are given both for the bibliographic reference and for the point at which the reference is cited in the text.

Acknowledgements

No work of this nature could be published without considerable effort by many people. To several of these people a special debt of gratitude is due. First, we are grateful to Torsten Husén and Neville Postlethwaite who guided the preparation of the first and second editions of the *International Encyclopedia of Education*. Second, we are grateful to the many authors who prepared entries, carefully checked galley proofs, revised their entries and in many cases acted as consultants for other entries in the volume. Third, we are very grateful to Barbara Barrett, Editorial Director of the Encyclopedias, and to Tony Seward who directed the work on the preparation of this volume, as well as to David Lamkin who supervised the many different aspects of the production task. Finally, we are grateful to

Frances Anderson and Teresa Hayton who have assisted with the typing of entries in connection with the preparation of this volume. To them all our sincere thanks are offered.

JOHN P. KEEVES
The Flinders University Institute of International Education
The Flinders University of South Australia

GABRIELE LAKOMSKI
The Faculty of Education
The University of Melbourne

Reference

Snow, C. P. 1964 *The Two Cultures: A Second Look.* Cambridge University Press, Cambridge.

Part I

Introduction

1 Overview of Issues in Educational Research

J. P. Keeves

The nature and purpose of educational research is the subject of ongoing debate not only in the columns of educational journals but also in the seminar rooms and at conferences where the findings of research into education and educational processes are presented. No course in educational research can fail to grapple with this problem, because of the consequences for approval of research studies for higher degrees, for the acceptance of theses, the selection of articles for publication and the allocation of funding for research. Simple dichotomies of research activity into "basic or applied", "discipline-oriented" or "policy oriented", "conclusion-oriented" or "decision-oriented", and "analytic" or "systemic" do not provide adequately for the complexity of the activities undertaken in educational research. Nevertheless, tensions exist between the proponents of alternative approaches into the investigation of educational problems. These tensions have been known to split schools of education, to lead to marked changes in the editorial policy of journals, to prejudice the funding of research in education, and to lead politicians and senior educational administrators to denigrate the field of educational inquiry.

It is an objective of this volume to present the alternative views of educational research for open debate and discussion in seminar rooms, and to encourage and facilitate the addressing of the many issues raised in student writings and conference addresses. However, it is also a purpose of the editors of this volume to present in this opening article and in the article that concludes this volume a view of educational research as a unified field that has been remarkably successful over recent decades in the accumulation of a substantial body of knowledge about education. The research enterprise in education draws on many disciplines and employs a wide variety of approaches to investigation, but this research activity has a unity of purpose and a unified epistemological basis that demands the rejection of alternative paradigms of inquiry. Morever, there is a rejection of the misleading dichotomy of research procedures into qualitative and quantitative methods, since it is argued that the choice of procedures to be employed depends on the nature of the problem under investigation.

The successes of educational research activity in the past half-century since the cessation of World War II, and more particularly the three decades since the mid-1960s, is seen in the compilations of knowledge about education that are presented in the first and second editions of the *International Encyclopedia of Education*. This corpus of knowledge is rather more than an accumulated body of wisdom and a related set of practices associated with education. Wisdom no longer refers to "knowledge of an abstruse kind", but rather to the "quality of being wise in relation to conduct and the choice of ends and means" in particular situations (New Shorter Oxford Dictionary, 1994, p. 3700). The knowledge generated by research activity must be debated among scholars and tested against evidence from the real world and stored and structured in a coherent way prior to further review and testing. Failure to view the products of educational research as a coherent body of knowledge would seem to misunderstand the nature of the research enterprise. Educational research, furthermore, has a unique function in this enterprise in so far as it not only involves the construction of a body of knowledge, but it also involves the investigation of the processes by which all knowledge is passed on to successive generations and by which the skills of inquiry are acquired, as well as the processes by which social action is initiated. These ideas about the functions of education and educational inquiry are developed in the pages that follow.

Nevertheless, it must be recognized from the outset that education involves practical activity, and that knowledge about the processes of education does not remain passive but is translated and implemented in educational practices and policies in many different forms and at many different levels. As a consequence, the ways in which the findings of educational research are applied are not only of considerable importance, but also warrant systematic investigation through educational research. The application of knowledge about education rarely takes place through technology and applied science, as do most of the findings of scientific research but rather through social action. These ideas are also developed in the following pages.

1   Concerning the nature of knowledge

Popper and Eccles (1997) have distinguished between three different worlds involved in human inquiry. The entities of the real world which include physical objects, as well as the various structures crated by human society and which include schools and universities, form **World 1**. The world of subjective experiences comprises **World 2**, a world of individual mental states, that comprises the states of conscious thought and psychological dispositions as well as the unconscious states of minds of individuals. Wisdom is an entity in World 2. There is, however, in addition, **World 3** which has been created as a new objective world, that is the product of human minds. It should be noted that World 3 not only contains the corporate body of propositional knowledge concerned with causal explanation, but also the works of art, music and literary writings that are all part of the world of shared knowledge. The important point is that World 3 objects have acquired a reality of their own.

The body of propositional knowledge that has been assembled by the natural sciences has been used to transform the real world through technology (Conant, 1947). It has been the marked success of research and development in the physical and biological sciences acting through technology that has advanced the standing of scientific inquiry. Figure 1 presents in diagrammatic form some of the relationships that exist between these three worlds of inquiry and technology.

Research is concerned with the processes of inquiry which involve interactions between World 1 – The Real World, World 2 – The Learner's Mind, and World 3 – The Body of Knowledge. The processes of inquiry involving relationships between World 1 and World 2 in which individuals employ the knowledge they possess to investigate the real world may be referred to as **Heurism**. The knowledge that research workers hold in their minds influences the ways in which they view the real world and the issues that they address in their research activities. Thus, there is a two way interaction between World 2 and World 1 in the heuristic process as indicated by the adjacent dotted and continuous lines in Figure 1.

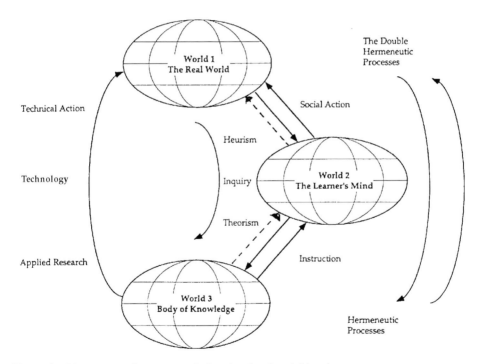

Figure 1   The nature and processes of educational and social inquiry.

Research is also concerned with the processes operating between World 2 and World 3 which may be referred to as **Theorism**. These processes include the formulation of generalizations, the building, testing and revising of models derived from theory and the subsequent advancement, modification or rejection of theory. The skills of theorism are largely taught in universities, while the skills of heurism are taught in schools as well as in higher education.

Again the interaction between World 2 and World 3 involves reciprocal processes that are indicated by adjacent dotted and continuous lines in Figure 1. Together heurism and theorism form the processes of inquiry. The manner and the context within which they work, or the manner in which the "messages of the gods are conveyed to human beings" for the formation of knowledge involve the **hermeneutic processes** (see *Hermeneutics*).

The hermeneutic examination of these processes in education and the social sciences has long been established in continental Europe. It involves the study of meaning and comprises the theory and practice of interpretation and the generation of understandings of the different social contexts in which human beings learn about the world in which they live and work. The hermeneutic method has developed from many different facets of scholarly inquiry in the social sciences, and its goal is that of understanding in the study of human actions within a social context. Moreover, this approach recognizes that in order to obtain meaning with respect to how and why humans act, it is necessary for an investigator to enter into dialogue with the human agents.

Giddens (1984) argues that a **double hermeneutic process** is also involved. There is not only the frame of meaning acquired by individuals in order to view the real world. This involves an interaction between World 2 and World 1 as shown in Figure 1. There is also a second frame of meaning constructed by the same individuals as they view the world of shared knowledge (World 3) and assimilate the ideas developed by social and behavioral scientists. In Figure 1 this would require interaction between World 3 and World 2. Thus, it is necessary to consider not only the meanings given by lay persons to the events of the real world (World 1), but also the ideas and relationships that are constructed from the body of knowledge (World 3), which is developed as the result of scholarly inquiry.

The accumulation of wisdom takes place in World 2 and in the minds of those individuals who, as a consequence of experience, develop wisdom which they can apply in particular contexts. Wisdom is fed by knowledge from World 3, but is not necessarily codified and structured as is stored knowledge and is not necessarily subjected to tests of coherence. Wisdom is unique to individuals, is slow to form, and is applied by individuals critically and practically. It is this individual knowledge that constructivist research is investigating.

It should be noted that education plays a highly significant role in these processes. It operates to transmit the essential ideas and relationships held in World 3 to the minds of the individuals who form World 2. However, education is not only involved in transmitting knowledge. Since the body of knowledge contained in World 3 is now so vast, there is the task of selecting or making simple and coherent the extensive and complex ideas and relationships of World 3, for communication in ways that permit the assimilation and structuring of these ideas and relationships in the minds of individuals. Educators are not only the purveyors of knowledge but they are also the gatekeepers of knowledge. It is these many processes that are referred to as the **double hermeneutic processes**, since the knowledge passes back from World 3 to influence perceptions of World 1. Furthermore, educators are responsible for training students in the skills of inquiry which include the processes of heurism and theorism.

2 The nature of social action

In the first half of the twentieth century, research workers in education and the social and behavioral sciences were conducting their inquiries within the perspectives of functionalism, positivism and naturalism. They sought universal generalizations about the social and behavioral world that could be applied to transform society in much the same way that scientific knowledge is applied through technology and technical action to change the physical and biological worlds. The dichotomy widely employed in the classification of research into **pure science** and **applied science** still reflects thinking that is largely inappropriate in education and the social and behavioral sciences. Earlier in this century the dream of many research workers in education and the social and behavioral sciences was that by obtaining knowledge about the processes of human life it would be possible to transform and control the social and behavioral world in much the same way as technology had transformed and controlled the physical world. However, politicians, administrators and natural scientists today accuse educational researchers for their failure to produce results that have direct application, because they view things in this way. This view of educational research and its application is both incomplete and inadequate.

In the mid-1950s and early 1960s it was possible to answer the critics of educational research with proposals for both increased funding and significant expansion of research activity. It was commonly claimed that with increased resources and effort both important generalizations and significant practical applications would emerge. There is no doubt that the increased resources provided for educational research, in particular, transformed this area of inquiry in the period of 20 years from the mid-1960s to the mid-1980s. An immense body of knowledge about educational, social, and psychological processes was assembled, that is only now being assimilated in a coherent and meaningful way. Nevertheless, it is also apparent that few universal generalizations have emerged that can be directly applied to benefit either educational practice or the operation of society.

Giddens (1984) has argued that there has been a failure to understand in an adequate way the nature of social action in the context of changes in social theory. He maintains that the technological view of the application of the findings of educational and social science research is grossly inadequate. Moreover, he contends that there is a sense in which such a view has seriously underestimated the practical impact of research in education and the social sciences on both daily life and on society.

In the quest for universal generalizations in the study of educational processes and in social research there has been a failure to recognize the existence of World 2 and the role of human agents in society. In the study of educational problems and societal processes, human beings as a group do not remain as passive subjects of inquiry. They comprehend the debate which arises during the formulation of ideas, and they not only assimilate these ideas, but they also accommodate to them and are changed. As Figure 1 shows, World 3, the world of shared knowledge, interacts with World 2, the world of personal knowledge, to such an extent that the views and perceptions held by human agents of World 1, the world of real things, are also changed.

Since the real world is itself unknowable without these views and perceptions which are held by human beings, the very foundations of human knowledge, are without certainty. Furthermore, a situation arises in which generalizations are advanced, but their existence has been generated from the educational and social theories held by research workers. Thus, perceptions of the educational and social world are changed by the theories that have been developed by research, and as a consequence the generalizations that are generated from research are also subject to change and are not universal or permanent laws and principles.

It is clear that Popper and Eccles (1977) are concerned with the same issues, approaching their problems from the perspective of the natural scientist. However, the problems are of greater magnitude in the social and behavioral sciences and in education, because human beings act as social agents. Furthermore, universal schooling and widespread higher and recurrent education have during recent decades facilitated the dissemination of the advances in educational, social and behavioral knowledge through paperback publications, journal articles, and the mass media. As a consequence the rate of change in both educational and social processes has been greatly increased, as has the perceptions and understandings of those processes.

3   Using the findings of educational research

There are, therefore, important reasons why it is not possible to point to a substantial number of universal generalizations that have been generated by educational, social and behavioral research. When from a study of human action, new ideas and concepts emerge which explain an educational or social process in a clearer way than members of society were previously able to provide, these ideas are appropriated by those members of society and incorporated back into their thinking and their social lives. These ideas have the effect of changing perceptions of education and social life, as well as the effect of subsequently changing the nature of the ideas and concepts of educational and social theory. Furthermore, the behavior and social actions that follow from these ideas and concepts are also changed, and as a consequence the initial and tentative generalizations that were formed from earlier research no longer hold. Such generalizations may need to be completely reformulated in terms of new ideas and new theory.

In many highly developed countries, including for example, the United States and Australia, the changing concepts of equality of educational opportunity and equity in education, as well as the ideas and theories of the melting-pot, cultural mosaic, and multiculturalism, reflect this relative rapid emergence of new ideas of relevance to education (see *Equality of Educational Opportunity: Philosophical Issues*). It is not the case that the initial views and generalizations associated with the educational and social processes were necessarily wrong, but rather that the ideas were so powerful that they changed the social processes themselves as well as the perceptions of them. The original ideas were not trivial or of little consequence, but as a result of their formulation, discussion and dissemination by educators, views of society were changed, society itself was changed by consequent social action, and the ideas themselves were subsequently subjected to change.

The impact of new ideas and theories in the social sciences depends upon how human agents assimilate and accommodate to new ideas through education. From these perspectives it would seem likely that educational and social theory may have had a more powerful and more rapid influence on daily life in societies throughout the world than has technological development. Moreover, the task of dissemination and discussion of ideas and developments in educational and social theory falls on education. Thus, education contributes to social change both as a source of ideas, as well as providing the key processes through which such ideas are introduced widely and change is subsequently implemented.

4 The unity of educational research

Since the early 1970s, a conflict has emerged in educational research concerning both the purposes and methods of inquiry. Alternative perspectives have been proposed and accepted by many. The value of alternative approaches is not to be denied, since the scholarly debate that follows and the exploratory use of these alternative approaches adds vitality to the field. The increased resources provided for educational research during the 1960s and 1970s led scholars from many different social science disciplines to study educational problems and to work alongside the historians and philosophers who had over a long period been interested in educational issues. These newcomers brought with them new methods and new perspectives.

Husén (see *Research Paradigms in Education*) argues that these many different perspectives constitute two main paradigms – the scientific and the humanistic which he contends "are not exclusive, but complementary to each other". Nevertheless, a case can be argued that the drawing of a distinction between these two approaches cannot be sustained to the extent that they are to be regarded as two different paradigms. It is necessary to recognize that these perspectives have their origins in long-standing philosophical traditions. Dilthey in the 1890s drew the distinctions, in connection with research conducted in the field of psychology, between interpretation or understanding (*Verstehen*) and explanation in causal terms (*Erklären*). Dilthey suggested that the former was the goal of humanistic research, and the latter the goal of scientific research. Von Wright (1971) subsequently traced the interpretative tradition with its emphasis on understanding back to Aristotle. This approach argued that things happen in the way that they do in terms of intentions, motives and expressed reasons. The alternative tradition of advancing a causal explanation was said by Von Wright to have originated with Galileo.

It must be recognized that these two traditions have been fed during the twentieth century by the specialization that has taken place in upper secondary schools and in universities into two major strands of learning – the humanities and the sciences. Snow (1964) advanced the view that this specialization had led to the formation of "two cultures", since the burden of developing skills and acquiring foundational knowledge in both areas had become so great that very few students could be expected to develop competence in both areas.

Since these distinctions between the humanistic and the scientific approaches which have emerged in educational research would appear to have had their origins in different philosophical traditions of long standing, it is necessary to ask:

(1) whether it is possible to bring these two traditions together in a unified approach;
(2) whether one approach should be superseded by the other;
(3) whether both must be abandoned, since neither can be meaningfully endorsed; or
(4) whether both should be maintained, because they each have different goals.

The position adopted by de Landsheere (see *History of Educational Research*) and by Husén (see *Research Paradigms in Education*) would seem to be the fourth option in which the two traditions are regarded as complementary. This position permits both lines of research to continue and to contribute. Other scholars (see *Naturalistic and Rationalistic Enquiry*) would seem to argue for the second position. They draw distinctions between the two paradigmatic approaches in such a way that there is no possibility of reconciliation between their naturalistic paradigm in which there are multiple perceptions of reality and the scientific paradigm, which is translated by them into a positivistic approach.

Evers and Walker (see *Research in Education: Epistemological Issues* and *From Foundations to Coherence in Educational Research*) are concerned with the basic question as to whether these two approaches involve "different ways of knowing or forms of knowledge". If the two approaches are associated with mutually incompatible ways of investigating World 1, then the educational research worker must of necessity make a choice between the two. In the course of time, it would be expected that one of the two ways of knowing would cease to provide meaningful answers to the problems investigated and the other would survive. In addition, they address the question as to whether or not the two paradigms can both be said to exist. Since each paradigm includes both substantive theories and the methods to be employed for assessing the strength of those theories, there is, unfortunately, no position from which a theory of paradigms could be assessed. The issue could not be resolved by the use of procedures employed by either or both.

If the view is accepted, as has already been done earlier in this article, that observations of the real world are greatly influenced by the knowledge about that world held by individuals and by groups, then there are no sound epistemological bases for differences between the extreme views of how educational research should be undertaken. If investigators working with both the scientific and humanistic approaches seek to investigate the real world and to build a simple and coherent body of knowledge about education and its processes, then they are engaging in a common enterprise of inquiry associated with the interactions between World 2 and World 1 and between World 2 and World 3 in order to add to the corpus of knowledge in World 3. If they do not seek to add to the knowledge stored in World 3, it might well be argued that they are not engaged in the research enterprise in the field of education.

If, however, they are engaged in adding to the body of knowledge, both of the long-standing traditions considered above must be rejected and in addition, the positivist and the naturalistic positions must also be abandoned (see *Positivism, Antipositivism and Empiricism*). Under these circumstances the idea of two or more paradigms can no longer be sustained and the case must be endorsed for unity in educational research. This does not mean a denial of the humanistic and scientific approaches to research. Nor does it imply any rejection of the well established disciplinary methods that are being employed with profit in educational research world-wide. However, it does lead to the adoption of a common approach to educational inquiry in which researchers and practitioners work together to solve educational problems.

Such a perspective, that acknowledges a unified approach, would also permit psychologists to work on educational problems in a laboratory setting and under experimental conditions in the search for a generalization that might be considered to be a universal finding. They would employ procedures similar to those used by the natural scientist. This perspective would also provide for classroom teachers to involve themselves in action research which is directed towards a very practical problem that had arisen in the classroom situation (see *Teachers as Researchers; Action Research*). Furthermore, it would incorporate within the field of educational research the ethnographer who sought an interpretative view of a specific school or classroom situation that would yield a deeper understanding of the school or classroom processes (see *Ethnographic Research Methods*). These educational researchers might not only seek new solutions to practical problems but also new ideas and new knowledge. It is important, moreover, that the ideas developed during such research and the relationships investigated and tested should be incorporated into the body of knowledge relating to education, and should not merely accumulate as the professional wisdom of a few privileged individuals.

5   Coherence – the test of knowledge

The issue remaining to be addressed is concerned with the testing, for inclusion in World 3, of the knowledge assembled, in the minds of individual persons in World 2. It is necessary to determine whether the assembled knowledge corresponds with events in the real world – World 1, which is viewed from the perspective of those individuals in World 2 who hold that knowledge. Educational knowledge, like knowledge in other domains, evolves in unsystematic and unplanned ways. In general, knowledge develops with several alternative and competing theories, each with limited usefulness. Sometimes these theories over-lap, sometimes they are very different. At different stages in the development of a sphere of knowledge, one theory may be given credence or may hold a dominant position, only to be superseded by an alternative theory as new evidence becomes available. The validation or verification of hypotheses and models derived from theory and subsequently of the theory itself is undertaken to varying degrees with five criteria that have been advanced by Quine and Ullian (1978) in an approach referred to as **coherentism**:

(1) **fruitfulness**, since theory gives rise to explanation and to new ideas;
(2) **testability**, since a theory that cannot be subjected to testing leads nowhere;
(3) **generality**, since a theory must have sufficient generality to address a range of related situations;
(4) **coherence**, since the various parts of a theory must link together to support each other; and
(5) **simplicity**, since a theory must not collapse under its own weight.

It is evident that the purposes of a theory are to unify and systematize knowledge. However, since a theory is never complete, these purposes are never fully achieved. Nevertheless, in the field of education remarkable progress has been made in the 30 years from the mid-1960s.

It is also necessary to ask whether research into educational problems demands an approach to inquiry which is different from that used in other domains of knowledge. Some argue that all knowledge of human activity is essentially subjective, since it involves unique events, the meanings ascribed to those events by individuals, and the responses made by individuals according to the nature of the events and the meanings ascribed. However, educational research is succeeding in building a corpus of theoretical knowledge about educational processes. In addition, educational research is engaged in a quest for evidence that ties the world of theory – World 3 to the real world – World 1, and in the testing of theory against evidence in order to reject or endorse the adequacy of the theory. The epistemological basis of this process does not differ whether quantitative or qualitative methods of inquiry are employed, and whether or not measuring instruments are developed and used (see *Measurement in Educational Research*).

There is in addition to the humanistic and scientific approaches to educational research a third approach that is directed towards social action, after taking into account the particular nature of an educational problem. This approach involves what has become known as **critical theory** or **critical action research**. However, critical theory is primarily engaged in social action and is concerned with the relationships between World 2 and World 1, and the assembling of sufficient supportive opinion in World 2 to effect change in World 1. Ideas may be derived from World 3, but critical theory does not generally seek to contribute to the body of knowledge in World 3, and would not seem to acknowledge the body of theory already available in World 3 (see *Critical Theory and Education; Action Research*). Nevertheless, research from this perspective does not seek to investigate a real world situation, prior to the introduction of change, in order to maximize the effects of change.

6   The alternatives: ectopia

Late twentieth century thought has given rise to scholarly activity that questions any attempts to build a unified body of knowledge. The gaining of knowledge, from this perspective, ceases to be an end in itself. Some supporters of this view contend that since there are many different perceptions of the real world there are many different versions of reality. The version of reality under consideration at any particular time is seen as relative to the perspective adopted. Moreover, relativism demands multiple views of reality. This position is adopted in opposition to empiricism, that argues that knowledge is tested by experience through the senses and introspection, and to rationalism that argues that reason underpins human knowledge (see *Positivism, Antipositivism, and Empiricism*). Supporters of this position commonly contend that they are rejecting positivism. However, there is often a misunderstanding of what positivism involves, since the philosophical approach of coherentism, outlined in the previous section of this article does not involve positivism. It merely requires that theory is tested against evidence drawn from the real world, and should satisfy the requirements of having generality, coherence and simplicity. As might be expected there are several strands of thought within postmodernism as this alternative approach has come to be known (see *Postmodernism*) Whether these different strands of postmodernism could achieve the level of fruitfulness necessary to ensure their survival, or whether they could maintain their strength merely as forces of opposition to economic rationalism and scientific empiricism remains to be seen. Nevertheless, their impact on educational institutions and the study of education, would appear to have led to a decline of interest in issues relating to the history of education, the philosophy of education and the study of the classics of literature. In their place ideas are introduced that have their origins in phenomenology and existentialism with a marked emphasis in education on the development of interpersonal relations, with the school as a social institution fostering these relationships (see *Phenomenology and Existentialism*).

7   A coherent approach to educational research

All research into educational problems necessarily lacks secure foundations in the real world, since what is observed is influenced by the theories that direct the observations being made. There is need in educational inquiry to reorient the issues addressed not to the foundations for the observations, but rather to the consequences of the observations. As Kaplan (1964) has pointed out, such an approach is prospective rather than retrospective. If the emphasis in educational research shifts from the foundations to the outcomes of the research, whether in terms of contributing to theory or towards social action or to both, then the choice of problems to be investigated is made in terms of the significance and consequences of the findings rather than the firmness of the foundations. However, in the choice of problems, the part played by values cannot be denied. Thus, values enter into inquiry not only in the selection of problems, but also in the order in which problems are treated, as well as the resources of time and money spent on their resolution through research (see *Research in Education, Nature, Needs and Priorities*).

In educational research, the conflict between the proponents of the scientific and humanistic approaches to inquiry lacks a sound epistemological basis. Although there are two different traditions involved, each of which is supported by the specialization occurring in schools and universities, a coherentist approach to inquiry rejects any maintenance of these distinctions at the level of two different paradigms. There are, however, a variety of methods that are available for the conduct of research, as well as an emerging synthesis in social theory that could guide research into educational problems. One of the newer forms of research activity involves the analysis of the specified problem, the review of known and relevant research and the development of policy alternatives for consideration, prior to the introduction of new policies or the provision of support for changed practices (see *Policy-Oriented Research*). The methods employed in educational inquiry should then be influenced by the nature of the problems being considered. Furthermore, the problems investigated should be those that contribute most, both to change in the real world, as well as to the building of a coherent body of knowledge about education and educational processes.

References

Conant, J. B. 1947 *On Understanding Science*. Oxford University Press, Oxford.
Giddens, A. 1984 *The Constitution of Society*. Polity Press, Cambridge and Blackwell, Oxford.
Kaplan, A. 1964 *The Conduct of Inquiry*. Chandler, San Francisco.
Popper, K. R. and Eccles, J. C. 1977 *The Self and its Brain*. Springer International, Berlin.
Quine, W. V. and Ullian, J. S. 1978 *The Web of Belief*. Random House, London.
Snow, C. P. 1964 *The Two Cultures: A Second Look*. Cambridge University Press, Cambridge.
Von Wright, G. H. 1971 *Explanation and Understanding*. Routledge and Kegan Paul, London.

2 History of Educational Research

G. de Landsheere

Educational research as disciplined inquiry with an empirical basis was first known as "experimental pedagogy". This term was analogous to that of "experimental psychology", an expression coined by Wundt in Leipzig around 1880. Experimental pedagogy was founded around 1900 by Lay and Meumann in Germany; Binet and Simon in France; Rice, Thorndike, and Judd in the United States; and Claparède in Switzerland. Some years earlier, three publications – *Die Steele des Kindes* by Preyer, a German medical doctor, in 1882; *The Study of Children* by Hall in the United States in 1883; and articles by an English psychologist, Sully, in 1884 concerned with children's language and imagination – marked the beginning of the child study movement. Although progress was slow during the 1880s, the foundations were laid through this movement for research into related educational problems. From 1900 onward, in the study of educational problems, four movements can be identified: (a) the child study movement, where educational research was associated with applied child psychology; (b) the New Education or progressive movement where philosophy took precedence over science, and life experience over experimentation; (c) the scientific research movement, with initially a positivist approach; and (d) the humanistic research movement which has emerged since the 1960s and draws on the methods of research employed in sociology, anthropology, politics, history, philosophy, and linguistics.

During the first period (1900–30), Cronbach and Suppes (1969) speak of a "heyday of empiricism", empirical educational research focused on rational management of instruction, that challenged the concept of transfer of training, and advanced the development of new curricula, psychological testing, administrative surveys (school attendance, failure rates, etc.), and normative achievement surveys. Descriptive statistics were already well-established, and in the 1920s and 1930s inferential statistics and data analysis developed rapidly.

In the second period (1930 to the late 1950s), however, the strict scientific approach to education lost impetus to make room, practically all over the developed world, for the more philosophically oriented and innovative progressivism. Behind this shift were three factors: (a) the atomistic character of most educational research; (b) a questioning of the

15

scientific approach to the management of education at a time when there was an economic crisis soon to be followed by war; and (c) the charisma of the progressive movement with its combination of empirical research and a social and political philosophy merging free enterprise and liberal spirit with humanistic socialism.

Nevertheless, during this period, interest in cognitive development and language studies continued with the work of Piaget in Switzerland, and Vygotsky, who died in 1934, and his associates Luria and Leontief in the Soviet Union. In addition, a new strand of enquiry was opened up in the field of the sociology of education with the publication in 1994 of *Who Shall be Educated*? by Warner *et al.* (1946) in the United States. These authors brought together a substantial body of research to establish that schooling in the United States favoured White children from an urban middle-class background. Studies into adolescence and adolescent development soon followed.

In the third period (1960s and 1970s) a knowledge "explosion" took place and its applications to all fields of research really began. Educational research was soon influenced by this dynamic development. In the United States, challenged by Soviet technological advances (e.g., Sputnik) and being economically affluent, governmental and private agencies supported educational research to an unprecedented extent. A similar development, although not so spectacular, occurred in other highly industrialized countries. During the 1960s the computer added a new dimension to educational research leading to the introduction of sophisticated experimental design and massive national and international surveys, since data processing and data analysis were no longer limited by calculation time as in the precomputer era. From this, new ways of thinking about educational issues developed, which were concerned with assessing probabilities, multivariate analysis of educational outcomes, and the introduction of mathematical and causal modeling to predict and explain educational phenomena.

The Anglo-Saxon world led the field in educational research while West European countries tended to move more slowly. The profound impact of the Anglo-Saxon research methodology has been felt all over the world since the 1960s. But the 1960s were also marked by the beginning of an epistemological debate in the social sciences, perhaps a reaction to the strident empiricism which had developed. It is now fully realized that the rigid scientific ideal, embodied in the neopositivist approach, cannot take into account the multifaceted aspects of human behavior and all its environment-bounded subtle nuances (see *Research Paradigms in Education*).

Confrontation took place. Just as the student movement and revolt can now be considered as part of an emerging, new human culture, the positivistic versus the humanistic or hermeneutic debate can be conceived as the beginning of a new and fourth era in the social sciences. However, the answer to educational researchers of the 1990s is not either-or, but both (Husén, 1988; Keeves, 1988). The scientific approach is seen to be complementary to the anthropological, historical, phenomenological, or humanistic approach.

In tracing the development of educational research, this article examines the successive periods: pre-1900 era, 1900 to 1930s, 1930s to late 1950s, the 1960s and 1970s, and developments in the 1980s and 1990s (see de Landsheere, 1982, 1986).

1   Pre-1990

It is not incidental that within a period of about 25 years, empirical educational research was born and began to tackle most of the pervasive educational problems which are, in the late twentieth century, still under study throughout the Western world. The foundations for this sudden rise were laid during centuries of educational experience and philosophical thinking, and were inspired by the progress of the natural sciences during the nineteenth century. More specifically, longitudinal observations of individual children were recorded during the nineteenth century and attained a high-quality level with the pioneering study, in 1882, by Preyer, *Die Seele des Kindes* (The Mind of the Child). This was the first textbook on developmental psychology. The idea of experimentation in education is present in the writings of Kant, Herbart, and Pestalozzi, but this idea implied field experience and not experimentation according to an elaborated design.

In the second part of the nineteenth century, several signs show that developments in the natural sciences slowly began to influence psychology and education. In 1859, in *The Emotions and the Will*, Bain considered the construction of aptitude tests. Five years later, Fisher proposed a set of scales for the rating of ability and knowledge in major school subjects including handwriting. Fisher also introduced statistics into educational research by using the arithmetic mean as an index of achievement of a group of students. In 1870, Bartholomäi administered a questionnaire to 2,000 children entering primary school in order to know the "content of their mind" at that moment. Three years later, the first experimental study of attention was published by Miller in Göttingen. In 1875, James opened the first psychological laboratory in the United States at Harvard in order to carry out systematic observation, but not experimentation. The year 1879 saw the publication of Bain's *Education as a Science*.

The origins of modern educational research and of experimental psychology are not to be found in the emerging social sciences, but in the natural sciences. With his *Origin of the Species* (1859) Darwin linked research on humans with physics, biology, zoology, and geography. Six years later, Bernard published his *Introduction to the Study of Experimental Medicine* – a guide to modern scientific research (see Bernard, 1932). In 1869, Galton in *Hereditary Genius*, began his work on the concepts of standardization, correlation, and operational definition by applying statistics to the study of human phenomena. Carroll (1978) sees in Galton's *Inquiry into Human Faculty and its Development* (1883) the invention of the idea of mental testing.

Experimental psychology – soon to be followed by experimental pedagogy – was created in German physics laboratories by scholars with a strong philosophical background. Wundt, a student of one of these scholars, Helmholtz, founded the first laboratory of experimental psychology in Leipzig in 1879. Wundt's laboratory had a considerable impact, and the scientific leadership of the German universities at the end of the 1800s must be recognized in order to understand what happened between 1880 and 1900.

At that time, many students, particularly from the United States, completed their advanced education at the universities of Berlin, Leipzig, Heidelberg, or Jena. This explains the extraordinarily rapid dissemination of Wundt's ideas: Cattell, Stanley Hall, Judd, Rice and Valentine were among his students. His work was immediately known in France by Ribot and Binet, in Russia by Nestschajeff, in Japan by Matsumoto, and in Santiago, Chile by Mann. Psychological laboratories were soon opened on both sides of the Atlantic.

In the meantime, certain key events were associated with the birth of modern educational research:

> 1885   Ebbinghaus's study on memory drew the attention of the educational world to the importance of associations in the learning process.
> 1888   Binet published his *Études de Psychologie Experimentales*: at that time he was already working in schools.
> 1890   The term "mental test" was coined by Cattell.
> 1891   Stanley Hall launched the journal *Pedagogical Seminary.*
> 1894   Rice developed a spelling test to be administered to 16,000 pupils. He published the results of his testing in his *Scientific Management of Education* in 1913.
> 1895   In the United States, the *National Society for the Scientific Study of Education* was founded (initially called the National Herbart Society for the Scientific Study of Teaching).
> 1896   In Belgium, Schuyten published a report of his first educational research study on the influence of temperature on school children's attention. Dewey, a student of Stanley Hall, opened a laboratory school at the University of Chicago.
> 1897   Thorndike studied under James at Harvard and there discovered the works of Galton and Binet.
> Ebbinghaus published his co-called completion test to measure the effect of fatigue on school performance. This can be considered to the first operational group test. In the same year Binet began to work on his intelligence scale.
> 1898   Lay suggested distinguishing experimental education from experimental psychology.
> Binet and Henri condemned traditional education in their book *La Fatigue Intellectuelle* and indicated the need for experimental education.

Who is the father of "experimental pedagogy"? The answer to this question differs when the activity covered by the term itself is considered. Empirical research in education definitely existed before 1900. Many American authors regard Rice as the founder because of his research on the effect of spelling drills (1895–97), but other names: Binet, Lay, Mercante, or Schuyten, could also qualify. As for the term itself, it was coined by

Meumann (Wundt's former student) in 1900, in the German *Zeitschrift für Pädagogik* where he dealt with the scientific study of schooling. In 1903, Lay published his *Experimentelle Didaktik* where he made his famous statement: " . . . experimental education will become all education." In 1906, Lay and Meumann together published the review *Die Experimentelle Pädagogik*. Subsequently, Meumann's three-volume work *Einfhrung in die Experimentelle Pädagogik* (1910, 1913, 1914) emphasized both the strict scientific and quantitative side of the laboratory, while Lay continued to emphasize both quantitative and qualitative approaches in classroom research.

When did modern educational research appear in France? There is no doubt that Binet inspired it. In his introduction to *La Fatigue Intellectuelle* (1898) he wrote:

> Education must rely on observation and experimentation. By experience, we do not mean vague impressions collected by persons who have seen many things. An experimental study includes all methodically collected documents with enough detail and precise information to enable the reader to replicate the study, to verify it and to draw conclusions that the first author had not identified. (cited by Simon, 1924, p. 5)

It is obvious throughout the whole psychological work of Binet that he had a strong interest in all education. In 1905, he founded the School Laboratory in Paris. With him were Vaney, who in 1907 published the first French reading scale, and Simon, the coauthor of the *Intelligence Scale* (1905) and later author of the *Pädagogie Expérimentale*. Binet and Simon's *Intelligence Scale* presented in Rome at the 1905 International Conference of Psychology was the first truly operational mental test covering higher cognitive processes. Like Wundt's ideas, Binet's test became known throughout the world within a few years. Beyond its intrinsic value, this test had a far greater historical significance. It was now acknowledged that a test could be a valid measurement instrument both in psychology and education.

In 1904, Claparède, a medical doctor, founded the Laboratory for Experimental Psychology at the University of Geneva with his uncle Flournoy. In 1892, Claparède had visited Binet in Paris and in the following year was, for a short time, Wundt's student in Leipzig. In 1905, he published the first version of his *Psychologie de l'enfant et pédagogie expérimentale* (1911) that was the only French educational research methods handbook until 1935 when the Belgian Buyse published his *Expérimentation en Pédagogie*. In 1912, Claparède established the J. J. Rousseau Institute in Geneva which over the next 50 years was to make a marked contribution to child study and education through the work of Piaget. However, Claparède remained mostly psychologically and philosophically oriented. With his theory of functional education, he was the European counterpart of Dewey. Together they were seen as the two main leaders of progressive education.

Among many interesting features in the work of Claparède (following Dilthey's work in 1892 on *Verstehen* vs. *Erklären*) is his analysis, in 1903, of the explaining (positivist, nomothetic) versus the understanding (hermeneutic) approach. This elicited a debate which still lasts at the end of the twentieth century.

At the end of *Les Idées Modernes sur les enfants*, Binet (1924, p. 300) mentioned that "it is specifically in the United States that the remodeling of education has been undertaken on a new, scientific basis." In fact, at the beginning of the twentieth century, educational research advanced at an extraordinarily quick pace in the United States.

At Columbia University, Cattell who had obtained his PhD under Wundt and had known Galton in Cambridge, had, in 1890, as mentioned above, coined the term "mental test" in the philosophical journal *Mind*. In 1891, he established his psychological laboratory. Under his supervision Thorndike completed his PhD in 1898 on animal intelligence. Like many psychologists of the time he soon developed a keen interest in education. In this period, so much attention was focused on objective measurement that the experimental education movement was sometimes called "the measurement movement" (Jonçich, 1962).

Thorndike can be considered as the most characteristic representative of the scientific orientation in education. During the following decades, he dealt with all aspects of educational research. He was the first person to conceive of teaching methods in terms of an explicitly formulated and experimentally tested learning theory. In so doing, he opened a new teaching era. The influence of Thorndike in the field of educational research can be compared with the influence of Wundt in experimental psychology.

2   The flourishing of quantitative research, from 1900 to 1930

During this period, most educational research was quantitatively oriented and geared to the study of effectiveness. For a while, Taylorism and the study of efficiency became a component of educational thinking. The behavioristic and antimentalist study of human behavior was regarded as the best weapon against the formalism of the past.

The following aspects of research activities are representative illustrations of the era.

2.1   Statistical theory

It has sometimes been said that there is an inconsistency between the limitations of measurement in the social and behavioral sciences and the rapidly increasing sophistication of the statistical techniques employed. However, it can be argued that many statistical advances were achieved by researchers in education, precisely because they were aware of the complexity and the instability of most phenomena they had under study, consequently they had to look for increasingly sophisticated methods of both measurement and statistical analysis to obtain results of sufficient strength or else indicate the limitations of their conclusions.

The applicability of the Gaussian probability curve to biological and social phenomena was suggested at the beginning of the 1800s by Quetelet, who coined the term "statistics". Galton was the first to make extensive use of the normal curve to study psychological problems. Galton also suggested percentile norms. In 1875, he drew the first regression line, and developed the concept of correlation in 1877. In 1896, Pearson, who worked under Galton, published the formula for the product–moment correlation coefficient. In the first decade of the 1900s, the essentials of the correlational method, including the theory of regression, were developed, especially by British statisticians, Pearson and Yule. In the same period, Pearson developed the chi-square technique and the multiple correlation coefficient. Reliability was measured with the Spearman–Brown formula. In 1904, Spearman published his analysis of a correlation matrix to sustain his two-factor theory and factor analysis began to emerge. Researchers were also aware of the statistical significance of differences. In 1908, under the name of Student, Gossett showed how to measure the standard error of the mean and the principle of the t-test was formulated.

Experimental design was also developed. In 1903, Schuyten used experimental and control groups. In 1916, McCall, a student of Thorndike and probably the first comprehensive theorist of experimentation in education, recommended the setting up of random experimental and control groups. In a research study with Thorndike and Chapman (Thorndike $et\ al.$, 1916), he applied 2×2 and 5×5 Latin square designs.

The contribution of Sir Ronald Fisher was critical. With the publication of his $Statistical\ Methods\ for\ Research\ Workers$ in 1925, small-sample inferential statistics became known, but were not immediately utilized. In the same work, Fisher reinforced Pearson's chi-square by adding the concept of degrees of freedom, demonstrated the t-test, and explained the technique of analysis of variance. In 1935, Fisher published his famous $The\ Design\ of\ Experiments$, originally conceived for agriculture, and not widely applied in educational research before the late 1940s.

A look at some of the statistical texts available in the 1920s is often a surprise for modern students: Thorndike (1913), McCall (1922), Otis (1926), Thurstone (1925) in the United States; Yule (1911), Brown and Thomson (1921) in the United Kingdom; Claparède (1911) in Switzerland; Decroly and Buyse (1929) in Belgium had a surprisingly good command of descriptive parametric statistics and also a keen awareness of the need for testing the significance of differences.

2.2   Testing and assessment

Both mental and achievement tests already existed around 1900. Between 1895 and 1905 tests were administered in schools in the United States, Germany, France, Belgium, and many other countries. Perhaps the critical event was the appearance in 1905 of Binet and Simon's test, the first valid and operational mental measurement instrument. Group testing began in England in Galton's laboratory in 1905, and Burt and Spearman assisted him. In 1911, the United States National Education Association approved the use of tests for school admission and final examinations. A breakthrough occurred with the development of widescale, efficient use of tests by the United States Army, which were quickly constructed in 1917 mostly by drawing upon existing mental tests. Soon after the First World War, these tests were modified for school use (Carroll, 1978).

The 1891 $Yearbook$ of the National Society for the Study of Education was entirely devoted to the measurement of educational products. In 1928, about 1,300 standardized tests were available in the United States. By the 1930s, normative-test construction techniques were fully developed; item formats, order of items, parallel forms, scoring stencils and machine scoring, norms, reliability, and validity. The psychometric advance of the United States, at that time, was such that standardized tests were often referred to as "American tests".

Mental tests were soon used in all industrialized countries. In particular, Binet's scale was used in Europe, North and South America, and Australia, and was tried out in some African countries. This was far from being the case with achievement tests. Some fairly crude tests were used as research instruments but frequently remained unknown to the classroom teacher. It is, for instance, surprising to observe the lack of sophistication of the achievement tests developed in France after Binet and Simon. This continued until the 1940s, and the situation is particularly well-illustrated in the book by Ferré, *Les Tests à l'école*, a fifth edition of which appeared in 1961. It is all the more surprising since in the 1930s traditional examinations (essay and oral tests) were sharply criticized in England and in France where Piéron coined the word *docimologie*, meaning "science of examinations". Lack of validity and reliability, and sociocultural bias were denounced with documented evidence. In Continental Europe, standardized achievement tests were not extensively used in schools.

2.3 Administrative and normative surveys

Among educational research endeavours, surveys are the oldest. In 1817, Jullien became the founder of comparative education by designing a 32-page national and international questionnaire covering all aspects of national systems of education. The questions were posed, but unfortunately not answered at that time.

The modern questionnaire technique was developed by Hall at the end of the 1800s to show, among other things, that what is obvious for an adult is not necessarily so for a child.

In 1892, Rice visited 36 towns in the United States and interviewed some 1,200 teachers about curriculum content and teaching methods. Subsequently he carried out a spelling survey (1895–97) on 16,000 pupils and found a low correlation between achievement and time invested in drill. This survey was repeated in 1908 and again in 1911 (Rice, 1913). Thorndike's 1907 survey of dropouts was followed by a series of other surveys of school characteristics: differences in curricula, failure rates, teaching staff qualifications, school equipment, and the like. The most comprehensive survey of the period was the Cleveland Schools Survey undertaken in 1915–16 by Ayres and a large team of assistants. The study was reported in 25 volumes each dealing with different aspects of urban life and education.

In Germany, France, Switzerland, and Belgium, similar but smaller surveys were carried out by "pedotechnical" offices such as the one that opened in 1906 in the Decroly School in Brussels.

Several large-scale psychological surveys were undertaken: the Berkeley Growth Study (in 1928), the Fell's Study of Human Development (in 1929), and the Fourth Harvard Study (1929). In 1932, the Scottish Council for Research in Education carried out its first *Mental Survey* on a whole school population which provided a baseline for later surveys and for determining the representativeness of samples of the population of the same age.

A landmark in the history of experimental education was the *Eight-Year Study* (1933–41) conducted in the United States by the Progressive Education Association. The initial purpose of the study, which was carried out using survey research methodology, was to examine to what extent the college entrance requirements hampered the reform of the high school curriculum and to demonstrate the relevance and effectiveness of progressive ideas at the high school level. In this study students from 30 experimental schools were admitted to college irrespective of the subjects they had studied in high school. The by-products of this project were probably more important than the project itself. Tests covering higher cognitive processes and affective outcomes were developed by an evaluation team directed by Tyler. The careful definition of educational objectives was advanced. In 1944, influenced by the *Eight-Year Study*, Tyler wrote *Basic Principles of Curriculum and Instruction*, in which he presented his model for the definition of objectives. This was followed by Bloom's first taxonomy in 1956, and this marked the beginning of the contemporary thinking on the definition of objectives and on curriculum development and evaluation.

2.4   Curriculum development and evaluation

Curriculum was one focus of attention of empirical educational research from its very beginning. The article, in 1900, in which Meumann used the term ”*Expérimentelle Pädagogik*” for the first time dealt with the scientific study of school subjects. Shortly afterwards, Thorndike introduced a radical change in curriculum development by conceptualizing teaching methods in terms of a "psychology of school branches", and by demonstrating through his work on the transfer of learning the lack of validity of the prevailing theories of formal education, and how it ignored the needs of contemporary society. This methodological approach was perfectly compatible with the new pragmatic philosophy and the attempts to rationalize work and labor. Some years later, Decroly and Buyse hoped to "Taylorize instruction to save time for education". The psychology of school subjects was also dealt with by other leading scholars such as Judd. But, as far as research on curriculum, in the broad sense of the word is concerned, the work of Thorndike on content, teaching methods, and evaluation of material is second to none.

During the same period, the progressive movement, partly inspired by Dewey, remained in close contact with these specific developments, although it soon rejected a strictly quantitative experimental approach to educational phenomena. According to Thorndike's scientific approach, there could be only one standard curriculum at a given time, the best one that scientific research could produce. Most important to the movement was the rejection of formalism for functionality. The main criteria for curriculum content became individual needs in a new society, as conceived by liberal, middle-class educators of the time.

In 1918, Bobbitt published *Curriculum*, soon to be followed by Charters' *Curriculum Construction* (in 1923). This led to a series of studies with increasingly strong emphasis on a systematic and operational definition of educational objectives. On the European side, the Belgian *Plan d'études* (1936) by Jeunehomme was built on contributions of both strict empirical research and the progressive philosophy.

3   From the 1930s to the late 1950s

The economic crisis of the 1930s made research funds scarce. The Second World War and the years immediately following froze most educational research activities in European countries. Freedom of research was (and still is) not acceptable to dictators. In the former Soviet Union, the utilization of tests (as incompatible with political decisions) and more generally the "pedalogical movement" were officially banned in 1936 by a decree of the Communist Party, and this situation lasted until Stalin's death. However, other forms of research continued, arising from the publication in 1938 of *Thought and Language* by Vygotsky four years after his death, and the subsequent work of his associates such as Luria and Leontief in the development of Pavlov's ideas. In occupied countries, school reorganization was planned by underground movements which tried to draw conclusions from previous experiments and to design educational systems for peace and democracy. The *Plan Langevin–Wallon*, for the introduction of comprehensive secondary education in France is an example.

Conditions were different in the United States, Australia, and Sweden. Even if no spectacular advances occurred in educational research in those countries, the maturation of ideas went on and prepared the way for the postwar developments. Warfare had again raised problems of recruitment and placement and the role of military psychology and the development of selection tests is exemplified by the work of Guilford (1967) in the United States and Husén and Boalt (1968) in Sweden.

The strong field of interest in the 1940s and 1950s was without doubt in sociological studies. The seminal investigations were those concerned with social status and its impact on educational opportunity. A series of studies in the United States showed the pervasive existence of the school's role in maintaining social distinctions and discriminatory practices. From this research it was argued that schools and teachers were the purveyors of middle-class attitudes and habits. These effects of schooling were particularly evident at the high-school stage, and this trend of research became closely linked to the study of adolescent development. This work spread to the United Kingdom in the mid-1950s and subsequently to other parts of the world and led to challenging the maintenance of selective schools and to establishing comprehensive high schools. This research emphasis on issues associated with educational disadvantage has continued subsequently, with concern for disparities in the educational opportunities provided for different racial and ethnic groups, for inner urban and rural groups and, in particular, for girls.

Educational reforms were launched in several European countries after the Second World War. The structural changes which took place were based on the outcomes, or rather the interpretations of the outcomes, of these research endeavors. In Sweden and the United Kingdom the debate on comprehensive versus selective secondary education was closely connected with several big studies (e.g., Svensson 1962). In Germany, the Max Planck Society decided to establish a research institute for education in Berlin in 1964, an institute which played an important role in the debate on German school reform. Moreover, a Federal Council (*Bildungsrat*) was set up in the 1960s which commissioned a series of studies pertaining to the German school reform.

4   The 1960s and 1970s

During the first part of the 1960s in affluent countries educational research enjoyed for the first time in its history the massive support necessary for it to have a significant impact. This development was particularly marked in the United States. At that time money for research and curriculum development, particularly in mathematics and science, was readily available. In 1954, federal funds were first devoted through the Cooperative Research Act to a program of research and development in education (Holtzmann, 1978). The big, private foundations also began to sponsor educational research on a large scale. The civil rights movement, Kennedy's New Frontier, and Johnson's Great Society continued the trend.

In 1965, the Elementary and Secondary Education Act was passed, which authorized funding over a five-year period for constructing and equipping regional research and development (R & D) centers and laboratories. President Johnson implemented developments that had been planned under Kennedy and, in 1968, federal support for educational research reached its peak, with 21 R & D centers, 20 regional laboratories, 100 graduate training programs in educational research, and thousands of demonstration projects, representing a total federal investment of close to 200 million dollars per year. On a much smaller scale, similar developments took place in the United Kingdom and elsewhere.

Expansion also took place in the former Soviet Union. Between 1960 and 1970 the professional staff engaged in educational research increased considerably. The Soviet Academy of Pedagogical Sciences, initially under the name of the Academy of the Russian Republic, was founded in 1943. In 1967, the *Institut Pédagogique National* of France, for the first time, received significant funding for educational research.

By the late 1960s, all highly industrialized countries were in the midst of cultural crises which had a deep impact on scientific epistemology and thus affected the research world. There was also talk about a "world crisis" (Coombs, 1968) in education which applied in the first place to the imbalance between demand and supply of education, particularly in

Third World countries. Deeply disappointed in their hope for general peace, wealth, and happiness, people realized that neither science and technology nor traditional – mostly middle-class – values had solved their problems. An anti-intellectualist counterculture developed, emphasizing freedom in all respects, rejecting strict rationality, and glorifying community life. The value of "traditional" education was questioned. "Deschooling", nondirectivity, group experience, and participation seemed to many the alpha and omega of all pedagogy. This trend did not leave socialist countries unaffected, and a group of researchers in the former Soviet Union regretted a too rationalistic approach in educational research (Novikov 1977).

At the same time, scholars also began to question science, some with great caution and strong argumentation, others superficially in line with the *Zeitgeist*. Kerlinger (1977) condemned the latter with ferocity: "mostly bizarre nonsense, bandwaggon climbing, and guruism, little related to what research is and should be."

This was not the case in the crucial epistemological debate inspired by scholars like Polanyi, Popper, Kuhn, and Piaget. Fundamentally, the world of learning acknowledged both the contemporary "explosion of knowledge" and the still very superficial comprehensions of natural, human phenomena. Piaget (1972) showed in his *Epistémologie des sciences de l'homme*, that nomothetic and historical (anthropological) approaches are not mutually exclusive but complementary.

In 1974, two of the best-known United States educational researchers, Cronbach (1974) and Campbell (1974), without previous mutual consultation, chose the annual meeting of the American Psychologist Association to react against the traditional positivist emphasis on quantitative methods and stressed the importance of alternative methods of inquiry. Cronbach also emphasized the importance of aptitude-treatment interaction (ATI).

Since the 1960s, the computer has become the daily companion of the researcher. For the first time in the history of humankind, the amount and complexity of calculation are no longer a major problem. Already existing statistical techniques, like multiple regression analysis, factor analysis, multivariate analysis of variance, that previously were too onerous for desk calculation, suddenly became accessible in a few moments. Large-scale research surveys became feasible. Simultaneously, new statistical methods and techniques were developed.

Huge surveys, such as Project Talent in the United States and the mathematics and six subject surveys of the International Association for the Evaluation of Educational Achievement (IEA) would have been unthinkable without powerful data-processing units.

The experience gained in the domain of large-scale achievement evaluation opened the way to systematic monitoring of school systems and to the periodical publication of accountability reports. A pioneer in this kind of evaluation was the United States National Assessment of Educational Progress (NEAP).

Campbell and Stanley's (1963) presentation of experimental and quasi-experimental design for educational research can also be considered to be a landmark. Advances in the field of educational research were not only stimulated by access to funds and to powerful technology, but also by the "explosion" of knowledge in the social sciences, especially in psychology, linguistics, economics, and sociology.

Many scientific achievements in the field of education can be mentioned for the 1960s: the new ideas on educational objectives, the new concepts of criterion-referenced testing, formative and summative evaluation, teacher–pupil interaction analysis, research on teacher effectiveness, compensatory education for socioculturally handicapped children, the study of cognitive and affective handicaps, research into the importance and methods of early education, social aspects of learning aptitudes, deschooling experiments, adult education, the development of new curricula, empirical methodology of curriculum development and evaluation, and advances in research methodology (Connell, 1980; Husén and Kogan, 1984).

5 Developments in the 1980s and 1990s

With the advent of the last quarter of the twentieth century, the status of educational research attained a level of quality comparable to that of other disciplines. The epistemological debate of the previous decade classified considerably the relative strengths and weaknesses of the qualitative and the quantitative approaches. It was widely acknowledged in the early 1990s that no one research paradigm could answer all the questions which arose in educational research. Moreover, it was generally recognized that the hardline distinction between quantitative and qualitative methods could not be sustained since complex statistical procedures have been developed for the analysis of qualitative data. There was also marked growth of the humanistic research movement which employed the methods of anthropology, sociology, history, and linguistics.

A widely used alternative research strategy is ethnomethodology (Spindler, 1988). The way individuals behave in their environment (home, classroom, etc.) is extensively observed (naturalistic observation) and described. Variables are not manipulated. Main research themes are, for instance, the daily life of a class or a school, the observation of classroom processes that may help understanding school failure, and the processes of the latent or hidden curriculum. Ethnography is broadening knowledge of educational processes and phenomena. Unfortunately, this research method takes much time, and since all events are supposed to be observed, accumulated details become hard to interpret.

It is furthermore acknowledged that neither explaining nor understanding paradigms rely on firm empirical foundations. A research method – be it qualitative or quantitative – cannot provide knowledge of the true nature of phenomenon. Contemporary transcendental (or criterial) realism tries to overcome this epistemological difficulty.

A clear impact of this maturity can also be observed in educational practice. Both the scientific quest for the most efficient standard teaching method and the progressive improvisation (for a while replaced by nondirectivity) have been succeeded by subtle classroom management including careful definition and negotiation of objectives, consideration of student and teacher characteristics, of cognitive and affective styles, and of economic and social needs. Thanks to the advancement of developmental and educational psychology it is now understood, for instance, how the Piagetian constructivist theory implies that many crucial educational objectives can only be defined by or with the learner, while interacting with his or her environment. Recent progress in the cognitive sciences, particularly in the study of the functioning of the brain, have opened new research perspectives that are being vigorously pursued.

The frontiers of educational research are constantly changing.

6   Conclusion

Like medicine, education is an art. That is why advances in research do not directly produce a science of education, in the positivist meaning of the term, but yield increasingly powerful foundations for practice and decision-making. In this perspective, it can be said that educational research has gathered a large body of knowledge containing valuable observations and conclusions that have had a very marked impact both on policy-making and practice.

See also: Research Paradigms in Education.

References

Ayres, L. P. 1912–16 *Scales for Measuring the Quality of Handwriting. Scales for Measuring the Quality of Spelling.* Russell Sage, New York.

Bain, A. 1879 *Education as a Science.* Kegan Paul, London.

Bain, A. 1859 *The Emotions and the Will.* Parker, London.

Bartholmäi, F. 1871 Psychologische Statistik. *Allgemeine Schulzeitung.*

Bernard, C. 1932 *Introduction l'Étude de la Médicine Expérimentale.* Doin, Paris.

Binet, A. 1924 *Les Idées Modernes sur les Enfants.* Flammarion, Paris.

Binet, A. and Henri, V. 1898 *La Fatigue Intellectuelle.* Schleicher, Paris.

Binet, A and Simon, T. 1905 Methode nouvelle pour le diagnostic de l'intelligence des anormaux. *L'année Psychologique* 11: 191–244.

Bobbitt, F. 1918 *The Curriculum.* Houghton Mifflin, Boston, Massachusetts.

Brown, W. and Thomson, G. H. 1921 *The Essentials of Mental Measurement.* Cambridge University Press, Cambridge.

Buyse, R. 1935 *L'Expérimentation en Pédagogie.* Lamertin, Brussels.

Campbell, D. T. 1974 Qualitative knowing in action-research. Paper delivered to Annual Meeting of the American Psychological Association, Los Angeles, California.

Campbell, D. T. and Stanley, J. C. 1963 Experimental and quasi-experimental designs for research on teaching. In: Gage N. L. (ed.) 1963 *Handbook of Research on Teaching.* Rand McNally, Chicago, Illinois.

Carroll, J. B. 1978 On the theory–practice interface in the measurement of intellectual abilities. In: Suppes P. (ed.) 1978 *Impact of Research of Education.* National Academy of Education, Washington, DC.

Cattell, J. M. 1890 Mental tests and measurement. *Mind* 15: 373–81.

Claparède, E. 1911 *Psychologie de l'Enfant et Pédagogie Expérimentale. Vol. 2: Les Méthodes.* Delachaux and Niestlé, Nauchâtel.

Connell, W. F. 1980 *A History of Education in the Twentieth Century World.* Teachers College Press, New York.

Coombs, P. H. 1968 *The World Educational Crisis: A Systems Analysis.* Oxford University Press, London.

Cronbach, L. J. 1974 Beyond the two disciplines of scientific psychology. Paper delivered to the Annual Meeting of the American Psychological Association, Los Angeles, California.

Cronbach, L. J. and Suppes P. (eds.) 1969 *Research for Tomorrow's Schools: Disciplined Inquiry for Education: Report.* Macmillan, New York.

de Landsheere, G. 1982 *Empirical Research in Education.* UNESCO, Paris.

de Landsheere, G. 1986 *La Recherche en Éducation dans le Monde.* Presses Universitaires de France, Paris.

Decroly, O. and Buyse, R. 1929 *Introduction à la Pédagogie Quantitative: Eléments de Statistiques Appliqués aux Problèmes Pédagogiques.* Lamertin, Brussels.

Ebbinghaus, H. 1897 Über eine neue Methode zur Prüfung feistiger Fähigkeiten. *Zeitschrift für Angewandte Psychologie.*

Ferré, A. 1961 Les tests à l'école, 5th edn. Bourrelier, Paris.

Fisher, R. A. 1925 *Statistical Methods for Research Workers.* Oliver and Boyd, Edinburgh.

Fisher, R. A. 1935 *The Design of Experiments.* Oliver and Boyd, Edinburgh.

Galton, F. 1869 *Hereditary Genius: An Enquiry into its Laws and Consequences.* Macmillan, London.

Galton, F. 1883 *Inquiries into Human Faculty and its Development.* Macmillan, London.

Guilford, J. P. 1967 *The Nature of Intelligence.* McGraw-Hill, New York.

Holtzman, W. H. 1978 Social change and the research and development movement. In: Glaser R. (ed.) 1978 *Research and Development and School Change.* Erlbaum, Hillsdale, New Jersey.

Husén, T. 1988 Research paradigms in education. *Interchange* 19(1): 2–13.

Husén, T. and Boalt, G. 1968 *Educational Research and Educational Change: The Case of Sweden.* Wiley, New York.

Husén, T. and Kogan, M. (eds.) 1984 *Educational Research and Policy: How Do They Relate?* Pergamon Press, Oxford.

Jeunehomme, L. 1936 *Plan d'Études.* Ministère de l'instruction publique, Brussels.

Jonçich, G. 1962 Whither thou, educational scientist? *Teach. Coll. Rec.* 64(1): 1–12.

Jullien, M.-A. 1817 *Esquisse d'un Ouvrage sur l'Éducation Comparée.* Colas, Paris.

Keeves, J. 1988 The unity of educational research. *Interchange* 19(1): 14–30.

Kerlinger, F. N. 1977 *The Influence of Research on Educational Practice.* University of Amsterdam, Amsterdam.

Lay, W. A. 1906 Über Kämpfe und Fortschritte der experimentallen Pädagogik. *Die Experimentelle Pädagogik* 2: 96–117.

McCall, W. A. 1922 *How to Measure in Education.* Macmillan, New York.

Meumann, E. 1920 *Abriss der Experimentellen Pädagogik.* Nemmick, Leipzig.

Novikov, L. 1977 Probleme der Planung und Organisation der pädagogischen Forschung in der Sowjetunion. In: Mitter, W. and Novikov, L. (eds.) 1977 *Pädagogische Forschung und Bildungspolitik in der Sowjetunion: Organisation, Gegenstand, Methoden.* Deutches Institut für Internationale Pädagogische Forshchung. Frankfurt/Main.

Otis, A. S. 1926 *Statistical Method in Educational Measurement.* World Books, Yonkers-on-Hudson, New York.

Pearson, K. 1896 Mathematical contribution to the theory of evolution. *Philosophical Transactions* 187: 253–318.

Piaget, J. 1972 *Epistémologie des Sciences de l'Homme.* Gallimard, Paris.

Rice, J. M. 1897 The futility of the spelling grind. *Forum* 23: 163–72.

Rice, J. M. 1913 *Scientific Management in Education.* Hinds, Noble and Eldredge, New York.

Schuyten, M. C. 1896 Sur les méthodes de mensuration de la fatigue des écoliers. *Archives de Psychologie* 2.

Simon, T. 1924 *Pédagogie Expérimentale: Ecriture, Lecture, Orthographe.* Colin, Paris.

Spearman, C. 1904 General intelligence objectively determined and measured. *Am. J. Psychol.* 15: 201–92

Spindler, G. 1988 *Doing the Ethnography of Schooling: Education and Anthropology in Action.* Waveland Press, Prospect Heights, Illinois.

Svensson, N.-E. 1962 *Ability Grouping and Scholastic Achievement: Report on a Five-Year Follow-up Study in Stockholm.* Almqvist and Wiksell, Stockholm.

Thorndike, E. L. 1906 *The Principles of Teaching Based on Psychology.* Seiler, New York.

Thorndike, E. L. 1913 *An Introduction to the Theory of Mental and Social Measurements.* 2nd edn. Teachers College Press, New York.

Thorndike, E. L., McCall, W. A. and Chapman J. C. 1916 *Ventilation in Relation to Mental Work.* Teachers College Press, New York.

Thurston, L. L. 1925 *The Fundamentals of Statistics.* Macmillan, New York.

Tyler, R. W. 1949 *Basic Principles of Curriculum and Instruction.* University Press, Chicago, Illinois.

Vaney, V. 1909 L'âge de la lecture. *Société Libre pour l'Étude de la Psycholgie de l'Enfant,* 53.

Vygotsky, L. S. 1962 *Thought and Language.* MIT Press, Cambridge, Massachusetts.

Yule, G. U. 1911 *An Introduction to the Theory of Statistics.* Griffin, London.

Warner, W. L., Havighurst R. J. and Loeb M. B. 1946 *Who Shall be Educated? The Challenge of Unequal Opportunities.* Kegan Paul, London.

3   Research Paradigms in Education

T. Husén

Thomas Kuhn, himself a historian of science, contributed to a fruitful development in the philosophy of science with his book *The Structure of Scientific Revolutions* published in 1962. It mapped out how established thinking, research strategies, and methods in a scientific field, in Kuhn's terminology "normal science", were established. It brought into focus two streams of thinking about what could be regarded as "scientific", the Aristotelian tradition with its teleological approach and the Galilean with its causal and mechanistic approach. It introduced the concept of "paradigm" into the philosophical debate.

"Paradigm" derives from the Greek verb for "exhibiting side by side." In lexica it is given with the translations "example" or "table of declensions and conjugations". Although Kuhn himself used paradigm rather ambiguously, the concept has turned out to be useful in inspiring critical thinking about "normal science" and the way shifts in basic scientific thinking occur. A paradigm determines the criteria according to which one selects and defines problems for inquiry and how one approaches them theoretically and methodologically. Young scientists tend to be socialized into the precepts of the prevailing paradigm which to them constitutes "normal science". In that respect a paradigm could be regarded as a cultural artifact, reflecting the dominant notions about scientific behavior in a particular scientific community, be it national or international, and at a particular point in time. Paradigms determine scientific approaches and procedures which stand out as exemplary to the new generation of scientists – as long as they do not oppose them.

A "revolution" in the world of scientific paradigms occurs when one or several researchers at a given time encounter anomalies, for instance, make observations, which in a striking way do not fit the prevailing paradigm. Such anomalies can give rise to a crisis after which the universe under study is perceived in an entirely new light. Previous theories and facts become subject to thorough rethinking and reevaluation.

In well-defined disciplines which have developed over centuries, such as the natural sciences, it is relatively easy to point out dramatic changes in paradigms, such as in astronomy from Ptolemy through Copernicus to Galileo or in physics from Aristotle via Galileo and Newton to Einstein. When the social sciences emerged in the nineteenth century, people like Compte tended to regard the natural sciences as scientific models, but without awareness that the social scientist is part of a process of social self-understanding. Educational research faces a particular problem, since education, as William James pointed out, is not a well-defined, unitary discipline but a practical art. Research into educational problems is conducted by scholars with many disciplinary affiliations. Most of them have a background in psychology or other behavioral sciences, but quite a few of them have a humanistic background in philosophy and history. Thus, there cannot be any prevailing paradigm or "normal science" in the very multifaceted field of educational research. However, when empirical research conducted by behavioral scientists, particularly in the Anglo-Saxon countries, in the 1960s and early 1970s began to be accused of dominating research with a positivist quantitatively oriented paradigm that prevented other paradigms of a humanistic or dialectical nature being employed, the accusations were directed at those with a behavioral science background.

1   The two classical paradigms

The twentieth century has seen the conflict between two main paradigms employed in researching educational problems. The one is modeled on the natural sciences with an emphasis on empirical quantifiable observations which lend themselves to analyses by means of mathematical tools. The task of research is to establish causal relationships, to explain (*Erklären*). The other paradigm is derived from the humanities with an emphasis on holistic and qualitative information and interpretive approaches (*Verstehen*).

Briefly, the two paradigms in educational research developed historically as follows. By the mid-nineteenth century, when Auguste Comte (1798–1857) developed positivism in sociology and John Stuart Mill (1806–1873) empiricism in psychology, there was a major breakthrough in the natural sciences at the universities with the development of a particular logic and methodology of experiments and hypothesis testing. They therefore came to serve as models and their prevailing paradigm was taken over by social scientists, particularly in the Anglo-Saxon countries (see, e.g., Pearson, 1892). However, on the European Continent there was another tradition from German idealism and Hegelianism. The "Galilean", mechanistic conception became the dominant one, particularly with mathematical physics as the methodological ideal. Positivism was characterized by methodological monism. Philosophers at the University of Vienna (such as Neurath), referred to as the "Vienna Circle", developed what is called "neopositivism" or "logical empiricism". Around 1950 they founded a series of publications devoted to the study of what they called "unified science." Positivism saw the main task for the social sciences as being the making of causal explanations and the prediction of future behavior on the basis of the study of present behavior. Neopositivism emanated from the strong influence of analytical philosophy.

There are at least three strands for the other main paradigm in educational research. The Continental idealism of the early nineteenth century has been mentioned. Around the turn of the century it had a dominant influence at German universities with philosophers, such as Wilhelm Dilthey (1833–1911), who in the 1890s published a classical treatise in which he made the distinction between *Verstehen* and *Erklären*. He maintained that the humanities had their own logic of research and pointed out that the difference between natural sciences and humanities was that the former tried to explain, whereas the latter tried to understand. He also maintained that there were to kinds of psychology, the one which by means of experimental methods attempted to generalize and predict, and the one that tried to understand the unique individual in his or her entire, concrete setting. Other philosophers with similar conceptions were Heinrich Rickert and Wilhelm Windelband. A counterpart in France was Henri Bergson (1859–1941) who maintained that the intellect was unable to grasp the living reality which could only be approached by means of intuition. In Sweden, John Landquist advanced an epistemology of humanities.

A second strand was represented by the phenomenological philosophy developed by Edmund Husserl (1859–1938) in Germany. It emphasized the importance of taking a widened perspective and of trying to "get to the roots" of human activity. The phenomenological, and later the hermeneutic, approach is holistic: it tries by means of empathy (*Einfühlung*) to understand the motives behind human reactions. By widening the perspective and trying to understand human beings as individuals in their entirety and in their proper context it also tries to avoid the fragmentation caused by the positivistic and experimental approach that takes out a small slice which it subjects to closer scrutiny.

The third strand in the humanistic paradigm consists of the critical philosophy, not least the one of the Frankfurt school (Adorno, Horckheimer, and Habermas) which developed with a certain amount of neo-Marxism. Marx himself would probably have felt rather ambivalent in an encounter between the two main scientific philosophies. On the one hand, he felt attracted to positivism. On the other hand, Marx belonged to the German philosophical tradition and the neo-Marxists have not had great difficulties in accepting hermeneutics and merging it with a dialectical approach.

The paradigm determines how a problem is formulated and methodologically tackled. According to the traditional positivist conception, problems that relate, for example, to classroom behavior should be investigated primarily in terms of the individual actor, either the pupils, who might be neurotic, or the teacher, who might be ill-prepared for his or her job. The other conception is to formulate the problem in terms of the larger setting, that of the school, or rather that of the society at large. Furthermore, one does not in the first place, by means of such mechanisms as testing, observation, and the like, try to find out why the pupil or the teacher deviates from the "normal". Rather an attempt is made to study the particular individual as a goal-directed human being with particular and unique motives.

The belief that science, particularly social science, would "save us" was expressed as late as in the 1940s by George Lundberg (1947), a sociologist who represented a consistent positivist approach. In the long run, the study of human beings would map out the social reality and provide a knowledge base for vastly improved methods of dealing with human beings, be they pupils in the classroom or workers in the factory. A similar hope still guided the establishment of research and development centers with massive resources at some North American universities in the 1960s. What experience and enlightened empathy could tell was something regarded as inferior to the knowledge provided by systematic observations and measurements.

2   A historical note

In his *Talks to Teachers on Psychology*, given in the 1890s, James (1899, p. 9) pointed out: "To know psychology . . . is absolutely no guarantee that we shall be good teachers." An additional ability is required, something that he calls the "happy tact and ingenuity", the "ingenuity in meeting and pursuing the pupil, the tact for the concrete situation." He mentions the demands of making systematic observations that some "enthusiasts for child study" have burdened the teachers with, including "compiling statistics and computing the percent." In order to avoid such endeavors resulting in trivialities they must be related to the "anecdotes and observations" which acquaint the teachers more intimately with the students.

What James refers to is something that in the terminology of the late twentieth century would be seen as a conflict between two main research paradigms. By the end of the nineteenth century, the scientific paradigm emerged that has since then been the prevailing one, at least in the Anglo-Saxon world. It was part of a larger movement toward "scientific management" in industry.

The new scientific approach emerging at the end of the nineteenth century was spelled out by the leading educational psychologist, Edward Lee Thorndike of Columbia University, in the preface to his seminal book *Educational Psychology* in 1903. He set out to apply "the methods of exact science" to educational problems, reject "speculative opinions", and emphasize "accurate quantitative treatment" of information collected (Clifford 1984). He acknowledged the influence on his thinking of people who have advocated the quantitative and experimental approach, like James McKeen Cattell and R. S. Woodworth in the United States and Francis Galton and Karl Pearson in England. In a brief concluding chapter he dealt with the problem of education as a science and presented the main characteristics of what he regarded as scientific in education:

> It is the vice or the misfortune of thinkers about education to have chosen the methods of philosophy or of popular thought instead of those of science . . . The chief duty of serious students of the theory of education today is to form the habit of inductive study and learn the logic of statistics. (Thorndike, 1903, p. 164)

Part of the new scientific paradigm was to make a clear-cut distinction between the descriptive and the normative. Research conducted according to "logic of science" was supposed to be neutral with regard to values and policy-making.

The prevailing paradigm in North America spelled out by Thorndike was further developed by John Franklin Bobbitt, professor at the University of Chicago, who in 1912 advanced the notion that schools could be operated according to the methods of "scientific management" which had been developed in industry by Frederick Taylor. Bobbitt also played an important role in attempts to determine empirically the content of curriculum by analyzing what people needed as holders of occupations and as citizens in order to arrive at a common denominator of skills and specific pieces of knowledge with which the school had to equip them.

With an eye on the natural sciences, social science has for more than a century made the claim to be an "objective" and "explaining" science. It purported to be able to make a clear-cut distinction between aims and means of achieving these aims. It maintained that in handling social realities it was able to do it without any moral commitments. Its representatives claim like in the natural sciences to reside outside the system they observe. Such a claim has been brought into question. Gunnar Myrdal (1969) did so in a book (first published in Swedish in the 1930s) on science and politics in economics. He showed that the social researcher could not be free from his or her own values and political convictions, but could arrive at more valid conclusions and gain in credibility by making his or her value premises explicit and by making clear what those biases were in describing reality. Thereby the researcher can also give the "consumers" of his or her research an instrument for correction.

Social research, not least that in education, consists of data collection and reflection about societal problems, with their dilemmas and paradoxes, tensions, and so on, as well as alternatives for political action which offer themselves. Not even in the ideal case can a consensus be expected around theoretical paradigms as separated from practical problems. Social science researchers are part of the social process which they set out to investigate. They share social and political values of the surrounding society. In a way, they participate in the process of social self-understanding. This means that there is no such thing as a "social technology" in the same sense as a technology based on natural science. This does not imply, however, that educational research endeavors are of very limited value or entirely futile. The "aloofness" of the researchers in terms of dependence on interest groups and politics with shared social values is a relative matter. The task of the academic of "seeking the truth" can become institutionalized. This is what happens when fundamental, discipline-oriented research is established in institutions where the researchers can pursue their tasks of critical review without jeopardizing their positions.

There were those who, in contrast to William James, thought that it would be possible to make education a science. One of them was Charles H Judd (a student of Wundt), who in *Introduction to the Scientific Study of Education* in 1918, tried to explain how research was related to teacher training and educational practice. In 1909 the Department of Education at the University of Chicago had abandoned course requirements for prospective teachers in the history of education and psychology. These courses had been replaced by one course called "Introduction to Education" and one in "Methods of

Teaching". Thereby the teacher candidates could be introduced to the school problems in "a more direct, concrete way." Each chapter in Judd's book presents practical school problems and gives sources of information for the solution of these problems. Much of this information is very incomplete, but as a whole Judd thinks that it is justified to speak about a "science of education". To use the term "science" he thinks would be justified, even when the information available is very scanty, "for the essence of science is its methods of investigation, not its ability to lay down a body of final rules of action" (Judd 1918, p. 299).

A research paradigm similar to the one advanced by Galton, Pearson, and Thorndike developed in Germany and France under the influence of experimental psychology. Ernst Meumann, a student of Wilhelm Wundt and a leading experimental psychologist, published at the beginning of the twentieth century his monumental three-volume work *Vorlesungen zur Einführung in die experimentelle Pädagogik* (Introduction to Experimental Pedagogy). He meant by "experimental education" largely the application of the systematic, empirical, and statistical methods to educational data. Alfred Binet in France had a similar influence in both child study and intelligence testing.

3   The two main paradigms and their compatibility

One can distinguish between two main paradigms in educational research planning and with different epistemological basis (Adams, 1988). On the one hand, there is the functional–structural, objective–rational, goal-directed, manipulative, hierarchical, and technocratic approach. On the other hand, there is the interpretivist, humanistic, consensual, subjective, and collegial one.

The first approach is derived from classical positivism. The second one, which in recent years has gained momentum, is partly derived from the critical theory of the Frankfurt school, particularly from Habermas's theory of communicative action. The first approach is "linear" and consists of a straight-forward rational action toward preconceived problems. The second approach leaves room for reinterpretation and reshaping of the problem during the process of dialogue prior to action and even during action.

Phillips (1983) has contributed to a valuable conceptual clarification of "positivism." He distinguishes between four varieties of it: (a) the classical Comtean positivism with its belief that the scientific method established in the natural sciences can be applied in the study of human behavior and human affairs in general; (b) logical positivism embodied by the Vienna Circle which had a strong impact among psychologists and sociologists in the middle of the twentieth century with its quest for verification and operational definitions; (c) behaviorism of the Watsonian or Skinnerian type; and (d) positivism as a general label for empiricism, which covers a broad spectrum of epistemological positions.

Phillips (1983) argues that some of the many ardent critics of allegedly positivist researchers are themselves "more positivistic than they recognize," some of them by using an instrumentalistic criterion of truth. They tend to make the mistake of "identifying positivism with particular research methods," such as experimental design or statistical analysis methods. Thus, there is basically not such an unbridgeable gap between the two paradigms as is often purported by representatives of the respective camps.

Keeves (1988) argues that the various research paradigms employed in education, the empirical–positivist, the hermeneutic or phenomenological, and the ethnographic–anthropological are complementary to each other. He talks about the "unity of educational research," makes a distinction between paradigms and approaches, and contends that there is, in the final analysis, only one paradigm but many approaches. The teacher–learning process can be observed and/or video-recorded. The observations can be quantified and the data analyzed by means of advanced statistical methods. Content can be studied in the light of national traditions and the philosophy underlying curriculum constructions. Both the teaching–learning process and its outcomes can be studied in a comparative, cross-national perspective.

Depending upon the *objective* of a particular research project, emphasis is laid more on the one or on the other paradigm. One could quote the following as an example of how quantitative and qualitative paradigms are complementary to each other. It is not possible to arrive at any valid information about a school or national system concerning the level of competence achieved in, for instance, science by visiting a number of classrooms and thereby trying to collect impressions. Even a highly experienced science teacher is not able to gain information that would allow accurate inferences about the quality of outcomes of science teaching in the entire system of education. Sample surveys like the ones conducted by the IEA (International Association for the Evaluation of Education Achievement) would be necessary instruments. But such surveys are too superficial when it comes to accounting for factors behind the differences between school systems. Here qualitative information of different kinds is required.

But the choice or "mix" of paradigm is also determined by what *kind of knowledge* one is searching for. The ultimate purpose of any knowledge arrived at in educational research is to provide a basis for action, be it policy action or methods of teaching in the classroom. The former type of knowledge must by definition be of a more general nature and apply to many local and individual situations, such as reforming the structure of the system or the relationship between home background and school attainments. But the classroom teacher deals with a unique child in a unique teaching–learning situation and is not very much helped by relying on generalized knowledge.

Policymakers, planners, and administrators want generalizations and rules which apply to a wide variety of institutions with children of rather diverse backgrounds. The policymaker and planner is more interested in the collectivity than in the individual child. They operate from the perspective of the whole system. Educational research has made significant contributions to reforms of entire national systems of education. Sweden and Germany are cases in point.

Classroom practitioners are not very much helped by generalizations which apply "on the whole" or 'by and large" because they are concerned with the timely, the particular child here and now. Research on the teaching–learning process can at best give them a perspective on the particular teaching–learning situation with which they are faced. The pedagogical steps taken have to be guided by the qualitative information that Eisner (1982) refers to as "connoisseurship" which is a body of experiences and critical analysis which may well also be guided by research insights.

4   The need for pluralism in approaches

In the late 1960s and early 1970s critical, dialectical, hermeneutical, and neo-Marxian paradigms were advanced as alternatives or even replacements for the prevailing neopositivist paradigm of quantification, hypothesis testing, and generalizations. The latter had dominated the scene of social science research in the Anglo-Saxon countries for many decades and had taken the lead at many Continental universities as well. The new approaches were espoused by many from these universities to the extent that a group of younger researchers in education even prepared an international handbook of educational research that deliberately challenged the prevailing Anglo-Saxon research paradigms. The behavioral sciences have equipped educational researchers with an arsenal of research tools, such as observational methods and tests, which help them to systematize observations which would otherwise not have been considered in the more holistic and intuitive attempts to make, for instance, informal observations or to conduct personal interviews.

Those who turn to social science research in order to find out about the "best" pedagogy or the most "efficient" methods of teaching are in a way victims of the traditional science which claimed to be able to arrive at generalizations applicable in practically every context. But, not least through critical philosophy, researchers have become increasingly aware that education does not take place in a social vacuum. Educational researchers have also begun to realize that educational practices are not independent of the cultural and social context in which they operate. Nor are they neutral to educational policies. Therefore, dogmatic evangelism for particular philosophies and ideologies espoused as "scientific" and not accessible to criticism is detrimental to the spirit of inquiry. The two main paradigms are not exclusive, but complementary to each other.

See also: Hermeneutics; Research in Education: Epistemological Issues; Positivism, Anti-positivism and Empiricism.

References

Adams, D. 1988 Extending the educational planning discussion: Conceptual and paradigmatic explorations. *Comp. Educ. Rev.* 32: 400–15.
Clifford, G. J. 1984 *The Sane Positivist: A Biography of Edward L. Thorndike.* Wesleyan University Press, Middletown, Connecticut.
Eisner, E. 1982 *Cognition and Curriculum: A Basis for Deciding What to Teach.* Longman, London.
James, W. 1899 *Talks to Teachers on Psychology: And to Students on Some of the Life's Ideals.* Longman Green, London.

Judd, C. H. 1918 *Introduction to the Scientific Study of Education.* Ginn, Boston, Massachusetts.
Keeves, J. P. 1988 The unity of educational research. *Interchange* 19(1): 14–30.
Kuhn, T. S. 1962 *The Structure of Scientific Revolutions.* University of Chicago Press, Chicago, Illinois.
Lundberg, G. 1947 *Can Science Save Us?* Longman Green, London.
Meumann, E. 1911 *Vorlesungen zur Einführung in die Experimentelle Pädagogik und Ihre Psychologischen Grundlagen.* Engelmann, Leipzig.
Myrdal, G. 1969 *Objectivity in Social Research.* Pantheon, New York.
Pearson, K. 1892 *The Grammar of Science.* Adam and Charles Black, London.
Phillips, D. C. 1983 After the wake: Postpositivistic educational thought. *Educ. Res.* 12(5): 4–14, 23–24.
Thorndike, E. L. 1903 *Educational Psychology.* Scientific Press, New York.

Further reading

Cronbach, L. J. 1975 Beyond the two disciplines of scientific psychology. *Am. Psychol.* (30): 116–27.
Eisner, E. (ed.) 1985a *The Educational Imagination.* Macmillan, New York.
Eisner, E. (ed.) 1985b Learning and teaching the ways of knowing. In; National Society for the Study of Education 1985 *Eighty-fourth Yearbook.* Chicago University Press, Chicago, Illinois.
Fritzell, C. 1981 *Teaching Science and Ideology: A Critical Inquiry into the Sociology of Pedagogy.* Gleerup, Lund.
Fromm, E. (ed.) 1965 *Socialist Humanism: An International Symposium.* Doubleday, Garden City, New York.
Gage, N. L. 1989 The paradigm wars and their aftermath: A "historical" sketch of research on teaching since 1989. *Educ. Res.* 18(7): 4–10.
Galtung, J. 1977 *Essays in Methodology, Vol. 1: Methodology and Ideology.* Ejlers, Copenhagen.
Guba, E. 1978 *Toward a Methodology of Naturalistic Inquiry in Educational Evaluation.* University of California, Center for Study in Evaluation. Los Angeles, California.
Habermas, J. 1972 *Knowledge and Human Interests.* Heinemann, London.
Heidegger, M. 1962 *Being and Time.* Harper, New York.
Home, K. R. 1988 Against the quantitative–qualitative incompatibility thesis or dogmas die hard. *Educ. Res.* 17(8): 10–16.
Husén, T. 1979 General theories in education: A twenty-five year perspective. *Int. Rev. Educ.* 25: 325–45.
Husén, T. 1988 Research paradigms in education. *Interchange* 19(1): 2–13.
Husén, T. 1989 Educational research at the crossroads? An exercise in self-criticism. *Prospects* 19(3): 351–60.
Jaeger R. M. 1988 *Complementary Methods of Research in Education.* American Educational Research Association (AERA), Washington, DC.
Landquist, J. 1920 *Människokunskap.* Bonniers, Stockholm.
Lindholm, S. 1981 *Paradigms, Science and Reality: On Dialectics, Hermeneutics and Positivism in the Social Sciences.* Department of Education, Stockholm University, Stockholm.
Landsheere, G. de 1986 *La Recherche on Education dans le Monde.* Presse Universitaire de France, Paris.
Palmer, R. E. 1969 *Hermeneutics: Interpretation Theory in Schleiermacher, Dilthey, Heidegger, and Gadamer.* Northwestern University Press, Evanston, Illinois.
Phillips, D. C. 1992 *The Social Scientist's Bestiary.* Pergamon Press, Oxford.
Rapaport, A. 1950 *Science and the Goals of Man: A Study in Semantic Orientation.* Harper, New York.
Rizo, F. M. 1991 The controversy about quantification in social research: An extension of Gage's "historical sketch." *Educ. Res..* 20: 9–12.
Shulman, L. S. 1986 Those who understand knowledge growth in teaching. *Educ. Res.* 15(2): 4–14.
Smith, J. K. and Heshusius, L. 1986 Closing down the conversation: The end of the quantitative–qualitative debate among educational inquirers. *Educ. Res.* 15(1): 4–12.
Soltis, J. F. 1984 On the nature of educational research. *Educ. Res.* 13(10): 5–10.
Tuthill, D. and Ashton, P. 1983 Improving educational research through the development of educational paradigms. *Educ. Res.* 12(10): 6–14.
Wright, G. H. von 1971 *Explanation and Understanding.* Routledge and Kegan Paul, London.

4 Research in Education: Epistemological Issues

J. C. Walker and C. W. Evers

Epistemology is the study of the nature, scope, and applicability of knowledge. Educational research, in being concerned with the conduct of educational inquiry and the development and evaluation of its methods and findings, embodies a commitment to epistemological assumptions – at least it does if its findings are expected to command attention, serve as a sound basis for action, or constitute legitimate knowledge claims. These matters are the subject of epistemological theories which deal more systematically with such general corresponding issues as justification, truth, and the accessibility of reality in the search for knowledge.

In educational research, obviously, there are different methods of inquiry, ranging from controlled laboratory experiments through participant observation to action research, from historical studies to logical analysis. These have been organized in different research traditions, such as "quantitative" and "qualitative", or associated with different theoretical positions, such as behaviorism and critical theory. In practice, the categories of method, tradition, and theoretical position cut across each other to some extent.

The major epistemological question here is whether these distinctions are associated with different ways of knowing or forms of knowledge, which partition educational research so that research traditions, for example, turn out to be radically distinct epistemologically, each having its own theories and rules of justification, meaning, and truth. If so, the next question is whether findings produced by the different traditions can be rationally integrated, rendered coherent, or even compared. For this to be possible, for traditions to be commensurable, there will have to be some shared concepts and standards of justification, meaning, and truth: some epistemological touchstone. If, however, the traditions are so fundamentally disparate that any choice between them in educational research is arbitrary or the result of non rational commitment – an act of faith – there is no touchstone. The research traditions are incommensurable.

There has long been controversy over these issues, in educational research and the social sciences generally, as advocates of research traditions variously described as "scientific", "humanistic", "quantitative", "qualitative", "positivist", and "interpretative" have tried to sort out the respective epistemological merits of these approaches and the methodological, practical, and even political relations between them.

There are three major views available, which have emerged in educational research in more or less the following historical order. First, it can be asserted that there are epistemologically different paradigms which are incommensurable in that neither educational research nor any other form of inquiry can provide a rational method for judging between them. Moreover, they are mutually incompatible, competitive ways of researching the same territory. This may be called the "oppositional diversity thesis". Second, it could be decided that there are epistemologically distinct paradigms, but that though incommensurable they are complementary, not competitive: equally appropriate ways of approaching different, overlapping, or perhaps even the same research problems. This may be called the "complementary diversity thesis". The first and second views agree that there is a fundamental epistemological diversity in educational research. The third alternative, the unity thesis, denies this. It disagrees with the view that different research methods can be grouped under incommensurable paradigms, and asserts that the very idea of such paradigms is mistaken, even incoherent. It claims there is touchstone for judging the respective merits of different research traditions and bringing them into a productive relationship with one another. It asserts a fundamental epistemological unity of educational research, derived from the practical problems addressed.

This article argues for the unity thesis. After a discussion of the term "paradigm", and of the oppositional and complementary diversity theses, it is shown that the theory that there are research paradigms – call it the "P"-theory – is largely responsible for both forms of diversity thesis. Some reasons are offered for believing that P-theory is incoherent, and it is argued that a coherentist epistemology sustains the thesis of the epistemological unity of educational research. A feature of this epistemology is its account of touchstone in educational research.

1   Epistemology and paradigms

Numerous educational researchers have been drawn to the view that research traditions are best regarded as different paradigms. Indeed, as Shulman (1986, p. 3) observed, in writing about the different research programs of communities of scholars engaged in the study of teaching, "the term most frequently employed to describe such research communities, and the conceptions of problem and method they share is *paradigm*."

As the quantitative/qualitative debate shows, many writers in education distinguish two fundamental paradigms of research: the "scientific" which is often erroneously identified with positivism, and the "interpretative" or "humanistic". Husén associates the distinction with divergent forms of explanation and understanding:

> The twentieth century has seen the conflict between two main paradigms employed in researching educational problems. The one is modeled on the natural sciences with an emphasis on empirical quantifiable observations which lend themselves to analyses by

means of mathematical tools. The task of research is to establish causal relationships, to explain (*Erklären*). The other paradigm is derived from the humanities with an emphasis on holistic and qualitative information and to interpretive approaches (*Verstehen*) (see *Research Paradigms in Education* p. 32)

In offering a broader, three-way taxonomy of research to account for diversity in enquiry, Popkewitz (1984, p. 35) says: "the concept of paradigm provides a way to consider this divergence in vision, custom and tradition. It enables us to consider science as having different sets of assumptions, commitments, procedures and theories of social affairs." He assumes that "in educational sciences, three paradigms have emerged to give definition and structure to the practice of research." After the fashion of "critical theory" (Habermas, 1972), he identifies the paradigms as "empirical–analytic" (roughly equivalent to quantitative science), "symbolic" (qualitative and interpretative or hermeneutical inquiry), and "critical" (where political criteria relating to human betterment are applied in research).

Noting the influence of positivism on the formation of research traditions and the paradigms debate, Lincoln and Guba (1984, p. 15) mention another common three-way distinction, which they apply to "paradigm eras," "periods in which certain sets of basic beliefs have guided inquiry in quite different ways," rather than directly to paradigms as such. They identify these paradigm eras as "prepositivist", "positivist", and "post-positivist". Now the term "positivist" also has a history of varied usage (Phillips, 1983) but, because of the practice common among educational researchers of defining their perspectives in relation to one or more of the varieties of positivism, it is important to note some of the issues involved in the transition to postpositivism (see *Positivism, Anti-positivism and Empiricism*).

In philosophy of science, views of the nature of science commonly described as positivist have characterized science as value-free, basing its theories and findings on logically simple and epistemically secure observation reports, and using empirical concepts themselves deriving directly from observation (Hooker, 1975). Positivism in this sense, as a form of empiricism, involves a foundational epistemology. Knowledge claims are justified when they are shown to be based on secure foundations, which for positivist empiricism are the sense data acquired through empirical observation. Some positivists – the logical positivists – maintained that only the sentences of science thus conceived, and the "conceptual truths" of logic and mathematics, were objectively meaningful, and that therefore here were to be drawn the limits of genuine knowledge, not simply scientific knowledge. Thus delimited, the domain of knowledge excluded morals, politics, and indeed any field where value judgments were made, which would include much educational research. The movement to postpositivist philosophy of science has occurred because of the undermining of all such doctrines (House, 1991).

This use of "positivist" needs to be clearly distinguished from use of the term to describe any view that science (and perhaps conceptual truths of logic and mathematics) is the only way to knowledge, and that the task of philosophy – which is not sharply distinguished from, but continuous with, empirical science – is to find general principles common to all sciences and even to extend the use of such principles to the regulation of human conduct and the organization of society. The move to a postpositivist (in the first sense) philosophy of science is quite compatible with such a view of the nature of science and its role in human affairs.

Unfortunately, this distinction is not always clearly observed in epistemological discussions of educational research. It is one thing to say, with Lincoln and Guba (1984), that since it has been recognized that science is more complex than building on theory-free and value-free observations, qualitative inquiry may be recognized as a legitimate approach; that the latest paradigm era sanctions more than one paradigm. It is another thing to identify science with positivism (in the first sense) and on the basis of this identification to attack all views suggesting an epistemological continuity between the natural and the social sciences including educational research. Ironically, many writers, while they claim to reject positivism (in both senses), retain a positivist (in the first sense) view of natural science (e.g. Habermas, 1972). In this entry "positivist" is used in the first sense, to refer to positivistic empiricism, including logical positivism.

In summary, the move from a positivist to a postpositivist philosophy of science has been paralleled by a move from a view of educational research dominated by the quantitative tradition to a more pluralistic view. The advent of the postpositivist era has been characterized by an acceptance of epistemological diversity which, however, insofar as it is formulated in terms of P-theory, leaves educational research epistemologically divided. The question, then, if there are such divisions as have been noted, is whether the diversity must be oppositional, or can it be harmonious?

2 The oppositional diversity thesis

Quantitative researchers have often seen qualitative research as lacking in objectivity, rigor, and scientific controls (Kerlinger, 1973, p. 401). Lacking the resources of quantification, qualitative research cannot produce the requisite generalizations to build up a set of laws of human behavior, nor can it apply adequate tests for validity and reliability. Moreover, the positivist fact/value distinction is often employed to discredit the claims of qualitative inquiry to produce knowledge, since knowledge is value-free whereas qualitative research is irreducibly value-laden and subjective. In short, qualitative research falls short of the high standards of objectivity and the tight criteria for truth of the quantitative, or "scientific", paradigm. Given the prestige of science, and a positivist view of science, it is easy to see why quantitative researchers have sometimes even seen qualitative research as opposed to sound scientific method.

In reply, many qualitative researchers, invoking the explanation/understanding distinction, claim that the genuinely and distinctively human dimension of education cannot be captured by statistical generalizations and causal laws. Knowledge of human affairs is irreducibly subjective. It must grasp the meanings of actions, the uniqueness of events, and the individuality of persons. From this perspective, it is easy to see the quantitative tradition as an intrusive, even alien and antihuman, approach to the study of education. "Science" may be appropriate to the study of nature, but it distorts the study of human affairs. It is easy to see why, given a perceived *de facto* domination of educational research by the quantitative tradition, qualitative researchers have sometimes seen it in oppositional, even antagonistic, terms.

Thus the debate over whether so-called qualitative research methodology is in conflict with qualitative research methodology does not revolve simply around the use of numbers, or mathematical and statistical procedures. Rather, it concerns the relation of quantification to more basic questions about objectivity, validity, reliability, and criteria for truth. For example, according to Smith and Heshusius (1986, p. 9), who have reasserted the oppositional diversity thesis against the increasing popularity of the other two: "For quantitative inquiry, a logic of justification that is epistemologically foundational leads to the position that certain sets of techniques are epistemologically privileged in that their correct application is necessary to achieve validity or to discover how things really are out there." They also state: "From the perspective of qualitative inquiry, this line of reasoning is unacceptable. The assumptions or logic of justification in this case are not foundationalist and, by extension, do not allow that certain sets of procedures are epistemologically privileged." There are two key epistemological distinctions here. First, "logic of justification" (grounds for making claims) is distinguished from research procedures (techniques used to gather, analyze, and interpret data). Second, foundational epistemologies, which provide a logic or justification basing knowledge claims on supposedly secure or certain foundations (such as empirical observations), are distinguished from nonfoundational epistemologies whose logic of justification involves no foundations. Later in this entry the assumption that quantitative inquiry must be foundationalist is queried.

The key epistemological dilemma posed by Smith and Heshusius is that for the quantitative researcher there exists a mind-independent reality "out there" that is to some extent knowable. Disciplined observation of it provides epistemic foundations. Qualitative researchers, they assert, are committed to denying this. By following certain practices of inquiry that enjoy a cluster of related theoretical advantages – the advantages of internal and external validity, reliability, and objectivity – the quantitative researcher increases the likelihood of discovering something important about that reality. Its properties and the causal structures governing the orderly behavior of its interrelated parts constitute typical goals of quantitative inquiry. What makes these goals possible, and indeed holds together the theoretical features of such inquiry, is a belief that people can know when a correspondence obtains between the sentences of a theory and the world "out there". It is this correspondence that makes knowledge claims true.

It is precisely this belief that is most often questioned by qualitative researchers. Reality, or at least social reality, they frequently maintain, is something constructed with the mind as a product of theorizing. Theorizing shapes reality, rather than the other way around. There is simply no mind-independent or theory-independent reality to match up with or correspond to sentences, to serve as a check on their acceptability. Under this assumption, the theoretical apparatus employed to characterize epistemically virtuous inquiry will apparently have little use for familiar quantitative notions. Instead, distinctly alternative networks of theoretical requirements for qualitative research will need to be devised, tied to procedures for getting at subjective, or intersubjective, symbols, meanings, and understandings.

Critical theorists go one step further in this philosophical opposition to the "intrusion" of the quantitative tradition into the search for knowledge of the "genuinely human". In addition to being unable to capture the necessary relation between the human mind and social reality, critical theorists maintain that the quantitative (or empirical-analytic) tradition cannot capture the essential role of values in that kind of knowledge needed to improve the human condition. Thus Bates (1980) argues that epistemically adequate educational research must be research that makes for "human betterment". The "praxis" tradition in epistemology, well-exemplified in the theoretical writings of Freire (1972), and more particularly in the action research tradition (Carr and Kemmis, 1983), provides a rich theoretical context for elaborating further nonquantitative criteria to replace quantitative notions of validity, reliability, and objectivity. In contrast to the usual lines drawn in the quantitative/qualitative debate, the elimination of social injustice, for example, is not merely a matter of constructing alternative realities, or alternative theories. Nor is validity simply a matter of establishing a correspondence between theory and the world, when the goal is social improvement. Rather, what counts as valid inquiry, as epistemically progressive, is limited to what surrounding epistemology counts as promoting human well-being.

3   The complementary diversity thesis

Within the epistemologically softer climate of the postpositivist era, many educational researchers believe that the various research traditions, even if incommensurable, are equally legitimate and in no necessary conflict. The "scientific" and "humanistic" approaches, "are not exclusive, but complementary to each other" (see *Research Paradigms in Education*). Indeed Shulman (1986, p. 4) goes so far as to suggest that "the danger for any field of social science or educational research lies in its potential corruption . . . by a single paradigmatic view." Against what they have regarded as the unwarranted "positivist", quantitative domination of educational research, proponents of the qualitative/ interpretative paradigm have succeeded in convincing a number of scholars whose work has been within the quantitative tradition (e.g., Campbell and Overman, 1988; Cronbach, 1975) that the qualitative approach has its own merits.

Some writers have suggested that complementarity must be recognized in view of various distinct desiderata in educational research, not all of which can be met by any one single paradigm. For example, there are pressing educational and social problems requiring policy and practical responses. The information necessary for policy formulation might not be available for controlled laboratory experiments of limited generalizability (or external validity), but might be provided by "quasi-experiments" (Cook and Campbell, 1979) or qualitative research. Moreover, given the rate of social change, or the constant interactive effects of educational treatments and student aptitudes, generalizations yielded by a quantitative approach might become rapidly out of date. The project of developing a stable set of scientific educational laws may not be viable (Cronbach, 1975).

For other writers espousing complementary diversity, the multifactorial complexity of educational problems supports epistemological pluralism. Keeves acknowledges that some approaches are more holistic, embracing greater complexity than others:

> The techniques employed in educational research must be capable of examining many variables at the same time, but not necessarily through the use of complex statistical procedures . . . although these have their place. Anthropologists have evolved procedures from analyzing and presenting information from a situation which involves many factors that are very different from those used by psychologists, and different again from those that might be employed by economists and sociologists. (1986, p. 390)

Nevertheless, according to Campbell and Overman (1988), P-theoretical differences are still unavoidable because there remains a need for the kind of research produced by the tools of descriptive science and formal logic, which cannot embrace the value judgments characteristic of much nonquantitative educational inquiry. For other writers, fundamental epistemological differences between explanation and interpretation, of course, remain.

In educational research acceptance of the epistemological integrity of a nonquantitative paradigm has largely been the result of efforts by qualitative researchers to spell out alternative networks of theoretical requirements for qualitative research. These have tended to run parallel to elements in the received epistemological scheme of quantitative research (validity, reliability, etc.). One influential example, elaborated by Lincoln and Guba (1984), employs the notions of credibility, applicability (or transferability), consistency, and neutrality, as analogies respectively for internal validity, external validity, reliability, and objectivity.

The point here, however, is not so much that there is some loose analogical connection between corresponding terms in these sets. Rather, despite détente, the point to note is the persisting apparent epistemological distinctiveness of these theoretically interanimated clusters and their respective embeddings in different epistemologies. Some complementary diversity theorists might think that they can have fundamental epistemological diversity without subscribing to something as strong as the P-theory and its incommensurability doctrine. Here, perhaps, epistemological diversity is being confused with methodological diversity, a diversity of techniques of inquiry. Of course the latter is possible but, in the opinion of the authors, is best underwritten by a touchstone account of epistemic justification, not several incommensurable epistemologies. Such an account does not have to be fixed and absolute; it can change. The point is that at any given time it embraces those epistemological commitments that are shared by researchers. This is the unity thesis. If complementary diversity theorists wish to eschew such epistemological touchstone, then they remain committed to P-theory.

It should be noted that many advocates of equal rights for qualitative research have wished to play down the epistemological differences (Lincoln and Guba, 1984; Miles and Huberman, 1984). It may be that exponents of the complementary diversity thesis who persist with the term "paradigm" do not embrace P-theory's doctrine of incommensurability, although this is rarely made explicit. If they disavow incommensurability, their position would seem to collapse into the unity thesis, with revisionary consequences for the way they draw the distinctions between paradigms. These may be more drastic than at first appears. Not all complementarists have recognized the seriousness of the problem, however. As Smith and Heshusius (1986, p. 7) put it, there has been a tendency to "de-epistemologize" the debate or even ignore paradigmatic differences. Given that paradigms exist, Smith and Heshusius may well be right – but do paradigms exist?

4   Criticisms of the paradigms theory

It is apparent that there is some confusion over both the term "paradigm" and the problem of unambiguously identifying paradigms of educational research. Some of the confusion comes from the ambiguity of the term "paradigm" itself. On the one hand, as Husén (1988, p. 17) points out, there would be wide agreement that the most influential use of "paradigm" stems from the work of Kuhn (1970). However, Masterman (1970) identified some 21 different uses of the term in Kuhn's book; Kuhn subsequently published revisions, some substantial, to his original theory (e.g., Kuhn, 1974); and finally, not all methodologists embrace Kuhn's ideas uncritically.

Kuhn has also put the principal argument for regarding paradigms as incommensurable, as incapable of being compared or measured against some touchstone standard:

> In learning a paradigm the scientist acquires theory, methods, and standards together, usually in an inextricable mixture. Therefore when paradigms change, there are usually significant shifts in the criteria determining the legitimacy both of problems and of proposed solutions.
>
>   That observation . . . provides our first explicit indication of why the choice between competing paradigms regularly raises questions that cannot be resolved by the criteria of normal science . . . will inevitably talk through each other when debating the relative merits of their respective paradigms. In the partially circular arguments that regularly result, each paradigm will be shown to satisfy more or less the criteria that it dictates for itself and to fall short of a few of those dictated by its opponent. (1970, pp. 109–10)

The key claim being made here is that paradigms include both substantive theories and the standards and criteria for evaluating those theories, or paradigm-specific epistemologies. As such, it is also claimed, there is no privileged epistemic vantage point from which different paradigms can be assessed; there are only the rival epistemic standards built into each paradigm.

Kuhn's early comments on the task of adjudicating the merits of competing paradigms are instructive: "the proponents of competing paradigms practise their trade in different worlds" (Kuhn, 1970, p. 150); "the transfer of allegiance from paradigm to paradigm is a conversion experience that cannot be forced" (Kuhn 1970, p. 151); such a transition occurs relatively suddenly, like a gestalt switch "just because it is a transition between incommensurables" (Kuhn, 1970, p. 150).

Moreover, the belief that some research traditions are incommensurable can be made to look initially plausible by noting the kind of tradition-specific vocabularies that are used to characterize matters epistemological. As has been seen, methodological reflection on quantitative research commonly trades in such terminology as "scientific", "positivist", "foundational", "correspondence-truth", "objective", "realist", "validity", "reliability", "reductionist", and "empiricist". The qualitative network of such terms includes "nonpositivist", "antifoundational", "interpretation", "understanding", "subjective", "idealist", "relativist", and "antireductionist". The fact that key terms of epistemic conduct in one cluster are formed by negating terms in the other cluster readily suggests no common basis for the conduct and assessment of inquiry, and hence the incommensurability of these traditions.

Clearly, for a defense of the epistemological unity of educational research, the most important obstacle is this P-theoretical analysis of research traditions. So the first point to make in a defense of the unity thesis is that in philosophy, and philosophy of science in particular, P-theory is widely regarded as false. In a major review of the literature following a 1969 symposium on the structure of scientific theories, Suppe (1977, p. 647) remarks: "Since the symposium Kuhn's views have undergone a sharply declining influence on contemporary work in philosophy of science." He goes on to claim that contemporary work in philosophy of science, that is, postpositivist philosophy in science, "increasingly subscribes to the position that it is a central aim of science to come to know how the world *really is*" (Suppe, 1977, p. 649). In social and educational research, however, especially among qualitative researchers and critical theorists, antirealist belief in paradigms remains strong. In the authors' opinion, the apparent ubiquity of "paradigms" in educational research occurs because the epistemological assumptions of the P-theory itself, or its P-epistemology, are largely responsible for structuring differences among research traditions into putative paradigms.

Of course epistemologists in general agree that inquiry structures knowledge of the objects of inquiry; this is part of what is involved in maintaining that all experience is theory-laden. Contrary to Smith and Heshusius (1986), it is not a feature peculiar to qualitative inquiry. The interesting question is whether there is any reason to believe that different research traditions partition into paradigms the way P-theory requires. However, it is rarely noted that whether it is even appropriate to give reasons, to marshal evidence, to analyze research practices and inquiry contexts in order to justify such a belief, will depend on whether P-theory is, by its own lights, a paradigm (or part of a paradigm), or not. If it is, then the relevant standards of reasoning, evidence, and analysis will be peculiar to P-theory (or its encompassing paradigm) and so will have rational epistemic purchase on none but the already committed. To the unbeliever, P-theory would literally have nothing to say for itself. For one to believe that educational research comes in paradigms would require an act of faith: to come to believe it after believing the contrary would require a conversion experience.

There are interesting problems with this view. For example, what happens if one is converted to it? Does one then say that it is true that educational research divides into paradigms? Unfortunately the term "true" is P-theoretical and so one needs to determine first whether, for example, the sentences of P-theory correspond to a world of real educational researchers really engaged in incommensurable research practices. If so, then P-theory is not after all a paradigm distinct from those that employ correspondence-truth. If not, then there is a genuine equivocation over the term "true" which will permit the following claims to be made without contradiction: (a) it is correspondence-true that the different research traditions are not epistemologically distinct; and (b) it is P-true that the different research traditions are epistemologically distinct.

In conceding the equal legitimacy of incommensurable rivals (whether oppositional or complementary), however, particularly a correspondence-truth rival, the P-theorist seems to be surrendering the capacity to say anything about actual educational research practices and the historical and theoretical context of current research traditions. Worse still, in eschewing any schema for determining the ontological commitments of P-theory, there seems to be no way of knowing what the P-theorist is talking about. As such, P-theory hardly provides a challenge to a realist view of the unity of educational research.

To avoid the dilemma that threatens when P-theory becomes self-referential, several options are available. Two are considered here. First, a less parsimonious attitude to rival epistemologies can be adopted by maintaining that correspondence-true theories, which caused all the trouble, are false, wrong, or, as hard-hitting relativists are fond of saying, inadequate. Indeed, getting rid of correspondence-truth may be a condition for meaningful P-theoretical claims about theorists' living in different worlds; after all, talk of a real world tends to make other worlds pale into nonexistence. A second, opposite, strategy is to say that P-theory is not a distinct paradigm at all, but rather a set of carefully argued, evidentially supported, correspondence-true claims about the existence of paradigmatic divisions among the major research traditions. It is instructive to note that some methodologists run both these strategies simultaneously (e.g., Lincoln and Guba, 1984; Eisner, 1979). (For damaging criticism of Eisner's running the two strategies together, see Phillips, 1983.)

Arguments for the first option are by now familiar enough. Correspondence-truth is assumed to be located in a network of terms usually associated with the quantitative research tradition. Valid and reliable knowledge about the world is said to be that which is, in some way, derivable from some epistemically secure (or even certain) foundation; in positivistic empiricism usually observations or first person sensory reports. Objectivity consists in intersubjectively agreed matchings between statements and experience. And, of course, these objectively known statements are correspondence-true just in case the required matching occurs (although often the only reality admitted was sense data).

There are many objections to foundational empiricist epistemologies (e.g. Hesse, 1974; Churchland, 1979), but a version of the earlier argument from self-reference will suffice to illustrate the problems. Although this is not widely recognized in positivistic empiricism, epistemology is a task that requires (as Kant saw) a theory of the powers of the mind. What one can know will depend, to some extent, on what sort of creature one is and, in particular, on what sort of perceptual and cognitive capacities one has. A theory of the mind, however, is something one has to get to know. In the case of empiricist foundationalism, it is necessary to know that one's own sensory experiences will provide one with epistemically secure foundations. Unfortunately for the foundationalist, the theory of mind required to underwrite this claim is not itself an item of sensory experience, nor an observation report. This means that knowledge of how the class of epistemically privileged items is known is not itself epistemically privileged. Indeed, the sophisticated neurophysiological models of brain functioning now typical of accounts of perception and cognition are quite ill-suited to serving the regress pattern of foundational justification. For they so far outrun the purported resources of any proposed foundation that the whole point of foundational justification here collapses. More generally, knowledge of perceptual powers, or possible foundations, like knowledge of everything, is theory-laden. The result is that there is no epistemically privileged, theory-free, way of viewing the world. There is thus no reality that can be seen independent of competing theoretical perspectives. This applied as much to the empirical sciences (and the quantitative tradition in educational research) as to other areas (see Walker and Evers, 1982, 1986).

From the fact that all experience is theory-laden, however, that what one believes exists depends on what theory one adopts, it does not follow that all theories are evidentially equivalent, or equally reasonable. There is more to evidence than observation, or as Churchland (1985, p. 35) argues: "observational excellence or 'empirical adequacy' is only one epistemic virtue among others of equal or comparable importance." The point is that some theories organize their interpretations of experience better than others. A humdrum example employing subjectivist scruples on evidence will illustrate this point. A theory which says that I can leave what I interpret to be my office by walking through what I interpret to be the wall will cohere less well with my interpreted desire to leave my office than a theory which counsels departure via what I take to be the door. It is all interpretative, of course, but some organized sets of interpretations, or theories, are better than others. The theory that enables a person to experience the desired success of departing the perceived enclosure of an office enjoys certain epistemic advantages over one that does not. With all experience interpreted, though, the correct conclusion to draw is not that there is no adequate objective standard of reality, but that objectivity involves more than empirical adequacy. Theoretically motivated success in getting in and out of rooms is about as basic as objectivity ever gets. There are superempirical, theoretical tests which can be couched in a "coherence epistemology." One advocate of coherence epistemology, the postpositivist philosopher Quine, sums up this standard of reality.

> Having noted that man has no evidence for the existence of bodies beyond the fact that their assumption helps him organize experience, we should have done well, instead of disclaiming evidence for the existence of bodies, to conclude: such, then, at bottom, is what evidence is both for ordinary bodies and molecules. (Quine, 1960a, p. 251)

Quine's point here foreshadows a significant epistemological consequence of this attack on foundationalism. According to Quine, and many coherence theorists, we need to distinguish sharply between the theory of evidence and the theory of truth (Quine, 1960a, 1960b, 1969, 1974; Williams, 1980). Theory of evidence is concerned with the global excellence of theory, and involves both empirical adequacy, inasmuch as this can be achieved and the superempirical virtues of simplicity, consistency, comprehensiveness, fecundity, familiarity or principle, and explanatory power. Once the best theory according to these coherence criteria has been established, it is the resulting theory itself that is used to state what exists and how the theory's sentences match up with that posited reality. What corresponds to true sentences is therefore something that is determined after the theory of evidence has done its work. It is not something that figures *a priori*, or in some privileged foundational way in the determination of the best theory.

The evidence suggests that P-theory critiques of foundationalism draw too radical a conclusion. In terms of the quantitative/qualitative debate, for example, the coherence epistemology sanctioned by the most powerful criticisms of empiricist foundationalism cuts across this familiar methodological (putatively paradigmatic) bifurcation. In acknowledging the theory-ladenness of all experience it is nonpositivist and non-foundational. It agrees that people's window on the world is mind-dependent and subject to the interpretations of theorists. On the other hand, it can be realist, scientific, objective, reductionist, and embrace correspondence-truth. This possibility raises serious doubts about P-theorists' claims concerning the diversity of educational research, whether oppositional or complementary.

A more systematic objection to P-theory can be raised, however, by examining the epistemological warrant for incommensurability. The belief that research methodologies comprising incommensurable networks of theoretical terms are epistemically autonomous is sustained in large measure by a particular theory of meaning, notably that terms gain what meaning they possess in virtue of their role in some network or conceptual scheme. Where conceptual schemes or theories are said to be systematically different, no basis exists for matching the terms of one theory with those of another. So expressions such as "validity" or "truth", which appear as orthographically equivalent across different schemes, are really equivocal, with systematic differences emerging as differences in conceptual role.

Both Kuhn and Feyerabend maintain versions of the conceptual role theory of meaning. The trouble, however, is that they maintain implausibly strong versions of it, for if meaning is determined entirely by conceptual role than incommensurable theories become unlearnable. This all turns on the modest empirical fact that as finite learners, people need some point of entry into an elaborate systematically interconnected vocabulary like a theory. In order to learn some small part of the theory, say a handful of expressions, however, P-epistemology requires mastery of the whole theory in order to appreciate the conceptual role played by these expressions. It is at this point that the theory of meaning begins to outrun its own epistemological resources: it posits learned antecedents of learning that cannot themselves be learned. The parts cannot be understood without mastery of the whole, and resources are lacking to master the whole without first scaling the parts. An implicit feature of the epistemology driving P-theory's account of meaning as conceptual role is thus an implausibly strong theory of the powers of the mind. (A P-theoretical attack on correspondence-truth appears to depend on a correspondence-true theory of mind.)

Once again P-theory may be observed getting into difficulty over self-reference. In this case an epistemology should come out knowable on its own account of knowledge. The chief advantage of arguments from self-reference is that they focus directly on the superempirical virtues or weaknesses of a theory.

Inasmuch as one is impressed by such theoretical shortcomings as inconsistency, lack of explanatory power in relation to rivals, use of *ad hoc* hypotheses, and so on, one is allowing these criteria to function as touchstone in the evaluation of epistemologies and research methodologies. Of course one can ignore these vices in theory-construction: they are not extratheoretical privileged foundations by which all theorizing can be assessed. Methodologists in the main research traditions, however, who expect their inquiries to command attention, serve as a sound basis for action, or constitute a particular or definite set of knowledge claims, have been unwilling to play fast and loose with such virtues as consistency (usually on the formal ground that a contradiction will sanction any conclusion whatever) or simplicity and comprehensiveness (on the ground that *ad hoc* or arbitrary addition of hypotheses can be used to explain anything whatsoever, and hence nothing at all). Indeed a theory cannot be empirically significant unless it is consistent. With P-theory's theory of meaning exhibiting the superempirical weakness of lack of explanatory power in relation to what it sets itself to explain, and with that weakness being traceable to a theory of mind, it should be observed that whether epistemologies or methodologies are incommensurable turns on such things as empirical theories of mind or brain functioning, or theories of learning and cognition. Epistemology itself is therefore continuous with, and relies upon, empirical science. In Quine's words (1969), epistemology is "naturalized". One consequence is that interpretative theorists, for example, must rely partly on the "scientific" paradigm in order to show the incommensurability of their own paradigm with the "scientific".

5   The unity thesis

Although the paradigms perspective is seriously flawed, some account of the kind of unity educational research actually enjoys still needs to be given. In arguing against P-theory, coherence epistemology has already been considered. To conclude this discussion a brief outline will be given of a particular version of coherentism, or epistemological holism, which has achieved considerable prominence in postpositivist philosophy (Quine, 1974), has been applied to educational philosophy (Walker and Evers, 1982), and systematically to educational administration (Evers and Lakomski, 1990) and research methodology (Lakomski, 1991).

A more positive epistemological agenda for educational research can be provided by responding to the second strategy a P-theorist can adopt in defending diversity. This strategy involved denying P-theory was a distinct paradigm, conceding correspondence-truth, but arguing that fundamental epistemological diversity still occurred in educational research. In replying to this claim it can be noted that the strategy will need to employ superempirical epistemic virtues to be persuasive. To be effective against a wide range of theoretical perspectives, these virtues (consistency, simplicity, fecundity, etc.) will need to be recognized as such by rival epistemologies and hence function as touchstone. As a result the P-theorists' strategy is already compromised. To complete the job, however, a coherence epistemology is needed that yields a touchstone-coherent account of itself and its own epistemic virtues, that is unproblematically self-referential in scope, and that can account for the touchstone-recognized successes of alternative epistemologies and their research extensions.

In the view of the authors, the epistemology that best accounts for knowledge, its growth, and evaluation is a form of holistic scientific naturalism (in Quine's "epistemology naturalized" sense of "naturalism") – a theory that makes ready use of the best or most coherent theories of perception and cognition. According to this view, people are acquiring their theory of the world from infancy onward. Indeed, as Quine (1960b) has shown, theory precedes all learning and hence commences with the innate complement of dispositions to respond selectively to the environment. What one can know is dependent on the kind of creature one is and, as human beings, everyone is one kind of creature. Everyone shares genetically derived, though culturally expressed, refined and modified touchstone standards and procedures. Added to these is further culturally produced touchstone that people acquire as social beings sharing material problems in concrete social contexts. Knowledge is made up of theories, whose existence is to be explained causally, as problem-solving devices. There are numerous philosophical accounts (e.g., Laudan, 1977) of how theories can be analyzed as problem-solving devices. In the case of epistemological theories, the problems arise from theoretical practice, including empirical (e.g., educational) research. Clearly, there are certain issues concerning whether a theory is addressing the right problems, and a theory is needed of how to distinguish between real problems and pseudoproblems, and between better and worse formulations of problems.

Here the epistemology would lean on a theory of evidence and experiment, on the pragmatic relations between "theory" and "practice" (Walker, 1985a).

One real problem, shared by all educational researchers, is how best to conduct inquiry into human learning itself. Without this problem there could be no debate about whether educational research is epistemologically diverse. For there to be an issue at all presupposes at least some sharing of language, including general epistemological terminology such as "truth", "meaning", "adequacy", "interpretation", "paradigm", and so on.

Competition remains, of course, but competition between theories, including theories of educational research methodology, not paradigms. Competition arises because, in addition to touchstone, there are unshared (which is not to say incommensurable) concepts, hypotheses, and rules of method. Indeed, this is part and parcel of being able to distinguish one theory from another in a competitive situation. There can be genuine competition between theories, however, only when they have an issue over which to compete, some shared problem(s). Theory A is in competition with theory B when one or more of its sentences is contrary to sentences in theory B. For this situation to obtain, theories A and B must be attempts at solving at least one common problem. To identify a shared problem involves some conceptual common ground and, if only implicitly at first, some shared method; the concepts have to be deployed. Thus one begins to discover and negotiate touchstone theory which, unlike the privileged epistemic units of foundational epistemologies, is merely the shifting historically explicable amount of theory that is shared by rival theories and theorists. Beginning with identification of common problems, one can proceed to identify further touchstone and elaborate the touchstone frameworks within which theories compete.

Having identified common ground between theories, their differences are next rigorously set out and tested against that touchstone by empirical research and theoretical analysis, seeking to identify the strengths and weaknesses of each, and reach a decision on the theory which is strongest under present circumstances (Walker, 1985b), taking into account past achievements and likely future problems (Churchland, 1979).

Other features of this epistemology include its capacity to survive its own test of self-reference (Quine, 1969), its unified account of validity and reliability (Evers, 1991), its denial that all science consists of sets of laws, and of any fundamental epistemological distinction between explanation and understanding (Walker, 1985c) or between fact and value judgments (Evers and Lakomski, 1990).

Finally, although in this entry it has been maintained that such a coherentist naturalist epistemology is a sound way of underwriting the epistemological unity of educational research, achieved through touchstone analysis, it should be stressed that it is as much a competing theory as any other, and subject to theory testing (Walker, 1985a). Granted that it shares touchstone with other epistemologies, arguments can of course be mounted against it; to engage in such arguments, however, all participations would be implicitly conceding the epistemological unity of research.

See also: Scientific Methods in Educational Research; History of Educational Research; Naturalistic and Rationalistic Enquiry.

References

Bates, R. J. 1980 New developments in the new sociology of education. *Br. J. Sociol. Educ.* 1(1): 67–79.

Campbell, D. T. and Overman S. E. 1988 *Methodology and Epistemology for Social Science: Selected Papers.* Chicago University Press, Chicago, Illinois.

Carr, W. and Kemmis, S. 1983 *Becoming Critical. Knowing Through Action Research.* Deakin University Press, Geelong.

Churchland, P. M. 1979 *Scientific Realism and the Plasticity of Mind.* Cambridge University Press, Cambridge.

Churchland, P. M. 1985 The ontological status of observables. In: Churchland P. M., Hooker C. A. (eds.) 1985 *Images of Science: Essays on Realism and Empiricism.* University of Chicago Press, Chicago, Illinois.

Cook, T. H. and Campbell, D. T. 1979 *Quasi-Experimentation. Design and Analysis Issues for Field Settings.* Rand McNally, Chicago, Illinois.

Cronbach, L. J. 1975 Beyond the two disciplines of scientific psychology. *Am. Psychol.* 30(2): 116–27.

Eisner, E. 1979 *The Educational Imagination.* Macmillan, New York.

Evers, C. W. 1991 Towards a coherentist theory of validity. *Int. J. Educ. Res.* 15(6): 521–35.

Evers, C. W. and Lakomski, G. 1990 *Knowing Educational Administration.* Pergamon Press, Oxford.

Freire, P. 1972 *Cultural Action for Freedom.* Penguin, Harmondsworth.

Giddens, A. 1984 *The Constitution of Society: Outline of the Theory of Structuration.* Polity Press, Cambridge.

Habermas, J. 1972 (trans. Shapiro J.) *Knowledge and Human Interests.* Heinemann, London.

Hesse, M. 1974 *The Structure of Scientific Inference.* Macmillan, London.

Hooker, C. A. 1975 Philosophy and meta-philosophy of science. Empiricism, Popperianism and realism. *Synthèse* 32: 177–231.

House, E. R. 1991 Realism in research. *Educ. Researcher* 20(6): 2–9.

Keeves, J. P. 1986 Theory, politics and experiment in educational research methodology. A response. *Int. Rev. Educ.* 32(4): 388–92.

Kerlinger, F. N. 1973 *Foundations of Behavioral Research. Educational and Psychological Inquiry.* 2nd edn. Holt, Rinehart and Winston, New York.

Kuhn, T. S. 1970 *The Structure of Scientific Revolutions,* 2nd edn. University of Chicago Press, Chicago, Illinois.

Kuhn, T. S. 1974 Second thoughts about paradigms. In: Suppe F. (ed.) 1977.

Lakomski, G (ed.) 1991 Beyond paradigms: Coherentism and holism in educational research. *Int. J. Educ. Res.* 15(6): 449–97.

Laudan, L. 1977 *Progress and its Problems. Towards a Theory of Scientific Growth.* Routledge and Kegan Paul, London.

Lincoln, Y. S., Guba E. G. 1984 *Naturalistic Inquiry.* Sage, Beverly Hills, California.

Masterman, M. 1970 The nature of a paradigm. In: Lakatos I, Musgrave A. (eds) 1970 *Criticism and the Growth of Knowledge.* Cambridge University Press, London.

Miles, M and Huberman, M. 1984 Drawing valid meaning from qualitative data. Towards a shared craft. *Educ. Researcher* 13(5): 20–30.

Phillips, D. C. 1983 After the wake: Postpositivistic educational thought: The social functions of the intellectual. *Educ. Researcher* 12(5): 4–12

Popkewitz, T. 1984 *Paradigm and Ideology in Educational Research.* Falmer Press, London.

Quine, W. V. 1960a Posits and reality. In: Uyeda S. (ed.) 1960 *Bases of Contemporary Philosophy,* Vol. 5. Waseda University Press, Tokyo.

Quine, W. V. 1960b *World and Object.* MIT Press, Cambridge, Massachusetts.

Quine, W. V. 1969 Epistemology naturalized. In: Quine W. V. 1969 *Ontological Relativity and Other Essays.* Columbia University Press, New York.

Quine, W. V. 1974 The nature of natural knowledge. In: Cuttenplan S. (ed.) 1975 *Mind and Language.* Clarendon Press, Oxford.

Shulman, L. 1986 Paradigms and research programs in the study of teaching. A contemporary perspective. In: Wittrock M. C. (ed.) 1986 *Handbook of Research on Teaching,* 3rd edn. Macmillan, New York.

Smith, J. K. and Heshusius, L. 1986 Closing down the conversation. The end of the qualitative/quantitative debate among educational inquirers. *Educ. Researcher* 15(1): 4–12.

Suppe, F. (ed.) 1977 *The Structure of Scientific Theories,* 2nd edn. University of Illinois Press, Chicago, Illinois.

Walker, J. C. 1985a The philosopher's touchstone. Towards pragmatic unity in educational studies. *J. Philos. Educ.* 19(2): 181–98.

Walker, J. C. 1985b Philosophy and the study of education. A critique of the commonsense consensus. *Aust. J. Educ.* 29(2): 101–14.

Walker, J. C. 1985c Materialist pragmatism and sociology of education. *Br. J. Social. Educ.* 6(1): 55–74.

Walker, J. C. and Evers C. W. 1982 Epistemology and justifying the curriculum of educational studies. *Br. J. Educ. Stud.* 30(2): 213–29.

Walker, J. C. and Evers C. W. 1986 Theory, politics, and experiment in educational research methodology. *Int. Rev. Educ.* 32(4): 373–87.

Williams, M. 1980 Coherence justification and truth. *Rev. Metaphys.* 34(2): 243–72.

Further reading

Chalmers, A. 1990 *Science and its Fabrication.* Open University Press, Buckingham.

Miller, S. I. and Fredericks M. 1991 Postpositivistic assumptions and educational research: Another view. *Educ. Researcher* 20(4): 2–8.

Phillips, D. C. 1987 *Philosophy, Science and Social Inquiry.* Pergamon Press, Oxford.

Salomon, G. 1991 Transcending the qualitative–quantitative debate: The analytic and systemic approaches to educational research. *Educ. Researcher* 20(6): 10–18.

5 Teachers as Researchers

S. Hollingsworth

The international movement to recognize, prepare, and learn from teachers as researchers has come of age in the years since Elliott's (1985) entry on the topic in *The International Encyclopedia of Education (1st edn)*. This article summarizes the breadth, diversity, and significance of the teacher-as-researcher movement across three interrelated areas: curriculum improvement, professional and structural critique, and societal reform. Since teacher researchers are concerned simultaneously with ways to (a) improve their practice, (b) change the situations in which they work, and (c) understand their practices within the larger society, the organization of this article is not intended to be linear or hierarchical. The discussion, instead, is framed in terms of different organizing focuses.

1 Curriculum improvement

Curriculum improvement research is a derivative of what was known as "action research" and which led to the conceptualisation of teachers as researchers within a process model (Stenhouse 1983). The work in this area produced both immediate curriculum changes on the part of teachers (first-order research), and observations about teacher research from collaborating academics (second-order research).

1.1 Action research

The use of experimental social science to investigate various programs of social action was popularized in the United States by social psychologist Kurt Lewin (1946). Corey (1953) adapted the concept to improve school practices. He and his faculty colleagues at Teachers College at Columbia University worked cooperatively with public-school personnel on curriculum projects in action. In the post-Sputnik climate of the late 1950s, however, primary funding went to curriculum projects which followed traditional research, development, and dissemination models. Action research, suspect as "unscientific" in such a climate, became "interactive R & D [research and development]", disseminating research results through inservice teacher training. Much of that federally funded work, however, supported regular seminars in which teachers were encouraged to investigate topics related to their practices. It was the curriculum reform movement in the United Kingdom, however, that first popularized teachers as researchers.

1.2 Teachers as researchers

Stenhouse (1983) is credited with developing the concept of teachers as researchers at the University of East Anglia. As director of the Schools Council's Humanities Project, Stenhouse came to see teachers' authority and autonomy as a basis for curriculum improvement and innovation. Like Corey, Stenhouse used the scientific method of developing and testing curricular hypotheses, but felt that its use to develop replicable results across classrooms was limited. He also questioned the ethical stance of separating the performance from the performer. Stenhouse thus rejected the "objectives model" of curriculum adoption (Tyler, 1949) and asked teachers to engage in a "process model" of curriculum innovation where professional and curricular development became part of the same enterprise.

1.3 Developing the process model

Three factors made action research in the process model a viable alternative in the late 1970s and 1980s: (a) the difficulties of disseminating quantitative, experimental methodologies to local educational settings; (b) an increasing acceptance of the concept of curriculum as integrated with human deliberation (Schwab, 1973); and (c) a professional and political reaction to post-Sputnik accountability as an approach for improving and changing curriculum. Elliott (1991), a colleague of Stenhouse, emphasized the interpretive-hermeneutic nature of inquiry. He saw action research as a pedagogical paradigm – a form of teaching. He argued that educational research should be modeled after action research: "a moral science paradigm to which teacher researchers would be the main contributors, rather than those in academic disciplines" (McKernan, 1991, p. 23).

1.4 The impact of first- and second-order research on curriculum improvement

First-order research examines changes in the curriculum made by teachers. Examples of such research are included in reports prepared by public-school teachers (Philadelphia Teachers Learning Collaborative, 1984), descriptions of university-level teachers' research on their curricular practices (Lampert, 1989), and summaries included in texts detailing the action of teacher researchers and academics (Clandinin et al., 1995). Examples of second-order research (that is, discussions about teacher research) can be found in outlines of skills needed by teacher researchers (Hopkins, 1985), in discussions of teacher researchers' cognitive development (Oja and Sumlyan, 1989), in descriptions of teacher networks (Smith et al., 1991), and in understandings gained from teacher–university collectives (Carini, 1988).

The cumulative effect of this work has changed the manner in which teachers are perceived as professional curriculum developers. It has also influenced collaborative research models and school restructuring plans which emphasize "teacher empowerment". One of the best examples of curriculum-based teacher research, one which improved practice and then led to theoretical, professional, and structural change, is the Bay Area Writing Project (BAWP). Reports from BAWP extensions across the United States range from first-order summaries (Fecho, 1992) to second-order analyses of project participants' ideological difference (Schecter, 1992).

2 Professional and structural critique

Emerging in the 1980s from the success of curriculum improvement research in the United Kingdom and the United States was an attempt to improve social environments and/or conditions of practice through structural and professional critique.

2.1 Structural critique

Kemmis and his colleagues at Deakin University in Australia and elsewhere have articulated a model of a critical educational science. Their basic premise is that "new ideas are not enough to generate better education. Educational practices and patterns of school and classroom organization must also be changed to secure improvement" (Kemmis and McTaggert, 1988, p. 34).

The critical stance of teachers as researchers, focusing on desired and possible changes in the educational structures, has also been noted within the United Kingdom and other countries. Simons (1992), for example, has argued for collaborative partnerships in the teacher research movement, which take into account the practice-oriented views of the curriculum researcher and the structural views of the critical researcher. She points out that reforming schools from the outside cannot work – neither can simple calls for collaboration. Existing structures privilege privacy, hierarchy, and territory within the institution and across collaborative boundaries; thus, structural and professional relationships must change.

2.2 Critiques of professionalism and professionalization

Sockett (1989) has drawn educational scholars' attention to the need for professionalism in teaching as well as the professionalization or socialization process by which one becomes a professional. Teacher research is an important part of both processes. Posch (1992) in Austria also speaks of the importance of teacher research for the profession. He argues that teacher professionalism involves teacher research on student professionalism.

Preparing student teachers and experienced teachers to be critical professionals who challenge and change the workplace conditions (including curriculum) is an important part of a professional and structural critique. Feminists involved in teacher education help teachers to develop radical pedagogies or "styles of teaching which help make visible to pupils the structural social inequities which constrain their lives" (Middleton, 1992, p. 18).

2.3   *Impact on the workplace and the profession*

Although the preparation of teachers as critical inquirers is not yet widespread, structural and professional changes influenced by this work have been widely noted in new policies for school and professional restructuring. In the United States, a Californian decision to retain and reshape the state-sponsored mentoring project followed teacher research investigations into its possibilities and limitations (see Ashton *et al.* 1990).

Many of the transformative results from the critical professional and structural stance, however, have been far less public and far more personal. The Boston Women's Teachers' Group (Freedman *et al.*, 1983), for example, met for three years to cope with the isolated struggle of their daily work and to study how their work conditions affected them as teachers. Like other groups who have created similar structures, their professional work was critical rather than curricular. They focused on the creation of conditions under which participants could consider their own interests and develop curriculum innovations.

3   Societal reform

The focus of teachers as researchers in the societal reform sense is on how schools and teaching are shaped in society and what epistemological views are needed for their transformation. In some countries, the societal focus resulted from an awareness of the increasing gap between the concept of democracy and the reality of domination and oppression. Fueled by the Civil Rights and Women's Movements in the United States, even popular teacher-promoted curricular projects challenging static views of knowledge and societal norms were not free from scrutiny (see, for example, Delpit's (1986) critique of the Bay Area Writing Project). Two broad areas of societal reform are epistemological critique and the problem of gender.

3.1   *Epistemological critique*

This view of teachers as researchers developed simultaneously with philosophical critiques of societal positions based on privileged conceptions of knowledge. Bruner (1985), for example, questioned the power ascribed the paradigmatic or "rational" view of knowledge and discussed the power of its antitheses: a narrative view of knowledge. Harding (1991) questioned natural science's position on objectivity as too protective of the power-dominant, White, male society. Belenky *et al.* (1986) raised questions about alternative ways of knowing which could privilege some women over others. Culturally diverse ways of knowing and representing knowledge, such as those pointed out by Lourde (1984), also critiqued societally accepted knowledge. Finally, many critiques either implicitly or explicitly questioned the separation of hierarchically powered social structures and inquiry methods (Winter, 1987).

3.2   The problem of gender

Zeichner (1990) challenged the problematic social and epistemological hierarchy by speaking of the importance of teachers as women in the second professional wave of educational reform. Zeichner stressed that "Teaching is not just work; it is gendered work" (p. 366). As he expressed hope for societal reform and emancipation in the press for teacher empowerment, he also offered caution. He pointed out the possibility of curricular reform missions being undermined unless teacher research is incorporated into, instead of added to, teacher's work.

For Hollingsworth (1992), the teacher-as-researcher movement takes on a perspective of feminist praxis. A consciousness of the teacher's personal position within society (i.e., most teachers throughout the world are women), an understanding of research, an appreciation of the teacher's ability to construct and critique knowledge, and the integration of those features in classroom teaching suggests that teaching itself is research. Thus, teachers are the researchers of educational and societal reform – a position Elliott (1991) had endorsed earlier from a curricular stance.

Weiner (1989) contrasts teacher research in the Schools Council Sex Differentiation Project with mainstream professional development or curricular teacher research. Rather than convince teachers of a need to change their practices, gender researchers in the United Kingdom wish to bring about improvements in the social and economic position of women. Similar research is being conducted in the United States (see McIntosh *et al.*, 1992).

3.3   Impact of societal reform

Excellent examples of first-order research from the societal reform stance are available (Newman, 1990). The publication of such work is indicative of the increasing involvement of teachers in emancipatory work. Further, not only are teacher researchers conducting their own professional meetings, but they are participating at national and international research conferences previously reserved for university researchers. For example, since 1989, the American Educational Research Association has registered a special interest group on teacher research. The National Research Center on Literature Teaching and Learning in the United States sponsored a Teacher Research Institute in 1992. These are but a few examples of how the teacher-as-researcher movement is resulting in societal reform.

The concept of teacher-as-researcher is at the center of international attention to reform in all areas of the educational enterprise: research, teaching, the profession, its moral purpose, and its impact on societies. Some might worry that the political implications of teacher empowerment and societal reform might lead to a new and unknown world with unfamiliar epistemological and social norms. Others might be concerned that the growing popularity of teachers-as-researchers will ensure that it becomes yet another form of power and hierarchy inside schools. If so, the concept may be mandated, measured, and become meaningless to actual improvement of practice. Conversely, it may become a new process for reproducing existing school structures and societal outcomes. The trends found in the literature fail to resolve either of those worries. What is clear is that the movement is part of the larger evolution of society into the postinformation age – and that teachers-as-researchers are no longer marginally involved.

References

Ashton, D. *et al.* 1990 *Where Do We Go From Here in the California Mentor Teacher Program?: Recommendations by Seven Mentors.* Stanford/Schools Collaborative, Stanford University, Stanford, California.

Belenky, M. F., Clinchy B. M., Goldberger N. R. and Tarule J. M. 1986 *Women's Ways of Knowing: The Development of Self, Voice and Mind.* Basic Books, New York.

Bruner, J. S. 1985 Narrative and paradigmatic modes of thought. In: Eisner E. (ed.) 1985 *Learning and Teaching the Ways of Knowing, 84th Yearbook of the National Society for the Study of Education.* University of Chicago Press, Chicago, Illinois.

Carini, P. 1988 Prospect's documentary processes. Unpublished manuscript, Bennington, Vermont.

Clandinin, D. J. Davies, A. Hogan, P. and Kennard, B. (1995) *Learning to Teach: Teaching to Learn Stories of Collaboration in Teacher Education.* Teachers' College Press, New York.

Corey, S. 1953 *Action Research to Improve School Practices.* Teachers College Press, New York.

Delpit, L. 1986 Skills and other dilemmas of a progressive Black educator. *Harv. Educ. Rev.* 56(4): 379–85.

Elliott, J. 1985 Teachers as researchers. In: Husén T. and Postlethwaite T. N. (eds.) 1985 *The International Encyclopedia of Education, 1st edn.* Pergamon Press, Oxford.

Elliott, J. 1991 *Action Research for Educational Change.* Open University Press, Milton Keynes.

Fecho, B. 1992 The way they talk: An English teacher ponders his role. Paper presented at the Ethnography in Education Research Forum, University of Pennsylvania, Philadelphia.

Freedman, S. Jackson, J and Boles, K. 1983 Teaching: An imperilled "profession." In Shulman L. S. and Sykes G. (eds.) 1983 *Handbook of Teaching and Policy.* Longman, New York.

Harding, S. 1991 *Whose Science? Whose Knowledge? Thinking from Women's Lives.* Cornell University Press, Ithaca, New York.

Hollingsworth, S. 1992 Learning to teach literacy through collaborative conversation: A feminist approach. *Am. Educ. Res. J.* 29(2): 373–404.

Hopkins, D. 1985 *A Teacher's Guide to Classroom Research.* Taylor and Francis, London.

Kemmis, S and McTaggart, R. 1988 *The Action Research Planner,* 3rd edn. Deakin University Press, Geelong, Victoria.

Lampert, M. 1989 Research into practice: Arithmetic as problem solving. *Arithmetic Teacher* 36(7): 34–36.

Lourde, A. 1984 *Sister Outsider.* The Crossing Press, Freedom, California.

Lewin, K. 1946 Action research and minority problems. *J. Soc. Iss.* 2(4): 24–46.

McIntosh, P, Style, E and Tsugawa, T. 1992 *Teacher as Researcher.* National SEED Seeking Educational Equity and Diversity, Wellesley College Center for Research on Women, Wellesley, Massachusetts.

McKernan, J. 1991 *Curriculum Action Research: A Handbook of Methods and Resources for the Reflective Practitioner.* St. Martin's Press, New York.

Newman, J. D. (ed.) 1990 *Finding our Own Way: Teachers Exploring their Assumptions.* Heinemann, Portsmouth, New Hampshire.

Oja, S. N. and Smulyan, L. (eds.) 1989 *Collaborative Action Research: A Developmental Process.* Falmer Press, London.

Philadelphia Teachers' Learning Cooperative 1984 On becoming teacher experts: Buying time. *Lang. Arts* 61(7): 731–36.

Posch, P. 1992 Teacher research and teacher professionalism. Paper presented at the Int. Conf. Teacher Research, Stanford University, Palo Alto, California.

Schecter, S. R. 1992 Ideological divergences in teacher research groups. Paper presented at the Ethnography in Education Research Forum, University of Pennsylvania, Philadelphia.

Schwab, J. 1983 The practical 4: Something for curriculum professors to do. *Curric. Inq.* 13(3): 239–65.

Simons, H. 1992 Teacher research and teacher professionalism. Paper presented at the Int. Conf. Teacher Research, Stanford University, Palo Alto, California.

Smith, H, Wigginton, E, Hocking, K and Jones, R. E. 1991 Foxfire teacher networks. In: Lieberman A and Miller L. (eds). 1991 *Staff Development for Education in the 1990s: New Demands, New Realities, New Perspectives,* 2nd edn. Teachers College Press, New York.

Sockett, H. 1989 Practical professionalism. In: Cass W. (ed.) 1989 *Quality in Teaching.* Falmer Press, New York.

Stenhouse L. 1983 Research as a basis for teaching. In: Stenhouse L. (ed.) 1983 *Authority, Education and Emancipation.* Heinemann, Portsmouth, New Hampshire.

Tyler, R. W. 1949 *Basic Principles of Curriculum and Instruction.* University of Chicago Press, Chicago, Illinois.

Weiner, G. 1989 Professional self-knowledge versus social justice: A critical analysis of the teacher-researcher movement. *Brit. Educ. Res. J.* 15(1): 41–51.

Winter, R. 1987 *Action-research and the Nature of Social Inquiry: Professional Innovation and Educational Work.* Gower, Brookfield, Vermont.

Zeichner, K. M. 1990 Contradictions and tensions in the professionalization of teaching and the democratization of schools. *Teach. Col. Rec.* 92: 363–379.

6   Policy-Oriented Research

J. Nisbet

Policy-oriented research is best defined in terms of its instrumental function rather than by its topics of study. When research in education is designed, managed, and reported with the specific purpose of informing a policy decision, or assisting or monitoring its implementation, or evaluating its effects, the term "policy-oriented" is used to distinguish this approach from "fundamental" research which is designed primarily to extend the frontiers of knowledge. This definition of policy-oriented research may be extended to include research which is closely tied to educational practice as well as policy.

The implicit model is that the function of research is to provide an information base for decision-making, to establish the "facts"; administrators, politicians, or teachers then add the necessary value judgments, supposedly so that policy and practice are firmly based on empirical evidence from experiment and survey. Thus "good" research provides answers to "relevant" problems. In this approach, educational issues which are of current concern are accepted as priority topics for research. This instrumental view of the function of research, however, makes naive and simplistic assumptions about how policy and practice are determined. If adopted uncritically, the emphasis on relevance constrains inquiry within the limits of existing policy and risks a trivialization of research and centralization of control over the choice of topics for inquiry. But with a clearer understanding of the relation of research and policy and with enlightened administration of research funding, the trend toward policy-oriented research could enable research to make a more effective contribution to educational practice.

1   Definitions

The definition of policy-oriented research is usually expressed by contrasting it with fundamental research, on the analogy of pure and applied science. A variety of terms can be used to express the contrast: applied versus basic research, policy-oriented versus curiosity-oriented studies, instrumental versus enlightenment functions, work directed toward decision or action versus work directed toward knowledge or theory. Less charitably, "relevant" research may be contrasted with "academic" research. Cronbach and

Suppes (1969) criticized these "popular labels", arguing instead for a distinction in terms of the audience to whom the research is directed. Their concepts of "decision-oriented" and "conclusion-oriented" research have been widely adopted. Decision-oriented research is designed to provide information wanted by a decision-maker; the findings of conclusion-oriented research are of interest primarily to the research community. "The distinction between decision-oriented and conclusion-oriented research lies in the origination of the inquiry and the constraints imposed by its institutional setting, not in topic or technique" (p. 23). Thus, Cooley and Bickel (1985) define decision-oriented research as "a form of educational research that is designed to be directly relevant to the current information requirements of those who are shaping educational policy or managing educational systems" (p. xi).

Whichever terms are used, they carry value judgments which can be misleading if they are not made explicit. The distinction between pure and applied research in education is itself misleading, in that theoretical studies provide concepts for the analysis of problems and may even help to identify and define problems. It may be argued that educational research must be set in the context of an educational system; if it is general, it may be better described as psychological or sociological or management research. "From one point of view, *all* educational research is applied research, designed to bring about changes in the way education is carried on, rather than simply to add to our existing stock of knowledge" (Taylor, 1973, p. 207). Defined narrowly, policy-oriented research is research which has direct application to current issues in educational policy or practice. A wider definition (and, to anticipate the argument of this analysis, a better one) is that policy-oriented research consists of careful, systematic attempts to understand the educational process and, through understanding, to improve its efficiency.

Listing the procedures involved is one way of defining. Policy-oriented research includes surveys or any comparable data-gathering which enables policymakers or practitioners to base their decisions on evidence rather than on prejudice or guesswork. This includes the search for solutions to pressing educational or social problems, identifying and resolving the problems involved in implementing policy decisions, pilot studies to test new initiatives, monitoring and evaluating initiatives in educational practice, and experimental studies to compare alternative educational methods. It also includes policy studies and retrospective analyses of past policy where the purpose is to help make better policy decisions in the future.

Thus the essential distinction between policy-oriented and other forms of educational research is in terms of purpose, rather than in choice of subject or method. Since the perception of educational issues as being of current concern is subject to volatile popular fashion, an aspect of learning may be regarded as a theoretical issue this year but a topic of policy-oriented research next year. The end products of policy-oriented research are recommendations for decision or action. The products of fundamental research are contributions to knowledge, understanding, or theory. Since decisions and action necessarily imply the adoption of some theory or interpretation, and theory likewise has long-term implications for action, the distinction between the two categories is not as sharp as is sometimes assumed. However, policy-oriented research usually operates within the context of accepted theory: it does not aim to modify theory, though it may do so incidentally. Similarly, fundamental research does not aim to affect practice, but it may do so indirectly. Policy-oriented research is responsive, whereas fundamental research is autonomous.

Autonomous educational research, which does not have to be accountable in the sense of producing useful or usable findings, runs the risk of producing results which are of interest only to other researchers. In its extreme, it is concerned with attacking other people's theories, irrespective of whether the points at issue are of any importance outside the research sphere. Responsive research, designed as a response to a practical need, is no less likely to raise and illuminate fundamental issues, and there is the added bonus that it can be useful at the same time. However, it runs the risk of being left behind by the rapid course of events, since by the time results are available the problem which they were designed to answer is liable to have changed or to be no longer seen as important. The resolution of this dilemma may lie in the concept of "strategic research" (Bondi, 1983): "that grey zone of researches that . . . are not immediately of use to the customer, but lay the foundations for being able to answer questions that may be put in the future" (p. 3). Unfortunately, however, the precise nature of strategic research remains uncertain.

Since responsive research operates within the context of existing policy or practice, it is limited in its generalizability, but it is more likely to have an impact on the specific policy or practice for which it is designed. The impact of this kind of research, however, is incremental rather than radical. Policy-oriented research modifies (and hopefully improves) the existing situation, protecting it from running into trouble by identifying or anticipating problems. It may challenge established policy by demonstrating its impracticability, or may develop or explore alternative policies. But it is essentially concerned with movement from a present situation, and therefore it obliges researchers to relate their work to "reality", usually in the form of empirical studies or fieldwork.

2 Trends

Although pressure toward policy-oriented research has increased since the early 1970s, many of the early educational research studies had a strong practical orientation. Binet's work, for example, which laid the foundations of psychometry, began with the problem of early identification of slow-learning children. The work of Thorndike and others in the 1920s on the psychology of the elementary school curriculum aimed to influence educational policy and classroom practice. The "scientific movement" in the 1930s envisaged the creation of a science of education based on experimentation, which would be used to improve decision-making at all levels, from day-to-day classroom practice to long-term educational planning. National studies in the 1930s, such as the Eight-year Study to test the feasibility of school accreditation and the international program of research on examinations, were directed to produce practical recommendations for improvement of the system. The distinction between practical and theoretical research was not stressed at this time. The two kinds of research were seen as complementary; and since there was practically no public funding of research, the choice of topic was left to academic researchers in universities and colleges.

The situation changed dramatically in the years after 1950, first with the growth of publicly financed research (1955–65) and a massive expansion of funding in 1965–70, and subsequently with the demand for accountability and a trend toward central control of research. Initially (and relatively slowly) there was acceptance that educational research could make a significant contribution to policy and practice. The social sciences had come of age and their potential value was recognized. (Perhaps it was merely that administrators found themselves at a disadvantage in controversies if they could not produce empirical evidence to support their decisions.) In Sweden, the linking of research to policy began in the 1940s. In the 1960s, in the United States and the United Kingdom (and subsequently in many other countries), formal institutional structures were created for channeling public funds into educational research and development, particularly for curriculum development and intervention programs. As a result, between 1964 and 1969, expenditure on research in education in the United Kingdom multiplied tenfold; and in the United States, expenditure doubled each year from 1964 through 1967. Almost all this funding was for policy-oriented research.

The increase in funding soon led to a demand for accountability, and for a greater say in how the funds were to be spent. Since public funding was for policy-oriented research, policymakers began to demand the right to decide which policy aspects should be researched, and also how the research should be oriented. In 1970 in the United Kingdom, for example, the Secretary of State for Education and Science demanded that research policy in education "had to move from a basis of patronage – the rather passive support of ideas which were essentially other people's, related to problems which were often of other's peoples choosing – to a basis of commission . . . the active initiation by the Department on problems of its own choosing, within a procedure and timetable which were relevant to its needs" (DES 1970). This was followed in 1971 by the crude customer–contractor formula of the Rothschild Report (1971): "The customer says what he wants; the contractor (the researcher) does it if he can; and the customer pays" (p. 3). This method of deciding how research should be funded was widely challenged at the time. But the protests could not survive the energy crisis of 1973 and the economic constraints of the years which followed. The need to cut back expenditure made decisions on priorities inevitable, and increasingly these decisions were made by central government. Perhaps too much had been expected, or promised, and disillusionment was allied with suspicion of "academic drift", in which preoccupation with theory was given priority over pressing practical issues. In the early 1990s, research which is not linked to policy is at risk of being seen as a dispensable luxury, and major policy issues are seen as the only topics worth studying.

Thus, to quote from a review of developments in eight countries (Nisbet, 1981a), "Across the world, educational research is now an integral part of modern administrative procedure. Increased investment in research has led to . . . a concern that the conduct, organisation and funding of research should be directed towards maximizing its effect on policy and practice. The major questions to which answers are still sought are, What forms of research should have priority? and, Who is to decide?" (p. 104).

Since then, decisions increasingly have been made centrally by those who control public funds, not only on what should be researched but also on the method and scale (everything short of the results expected), and often with restrictions on the right to publish without official approval. Central decision-making on research priorities runs the risk of restricting the scope of inquiry. The Organisation for Economic Co-operation and Development in a report (OECD, 1988, p. 23) expressed its concern at the trend toward a "practical, short-term and commercial orientation" in the national research programs of its member states. However, as Cuban (1992) noted, "the frameworks which educational researchers use . . . often overlook unwittingly the enduring tension-ridden dilemmas that practitioners and policymakers must manage in their organizations" (p. 7). Restrictions on dissemination, though increasingly common in research contracts, run counter to the basic principle of "critical debate", defined in a policy statement of the British Educational Research Association (Bassey 1992) as "opening one's work to the scrutiny of others in order first to search for errors and fallacies, and secondly to seek creative insights into its future development" (p. 8).

If policy-oriented research is to be effective, it needs cooperation between policymakers and researchers; but it also requires a degree of independence. A warning of the danger inherent in central control was given in the United Kingdom in 1982, when a second Rothschild Report (1982) was published, on the work of the government-sponsored Social Science Research Council: "The need for independence from government departments is particularly important because so much social science is the stuff of political debate . . . It would be too much to expect Ministers to show enthusiasm for research designed to show that their policies were misconceived. But it seems obvious that their policies were misconceived. But it seems obvious that in many cases the public interest will be served by such research being undertaken" (p. 12). This raises the issue of how research can best be used in the framing and monitoring of policy.

3   Utilization

How can research best contribute to policy and practice in education? This question is the central theme of the 1985 *World Yearbook of Education* (Nisbet *et al.*, 1985), which reviews contrasting perspectives in 14 countries. People have different expectations of research, and these are often unrealistic. Policy-makers and teachers tend to look to research to provide answers to their problems; but research can perform this function only when there is consensus on values, within the framework of accepted policy or in the context of established practice. Researchers are more likely to see the role of research as identifying new problems, or new perspectives on problems – problem-setting rather than problem-solving (Rein and Schon, 1977). But implementation will happen only when the findings are seen as relevant to the issues which concern those with the responsibility of action. If it is not to be just an esoteric activity, research in education must have a context. But whose context is it to be?

If research is undertaken in the context of those who are expected to make use of the findings, the likelihood of implementation is much greater. The Australian *Karmel Report* (Karmel, 1973) summarized the requirements for impact: "The effectiveness of innovation . . . is dependent on the extent to which the people concerned perceive a problem . . . , are knowledgeable about a range of alternative solutions, and feel themselves to be in a congenial climate" (p. 126). How people perceive a problem is itself influenced by research publications. Thus research shapes people's perceptions, and provides them with concepts to use in thinking about the work they do. In this way, research creates an agenda of concern.

Weiss (1979), reviewing the contribution of social research to public policy, identified seven models of research utilization:

(a) the *linear model*, which assumes that basic research leads into applied research, followed by development and implementation;

(b) the *problem-solving model*, in which research identifies the missing knowledge to guide action;

(c) the *interactive model*, involving researchers and policymakers in constructive cooperative dialogue;

(d) the *political model*, where research is used to provide justification for an already favored policy;

(e) the *tactical model*, in which the need for research is used as an excuse to delay decision or action;

(f) the *enlightenment model*, envisaging research ideas filtering through and shaping how people think;

(g) the *intellectual model*, by which the activity of research widens horizons and raises the quality of public debate.

The first two models are naive, the third and seventh over-hopeful; the fourth and fifth cynical. In an earlier work, Weiss (1977) argued for the sixth of these models – the enlightenment model – seeing the most important effect of research as indirect and long-term, though "a gradual accumulation of research results" (p. 16), shaping the context within which policy decisions are made. Husén and Kogan (1984) in *Educational*

Research and Policy: How Do They Relate?, the most comprehensive review of the issue in the 1980s, accept this "percolation" model, but ask how the percolation of ideas can be engineered. Research can clarify issues, raise awareness and create space for testing policies before they are put into action; but there is a lack of institutional structures for independent research to have impact on the formulation of policy.

The problem-solving model is implicit in one of the most widely read educational publications of the 1980s, *What Works: Research About Teaching and Learning* (US Department of Education 1986). This 65-page booklet listed 41 research findings about how best to teach and improve learning. Each finding was stated, briefly elaborated, and supported by five references to research literature. In the Preface, the President of the United States commended it as providing practical knowledge based on "some of the best available research for use by the American public." Published in January 1986, 300,000 copies were in circulation within 6 months. Glass (1987) criticized this selection of "useful findings" as "an expression of conservative philosophy" (p. 6), arguing that its popular appeal was due to the possibility of applying the findings within the existing framework of educational assumptions.

Husén and Kogan (1984) identify a major dilemma in the different worlds of policy and research. The two worlds have different and conflicting values, different reference groups and reward systems, and even different languages. Policy decision-making must be firm and authoritative, whereas research is essentially questioning and uncertain.

> A political design will lead to closure on an issue. Research findings add to, rather than reduce, uncertainty for decision-makers. The interplay between decision-making which must be authoritative and firm and the questioning and uncertainty implicit in the research is an important phenomenon. It leads to a central policy question: can national authorities sponsor the generation of uncertainty? . . . Policy-makers may foreclose on issues too quickly: social science can keep open the space between the dissemination of ideas which might lead to policy changes and their enforcement. (p. 52)

Bell and Raffe (1991) offer a resolution of this dilemma by distinguishing a changing balance between research and policy in three phases of the policy cycle:

(a) recognition of a problem and shaping a policy;
(b) implementing a policy;
(c) evaluating the outcomes and reshaping the policy.

In the first phase, before outlines of a new policy have emerged, "wide-ranging critical research is welcomed, because it will help to win support for change." In the second phase, the government needs to build support for its chosen policy: "research which calls into question the wisdom of the policy or the assumptions on which it is based is not welcome." Here the policy world is most restrictive and control tightest. In the third phase, "there is a degree of relaxation: the policy is no longer so politically sensitive (it is now the flavour of last month) . . . and critical research findings are less potentially damaging" (p. 141). Bell and Raffe ask why so little policy-related research is commissioned in the first phase of the policy cycle.

The answer lies in who is seen as holding power. The policymakers seek to establish a policy which is acceptable to those with power to influence its implementation. Their concern is not so much a matter of being "right" (for there are different "right" solutions, depending on one's values), but rather of reconciling divergent views in a solution which is seen as "fair" by a maximum number of those affected by it. In this, the aims and values of those with access to power must carry greatest weight.

In the amorphous process of policy-making, there are several functions which research can perform. First, insofar as information conveys power, research strengthens the hand of any group which can produce research findings to support its preferred viewpoint. (Even to describe assertions as "research" strengthens their impact.) Coleman (1984) noted that this strategy "is most often used by those without direct control over policy, who challenge the policies of those in positions of authority" (p. 132); and this may be one reason for policymakers' hostility to research. Administrators commission policy-oriented research to strength their hand against the many pressure groups in the policy-making arena. In the view of the administrators, pressure groups are those who seek to further their own policies, whereas administrators see themselves as neutral to the policy they implement. Information thus weakens the power of those who play on ignorance or twist facts to suit their private ends. This, however, assumes that research is value-free, or at least that research makes explicit the values on which it is based.

A second function for research is to ensure that action will achieve what is intended in a policy. For this purpose, research is used to work out the details of how to implement decisions, by identifying obstacles, including the opinions and attitudes of those who might oppose the policy, and by testing out solutions to overcome these obstacles in trials with pilot groups. Using Bell and Raffe's three phases of the policy cycle: in phase 1, surveys gather relevant "facts" as a database for decision; in phase 2, pilot studies establish feasibility and identify likely obstacles; and in phase 3, evaluation provides monitoring and guidance for future decision or modification.

In all three phases, the most valuable research design is one which focuses on analysis of problems, rather than simply seeking to supply answers to questions. There are of course some who still hold the unrealistic expectation that research should provide ready-made incontrovertible solutions. The Secretary of State of the Department of Education and Science for England and Wales, for example, once complained: "It is exceptional to find a piece of research that really hits the nail on the head and tells you pretty clearly what is wrong or what should be done" (Pile, 1976, p. 3). Weiss (1977) describes this as the "linear model" of research utilization and criticizes its "instrumental naivety." The sequence implied is: "A problem exists: information or understanding is lacking; research provides the missing knowledge; a solution is reached" (pp. 11–12). There are relatively few situations in which this model is applicable. Halsey's (1972) interpretation is nearer the truth: "Action research is unlikely ever to yield neat and definitive prescriptions from field-tested plans. What it offers is an aid to intelligent decision-making, not a substitute for it. Research brings relevant information rather than uniquely exclusive conditions" (p. 179).

However, the claim that the prime use of research lies in the analysis of problems may be seen only as an academic abdication of responsibility, and may encourage the suspicion that the only ones who derive benefit from investment in research are the researchers themselves. Being isolated from the practical realities of the "real world", as it is termed, they divert public money to academic interests of their own instead of to the problems which require solutions. The solution adopted has been to take the decisions on research priorities out of the hands of the administrators. If research cannot give direction to policy, then the influence should be reserved and policymakers should be given control of research, allowing policy priorities to determine the choice and design of research. If those who are in contact with the "real world" take over the management of research, so the assumption goes, impact will be improved, relevance will be greater, and the risk of wasted money will be avoided.

Consequently, decisions on research priorities are often made by those who are not themselves directly involved in research. This mode of working is familiar to the economist, the engineer, and the agricultural specialist; it is not accepted generally in legal and medical matters. The administrator who controls research funds now expects to be involved in the initial decisions on the topic of inquiry, the design, the time scale, the personnel required, and of course the cost. When a project is funded, there will be continuing interest (or interference, as it may seem to the researcher) in monitoring what is being done through an advisory committee) and regular reporting on progress. Tighter control may be imposed by "stepped funding", in which funds for each stage are conditional on approval of a report on the previous one. Arrangements for publishing and discussing the findings will be specified in the contract, which may require surrender of copyright and "moral rights" to the sponsor and acceptance of their right of veto should they find the results not to their liking.

It is difficult to stand against these pressures. Not only can sponsors withhold funds; even access to school is usually made conditional on approval of the research project as a whole and of the research instruments in detail. Thus policy-oriented research can become wholly directed and censored by people who are not themselves researchers and who have a vested interest in the outcomes. Clearly, the dangers here are that criticism of a policy is not likely to be encouraged and that important issues are organized out of debate. Fortunately, many of those responsible for the funding of research are aware of these dangers. In some countries at least, the relationship between researchers and the providers of funds is quite close; both sides understanding the requirements and constraints of the other.

4   Conclusion

Two functions of research in education can be distinguished: one long-term, creating the theoretical context in which day-to-day issues are perceived, writing an agenda of concern; the other more immediate, working out routine problems within the context of the current educational provision and prevailing views. These are the basic and policy-oriented modes of research, but the distinction between them is not as sharp as might appear. The applied sciences have often resulted in significant contributions to theory, and theoretical studies may have profound impact on perceptions of practical needs.

Academic status tends to be accorded to those who make contributions to theory. In the social sciences, their ideas and new concepts are gradually absorbed into popular thought and discussion until they become a new climate of opinion, variously described as a "prevailing view" (Cronbach and Suppes), "a cumulative altering of conceptions of human behavior" (Getzels), "sensitizing" (Taylor), or "ideas in good currency" (Schon). Administrators and politicians respond to the "resonance" of research findings, often to a filtered, out-of-date perception. In the early 1990s, however, research funding is available almost exclusively for policy-oriented studies. Research of this kind can be a powerful instrument of reform, testing out new ideas, modifying them or rejecting them if they are at fault, and if the evidence shows them to be feasible, establishing their credibility all the more widely and quickly. The results are more likely to have impact and thus create in the long term a favorable climate of opinion as to the value of educational research. In a time of financial constraint and accountability, it is difficult to justify the expenditure of public funds on any other kind of research in education.

The danger, however, is that if research is too closely tied to existing educational provision and practice, where the concept of "relevance" implies implementation without radical change, the effects may be only marginal and may even be an obstacle to reform. The restrictions increasingly imposed on researchers in policy-oriented funding are seen by many as running counter to the basic requirement of open, critical study. There is also a danger of accepting a purely technocratic role for research, creating an elite group of researchers in alliance with bureaucrats to manager the system. Though at first sight this may seem an attractive role for the researcher, it is potentially divisive, since it divides the researcher and his or her powerful partner from the teaching profession and the public. An alternative style of research is the "teachers as researchers" movement (see *Teachers as Researchers*) or "action research" (see *Action Research*). In this school-based research, teachers are encouraged to apply the techniques of research to their own work: they define the problems to be researched and they investigate and reflect on their own practice. This style of research also has its risks, of restricting research within the limits of inflexible classroom traditions and narrow professional perspectives. But it could also "be the most fertile soil for educational research to grow in . . . If it can be developed so as to provide teachers (and administrators and parents and all those concerned with education) with the means of improving their own understanding, then its effect will be to put educational studies into a questioning framework" (Broadfoot and Nisbet, 1981, p. 121).

An interactionist model of this kind for educational research applies also to the relation of research to policy. The association of policy, administration, and research could be developed in such a way that each illuminates the others. Cronbach *et al.* (1980) argue for an intermediate structure between research and application to promote this interaction, some institutional means of arguing about the policy relevance of ambiguous results in a "context of accommodation" rather than a "context of command" (pp. 83–84). If policy-oriented studies can be developed in this enlightened way, educational research stands to gain from its closer association with both policy and practice. "Two worlds of educational research may be distinguished, the practical and the theoretical, pure and applied; but we are more likely to have a balanced attitude if we have a foot in both worlds" (Nisbel, 1981b, p. 175). The contributions of research to policy, to practice, and to theory are not easily reconciled; but the research enterprise would suffer if any one of these three is regarded as of lesser importance.

References

Bassey, M. 1992 Educational research and politics: A viewpoint. *Research Intelligence* 43: 8–9.

Bell, C. and Raffe, D. 1991 Working together: Research, policy and practice. In: Walford G. (ed.) 1991 *Doing Educational Research.* Routledge, London.

Bondi, H. 1983 Research funding scrutinized. *THES* August 19: 3.

Broadfoot, P. M. and Nisbet, J. 1981 The impact of research on educational studies. *Br. J. Educ. Stud.* 29(2): 115–22.

Coleman, J. S. 1984 Issues in the institutionalisation of social policy. In Husén T. H. and Kogan M. (eds.) 1984.

Cooley, W. and Bickel, W. 1985 *Decision-oriented Educational Research.* Kluwer-Nijhoff, Boston, Massachusetts.

Cronbach, L. J. and Suppes, P. (eds.) 1969 *Research for Tomorrow's Schools: Disciplined Inquiry for Education.* Macmillan, New York.

Cronbach, L. J. *et al.* 1980 *Toward Reform of Program Evaluation.* Jossey-Bass, San Francisco, California.

Cuban, L. 1992 Managing dilemmas while building professional communities. *Educ. Researcher* 21(1): 4–11.

Department of Education and Science (DES) 1970 Press release December 1, 1970, for speech to National Foundation for Educational Research. In: Taylor W. (ed.) 1973 *Research Perspectives in Education.* Routledge and Kegan Paul, London.

Glass, G. V. 1987 What works: Politics and research. *Educ. Researcher* 16(3): 5–10.

Halsey, A. H. 1972 *Educational Priority*, Vol. 1. HMSO, London.

Husén, T. and Kogan, M. (eds.) 1984 *Educational Research and Policy: How Do They Relate?* Pergamon Press, Oxford.

Karmel, P. H. (Chair) 1973 *Schools in Australia.* Australian Government Printing Service, Canberra.

Nisbet, J. 1981a The impact of research on policy and practice in education. *Int. Rev. Educ.* 27(2): 101–04.

Nisbet, J. 1981b Educational research and educational practice. In: Simon B. and Taylor W. (eds) 1981 *Education in the Eighties: The Central Issues.* Batsford, London.

Nisbet J, Megarry J, Nisbet S (eds.) 1985 *World Yearbook of Education 1985: Research, Policy and Practice.* Kogan Page, London.

OECD 1988 *Science and Technology Policy Outlook.* OECD, Paris.

Pile, W. 1976 Some research called "rubbish." *THES* January 23: 3.

Rein, M. and Schön D. A. 1977 Problem setting in policy research. In: Weiss C. (ed.) 1977.

Rothschild Report 1971 *A Framework for Government Research and Development.* HMSO (Cmnd 4814), London.
Rothschild Report 1982 *An Enquiry into the Social Science Research Council.* HMSO (Cmd 8554), London.
Taylor, W. (ed.) 1973 *Research Perspectives in Education.* Routledge and Kegan Paul, London.
US Department of Education 1986 *What Works: Research about Teaching and Learning.* Washington, DC.
Weiss, C. (ed.) 1977 *Using Social Research in Public Policy Making.* Heath, Lexington, Massachusetts.
Weiss, C. 1979 The many meanings of research utilization. *Public Administration Review* (Sept/Oct): 426–31.

Part II

The Range of Approaches

7   Scientific Methods in Educational Research

A. Kaplan

Methodology as a discipline lies between two poles. On the one hand is technics, the study of specific techniques of research – interpreting a Rorschach protocol, conducting a public opinion survey, or calculating a correlation coefficient. On the other hand is philosophy of science, the logical analysis of concepts presupposed in the scientific enterprise as a whole – evidence, objectivity, truth, or inductive inference. Technics has an immediate practical bearing, but only on the use of specific techniques. Philosophy of science, though quite general in application, has only remote and indirect practical bearings. Though philosophy is much exercised about the problem of induction, for instance, educational researchers and behavioral scientists would be quite content to arrive at conclusions acceptable with the same confidence as the proposition that the sun will rise tomorrow.

Methodology is a generalization of technics and a concretization of philosophy. It deals with the resources and limitations of general research methods – such as observation, experiment, measurement, and model building – with reference to concrete contexts of inquiry. No sharp lines divide methodology from technics or from philosophy; particular discussions are likely to involve elements of all three.

The concern with methodology has lessened: more and more the researchers do their work rather than working on how they should do it. There has been a corresponding lessening of belief in the myth of methodology, the notion that if only the student of adult education could find "the right way" to go about research, the findings would be undeniably "scientific".

Anxious defensiveness heightened vulnerability to the pressure of scientific fashions. Scientism is an exaggerated regard for techniques which have succeeded elsewhere, in contrast to the scientific temper, which is open to whatever techniques hold promise for the particular inquiry at hand. Computers, mathematical models, and brass instruments are not limited to one subject matter or another; neither is their use necessary for scientific respectability.

Methodology does not dictate that the educational disciplines be hardened or abandoned. Neither does methodology exclude human behavior from scientific treatment.

The task is to do as well as is made possible by the nature of the problem and the given state of knowledge and technology.

Fashions in science are not intrinsically objectionable, any more than fashions in dress, nor are they intrinsically praiseworthy. What is fashionable is only one particular way of doing things; that it is in the mode neither guarantees nor precludes effectiveness. Cognitive style is a characteristic way of attaining knowledge; it varies with persons, periods, cultures, schools of thought, and entire disciplines. Many different styles are identifiable in the scientific enterprise; at different times and places some styles are more fashionable than others. Successful scientists include analysts and synthesizers; experimenters and theoreticians; model builders and data collectors; technicians and interpreters. Problems are often formulated to suit a style imposed either by fashion or by personal predilection, and are investigated in predetermined ways. Scientism is marked by the drunkard's search – the drunkard hunts for the dropped house key, not at the door, but under the corner streetlamp, "because it's lighter there." Widespread throughout the sciences is the law of the instrument: give a small child a hammer and it turns out that everything the child sees needs pounding. It is not unreasonable to do what is possible with given instruments; what is unreasonable is to view them as infallible and all-powerful.

1   Scientific terms

Closely associated with the myth of methodology is the semantic myth – that all would be well in (adult) educational research if only their terms were defined with clarity and precision. The myth does not make clear precisely how this is to be done. Scientists agree that scientific terms must bear some relation to observations. There is no consensus on exactly what relation, nor even on whether a useful scientific purpose would be served by a general formulation of a criterion of cognitive meaning. In particular cases the issue is not whether a term has meaning but just what its meaning might be.

For some decades education was dominated by operationism, which held that terms have meaning only if definite operation can be performed to decide whether the terms apply in any given case, and that the meaning of the terms is determined by these operations. "Intelligence" is what is measured by an intelligence test; "public opinion" is what is disclosed in a survey. Which details are essential to the operation called for and which are irrelevant presupposes some notion of what concept the operations are meant to delimit. The same presupposition underlies attempts to improve adult literacy tests and measures. A more serious objection is that the validation of scientific findings relies heavily on the circumstances that widely different measuring operations yield substantially the same results. It is hard to avoid the conclusion that they are measuring the same magnitude. Most operations relate terms to observations only by way of other terms; once "symbolic operations" are countenanced, the semantic problems which operationism was meant to solve are reinstated.

Ambiguities abound in the behavioral sciences, as in the field of education. The behavioral scientist is involved with the subject matter in distinctive ways, justifiably so. The involvement makes for widespread normative ambiguity, the same term being used both normatively and descriptively – "abnormal" behavior, for example, may be pathological or merely deviant. Also widespread is functional ambiguity, the same term having both a descriptive sense and an explanatory sense – the Freudian "unconscious" may be topographical or dynamic. Ambiguity is a species of openness of meaning, perhaps the most objectionable. Vagueness is another species. All terms are more or less vague, allowing for borderline cases to which it is uncertain whether the term applies – not because what is known about the case is insufficient, but because the meaning of the term is not sufficiently determinate. All terms have some degree of internal vagueness, uncertainties of application, not at the borderline but squarely within the designation; some instances are better specimens of what the term designates than others (closer to the "ideal type"), and how good a specimen is meant is not wholly determinate. Most terms have also a systemic vagueness: meanings come not singly but in more or less orderly battalions, and the term itself does not identify in what system of meanings (notably, a theory) it is to be interpreted. Significant terms are also likely to exhibit dynamic openness, changing their meanings as contexts of application multiply and knowledge grows.

As dangerous as openness is the premature closure of meanings. The progressive improvement of meanings – the semantic approximation – is interwoven with the growth of knowledge – the epistemic approximation. The advance of science does not consist only of arriving at more warranted judgments but also of arriving at more appropriate concepts. The interdependence of the two constitutes the paradox of conceptualization: formulating sound theories depends on having suitable concepts, but suitable concepts are not to be had without sound theoretical understanding. The circle is not vicious; it is broken by successive approximations, now semantic and now epistemic.

Meanings are made more determinate by a process of specification of meaning. This is sometimes loosely called "definition"; in a strict sense of definition is only one way of specifying meanings – providing a combination of terms, whose meaning is presumed to be already known, which in that combination have a meaning equivalent to that of the given term. Definitions are useful for formal disciplines, like mathematics; for empirical disciplines, their usefulness varies inversely with the importance of the term.

In simple cases, meanings can be specified by ostension: making what is meant available to direct experience. Empiricism regards ostensions as the fundamental anchorage for theoretical abstractions. Meanings in the educational and behavioral sciences are often specified by description of the thing meant, especially when this is included in or is close to everyday experience. Most scientific terms have a meaning specified by indication: a set of indices, concrete or abstract, often the outcomes of specified tests and measures, which constitute, not *the* meaning of the term, but some of the conditions which provide ground for applying the term. Each index carries its own weight; each case exhibits a profile, whose weight is not necessarily the sum of the weights of the constituent indices. As contexts of application change as well as what knowledge is available, so do the indications and their weight, and thereby also the meaning specified. Premature closure of meaning by definition is likely to provide false precision, groundless or unusable.

Which type of specification is appropriate depends on the scientific purposes the term is meant to serve. Observables, terms denoting what can be experienced more or less directly, invite ostension. Indirect observables lend themselves to description of what would be observed if our senses or other circumstances were different from what they are: such terms are sometimes known as "intervening variables". Constructs have meanings built up from structures of other terms, and so are subject to definition. Theoretical terms have a core of systemic meaning which can be specified only by an open and ever-changing set of indications. Many terms have sufficient functional ambiguity to exhibit characteristics of several or all of these types of terms; they call for various types of specification of meaning. "Lifelong learning" is a good example of such an ambiguous, all-encompassing concept.

2   Classes

Empirical terms determine classes; because of openness of meaning these classes are only approximations to well-defined sets in the sense of mathematical logic, where everything in the universe of discourse definitely belongs to or is excluded from the class. The approximation to a set can be made closer (the term made more precise) by restricting its meaning to what is specifiable by easily observable and measurable indices. The danger is that such classes are only artificial, delimiting a domain which contributes to science little more than knowledge of the characteristics by which it is delimited. Natural classes correspond to an articulation of the subject matter which figures in theories, laws, or at least in empirical generalizations inviting and guiding further research. Artificial and natural classes lie at two poles of a continuum. A classification closer to being artificial is a descriptive taxonomy; one closer to being natural is an explanatory typology. Growth of concepts as science progresses is a movement from taxonomies to typologies – Linnaeus to Darwin, Mendeleef to the modern periodic table, humors to Freudian characterology.

3   Propositions

Knowledge of a subject matter is implicit in how it is conceptualized; knowledge is explicit in propositions. Propositions perform a number of different functions in science.

First are identifications, specifying the field with which a given discipline deals, and identifying the unit elements of the field. In the behavioral sciences "idiographic" disciplines have been distinguished from "nomothetic," the former dealing with individuals, the latter with general relationships among individuals (history and sociology, for instance, or clinical and dynamic psychology). Both equally involve generalizations, because both demand identifications – the same "state" with a new government, or different personalities of the same "person": sameness and difference can be specified only by way of generalizations. Which units are to be selected is the locus problem; political science, for instance, can be pursued as the study of governments, of power, or of political behavior. What is to be the starting point of any given inquiry cannot be prejudged by other disciplines, certainly not by methodology. It is determinable only in the course of the inquiry itself – the principle of the autonomy of the conceptual base.

Other propositions serve as presuppositions of a given inquiry – what is taken for granted about the conceptual and empirical framework of the inquiry. Nothing is intrinsically indubitable but in each context there is always something undoubted. Assumptions are not taken for granted but are taken as starting points of the inquiry or as special conditions in the problem being dealt with. Assumptions are often known to be false, but are made nevertheless because of their heuristic usefulness. Hypotheses are the propositions being investigated.

4   Generalizations

Conclusions of an inquiry, if they are to be applicable to more than the particular context of the inquiry, are stated as generalizations. According to the logical reconstruction prevailing in philosophy of science for some decades (but recently coming under increasing criticism), generalizations have the form: "For all x, if x has the property f, then it has the property g." The content of the generalization can be specified only in terms of its place in a more comprehensive system of propositions.

A simple generalization moves from a set of propositions about a number of individual cases to all cases of that class. An extensional generalization moves from a narrower class to a broader one. Both these types are likely to be only descriptive. An intermediate generalization moves from propositions affirming relations of either of the preceding types to one affirming a relation of both relata to some intermediate term. It begins to be explanatory, invoking the intermediate term to account for the linkage recorded in its premises. A theoretical generalization is fully explanatory, putting the original relata and their intermediates into a meaningful structure. The conclusion of a successful inquiry may produce any of these types of generalization, not only the last.

All empirical findings, whether appearing as premises or as conclusions, are provisional, subject to rejection in the light of later findings. Philosophy of science divides propositions into *a priori* and *a posteriori*; for methodology it is more useful to replace the dichotomy by degrees of priority, the weight of evidence required before a finding is likely to be rejected. In increasing order of priority are conjectures, hypotheses, and scientific laws. A law strongly supported by theory as well as by the empirical evidence may have a very high degree of priority, often marked by calling the law a principle. In a logical reconstruction of the discipline in which it appears it may be incorporated in definitions, and so become *a priori* in the strict sense.

5   Observations and data

Unless a proposition is a definition or a logical consequence of definition, it must be validated by reference, sooner or later, to observations. Reports of observation – data – must themselves be validated; what was reported might not in fact have been observed. A magician's performance can never be explained from a description of the effect, for the effect is an illusion; a correct description would not call for an explanation.

Errors of observation are virtually inevitable, especially in observations of human behavior; in the fashionable idiom, there is noise in every channel through which nature tells us something. In some contexts, observation can be insulated, to a degree, from error – it might be made, for instance, through a one-way mirror, so that data would not be contaminated by the intrusiveness of the observer. Error can sometimes be cancelled – reports from a large number of observers are likely to cancel out personal bias or idiosyncracy. In special cases error can be discounted: its magnitude or at least its direction, can be taken into account in drawing conclusions from the data – memories are likely to be distorted in predictable ways.

There is a mistaken notion that the validity of data would be guaranteed if interpretations were scrupulously excluded from reports of what is actually seen. This mistake has been called "the dogma of immaculate perception." Observation is inseparable from a grasp of meanings; interpretation is intrinsic to perception, not an afterthought. It has been well said that there is more to observation than meets the eye.

Two levels of interpretation can be discriminated (in the abstract) in behavioral science. First is the interpretation of bodily movements as the performance of certain acts – the grasp of an act meaning. Raised hands may be interpreted as voting behavior rather than as involuntary muscular contractions (such contractions may be act meanings for a physiologist). A second level of interpretation sees observed acts in the light of some theory of their causes or functions – the grasp of an action meaning. Dress and hairstyle may be seen as adolescent rebelliousness.

Both levels of interpretation are hypothetical in the literal sense – they rest on hypotheses as to what is going on. Such hypotheses in turn rest on previous observations. This is the paradox of data: hypotheses are necessary to arrive at meaningful data, but valid hypotheses can be arrived at only on the basis of the data. As with the paradox of conceptualization, the circle is broken by successive approximation.

Because observation is interwoven with interpretation, what is observed depends on the concepts and theories through which the world is being seen. Whatever does not fit into the interpretative frame remains unseen – invisible data, like pre-Freudian male hysteria and infantile sexuality. The data may be noted but be dismissed as meaningless – cryptic data, like dreams and slips of the tongue. Observation also depends on what instruments of observation are available. Techniques like mazes, projective tests, and opinion surveys have had enormous impact on research.

6   Experiments

Creating circumstances especially conducive to observation is an experiment. Not all experiments are probative, meant to establish a given hypothesis or to select between alternative hypotheses (crucial experiment). Some may be methodological, like pilot studies or the secondary experiments performed to determine factors restricting the interpretation of the primary experiment. Heuristic experiments may be fact finding or exploratory. Other experiments are illustrative, used for pedagogy or to generate ideas, a common function of simulations.

The significance of experiments sometimes appears only long after they were performed. Experiments have meaning only in a conceptual frame. Scientific advance may provide a new frame in which the old experiment has a new and more important meaning. The secondary analysis of an experiment already performed may be more valuable than a new experiment.

Experiments in education and the behavioral sciences have often been criticized on the basis of an unfounded distinction between the laboratory and "life." There are important differences between the laboratory and other life situations – for instance, significant differences in scale. Only moderate stresses are produced – subjects may be given, say, only a small amount of money with which to play an experimental game, whose outcome may therefore have only questionable bearings on decisions about marriage, surgery, or war. Secondary experiments may be useful to assess the effect of the differences in scale. All observations, whether in the laboratory or not, are of particular circumstances; applying the findings to other circumstances always needs validation.

Not all experiments are manipulative; in some, the manipulation is only of verbal stimuli – administering a questionnaire can be regarded as an experiment. Events especially conductive to observation even though they were not brought about for that purpose are sometimes called nature's experiments – disaster situations or identical twins separated at birth. The relocation of workers or refugees, school bussing, and changes in the penal code are instances of social experiments. Experimentation and fieldwork shade off into one another.

7   Measurement

The more exact the observations, the greater their possible usefulness (possible, but not necessary). Widespread is a mystique of quality – the notion that quantitative description is inappropriate to the study of human behavior. True, quantitative description "leaves something out" – precision demands a sharp focus. But what *is* being described is more fully described by a quantitative description. Income leaves out of account many important components of a standard of living, but a quantitative description says more about income than "high" or "low".

There is a complementary mystique of quantity – the notion that nothing is known till it has been weighed and measured. Precision may be greater than is usable in the context or even be altogether irrelevant. Because quantitative data are more easily processed, they may be taken more seriously than the actually more important imponderables. The precision may be spurious, accurate in itself but combined with impressionistic data. Fashion in the behavioral sciences may invite the use of quantitative idioms even if no measurements are available to determine the implied quantities.

Measurement is the mapping of numbers to a set of elements in such a way that certain operations on the numbers yield results which consistently correspond to certain relations among the elements. The conditions specifying the mapping define a scale; applications of the scale produce measures which correspond to magnitudes. Just what logical operations on the numbers can be performed to yield empirical correspondence depends on the scale.

Numbers may be used only as names – a nominal scale – in which case nothing can be inferred about the elements save that they are the same or different if their names are such. The numbers may be used so as to take into account relations of greater and less – an ordinal scale – allowing the corresponding elements to be put into a definite order. An interval scale defines a relation of greater and less among differences in the order. Operations may be defined allowing measures to be combined arithmetically, by which magnitudes can be compared quantitatively – a ratio or additive scale. Scales can be freely constructed, but there is no freedom to choose what they logically entail. Equally restrictive are the empirical constraints imposed by the operations coordinating measures and magnitudes.

One measuring operation or instrument is more sensitive than another if it can deal with smaller differences in the magnitudes. One is more reliable than another if repetitions of the measures it yields are closer to one another. Accuracy combines both sensitivity and reliability. An accurate measure is without significance if it does not allow for any inferences about the magnitudes save that they result from just such and other operations. The usefulness of the measure for other inferences, especially those presupposed or hypothesized in the given enquiry, is its validity.

8 Statistics and probability

No measures are wholly accurate. Observations are multiple, both because data are manifold and because findings, to be scientific, must be capable of replication by other observers. Inevitably, not all the findings are exactly alike. Inferences drawn from any measure are correspondingly inconclusive. Statistics are the set of mathematical techniques developed to cope with these difficulties.

A problematic situation is one inviting inquiry. The situation itself does not predetermine how the problem is to be formulated; the investigator must formulate it. A problem well-formulated is half solved; badly formulated, it may be quite insoluble. The indeterminacy of a situation, from the point of view of statistics, is its uncertainty. When a specific problem has been formulated, the situation is transformed to one of risk. A card game involves risk; playing with strangers, uncertainty. Moving from uncertainty to risk is the structuring problem; it may be more important than computing and coping with risk once that has been defined. How to compute risk is the subject matter of the theory of probability; how to cope with it, the theory of games, and more generally, decision theory.

The calculation of probabilities rests on three different foundations; alternatively, three different conceptions of probability may be invoked. Mathematical probability is expressed as the ratio of "favorable" cases (those being calculated) to the total number of (equally likely) cases. Statistical probability is the (long-run) frequency of favorable cases in the sequence of observations. Personal probability is an expression of judgments of likelihood (or degree of confidence) made in accord with certain rules to guarantee consistency. For different problems different approaches are appropriate. Mendelian genetics or the study of kinship systems makes use of mathematical probability. Studies of traffic accidents or suicides call for statistical probabilities. Prediction of the outcome of a particular war or labor dispute is a matter of personal probability.

Statistics begin where assignment of probabilities leaves off. A multiplicity of data are given. The first task is that of statistical description: how to reduce the multiplicity to a manageable unity with minimal distortion. This is usually done by giving some measure of the central tendency of the data, and specifying in one way or another the dispersion of the data around that central measure (like the mean and the standard deviation). Inferences drawn from the data are statable as statistical hypotheses, whose weight is estimated from the relation between the data and the population about which inferences are being made (sampling theory). Depending on the nature of the sample and of its dispersion, statistical tests assign a measure of the likelihood of the hypothesis in question. Explanatory statistics address themselves to the use of statistical descriptions and hypotheses in formulating explanations (for instance, by way of correlations).

9   Theories and models

Once a problematic situation has been structured and the data measured and counted, a set of hypotheses may be formulated as possible solutions to the problem. Generalized, the hypotheses are said to constitute a theory. Alternatively, it is possible to begin with a set of hypotheses formulated in the abstract, then interpret them as applying to one or another problematic situation. Such a set is called a model.

Often the result of structuring the problematic situation is called a model. Structure is the essential feature of a model. In an interpretation of the model, a correspondence is specified between the elements of the model and those of some situation, and between certain relations holding within each set of elements, so that when two elements of the model are in a certain relation the corresponding elements stand in the corresponding relation, and vice versa. A set of elements related in certain ways is a system; a structure is what is shared by corresponding systems (or it may be identified with the set of all possible systems corresponding to a given one and thus to each other).

A model can be a physical system (like an airplane model in a wind tunnel), in which case it is an analog. An analog computer is a device which allows such systems to be easily constructed – systems consisting, for instance, of electrical networks with certain voltages, resistances, and current flow. Operations on the analog which preserve its structure show what would happen in any other system having the same structure. If the model is a system of symbols it may be called a map. Behavioral science models are maps of human systems.

When the correspondences are only suggested rather than being explicitly defined, the symbolic system is an extended metaphor; intermediate between a metaphor and a model is an analogy, in which correspondences are explicit but inexact. All three have roles in the actual conduct of inquiry; the view that only models have a place in science makes both terms honorific.

In another honorific usage "model" is a synonym for "theory" or even "hypothesis." The term is useful only when the symbolic system it refers to is significant as a structure – a system which allows for exact deductions and explicit correspondences. The value of a model lies in part in its abstractness, so that it can be given many interpretations, which thereby reveal unexpected similarities. The value lies also in the deductive fertility of the model, so that unexpected consequences can be predicted and then tested by observation and experiment. Here digital computers have already shown themselves to be important, and promise to become invaluable.

Two dangers in the use of models are to be noted. One is map reading, attaching significance to features of the model which do not belong to its structure but only to the particular symbolization of the structure (countries are not colored like their maps; psychoanalytic models do not describe hydrodynamic processes of a psychic fluid: "psychic energy" is not equal to mc^2).

The other danger is, not that something is read into the map which does not belong to the structure, but that something is omitted from the map which does. This error is called oversimplification. All models simplify, or they would not have the abstractness which makes them models. The model is oversimplified when it is not known by how much nor even in what direction to correct the outcomes of the model so that they apply to the situation modeled. In an economic model, ignoring differences in the worth of money to the rich and to the poor is likely to be an oversimplification; ignoring what exactly the money is spent on may not be.

Theories need not be models; they may present a significant content even though lacking an exactly specified structure – as was done by the theory of evolution, the germ theory of disease, and the psychoanalytic theory of the neuroses. A theory is a concatenation of hypotheses so bound up with one another that the proof or disproof of any of them affects that of all the others. The terms in which the hypotheses are couched are likely to have systemic meanings, specifiable only by reference to the entire theory. Knowledge may grow by extension – applying a theory to wider domains. It may also grow by intention – deepening the theory, specifying more exactly details previously only sketched in or even glossed over.

Theory is not usefully counterposed to practice; if it is sound, a theory is of practice, though the theoretical problems may be so simplified that the theory provides only an approximate solution to the problems of practice, and then only under certain conditions. A theory, it has been said, is a policy, not a creed. It does not purport to provide a picture of the world but only a map. It guides decisions on how best to deal with the world, including decisions on how to continue fruitful inquiry. It raises as many questions as it answers; the answers themselves are proposed directives for action rather than assertions for belief.

10   Explanation, interpretation, and validation

Validation of a theory is a matter, first, of coherence with knowledge already established. A new theory may raise difficulties of its own, but it must at least do justice to the facts the older theory accounted for. Validation means, second, a certain correspondence with the world as revealed in the continually growing body of data – it must successfully map its domain. Validation, finally, lies in the continued usefulness of the theory in practice, especially in the conduct of further inquiry.

A valid theory provides an explanation of the data, not merely a shorthand description of them. The latter, even if comprehensive, is only an empirical generalization; a theory gives grounds for expecting the generalization to be indefinitely extendable to data of the same kind. A dynamic tendency is quite different from a statistical trend. The theory may allow the prediction of data not yet observed, though it may be valid without successful prediction if this is precluded by the intervention of factors outside the theory, or by cumulation of the inexactness to be found in all theories when applied to empirical findings. Conversely, an empirical generalization may suggest successful predictions even though it is unable to say why the predictions should succeed.

Deductive explanation deduces predictions from the premises postulated by the theory (together with the initial conditions of the particular situation). This type of explanation is characteristic of models. Pattern explanation makes the data intelligible by fitting them into a meaningful whole (predictions might then be made of what would fit the gaps). This is characteristic of disciplines concerned with action meanings.

Behavioral interpretation is grasping such meanings, as distinguished from model interpretation, which is setting up correspondences that give content to an abstract structure. In behavioral interpretation actions are understood as purposive, goal directed.

Goals need not be conscious, deliberate, intentional – in short, motivational; they may be purely functional, as are the telic mechanisms of cybernetic systems. Interpretation in the behavioral sciences often suffers from mistaking functions for motives, then introducing abstract agents to have the putative motives – neuroses are said to defend themselves, ruling classes to perpetuate a social order, economies to seek to expand.

All explanations, at best, leave something to be desired. They are partial, dealing with only a limited class of situations. They are conditional, depending on special circumstances in those situations. They are approximate – no explanation is wholly precise. They are indeterminate, having only a statistical validity – there are always apparent exceptions. They are inconclusive, never validated beyond any possibility of replacement or correction. They are intermediate, pointing always to something which needs to be explained in turn. They are limited, serving in each instance only some of the purposes for which explanations might be sought – a psychologist's explanation of a death (as, say, a suicide) is very different from a pathologist's explanation (as, say, a poisoning). Both explanations may be equally valid. All this openness of theory corresponds in the epistemic approximation to the openness of meaning in the semantic approximation.

11   Values and bias

Inquiry itself is purposive behavior and so is subject to behavioral interpretation. The interpretation consists in part in specifying the values implicated in specific processes of conceptualization, observation, measurement, and theory construction. That values play a part in these processes does not in itself make the outcomes of these processes pejoratively subjective, nor otherwise invalidate them. A value which interferes with inquiry is a bias. Not all values are biases; on the contrary, inquiry is impossible without values.

A distinction between facts and values remains; the distinction is functional and contextual, not intrinsic to any given content. Descriptions may be used normatively. They are also shaped by norms which guide not only what is worth describing but also what form the description should take – for instance, the degree of precision which is worthwhile, the size of sample which is worth taking, the confidence level to be demanded, and the like. Values play a part not only in choosing problems but also in choosing patterns of inquiry into them. The behavioral sciences have rightly become concerned with the ethics of the profession, as bearing, for instance, on experimentation with human beings.

A myth of neutralism supposes that scientific status requires rigorous exclusion of values from the scientific enterprise. Even if this exclusion were desirable (a value!), it is impossible. The exclusion of bias, on the other hand, *is* an operative ideal. Bias is only hidden by the pretense of neutrality; it is effectively minimized only by making values explicit and subjecting them in turn to careful inquiry.

The danger that values become biases is especially great when values enter into the assessment of the results of inquiry as distinct from what is being inquired into and how.

A truth may be unpleasant, even downright objectionable, yet remain true for all that. Science must be granted autonomy from the dictates of political, religious, and other extra scientific institutions. The content of the pursuit of truth is accountable to nothing and no one not a part of that pursuit.

All inquiries are carried out in specific contexts. Validation of the results of any particular inquiry by reference to the outcomes of other inquiries is important. How important varies with the distance between their respective subject matters, concepts, data, and other components of the process of inquiry. The behavioral sciences have become increasingly willing to affirm their autonomy with respect to the physical and biological sciences. Science suffers not only from the attempts of church, state, and society to control its findings but also from the repressiveness of the scientific establishment itself. In the end, each scientist must walk alone, not in defiance but with the independence demanded by intellectual integrity. That is what it means to have a scientific temper of mind.

See also: Empirism, Positivism and Antipositivism; Research in Education: Epistemological Issues.

References

Bailey, K. D. 1978 *Methods of Social Research.* Free Press, New York.
Black, J. A. and Champion, D. J. 1976 *Methods and Issues in Social Research.* Wiley, New York.
Braithwaite, R. B. 1953 *Scientific Explanation: A Study of the Function of Theory Probability and Law in Science.* Cambridge University Press, Cambridge.
Campbell, N. R. 1928 *Measurement and Calculation.* Longman, New York.
Durkheim, E. 1950 *The Rules of Sociological Method,* 8th edn. Free Press, New York.
Ellingstad, V. S. and Heimstra, N. W. 1974 *Methods in the Study of Human Behavior.* Brooks Cole, Monterey, California.
Gellner, E. 1973 *Cause and Meaning in the Social Sciences.* Routledge and Kegan Paul, London.
Hanson, N. R. 1972 *Observation and Explanation: A Guide to Philosophy of Science.* Harper and Row, New York.
Hempel, C. G. 1965 *Aspects of Scientific Explanation, and Other Essays in the Philosophy of Science.* Free Press, New York.
Kaplan, A. 1964 *The Conduct of Inquiry: Methodology for Behavioral Science.* Chandler, New York.
Kuhn, T. S. 1970 *The Structure of Scientific Revolutions.* University of Chicago Press, Chicago, Illinois.
Lachenmeyer, C. W. 1973 *Essence of Social Research: A Copernican Revolution.* Free Press, New York.
Myrdal, G. 1969 *Objectivity in Social Research.* Pantheon, Westminster, Maryland.
Nachmias, D. and Nachmias C. 1976 *Research Methods in the Social Sciences.* St. Martin's Press, New York.
Nagel, E. 1961 *The Structure of Science: Problems in the Logic of Scientific Explanation.* Harcourt Brace, and World, New York.
Nerale, J. M. and Liebert, R. M. 1973 *Science and Behavior: An Introduction to Methods of Research.* Prentice-Hall, Englewood Cliffs, New Jersey.
Popper, K. R. 1959 *The Logic of Scientific Discovery.* Basic Books, New York.
Popper, K. R. and Eccles, J. C. 1983 *The Self and its Brain.* Routledge and Kegan Paul, London.
Quine, W. V. and Ullian, J. S. 1978 *The Web of Belief,* 2nd edn. Random House, New York.
Runkel, P. J. and McGrath, J. E. 1972 *Research on Human Behavior: A Systematic Guide to Method.* Holt, Rinehart and Winston, New York.
Weber, M. 1949 *Methodology in the Social Sciences.* Free Press, New York.

8 Biographical Research Methods

N. K. Denzin

The biographical method, which is considered in this article, is defined as the studied use and collection of life documents, or documents of life that describe turning-point moments in individuals' lives. These documents include autobiographies, biographies, diaries, letters, obituaries, life histories, life stories, personal experience stories, oral histories, and personal histories. The subject matter of the biographical method is the life experiences of a person, and biographical methods provide the very foundations for the study of educative processes. When written in the first person it is called "autobiography", life story, or life history. When written by another person it is called a "biography". Sociologist John M Johnson has coined the term "burography" to describe an autobiography that analyzes the intersections of biography, personal experience, and bureaucratic, or organizational structures. An "autoethnography" is a partial first-person text, based on the cultural study of the person's own group. There are many biographical methods, or many ways of writing about a life. Each form presents different textual problems and leaves the reader with different messages and understandings. A life or a biography is only ever given in the words that are written about it.

1 Historical development

The biographical, life history, case study, case history, or ethnographic method has been a part of sociology's history since the 1920s and 1930s when University of Chicago sociologists, under the influence of Robert E Park and others were trained in the qualitative, interpretative, interactionist approach to human group life. Sociologists in succeeding generations turned away from the method. They gave their attention to problems of measurement, validity, reliability, responses to attitude questionnaires, survey methodologies, laboratory experiments, theory development, and conceptual indicators. Many researchers combined these interests and problems with the use of the life history, biographical method. The result often produced a trivialization, and distortion of the original intents of the method.

In the 1980s and 1990s sociologists and scholars in other disciplines have evidenced a renewed interest in the biographical method, coupled with a resurgence of interest in interpretative approaches to the study of culture, biography, and human group life. In 1978 a "Biography and Society Group" formed within the International Sociological Association (ISA) and met in Uppsala, Sweden. In 1986 that Group became a research committee within the ISA (see *Current Sociology*, 1995). The journal *Oral History*, of the Oral History Society, also regularly publishes life history, biographical materials. Within sociology and anthropology *Qualitative Inquiry/Qualitative Sociology*, The *Journal of Contemporary Ethnography, Dialectical Anthropology,* and *Current Anthropology* frequently published biographically related articles, as does *Signs*. The autobiography has become a topic of renewed interest in literary criticism. Feminists and post colonial theorists (Trinh, 1991, 1989) have led the way in this discussion (Personal Narratives Group, 1989); moreover, a number of sociological monographs using the method have appeared. In short, the method has returned to the human disciplines.

Central to the biographical–interpretative view has been the argument that societies, cultures, and the expressions of human experience can be read as social texts; that is, as structures of representation that require symbolic statement. These texts, whether oral or written, have taken on a problematic status in the interpretative project. Questions concerning how texts are authored, read, and interpreted have emerged. How authors, lives, societies, and cultures get inside interpretative texts are now hotly debated topics.

In 1959 Mills in *The Sociological Imagination* argued that the sociological imagination "enables us to grasp history and biography and the relations between the two within society." He then suggested that "No social study that does not come back to the problems of biography, of history and of their intersections within a society has completed its intellectual journey" (Mills, 1959).

A basic question drives the interpretative project in the human disciplines: how do men and women live and give meaning to their lives, and capture these meanings in written, narrative, and oral forms? As Karl Marx observed, men and women "make their own history, but not . . . under conditions they have chosen for themselves; rather on terms immediately existing, given and handed down to them." How are these lives, their histories and their meanings to be studied? Who are these people who make their own history? What does history mean to them? How do sociologists, anthropologists, historians, and literary critics read, write, and make sense of their lives?

2   The subject and the biographical method

From its birth, modern, qualitative, interpretative sociology, which links with Max Weber's mediations on *verstehen* (understanding) and method, has been haunted by a "metaphysics of presence" which asserts that real, concrete subjects live lives with meaning and these meanings have a concrete presence in the lives of these people. This belief in a real subject, who is present in the world, has led sociologists to continue to search for a method that would allow them to uncover how these subjects give subjective meaning to their life experiences. This method would rely upon the subjective, verbal, and written expressions of meaning given by the individuals being studied; these expressions being windows into the inner life of the person. Since Wilhelm Dilthey (1833–1911) this search has led to a perennial focus in the human sciences on the autobiographical approach and its interpretative biographical variants, including hermeneutics (see *Hermeneutics*).

Jacques Derrida has contributed to the understanding that there is no clear window into the inner life of a person, for any window is always filtered through the glaze of language, signs, and the process of signification. Moreover, language, in both its written and spoken forms, is always inherently unstable, in flux, and made up of the traces of other signs and symbolic statements. Hence there can never be a clear, unambiguous statement of anything, including an intention or a meaning. The researcher's task is to reconcile this concern with the metaphysics of presence, and its representations, with a commitment to the position that interpretative sociologists and anthropologists study real people who have real lived experiences in the social world.

3   A clarification of terms

A family of terms combine to shape the biographical method. The terms are: method, life, self, experience, epiphany, case, autobiography, autoethnography, biography, story, discourse, narrative, narrator, fiction, history, personal history, oral history, case history, case study, writing presence, difference, life history, life story, self-story, and personal experience story. Table 1 summarizes these concepts and terms which have historically defined the biographical method.

The above terms require discussion. The word "method" will be understood to refer to a way of knowing about the world. A way of knowing may proceed from subjective or objective grounds. Subjective knowing involves drawing on personal experience, or the personal experiences of others, in an effort to form an understanding and interpretation of a particular phenomenon. Objective knowing assumes that an individual can stand outside an experience and understand it, independent of the persons experiencing the phenomenon in question. Intersubjective knowing rests on shared experiences and the knowledge gained from having participated in a common experience with another person. The biographical method rests on subjective and intersubjectively gained knowledge and understandings of the life experiences of individuals, including a person's own life. Such understandings rest on an interpretative process that leads a person to enter into the emotional life of another. "Interpretation" – the act of interpreting and making sense of something – creates the conditions for "understanding", which involves being able to grasp the meanings of an interpreted experience for another individual. Understanding is an intersubjective, emotional process. Its goal is to build shareable understandings of the

Table 1 Terms/forms and varieties of the biographical method[a]

Term/method	Key features	Forms/variations
1 Method	A way of knowing	subjective/objective
2 Life	Period of existence; lived experiences	Partial/complete/edited/ public/private
3 Self	Ideas, images and thoughts of self	Self-stories, autobiographies
4 Experience	Confronting and passing through events	Problematic, routine, ritual
5 Epiphany	Moment of revelation in a life	Major, minor, relived, illuminative
6 Autobiography	Personal history of one's life	Complete, edited, topical
7 Ethnography	Written account of a culture, or group	Realist, interpretative, descriptive
8 Autoethnography	Account of one's life as an ethnographer	Complete, edited, partial
9 Biography	History of a life	Autobiography
10 Story	A fiction, narrative	First, third person
11 Fiction	An account, something made up, fashioned	Story (life, self)
12 History	Account of how something happened	Personal, oral, case
13 Discourse	Telling a story, talk about a text, a text	First, third person
14 Narrator	Teller of a story	First, third person
15 Narrative	A story, having a plot and existence separate from life of teller	Fiction, epic, science, folklore, myth
16 Writing	Inscribing, creating a written text	Logocentric, deconstructive
17 *Différance*	Every word carries traces of another word	Writing, speech
18 Personal history	Reconstruction of life based on interviews and conversations	Life history, life story
20 Oral history	Personal recollections of events, their causes, and effects	Work, ethnic, religious personal, musical, etc.
21 Case history	History of an event or social process, not of a person	Single, multiple, medical, legal
22 Life history	Account of a life based on interviews and conversations	Personal, edited, topical, complete
23 Life story	A person's story of his or her life, or a part thereof	Edited, complete, topical, fictional
24 Self-story [mystory]	Story of self in relation to an event	Personal experience, fictional, true
25 Personal experience story	Stories about personal experience	Single, multiple episode, private or communal folklore
26 Case study	Analysis and record of single case	Single, multiple

[a] Adapted from Denzin (1989)

life experiences of another. This is also called creating verisimilitudes or "truth-like" intersubjectively shareable emotional feelings and cognitive understandings.

3.1 Lifes, persons, selves, experiences

All biographical studies presume a life that has been lived, or a life that can be studied, constructed, reconstructed, and written about. In the present context a "life" refers to two phenomena: (a) lived experiences, or conscious existence, and person (a person is a self-conscious being, as well as a named, cultural object); or (b) cultural creation. The consciousness of the person is simultaneously directed to "an inner world of thought and experience and to an outer world of events and experience." These two worlds, the inner and the outer, are termed the "phenomenological stream of consciousness" and the "interactional stream of experience." The phenomenological stream describes the person caught up in thoughts and the flow of inner experience. The outer, interactional stream locates the person in the world of others. These two streams are opposite sides of the same process, or chiasma, for there can be no firm dividing line between inner and outer experience. The biographical method recognizes this facticity about human existence, for its hallmark is the joining and recording of these two structures of experience in a personal document.

"Epiphanies" are interactional moments and experiences that leave marks on people's lives. In them personal character is manifested. They are often moments of crisis. They alter the fundamental meaning structures in a person's life. Their effects may be positive or negative. They are like the historian Victor Turner's "liminal phase of experience." In the liminal, or threshold moment of experience, the person is in a "no-man's land betwixt and between ... the past and the ... future". These are existential acts. Some are ritualized, as in status passages; others are even routinized, as when a person daily batters and beats his or her spouse. Still others are totally emergent and unstructured, and the person enters them with few – if any – prior understandings of what is going to happen. The meanings of these experiences are always given retrospectively, as they are relived and re-experienced in the stories persons tell about what has happened to them.

There are four forms of the epiphany: (a) the major event which touches every fabric of a person's life; (b) the cumulative or representative event which signifies eruptions or reactions to experiences that have been going on for a long period of time; (c) the minor epiphany which symbolically represents a major, problematic moment in a relationship, or a person's life; and (d) those episodes whose meanings are given in the reliving of the experience. These are called, respectively, the "major epiphany", the "cumulative epiphany", the "illuminative or minor epiphany", and the "relived epiphany".

A "case", as indicated in Table 1, describes an instance of a phenomenon. A case may even be a process or a person. Often a case overlaps with a person; for example, the number of AIDS cases in a local community. "History" is an account of an event and involves determining how a particular event, process, or set of experiences occurred. A "case history" refers to the history of an event or a process; for example, the history of

AIDS as an epidemic in the United States. A "case study" is the analysis of a single case, or of multiple instances of the same process, as it is embodied in the life experiences of a community, a group, or a person (see *Case Study Methods*).

An "autobiography", as noted earlier, is a first-person account (which actually takes the third-person form) of a set of life experiences. A "biography" is an account of a life, written by a third party. The poet John Dryden (1631–1700) defined the word biography in 1683 as "the history of particular men's lives." A biographer, then, is a historian of selves and lives. Autobiographies and biographies are structured by a set of literary, sociological, and interpretative conventions. They are formalized expressions of experience. An "autoethnography" is an ethnographic statement which writes the ethnographer into the text in an autobiographical manner. This is an important variant in the traditional ethnographic account, which positions the writer as an objective outsider in the texts that are written about the culture, group, or person in question. A fully grounded biographical study would be autoethnographic, and contain elements of the writer's own biography and personal history. Such an autoethnography would be descriptive and interpretative (see Ellis, 1995, 1996).

Several critical points concerning the autobiographical and biographical method may be drawn from these extended excerpts. Autobiographies and biographies are conventionalized, narrative expressions of life experiences. These conventions, which structure how lives are told and written about, involve the following problematic presuppositions, and assumptions that are taken for granted: (a) the existence of others; (b) the influence and importance of gender and class; (c) family beginnings; (d) starting points; (e) known, and knowing authors and observers; (f) objective life markers; (g) real persons with real lives; (h) turning point experiences, and (i) truthful statements distinguished from fictions.

These conventions serve to define the biographical method as a distinct approach to the study of human experience. They are the methods by which the "real" appearances of "real" people are created. They are Western literary conventions and have been present since the invention of the biographical form. Some are more central than others, although they all appear to be universal, while they change and take different form, depending on the writer, the place of writing, and the historical moment. They shape how lives are told. In so doing they create the subject matter of the biographical approach. They were each present in the biographical and autobiographical excerpts just presented. Each is treated in turn below.

Ethnographies, biographies, and autobiographies rest on "stories" which are fictional, narrative accounts of how something happened. Stories are fictions. A "fiction" is something made, or fashioned, out of real and imagined events. History, in this sense, is fiction. A story has a beginning, a middle, and an end. Stories take the form of texts. They can be transcribed, written down, and studied. They are "narratives" with a plot and a story line that exists independently of the life of the storyteller, or "narrator". Every narrative contains a reason, or set of justification for its telling. Narrators report stories as narratives.

A story is told in and through "discourse", or talk, just as there can be discourse about the text of a story. A text can be part of a larger body of discourse.

A "life history" or "personal history" is a written account of a person's life based on spoken conversations and interviews. In its expanded form the life history may pertain to the collective life of a group, organization, or community. An "oral history" focuses chiefly on events, processes, causes, and effects, rather than on individuals whose recollections furnish oral history with its raw data. Since oral histories are typically obtained through spoken conversations and interviews, they often furnish the materials for life histories, and case histories. Oral histories should not be confused, however, with personal histories, for the latter attempt to reconstruct lives based on interviews and conversations. Life histories and personal histories may be topical, focusing on only one portion of a life, or compete, attempting to tell the full details of a life as it is recollected.

"Life Stories" examine a life, or a segment of a life, as reported by the individual in question. A life story is a person's story of his or her life, or of what he or she thinks is a significant part of that life. It is therefore a personal narrative, a story of personal experience. A life story may be written or published as an autobiography. Its narrative, story-telling form gives it the flavor of fiction, or of fictional accounts of what happened in a person's life.

The life story turns the subject into an author; an author, or authoress being one who brings a story into existence. The subject-as-author is given an authority over the life that is written about. After all it is their life. This means the author has an authority in the text that is given by the very conventions that structure the writing or telling of the story in the first place. But where in the text of the story is the author? Clearly he or she is everywhere and nowhere. For an author is always present in personal name, and signified in the words that he or she uses. But the author is not in those words; they are only signs of the author, the self, and the life in question. They are inscriptions on and of the self or life that is being told about. The author is in the text only through the words and the conventions he or she uses. The languages of biography structure how biographies are written. There is no fixed, ever-present author.

"Self-stories" are told by a person in the context of a specific set of experiences. A self-story positions the self of the teller centrally in the narrative that is given. It is literally a story of and about the self in relation to an experience. The self-story is made up as it is told. It does not exist as a story independent of its telling; although after it has been told, it can take on the status of a story that can be retold. Its narrative form typically follows the linear format; that is, beginning, middle, end. These tellings build on the assumption that each person is a storyteller of self-experiences. These oral histories of self are often mandated by social groups. When a self-story joins with an author's account of popular culture and scholarly discourse on the individual's life experiences it becomes a "mystory"; that is, my story about how my life has been represented by others. ("Mystory" is Gregory Ulmer's term.)

"Personal experience narratives" are stories people tell about their personal experience. They often draw upon the public, oral story-telling tradition of a group. These stories are based on personal experience. They have the narrative structure of a story (i.e., a beginning, middle, and end). They describe a set of events that exist independently of the telling. The experiences that are described draw their meaning from the common understandings that exist in a group, although they do express the "private" folklore, or meanings of the teller. When told, they create an emotional bond between listener and teller. They express a part of the "inner life" of the storyteller.

Personal experience narratives differ from self-stories in several ways. These narratives do not necessarily position the self of the teller in the center of the story, as self-stories do. Their focus is on shareable experience. Personal experience narratives are more likely to be based on anecdotal, everyday, commonplace experiences, while self-stories involve pivotal, often critical life experiences. Self-stories need not be coherent, linear accounts. They need not be entertaining, or recreate cherished values and memories of a group, while personal experience narratives do. Self-stories are often mandated by a group; personal experience narratives are not. Self-stories are often told to groups, while personal experience narratives may only be told to another individual. These two biographical forms are alike, however, in that they both rest on personal experiences.

4   Representing lives

Lives and their experiences are represented in stories. They are like pictures that have been painted over, and when paint is scraped off an old picture something new becomes visible. What is new is what was previously covered up. A life and the stories about it have the qualities of pentimento: something painted out of a picture which later becomes visible again. Something new is always coming into sight, displacing what was previously certain and seen. There is no truth in the painting of a life, only multiple images and traces of what has been, what could have been, and what now is.

These stories move outward from the selves of the person and inward to the groups that give them meaning and structure. Persons are arbitrators of their own presence in the world, and they should have the last word on this problem. Texts must always return to and reflect the words that persons speak as they attempt to give meaning and shape to the lives they lead. The materials of the biographical method resolve, in the final analysis, into the stories that persons tell one another.

These stories are learned and told in cultural groups. The stories that members of groups pass on to one another are reflective of understandings and practices that are at work in the larger system of cultural understandings that are acted upon by group members. These understandings contain conceptions of persons, lives, meaningful and subjective experience, and notions of how persons and their experiences are to be represented. There are only stories to be told, and listened to. These stories resolve the dilemmas surrounding the metaphysics of presence that haunts the individual as he or she attempts to give shape to this thing called a life and a biography. A person becomes the stories he or she tells. The elusive nature of these stories calls the person back to the understanding that this business of a life story is just that, a story that can never be completed.

Stories then, like the lives they relate, are always open ended, inconclusive, and ambiguous, subject to multiple interpretations. Some are big, others are little. Some take on heroic, folktale proportions in the cultural lives of groups' members; others are tragic; and all too few are comic. Some break fast and run to rapid conclusions. Most slowly unwind and twist back on themselves as persons seek to find meaning for themselves in the experiences they call their own. Some are told for the person by others who are called experts, be these journalists, or professional biographers. Some the person keeps to herself or himself and tells to no one else. Many individuals are at a loss as to what story to tell, feeling that they have nothing worthwhile to talk about. Within this group there are persons who have no voice, and no one to whom to tell their story.

This means that biographical work must always be interventionist, seeking to give voice to those who may otherwise not be allowed to tell their story, or who are denied a voice to speak. This is what *écriture feminine* attempts; a radical form of feminist writing which "transgresses structures of . . . domination – a kind of writing which reproduces the struggle for voice of those on the wrong side of the power relationship." This stance disrupts the classical oedipal logic of the life-history method which situates subjectivity and self-development in the patriarchal system of marriage, kinship, and sexuality (Clough, 1994). This logic underwrites the scientistic, positivistic use of life histories, and supports institutionalized sociological discourse on human subjects as individuals who can tell true stories about their lives. *Écriture feminine* and certain versions of "queer theory" (Clough, 1994) moving from a deconstructive stance, make no attempt at the production of biographical narratives which fill out the sociologist's version of what a life and its stories should look like. It accepts sociology as fictive writing, and biographical work as the search for partial, not full identities.

Students of the method must begin to assemble a body of work that is grounded in the workings of these various cultural groups. This is the challenge and the promise of this project. In order to speak to the Fourth Epoch, so called by Mills as the "post-modern period", it is necessary to begin to listen to the workings of these groups that make up our time. It is necessary also to learn how to connect biographies and lived experiences, the epiphanies of lives, to the groups and social relationships that surround and shape persons.

5   Personal writing

As we write about our lives, we bring the world of others into our texts. We create differences, oppositions, and presences which allow us to maintain the illusion that we have captured the "real" experiences of "real" people. In fact, we create the persons we write about, just as they create themselves when they engage in story-telling practices. As students of the biographical method we must become more sensitive to the writing strategies we use when we attempt to accomplish these ends. And, as readers, we can only have trust, or mistrust in the writers that we read, for there is no way to stuff a real-live person between the two covers of a text.

Biographical studies should attempt to articulate how each subject deals with the problems of coherence, illusion, consubstantiality, presence, deep, inner selves, others, gender, class, starting and ending points, epiphanies, fictions, truths, and final causes. These recurring, obdurate, culturally constructed dimensions of Western lives provide framing devices for the stories that are told about the lives that we study. They are, however, no more than artifices; contrivances that writers and tellers are differentially skilled at using. As writers we must not be trapped into thinking that they are any more than cultural practice.

As we learn to do this we must remember that our primary obligation is always to the people we study, not to our project, or to a larger discipline. The lives and stories that we hear and study are given to us under a promise. That promise being that we protect those who have shared with us. In return, this sharing will allow us to write life documents, that speak to the human dignity, the suffering, the hopes, the dreams, the lives gained and the lives lost by the people we study. These documents will become testimonies to the ability of the human being to endure, to prevail, and to triumph over the structural forces that we threaten, at any moment, to annihilate all of us. If we foster the illusion that we understand when we do not, or that we have found meaningful, coherent lives where none exist, then we engage in a cultural practice that is just as repressive as the most repressive of political regimes.

See also: Historical Methods in Educational Research; Hermeneutics; Postmodernism.

References

Clough, Patricia Ticineto. 1994 *Feminist Thought: Desire, Power and Academic Discourse.* Blackwell, Cambridge, Mass.

Current Sociology 1995 Special Issue: Biographical Research. 43, No. 2/3. Autumn/Winter. Daniel Simeoni and Marco Doana, Issue Editors.

Ellis, Carolyn 1996 "Evocative Autoethnography: Writing Emotionally About Our Lives." Forthcoming in Yvonna S. Lincoln and William Tierney (eds.), *Representation and the Text: Reframing the Narrative Voice.* SUNY Press, Albany, NY.

Ellis, Carolyn 1995 *Final Negotiations.* Temple University Press, Philadelphia.

Mills C. W. 1959 *The Sociological Imagination.* Oxford University Press, New York.

Personal Narratives Group 1989 *Interpreting Women's Lives: Feminist Theory and Personal Narratives.* Indiana University Press, Bloomington, Indiana.

Trinh T. Minh-ha 1991 *When the Moon Waxes Red: Representation, Gender and Cultural Politics.* Routledge, New York.

Trinh T. Minn-ha 1989 *Women, Native, Other: Writing Postcoloniality and Feminism.* Indiana University Press, Bloomington.

Further reading

Denzin N. K. 1987 *Interpretative Biography.* Sage, Newbury Park, California.

Denzin N. K. 1989 *The Research Act: A Theoretical Introduction to Sociological Methods.* 3rd edn. Prentice-Hall, Englewood Cliffs, New Jersey.

Denzin N. K. 1989 *Interpretative Interactionism.* Sage, Newbury Park, California.

Feagin J. R., Orum A. M. and Sjoberg G. (eds.) 1991 *A Case for the Case Study.* University of North Carolina Press, Chapel Hill, North Carolina.

Journal of Applied Behavioral Science 1989 vol. 25 (4) (issue devoted to Autobiography, Social Research, and the Organizational context).

Reinharz S. and Davidson L. 1992 *Feminist Methods in Social Research.* Oxford University Press, New York.

Roman L. G. 1992 The political significance of other ways of narrating ethnography: A feminist materialist approach. In: LeCompte M. D. and Millroy W. L. and Preissle J. (eds.) 1992 *Handbook of Qualitative Research in Education.* Academic Press, San Diego.

Smith L. M. 1994 Biographical methods. In: Denzin N. K. and Lincoln Y. S. (eds.) 1993 *Handbook of Qualitative Research.* Sage, Newbury Park, California, pp 286–305.

9 Case Study Methods

A. Sturman

"Case study" is a generic term for the investigation of an individual group, or phenomenon. While the techniques used in the investigation may be varied, and may include both qualitative and quantitative approaches, the distinguishing feature of case study is the belief that human systems develop a characteristic wholeness or integrity and are not simply a loose collection of traits. As a consequence of this belief, case study researchers hold that to understand a case, to explain why things happen as they do, and to generalize or predict from a single example requires an in-depth investigation of the interdependencies of parts and of the patterns that emerge.

Kaplan refers to methodology as a "generalization of technics and a concretization of philosophy" (*Scientific Methods in Educational Research*, p. 79). While the techniques relate to the specific strategies that are used in different types of case study, the philosophy is concerned with the place that case study has in educational inquiry, such as the extent to which it can be used to generalize, predict, or explain as opposed to being used to understand or simply to describe.

The following section deals with the philosophical dimension of case study and this is followed by a discussion of the technical dimension.

1 Case study and the "concretization of philosophy"

Diesing (1972) places case study within the holist tradition of scientific inquiry. According to this tradition, the characteristics of a part are seen to be largely determined by the whole to which it belongs. The holist argues that to understand these parts requires an understanding of their interrelationships, and accounts of wholes need to capture and express this holistic quality.

This view is expressed in a different way by Salomon (1991) who has distinguished the analytical and systemic approaches to educational research. The analytic approach mainly assumes that discrete elements of complex educational phenomena can be isolated for study leaving all else unchanged. The systemic approach, on the other hand, mainly assumes that elements are interdependent and inseparable and a change in one element changes everything else. It follows, therefore, that what is required is a study of patterns not single variables.

A holistic or systemic approach quite often entails qualitative techniques in order to tease out the interrelationships of complex variables. Quantitative research also addresses the interrelationships between variables, and statistical modeling procedures enable the testing of complex theories on the way systems operate. While it may be true that much quantitative research has failed to take account of the complexities of human systems and has reduced them to simplistic hypotheses and law-like relations, this is a failure of the research design and not of quantitative research *per se*. In addition, although holists frequently use qualitative techniques, they are not a distinguishing feature of case study.

While there are those who still argue that qualitative and quantitative approaches are incompatible because of the different philosophical traditions from which they draw their credibility and in particular because of the underlying assumptions that each make about the validity or dependability of findings, in general there is an acceptance that the two traditions can work together. It is accepted that qualitative research is useful both in developing concepts and theories that can be further tested through quantitative approaches – the approach used in the 150 Schools Project, a current Australian study of effective schooling – and also in explaining more fully findings from quantitative research – the approach adopted in the Australian Staffing and Resources Study (see Sturman, 1982).

1.1   Case study and the development of theory

Glaser and Strauss (1968) distinguished "grounded theory", that is, theory grounded in the data collected, from theory generated from logical deduction from *a priori* assumptions. They argued that grounded theory is likely to generate more useful hypotheses in that it has been inductively developed from observational research in the real world. Similarly, Wilson (1977) argued that there is room in research for more inductive approaches where the role of performed hypotheses is reduced to a minimum.

While case study is an ideal methodology for grounding theory, it does not follow that case study researchers approach or should approach settings without guiding theories and hypotheses. In fact, it is unlikely that they would be able to do this even if they wished. Popper (1963) argues that it is impossible to start with pure observation, that is, without anything in the nature of a theory. Selection within observation takes place and this selection is based on conjectures and anticipations and on other theories which act as a frame of reference for investigators.

Glaser and Strauss (1968) also acknowledged that researchers entered settings with a "general sociological perspective." However, what they were warning against was allowing preconceived theories or ideas to dictate relevances in concepts and hypotheses in the conduct of research. Wilson (1977) talked of "suspending" or "bracketing" preconceptions. Researchers should not be expected to be free of conjectures, but these should not preclude other avenues of inquiry.

Where case studies are providing a detailed description and understanding of a case and where researchers are open to new ideas that may challenge existing propositions, they provide not only the means by which existing conjectures and theories can be tested, but also the capacity to develop new theoretical positions. The process involved is what Kemmis (1980) called "iterative retroduction":

> With each cycle of retroduction, new "surprises" . . . are encountered and new hypotheses (interpretations) are advanced. These, in turn, suggest new implications and avenues for disconfirmation which, when pursued may generate new surprises. (p. 115)

1.2   Case study and explanation, understanding, and description

Kaplan (1964) has distinguished explanation from understanding: the difference between having an explanation and "seeing" it. He argued that the reason for something is known either when it can be fitted into a known pattern (the pattern model) or when it can be deducted from other known truths (the deductive model). According to the pattern model, something is explained when it is so related to a set of other elements that together they constitute a unified system. In other words, an explanation exists for something when it can be understood.

Case study researchers or holists are more likely to be concerned with pattern explanation than deductive explanation because the pattern model is more appropriate when there are many diverse factors and where the pattern of relations between them is important. To arrive at an explanation, therefore, requires a rich description of the case and an understanding of it, in particular the relationship of its parts.

1.3   Case study and prediction and generalization

Diesing (1972) held the view that because it is not possible to deduce an unknown part of a pattern from a known part, the symmetry of prediction and explanation that occurs in the deductive model, (i.e., in a model where one or more basic factors or laws determine what is to be explained) is not present.

However, this distinction does not always hold. Parsons (1976) commented, for example:

> Interpretation, explanation and understanding in social science contribute to prediction – they are not at odds with it. If one understands, one can attempt prediction and hopefully thereby plan better for the future. Theory organizes description, explanation and prediction in a multi-symbiotic process. (p. 133)

One of the earliest and lingering criticisms of case study methodology relates to the extent that it can be used to generalize to other cases or other settings. In 1975, Campbell referred to this problem in an article entitled *Degrees of Freedom and the Case Study*. The title of his article reflected what was at that time one of the major concerns about case study held by some quantitative researchers. Campbell (1975, p. 175) argued that the difference between qualitative and quantitative research had nothing to do with legitimacy of knowing – he argued that comparative social science engaged in "commonsense knowing" – but was related to confidence in the findings:

> If we achieve a meaningful quantitative 100-nation correlation, it is by dependence on this kind of knowing at every point, not by replacing it with a "scientific" quantitative methodology which substitutes for such knowing. The quantitative multination generalization will contradict such anecdotal, single-case, naturalistic observation at some points, but it will do so only by trusting a much larger body of such anecdotal, single-case, naturalistic observations.

The development of multisite case study, where case study methodology is applied to a number of settings or cases, makes such criticism too simplistic but, in any case, the holist argues that even single case study can be used for generalizations.

For example, Diesing (1972) argued that science deals with uniqueness and regularities: if the primary focus is on regularities, the unique shows up, and if it is on particulars, regularities show up. Case study methods include both the particular and the universal instead of segregating the two, and moves from the particular to the universal and back in graded steps.

Stake (1980, p. 69) has also advocated a process of naturalistic generalization arrived at "from the tacit knowledge of how things are, why they are, how people feel about them, and how these things are likely to be, later on or in other places with which this person is familiar. "Naturalistic generalization is arrived at, therefore, by recognizing the similarities of the objects and issues in different contexts and "sensing the covariations of happenings." Stake argued that policymakers attain and amend their understandings, for the most part, through personal experience, and knowledge is often transferred through a process of empathetic understanding. Therefore, demands for typicality and representativeness often yield to needs for assurance that the target case is properly described.

For naturalistic generalizations to be possible, it is essential to ensure that the salient features of a case are documented so that a new situation can be illuminated by a very thorough understanding of a known case. This is so whether it is the researcher who is attempting the generalization or practitioners using the description of the known case and applying it to their settings.

2   Case study and the "generalization of technics"

The specific techniques that are employed in case study depend on the type of study that is being conducted. These types can vary considerably, in part because case study embraces both the quantitative and qualitative approaches.

2.1   Types of case study

Leaving aside narrative historical studies, documentary films, and personal case studies such as those used in medical diagnosis and psychology, Stenhouse (1985) has referred to four styles of case study methodology:

(a) Ethnographic case study which involves single in-depth study usually by means of participant observation and interview. An example from the United Kingdom is the study by Hargreaves (1967).
(b) Action research case study where the focus is on bringing about change in the case under study. An example from a developing country is the group of projects initiated under the Collaborative Action Research in Education (CARE) program in Sierra Leone and reported by Wright (1988).
(c) Evaluative case study which involves the evaluation of programs and where quite often condensed fieldwork replaces the more lengthy ethnographic approach. An example from the United States is the study by Stake and Gjerde (1974).
(d) Educational case study which is designed to enhance the understanding of educational action. An example from Australia is the study by Sturman (1989).

While the first and second styles – ethnographic case study and action research case study – are likely, because of the in-depth nature of such research, to be single case study, evaluation and educational case study can involve a single case or can be incorporated into multisite methods. The introduction of multisite methods is particularly noticeable in policy research, which has led Herriott and Firestone (1983) to refer to this as "multisite qualitative policy research."

2.2   Dimensions of variation in techniques in case study methods

The degree to which case study research can be structured or unstructured is often ignored in methodological discussions. Louis (1982) has noted:

> In an increasing number of cases, data collected through very unstructured techniques may be transformed through coding into quantitative data bases, which are then analyzed using descriptive or inferential statistical techniques. Conversely, data may be collected through open-ended survey methods and analyzed "holistically" by site. In fact, to understand the variety of methods currently being employed, we must examine the nature of the design and practice at three points in the study: during data collection, during database formulation, and during the actual data analysis. (p. 9)

Figure 1, taken from Louis (1982), depicts this. The data collection phase ranges from the unstructured to the structured and can include ethnography, structured or unstructured interviews or surveys, and census data. The data formation stage ranges from the narrative to the numeric and includes the use of field notes; site reports; and nominal, interval, and ratio scales. Similarly, the data analysis phase ranges from the journalistic to the statistical

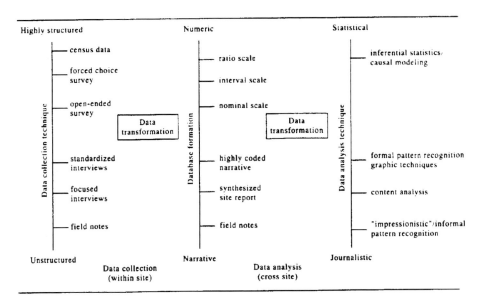

Figure 1   Dimensions of variation in multisite/multimethod studies.

Source: Louis K. S. 1982 Multisite/multimethod studies: An introduction. *American Behavioral Scientist* 26(1): 10, © Sage Publications, Inc. (Reprinted by permission of Sage Publication, Inc.)

and may include impressionistic analysis, content analysis, or inferential statistics and causal modeling.

2.3   Techniques in multisite case studies

Multisite methodology emerged in response to the perceived limitations of much policy and evaluation research for policymakers. Firestone and Herriott (1983, p. 438) have discussed the demands on policy researchers and the implications that these have for case study. They refer to the formalization of qualitative research and they list five major elements of this:

(a) Whereas traditional qualitative research tends to emphasize in-depth description, formalized qualitative research emphasizes explanation.

(b) Whereas traditional qualitative research tends to emphasize the conduct of inquiry by a single individual, formalized qualitative research emphasizes the use of a multiperson team.

(c) Whereas traditional qualitative research tends to emphasize the discovery of relevant questions and variables within the field, formalized qualitative research emphasizes the codification of questions and variables before beginning fieldwork.

(d) Whereas traditional qualitative research tends to emphasize unstructured questioning and observation, formalized qualitative research emphasizes the standardization of data collection procedures through the use of semistructured interview and observation protocols.

(e) Whereas traditional qualitative research tends to emphasize extended preservation of verbal narrative, formalized, qualitative research emphasizes the systematic reduction of verbal narratives to codes and categories.

In response to demands of policymakers, one of the major outcomes of such techniques, compared with ethnographic case study, is that researchers engaged in multisite case study usually spend much less time in each site. They trade in-depth inquiry for comparisons across a number of sites.

2.4 Case study and credibility

One concern that has been expressed about case study techniques, in particular ethnographic case study, is the credibility of what is seen as subjective research techniques. Although Wilson (1977) has argued that ethnographic case study challenges the traditional stance of the objective outsider, personal judgment forms an essential part of all science and is neither objective or subjective.

An assertion is an act of believing – to this extent it is subjective – but that assertion, whether it emerges from ethnographic research or multivariate statistical modeling, rests on personal judgment which includes an appraisal of evidence within the tenets of acceptable practice as perceived by the research community – to this extent it is objective. To say that science is more than its practitioners and their skills and judgments is a failure to perceive how science and its methods have historically progressed.

At the root of case study research as in all science lays the problem of "justified true belief":

> In every case in which someone would want to claim – however tentatively – to have established a scientific truth, he does so by making one set of assumptions about what counts as justification, along with another set of assumptions about the nature of belief. (Kemmis, 1980, p. 102).

The problem of justified true belief is then a double problem which involves reconciling the beliefs (private knowledge) of researchers and readers with the forms of knowledge of public discourse.

Instead of the blanket condemnation of subjectivity or the universal approbation of objectivity, what is needed is an opportunity to appraise those personal judgments being made by scientific colleagues. Case study methodology can achieve its own form of precision. Wilson (1977) has referred to this as "disciplined subjectivity". This requires that evidence must be open to scrutiny, and that the study must be reported in a way capable of "conveying credibility" (Glaser and Strauss, 1968) and subjected to standards of "trustworthiness", that is, credibility, transferability, dependability, and confirmability (Guba and Lincoln, 1985).

Among the strategies that practitioners have suggested for achieving credibility in case study are the following:

(a) Procedures for data collection should be explained.
(b) Data collected should be displayed and ready for re-analysis.
(c) Negative instances should be reported.
(d) Biases should be acknowledged.
(e) Fieldwork analyses need to be documented.
(f) The relationship between assertion and evidence should be clarified.
(g) Primary evidence should be distinguished from secondary and description from interpretation.
(h) Diaries or logs should track what was actually done during different stages of the study.
(i) Methods should be devised to check the quality of data.

The concept of "triangulation" (Tawney, 1975) is central to achieving credibility. Triangulation may involve the use of different data sources, different perspectives or theories, different investigators, or different methods. This process is, according to Diesing (1972), the holist's response to the issue of validity and reliability in survey research. The holist is concerned with contextual validity. This can take two forms: the validity of a piece of evidence which can be assessed by comparing it with other kinds of evidence on the same point, and the validity of the source of the evidence which can be evaluated by collecting other kinds of evidence about that source.

To distinguish contextual validity from the validity important to the survey researcher, Diesing referred to the dependability of a source of evidence.

2.5   Case study and data handling and retrieval

Where case study involves in-depth observations and interviews, one of the problems faced by the researcher is how to store and retrieve such information.

Examples of how to address these issues come mainly from the fields of information and library science (see, e.g., Levine, 1985), although the sourcebook prepared by Miles and Huberman (1984) provides one model for preparing qualitative data for analysis.

3   Ethics and the conduct of case study

The problem of ethics is not unique to case study methodology, but where case study involves the portrayal of persons or institutions in forms that may enable recognition, the ethical issues are paramount.

These problems are usually resolved through negotiations between researchers and those researched. This may take the form of an official contract or may be more informal, involving discussions over the content of written reports. While it may not be possible to have one set of rules that governs all situations, there is a responsibility on case study researchers to address in a responsible way ethical issues that emerge in their work.

4   Linking research methodologies

While conflicts about different methodologies have not disappeared, in recent years there has developed in the research community a suspicion of "scientism", that is, an exaggerated regard for techniques which have succeeded elsewhere in contrast to a scientific temper which is open to whatever techniques hold promise for the inquiry in hand (Kaplan, 1964).

There has also developed a recognition of the value of blending different methodologies. In one major study into the characteristics of effective schools in Australia, key concepts and variables were defined through reference both to prior quantitative studies as well as case studies of selected schools. From this a quantitative study of 150 schools was conducted, but case studies were also used to complement and help to illuminate the findings from this study. The process is cyclical and case study methodology enters the process at various stages.

See also: Research Paradigms in Education.

References

Campbell, D. 1975 Degrees of freedom and the case study. *Comparative Political Studies* 8(2): 178–93.

Diesing, P. 1972 *Patterns of Discovery in the Social Sciences.* Routledge and Kegan Paul, London

Firestone, W. A. and Herriott, R. E. 1983 The formalization of qualitative research: An adaptation of "soft" science to the policy world. *Eval. Rev.* 7(4): 437–66.

Glaser, B. G. and Strauss, A. L. 1968 *The Discovery of Grounded Theory: Strategies for Qualitative Research.* Weidenfield and Nicolson, London.

Guba, E. G. and Lincoln, Y. S. 1985 Naturalistic and rationalistic enquiry. In: Husén T. and Postlethwaite T. N. (eds.) 1985 *International Encyclopedia of Education,* 1st edn. Pergamon Press, Oxford.

Hargreaves, D. H. 1967 *Social Relations in a Secondary School.* Routledge and Kegan Paul, London.

Herriott, R. E. and Firestone, W. A. 1983 Multisite qualitative policy research: Optimizing descriptions and generalizability. *Educ. Researcher* 12(2): 14–19.

Kaplan, A. 1964 *The Conduct of Inquiry: Methodology for Behavioral Science.* Chandler, San Francisco, California.

Kemmis, S. 1980 The imagination of the case and the invention of the study. In: Simons H. (ed.) 1980.

Levine, H. G. 1985 Principles of data storage and retrieval for use in qualitative evaluations. *Educ. Eval. Policy Anal.* 7(2): 169–86.

Louis, K. S. 1982 Multisite/multimethod studies. An introduction. *American Behavioral Scientist* 26(1): 6–22.

Miles, M. B. and Huberman, A. M. 1984 *Qualitative Data Analysis: A Sourcebook of New Methods.* Sage, Beverly Hills, California.

Parsons, C. 1976 The new evaluation: A cautionary note. *J. Curric. St.* 8(2): 125–38.

Popper, K. R. 1963 *Conjectures and Refutations: The Growth of Scientific Knowledge.* Routledge and Kegan Paul, London.

Salomon, G. 1991 Transcending the qualitative-quantitative debate: The analytic and systemic approaches to educational research. *Educ. Researcher* 20(6): 10–18.

Stake, R. E. 1980 The case study in social inquiry. In: Simons H. (ed.) 1980

Stake, R. E. and Gjerde, C. 1974 *An Evaluation of T. City.* American Educational Research Association (AERA) Monograph Series in Curriculum Evaluation No. 7. Rand McNally, Chicago, Illinois.

Stenhouse, L. 1985 Case study methods. In: Husén T. and Postlethwaite T. N. (eds.) 1985 *International Encyclopedia of Education*. 1st edn. Pergamon Press, Oxford.

Sturman, A. 1982 *Patterns of School Organization: Resources and Responses in Sixteen Schools*. ACER Research Monograph No. 18. ACER, Hawthorn.

Sturman, A. 1989 *Decentralisation and the Curriculum: Effects of the Devolution of Curriculum Decision Making in Australia*. ACER Research Monograph No. 35, ACER, Hawthorn.

Tawney, D. A. 1975 Evaluation and science curriculum projects in the UK. *Stud. Sci. Educ.* 3: 31–54.

Wilson, S. 1977 The use of ethnographic techniques in educational research. *Rev. of Educ. Res.* 47(2): 245–65.

Wright, C. A. H. 1988 Collaborative action research in education (CARE) – reflections on an innovative paradigm. *Int. J. Educ. Dev.* 8(4): 279–92.

Further reading

Adelman, C., Jenkins, D. and Kemmis, S. 1976 Re-thinking case study: Notes from the second Cambridge Conference. *Camb. J. Educ.* 6(3): 139–50.

Hamilton, D., Jenkins, D., King, C., MacDonald, B. and Parlett, M. (eds.) 1977 *Beyond the Numbers Game: A Reader in Educational Evaluation*. MacMillan Education, Basingstoke.

Husén, T. 1988 Research paradigms in education. *Interchange* 19(1): 2–13.

Keeves, J. 1988 The unity of educational research. *Interchange* 19(1): 14–30.

Marshall, C. 1985 Appropriate criteria of trustworthiness and goodness for qualitative research on education organizations. *Quality and Quantity* 19: 353–73.

Simons, H. (ed.) 1980 *Towards a Science of the Singular: Essays about Case Study in Educational Research and Evaluation*. Occasional Publications No. 10. Centre for Applied Research in Education, University of East Anglia, Norwich.

Smith, J. K. and Heshusius L. 1986 Closing down the conversation: The end of the quantitative-qualitative debate among educational inquirers. *Educ. Researcher* 15(1): 4–12.

Tripp, D. H. 1985 Case study generalization: An agenda for action. *Br. Educ. Res. J.* 11(1): 33–43.

10   Ethnographic Research Methods

R. Taft

Some educational researchers have advocated the adoption of the ethnographic methods employed by cultural and social anthropologists in their field studies of social groups and communities. These methods are considered to be particularly appropriate for empirical research on the relatively bounded system of a school or classroom but they also have their place in the study of the role of the family, social organizations, or ethnic communities in education. Ethnographic research consists essentially of a description of events that occur within the life of a group with special regard to social structures and the behavior of individuals with respect to their group membership, and an interpretation of the meaning of these for the culture of the group. Ethnography is used both to record primary data and to interpret its meaning. It is naturalistic enquiry as opposed to controlled, and a qualitative as opposed to quantitative, method. In ethnography the researcher participates in some part of the normal life of the group and uses what he or she learns from that participation to produce the research findings. It is consequently often treated as being equivalent to participant observation, in contrast with nonparticipant observation in which the observer as an outsider records the overt behavior of the subjects, but it involves more than that. Participation in a group provides investigators with an understanding of the culture and the interactions between the members that is different from that which can be obtained from merely observing or conducting a questionnaire survey or an analysis of documents. The investigators' involvement in the normal activities of the group may be treated as a case of partial acculturation in which they acquire an insider's knowledge of the group through their direct experience with it. These experiences provide them with tacit knowledge which helps them to understand the significance to the group members of their own behavior and that of others and enables them to integrate their observations about that behavior with information obtained from other sources such as interviews with informants and documentary material.

1   The development of ethnographic methods

Field research was employed by anthropologists and sociologists in the nineteenth and early twentieth centuries, but the first to stress the need for a systematic approach to its conduct was the Polish-British scholar Malinowski, who emphasized the need for ethnographers to employ controls in their assembly of data in a manner that he described as analogous, although by no means similar, to those of the natural scientists. Malinowski laid down the requirement that observers should tabulate the data on which their conclusions are based, including verbatim statements, and should indicate whether they are derived from direct or indirect sources, a method that he called "concrete statistical documentation" (see the introductory chapter on Methodology in Malinowski, 1922). He stressed the need for the investigator to establish "trustworthiness" in respect of the study. Malinowski described the goal of ethnographic studies as "to grasp the native's point of view, his relation to life, to realise his view of his world" (p. 25). In order to achieve this, the investigator should learn the language of the community being studied, reside for a protracted period in the community – preferably out of contact with "white" people, and use both observation and informed interviews with selected informants from within the community as sources of data.

The field methods laid down by Malinowski have, to a greater or lesser degree, been used in studies of segments of modern, urbanized societies which have provided a model for the application of the methods to educational research. For example, studies were carried out of the unemployed in Austria, industrial organizations (Tavistock Institute), urban areas in the United States (Middletown, Yankee City), hobos, gangs, and dance musicians, to name just a few. These studies each raised their own peculiar problems of research strategy, but what they all have in common is their method of research in which the investigator becomes closely involved over a prolonged period in the everyday life of the members of a designated group or community in order to understand its culture. This contact enables the researchers not only to obtain an intimate and a broad knowledge of the group but also to test and refine hypotheses about the phenomena being studied.

Ethnographic methods of research came to education fairly late. The team of sociologists from the University of Chicago who studied medical students (Becker *et al.*, 1961) were probably the pioneers in the field of education, while Smith and Geoffrey (1968) were the first to base a study of classroom processes on anthropological field studies using a method which they described as microethnography. They stated that their "primary intent was to describe the silent language of a culture, a classroom in a slum school, so that those who have not lived in it will appreciate its subtleties and complexities" (p. 2). Smith observed the classroom every day for one semester and kept copious field notes, which he used as a basis for his daily discussions with the class teacher, Geoffrey, with the purpose of clarifying the intentions and motives behind the teacher's behavior in order to move towards a conceptualization in abstract terms of the teaching process. Both of the investigators were participants in the classroom, although one was more of an observer and the other more of an initiator and an informant.

A word should be added about the terms used in describing ethnographic studies in education. Smith and Geoffrey seem to have simply meant an intensive field study by their term microethnography, while Erickson (1975) confines it more narrowly to studies that use extensive observation and recording to establish the interactional structures in the classroom. For the purposes of this present article, the term ethnography is interpreted liberally to include case studies, the concept preferred by the ethnographers in the United Kingdom. The intensive study of a bounded community is a clear example of a simple case study, even though there are many individuals who make up that community.

2   The scientific status of the ethnographic method

There is some skepticism about the place of a positivist model or research in the social sciences according to which a detached scholar objectively studies an objective reality. Ethnographers are not detached; they influence their data and they are influenced by it in all stages of observing, interpreting and reporting. Their reports are constructions which are determined by their personal outlook and socio-cultural forces. (The issues are fully discussed in Denzin and Lincoln, 1994.) Some scholars argue that the reports of ethnographers should be viewed as "tales" or "narratives" which should be studied for their own sake. In contrast the post-positivist approach adopted here, while it does not ignore the constructionist aspects of ethnographic research, makes the assumption that there is an objective social reality and that ethnography is an appropriate method for studying it.

2.1   The social role of the investigator

The description of the investigator as a participant in the life of the group implies that he or she has some role in it which is recognized by the group. Sometimes this role is simply that of participant observer, a role which does not usually exist in most formal group structures, but one which does have a meaning in many classrooms where outsiders come to observe the class on occasions for one purpose or another. Thus, Louis Smith was introduced to both the children and the teachers as someone from the university who was interested in children's learning, a role which is understood and accepted in modern classrooms. In other cases the investigator fills a normal role in the group other than that of a researcher. For example, the researcher may be a regular classroom teacher in the school, a situation that represents participant observation in the fullest sense of the word. The role of participant observer has some advantages as a viewing point over that of the participant who plays the additional role of observer. The former is expected by the group to share, probe, ask questions, take notes, and so on because this is consistent with his or her role as an observer whereas the latter has tactical and ethical problems in doing so because of his or her obligations as a participant. On the other hand there is a danger that a participant observer can become so much absorbed into the group after a time that his or her status as an observer may be compromised.

A group member who also acts as a research observer may carry out that latter role overtly or covertly – or as a mixture of both where the member's role as an investigator is known to some but not all members of the group. A participant observer, by definition, plays an obtrusive role in the group process. Where the role of a group member as a researcher is overt, that person's role within the group can be compromised by the other groups members' awareness of that fact and the latter are likely to control their behavior in order to enhance or defend their public image. Thus, it can become difficult for the participant observer to carry out either of the roles – participant or observer. For this reason an investigator is tempted to engage in covert observation in which the observer role is not known to the members of the group. This type of research raises serious ethical issues and in many universities and research institutions an application for approval of support for a covert ethnographic study would be subject to rejection on ethical grounds.

2.2   The inside-outside view

One of the main advantages of the ethnographic method is that, in the course of becoming involved in the group, the investigator becomes acculturated to it. This means that he or she develops personal knowledge about the rules of the group and begins to perceive the same meanings of events as do the members of the group. The investigator learns what behavior is expected when, where, and in response to what situations. This process of acculturation is sometimes described as transition from the status of a "stranger" to that of a "friend", that is, a person who knows the "silent language" of the group and is in intimate communication with its members. It is, however, significant that a scholar who is studying the subculture of a school in his or her own society is unlikely to be as complete a stranger at the beginning as an anthropologist studying a traditional society.

Nevertheless, being an insider has its drawbacks as a method of studying a group. First, as already indicated, there are constraints imposed by propriety and ethics on an insider revealing to others the secrets of the group. There may, of course, be the same constraints on an outsider but, at least, the group can usually control his or her access to information by barring entry.

Second, the insider may not always have even as much access to information as an outsider. The investigator may have personal knowledge of only a segment of the group's life, sometimes without being aware of the limitation. He or she may even be denied access to the other segments: for example, a teacher may not be permitted to study the classroom of a colleague. In contrast, a stranger who is accepted as an observer may be deliberately informed and invited to observe just because he or she is a stranger. Furthermore, an outsider is more likely to be able to take steps to obtain a representative sampling of people, occasions, and settings in the group and thus can help to offset the suspicion of biased observation. A third drawback that may arise as a result of being an insider is that highly salient data may be overlooked just because it is so familiar. Strangers will notice events that stand out as a result of their contrast with the expectations that they have brought with them from their own cultural background and may therefore be better placed to infer their meaning and significance for other events in the group. Some element of surprise aids awareness. A further problem is the one mentioned earlier of the subjects' reactivity to being studied, particularly when the observer is a full participant in the group. Whether or not the observation is obtrusive, it is reactive observation; that is, the observer affects the behavior of the people being studied and consequently will have to take into account his or her own influence when assessing the group. As Everhart puts it "the fieldworker, rather than appearing to be one of many in the audience observing the drama on stage, is himself on stage, interacting with the other actors in 'his' setting and playing a role in the resolution of the production" (1977, p. 14). In order to take into account their own contributions and to assess what the situation would be if it were not for the fact that their presence is influencing the group, investigators need a great deal of self-awareness and a thorough understanding of the group processes. This necessity for playing the dual roles of participant and detached observer can impose a severe strain on the ethnographic investigator and it calls for continual monitoring of the effect the investigator has on others.

2.3   Subjectivity, reliability, and validity

The fact that investigators have a role in the group not only requires them to be aware of their own influence but also may give them an emotional stake in a particular research outcome. For example, if the observer is also a teacher, there may be a tendency for observation to be slanted towards a justification of the style of teaching normally used. Since ethnographic researchers use themselves as the instrument through which they observe the group, the method lends itself to extreme subjectivity; that is, the interpretation may be idiosyncratic to the observer with all of the associated limitations, eccentricities, and biases and is not matched by the interpretation of other observers. This raises questions concerning the reliability of the observations and the validity of the conclusions. Observations and interpretations are by their very nature subjective but they still can be made susceptible to reliability checks and it is still possible for the investigation to follow rules that can increase the validity of the conclusions.

Reliability, that is accuracy, of the observations can be enhanced by following the prescription laid down by Malinowski of recording wherever possible the concrete data in the form of a "synoptic chart" on which the inferences are to be based, including verbatim utterances and opinions. Modern methods of recording events so that they can be examined at leisure offer ethnographers unprecedented possibilities of attaining accuracy, but there are still sampling problems in the selection of the data and limitations to accuracy due to bias and lack of opportunity, as well as tactical and ethical considerations in making the recordings.

The reliability of the observations is assisted by the long period of exposure to the data in ethnographic research which provides opportunities for investigators to cross check their observations over time and to reconcile inconsistencies. Cross checks may also be made by triangulation, a procedure in which multiple sources are used to obtain evidence on the same phenomenon. Thus, the observations may be supplemented by interviews, feedback to the members of the group for their comment, and documentary evidence such as school notices, correspondence, minutes, and other archives. An additional source of reliability is to have more than one observer as, for example, in the study by Smith and Geoffrey (1968), a situation which is relatively rare in traditional anthropological studies. In the typical case, the multiple observers may be members of a team who are exposed to the same events and are then able to cross check each other's data.

Validity is a quality of the conclusions and the processes through which these were reached, but its exact meaning is dependent on the particular criterion of truth that is adopted. In ethnographic research the most appropriate criterion is credibility although even that term is subject to fuzziness in meaning. Some authors would add "plausibility" as a further criterion of validity but this is implied by the term "credibility" which is a socially defined concept as far as ethnographic research is concerned. The community of scholars within which an ethnographic researcher operates and to whom the results of the research are communicated has a collective understanding of what makes it acceptable as valid. Credibility is dependent on the apparent accuracy of the data, and all the steps described above that are intended to increase reliability are relevant. Much depends on the way in which the study is communicated to the scientific audience. A report in which the investigator describes the precautions that have been taken to ensure the accuracy of the observations has more credibility than one in which the reader is merely asked to take the data and findings "on faith". The report should contain indications that the investigator is aware of the need to convince the audience of the validity of the study. The interpretations made from the data are more credible when the researcher describes the evidence on which they are based and also any efforts made to test for evidence that would tend to disconfirm any tentative conclusions. One of the procedures that is often followed in ethnographic studies to confirm the validity of interpretations is to feed them back for comment to selected members of the group or to other persons who know the group. If necessary, the interpretations can be "negotiated" with the participants so that the final product is more likely to represent the situation as they see it, but there is always a danger in this procedure that the participants may exercise distortion and cover-up for their own reasons or that the researcher finds it impossible to obtain consensus. Different members of the group may hold different perceptions of the events, for example, teachers and students, or boys and girls. Some researchers have attempted to overcome these problems by setting up small groups of about four participants to engage in discussions towards establishing their shared meanings by acting as "checks, balances, and prompts" for each other, but in practice there are distinct limitations to the possible application of this procedure.

2.4   The role of theory, hypotheses, and generalization

Malinowski specifically recommends that field workers should commence with "fore-shadowed problems" arising from their knowledge of theory, but should not have "preconceived ideas" in which they aim to prove certain hypotheses. The ethnographic method is qualitative and holistic, making use of the investigator's intuition, empathy, and general ability to learn another culture. The investigator is more concerned with discovery than with verification and this requires preparedness to formulate, test, and, if necessary, discard a series of hunches. As investigators develop hypotheses in the course of pursuing a foreshadowed problem, they should be alert for data which refute, support, or cast doubts on their hypotheses and should be prepared to alter them in accordance with increased acquaintance with the phenomena. Research workers as they puzzle over the meaning of the behavior of the group, and perhaps seek help from informants, are likely to obtain illumination through a sudden shaft of understanding. Thus there is a continual dialogue between an orientation towards discovery and one towards verification. Gradually a theoretical basis for the understanding of the group processes may emerge through the process often described as grounded theory, that is, grounded in the research process itself. Theory that emerges from exposure to the data is more likely to fit the requirements than theory that is preconceived on an abstract basis. Also the actual data are more likely to produce categories that are appropriate for describing the particular case. The main problem that arises from grounded theory derived from a case study is that of making generalizations beyond the particular case viewed at a particular time. A straight out description of concrete happenings has some value as an addition to the corpus of information that is available to the investigator and to other interested people – including members of the group itself. However, its value is greatly enhanced when the case can be "located as an instance of a more general class of events" Smith (1978, p. 335). To achieve this, the investigator treats the case in point as either a representative of, or a departure from, a particular type. Sometimes the actual group or groups that are studied have been chosen initially as representatives of a designated type of case and this facilitates generalizations based on it but they should still be treated with reserve.

2.5   Ethnography as a case study method

The problem of the relationship between the One and the Many, a perennial one in philosophy, arises in different guises in the social sciences – idiographic versus nomothetic treatment of data, -emic versus -etic approaches to comparative studies, and the case study versus the sample survey research design. In order to generalize from an individual case study of behavior in one group to behavior in others it is necessary to reach sufficient understanding about the significance of the events in relation to the context in which they occur in order to extend interpretations to other contexts and other groups. In the process of generalizing it is necessary to violate somewhat the full integrity of any one group by describing events in some language that extends beyond the bounds of the culture of that group. Ethnographers are partially acculturated to the group that they are studying, but they are also familiar with other groups with which they compare their experience of the group. To maintain the analogy, an ethnographer is multicultural with respect to the object of study. When an investigator attempts to understand one group, he or she is aided by knowledge of other ones and his or her impressions are partially consolidated with the others. Thus, generalizations are built up through the investigator being able to mediate between one group and others; an ethnographic account of a school, then, derives its value largely from the fact that the investigator – and also the readers – are familiar with other schools, and with schools in general. Diesing refers to this as "pluralism" which he describes as follows: "one might say the method is relativistic in its treatment of individual cases and becomes gradually absolutistic as it moves toward broader generalizations" (1971, pp. 297–98).

In ethnographic studies no generalization can be treated as final, only as a working hypothesis for further studies which may again be ethnographic, or may consist of a survey by means of interviews, questionnaires, or tests. The ethnographic method gains credibility when it combines both subjective and objective methods but it need not be regarded as deriving its value only as a preliminary and exploratory procedure prior to the use of more conventional semiobjective techniques. It can make its own legitimate independent contribution at any stage of a research including the confirmation of hypotheses that have emerged out of other sources provided that the basic principles on which its credibility rests are observed.

See also: Case Study Methods.

References

Becker, G. S., Beer, B. Hughes, E. and Strauss, A. 1961 *Boys in White: Student Culture in Medical School.* University of Chicago Press, Chicago, Illinois.

Denzin, N. K. and Lincoln, Y. S. (eds.) 1994 *Handbook of Qualitative Research.* Sage, London.

Diesing, P. 1971 *Patterns of Discovery in the Social Sciences.* Aldine-Atherton, Chicago, Illinois.

Erickson, F. 1975 Gatekeeping and the melting Pot: Interaction in counseling encounters. *Harvard Educ. Rev.* 45: 44–70.

Everhart, R. B. 1977 Between stranger and friend: Some consequences of "long term" fieldwork in schools. *Am. Educ. Res. J.* 14: 1–15.

Malinowski, B. 1922 *Argonauts of the Western Pacific: An Account of Native Enterprise and Adventure in the Archipelagoes of Melanesian New Guinea.* Routledge, London.

Smith, L. M. 1978 An evolving logic of participant observation, educational ethnography, and other case studies. In: Shulman L. S. (ed.) 1978 *Review of Research in Education,* Vol. 6. Peacock, Ithaca, Illinois, pp. 316–77.

Smith, L. M. and Geoffrey, W. 1968 *The Complexities of an Urban Classroom: An Analysis Toward a General Theory of Teaching.* Holt, Rinehart and Winston, New York.

Further reading

Eisner, E. W. and Peshkin, A. (eds.) 1990 *Qualitative Inquiry in Education.* Teachers College Press, New York.

Wilson, S. 1977 The use of ethnographic techniques in educational research. *Rev. Educ. Res.* 47: 245–65.

11 Historical Methods in Educational Research

C. F. Kaestle

Historians often observe that their discipline is both a science and an art. When they say that history is a science, they mean that historians adhere to certain procedures of investigation and argument that allow them to agree on some generalizations about the past, even though their personal values and their understanding of human nature may differ. In many cases they can agree simply because the evidence is ample and clear, and because they agree on the ground rules. Factual statements like "Jean-Jacques Rousseau was born in 1712" occasion little debate as long as it is the same Rousseau being spoken about and as long as the surviving records are not contradictory. More complex statements are also capable of verification and may attract wide consensus among historians. Examples are such statements as the following: "The average White fertility rate was declining during the period from 1800 to 1860," or "Most educators in 1840 believed that state-funded schooling would reduce crime."

However, the rules of investigation and analysis help less and less as historians attempt to make broader generalizations about the past, or make judgments about its relation to the present, and this is part of what is meant by saying that history is also an art. Consider such statements as: "Slavery destroyed the American Black family," or "Schooling was a major avenue of social mobility in France." These claims are not only immensely difficult to study empirically; they also involve problems of definition and problems of implicit value judgments. The process of broad generalization is thus not simply inductive; it remains an act of creative and often normative interpretation, within the limits established by the evidence. To a considerable degree, history remains stubbornly subjective.

The history of education shares the methodological problems of the field of history in general. There is no single, definable method of inquiry, and important historical generalizations are rarely beyond dispute. Rather they are the result of an interaction between fragmentary evidence and the values and experiences of the historian. It is a challenging and creative interaction, part science, part art.

It is important for educators to understand this problematic nature of historical methodology because historical statements about education abound far beyond textbooks or required history courses in schools of education. Beliefs about the historical role of schooling in America are encountered every day as arguments for educational policies. For example, during the debates in America about the decentralization of urban school control in the 1960s, advocates of decentralization argued that centralization was a device by which social elites in the early twentieth century had gained control of urban education, protected the social structure, and tried to impose their particular values on public school children. The decentralizers argued that centralization had been an undemocratic means of social control, and therefore it deserved to be reversed. Opponents of decentralization claimed that it would lead to inefficiency and corruption. Besides, they said, a common, uniform school system has been a successful tool in creating a cohesive, democratic society in America. They too cited history as their authority. Behind these contending positions is a mass of complex evidence and conflicting values. The historian has no magic formula to tell you which analysis is correct.

The uncertain nature of historical generalization has been particularly apparent in the history of education since the early 1960s. During this period the traditional methods and assumptions of educational historians have come increasingly under attack. The controversy has led to fresh insights, new questions and, more than ever, a heightened sense of the precariousness of historical generalizations.

1 The traditional framework

Current methodological issues in the history of education are best understood in the light of the assumptions and conclusions of traditional educational historians. Until the 1950s most writers of educational history shared two basic assumptions: first, that the history of education was concerned centrally, indeed, almost exclusively, with the history of school systems; and second, that state-regulated, free, tax-supported, universal schooling was a good thing. These assumptions were largely unquestioned, partly because many educational historians performed a dual role as educational administrators or professors of education, and therefore they had a vested interest in seeing state schooling in a good light. But also there was widespread popular agreement that free, universal schooling was an unquestionably positive institution.

There were several unstated corollaries to these assumptions, and they provided the framework – what some might call the paradigm – for research in educational history. Four elements will be mentioned in this paradigm which helped determine methodology and which occasioned later criticism. The first has to do with the focus on schooling. Because they tended to equate education with schooling, traditional historians rated the educational well-being and enlightenment of earlier societies by assessing how much formal schooling there was, and to what extent it was organized under state control. Because their view of historical development was dominated by their present conception of desirable educational policy, they spent much effort trying to explain the lack of enthusiasm for state-regulated schooling prior to the 1830s, and they underestimated the importance of the family, the workplace, the churches, and other educational agencies in preindustrial society.

Related to this problem of focus is the problem of intent. Traditional historians of education saw those who favored state-regulated school systems as enlightened leaders working for the common good; they portrayed people who opposed educational reform as ignorant, misled, or selfish. The attribution of human motivation is a very difficult methodological problem in historical writing; it involves careful comparison of public and private statements; and it requires the separation, if possible, of attempts to determine the historical actor's personal motivation from moral judgments on the effects of an event or a policy. Moral judgments may be timeless, but the historical actor's motivation must be understood in the context of the social values and scientific knowledge of the day. The value bias of most traditional educational historians prejudiced them against recognizing self-interest on the part of school reformers or legitimate, principled objection on the part of their opponents. On the other hand, some recent so-called "revisionist" historians have simply reversed the bias, making school reformers the villains and their opponents the heroes. Either value bias tends to collapse the complexity of educational history and to side-step methodological problems in determining intent.

A third corollary of the assumption that state schooling was a good thing is the equation of growth with progress. Methodologically this prompted historians to glory in numerical growth, often without controlling for parallel population growth or monetary inflation, and without taking seriously the differential educational opportunities of different groups. The tendency is seen equally in the traditional history of Roman Catholic schooling, which is largely a chronicle of increasing schools, children, and budgets.

A fourth corollary of the goodness theme is the focus on leadership and organization rather than on the educational behavior and attitudes of ordinary people. The methodological implication of this focus on the governors rather than on the clients of schooling is to give central attention to public records created by elites rather than attempting to tease out of scanty evidence some inkling of the educational lives of the inarticulate, as recent social historians of education have been attempting to do.

The great majority of books and doctoral dissertations written prior to 1950 on the history of education adhered to this paradigm, focusing on the progressive and beneficial evolution of state school systems. There were some notable exceptions, and even within the paradigm, many excellent legal, institutional, and intellectual studies were written. Nonetheless, the traditional framework had long outlived its usefulness by the late 1950s and early 1960s, when it came under attack.

2   Two strands of revisionism

The two major thrusts of revision in the history of education resulted from rather distinct critiques of the two major tenets of the traditional paradigm: that is, that the history of education is essentially the history of schooling and second, that state-regulated schooling was benign and desirable. The first critique broadened the focus of educational history to look at various agencies of instruction other than schools in America; it has yielded its finest fruits in the works of Bernard Bailyn and Lawrence Cremin on the colonial period, when schooling was much less important than today in the transmission of knowledge. It remains to be seen whether this broader focus can be applied successfully to the history of education in more recent periods. It will be more difficult to research and construct a coherent account of all the ways children learn in twentieth-century society. Merely broadening the definition to include every aspect of socialization would leave the historian of education hopelessly adrift; each historian must therefore now decide carefully what definition of education lurks in his or her work, and this must depend upon what questions are being asked. If one is asking questions about how children acquire skills and beliefs in a society, then the definition of education must be quite broad indeed. If, on the other hand, one is asking questions about the origins of state policy toward education, it is legitimate to focus on schooling, because past policymakers, like past historians, have equated schooling with education. Society as a whole educates in many ways; but the state educates through schools.

There has been a second, quite different, strand of revision in recent educational history, one which has caused considerable commotion among educators. These revisionists have questioned the assumption that state-regulated schooling has been generated by democratic and humanitarian impulses, and the assumption that it has resulted in democratic opportunity. Their work has emphasized variously the exploitative nature of capitalism and how schools relate to it, the culturally abusive nature of values asserted by the schools, and the negative aspects of increasingly bureaucratic school systems. This reversal of ideological perspective on the development of school systems has not always resulted in methodologically sophisticated work, although as a while the works labeled "radical revisionism" have raised important questions about the gloomier aspects of educational systems and have made some persuasive statements about the educational failures of state schooling in industrial nations. Since this entry is about methodology, not ideology, it is not the place to argue the merits of the radical view of school history.

3   Quantitative methods

A newer brand of revisionism has been pursued by historians of various ideological persuasions. Their methods and their subject matter may help answer some of the questions raised by the radicals. These quantitative, social historians have devised the most substantial and problematic methodological innovations. Two aspects of the inadequate traditional framework summarized above were a naive use of numerical data and a focus on the leaders rather than on the clients of educational institutions. Recent social historians of education have taken these problems as their starting-point. They have adopted techniques from sociology and statistics to map out in some detail patterns of literacy, school attendance, years of schooling, school expenditures, voter characteristics on school issues, and other characteristics and have tried to chart changes over time. Much of this work would have been impossible in the early 1960s. It has been made possible by the development of computer programs for social scientists and by the availability of microfilmed sources of information, such as the manuscript United States censuses of the nineteenth century. The inspiration and the models have been provided by historical demographers and by other social historians, who have been charting changing family structures, mobility patterns, wealth distribution, and other phenomena that affect common people. The new emphasis on parents and children in educational history also parallels similar emphases in other fields of educational research: sociologists are studying family background and schooling outcomes, lawyers are studying students' rights, and philosophers are studying the ethics of child–adult relations.

Hopefully, the complex description provided by quantitative historical studies will help develop understanding about educational supply and demand in the past, about the role of schooling in different types of communities, about the different school experiences of different social groups, and about the impact of schooling on later life in different historical periods. The great virtue of quantitative education history is that it places historians in touch with the realities of schooling in the past; it provides a way to start doing history from the bottom up, as it were, and a way to compare popular behavioral patterns with the opinions and policies of educational leaders. However, the quantitative social historian of education also faces problems, problems so numerous and frustrating that they cause some researchers to shun the techniques altogether. Others feel compelled by questions that demand quantitative answers, and they are groping toward a more adequate descriptive social history of education, and to theories that will help explain the patterns they are discovering.

Here is a short list of the problems they encounter. First, statistics and computers are unfamiliar, even alien, to many historians. Even for those who learn the techniques, the work is still very time-consuming and expensive. Experts are constantly devising improved and more arcane statistical techniques. Social historians have trailed along behind sociologists and economists, picking and choosing the techniques that seem most appropriate. Some have moved from simple cross-tabulations and graphs into multiple regression analysis and its various offspring. The social historian who can solve these problems of time, money, and expertise then has to worry about the audience. Most readers of history balk at simple tables; but statistical adequacy demands detailed documentation and detailed presentation of results. This creates problems of style. Methodological sophistication is not worth much if it cannot reach the audience it is aimed at, but it is difficult to serve a technical audience and a general audience in the same work.

As serious as these matters of training and style are, there are more substantive methodological problems in quantitative educational history. First, the data are crude and incomplete. Often the available school and population censuses were ambiguous on crucial matters, or failed to ask the questions that are of most interest now. Most of the data are cross-sectional; they provide only a snapshot of a group at a given moment; but education is a process, and many important questions about educational careers, or the influenced of education on people's lives, can be answered only by data that trace individuals over time. Similarly, questions about the role of education in economic development require comparable aggregate data over time. Some historians have taken up this challenge and have developed longitudinal files by linking data from different sources, but that task is prodigious, and the attrition rate in studies of individuals (the cases lost by geographical mobility, death, and the ambiguity of common names) is so great as to render many conclusions dubious. More commonly, historians have tried to infer process from cross-sectional data. For example, they have examined length of schooling among different social groups by calculating the school-entry and school-leaving ages of different individuals in sample years; or, they have made inferences about the impact of industrialization on communities' educational practices by comparing communities at different stages of industrialization in a given year. Although the questions are about process, in neither case do the data trace individual children or communities over time. The logical and methodological problems of inferring process from static information are serious, and they constitute a central problem in quantitative history today.

Even within legitimate cross-sectional analysis – that is, in pursuing questions about a population at a given moment in time – there is a conflict between statistical adequacy and conceptual adequacy. Limits on research resources and on available data often result in small historical samples. In order to attain statistically significant results, it is sometimes necessary to collapse categories that should remain distinct. For example, if an attempt is being made to relate ethnic background and teenage school attendance while controlling for parental occupation, it may be necessary to combine immigrant groups with quite different cultural and economic features, in order to achieve statistically significant comparisons between children of immigrants and nonimmigrants. The best solution, of course, is to provide the reader with both the significant statistics for the grossly aggregated categories, as well as the descriptively useful information about the smaller subcategories. Here again, though, there are problems of space limits or sheer tedium in presentation.

There are numerous other problems in this new area of research in educational history. For instance, it is difficult to know how conscientiously the data were reported in the first place, or what biases operated; caution on this matter is reinforced when substantial contradictions are found between different sources that claim to measure the same variable in the same population. It is also difficult to create time series on educational variables like attendance, teachers' salaries, educational expenditures, or length of school year, because often the items were defined differently in different periods or omitted altogether.

Despite these many problems, however, some impressive work is beginning to emerge, work which helps to locate the history of education more solidly in the context of social structure and economic development. It is hardly a time for methodological self-congratulation, but neither is it a time for despair. One of the important by-products of this quantitative work in educational history has been to sustain the methodological self-consciousness that began with the critiques of the traditional paradigm in the early 1960s. When the historian does not take methodology for granted, and when his or her methodology is critically scrutinized by other researchers, and when historians are constantly searching for new sources of evidence and techniques of analysis, better work should result.

Not all questions are amenable to quantitative research. It is important to remember that history of education is still vitally concerned with the history of educational ideas. Much good work remains to be done on popular attitudes, on the quality of educational experience in the past, and on the intellectual and institutional history of education. The excitement since the early 1960s has not resulted in a new single methodology, nor in a new, broadly accepted interpretation of educational history. However, the collapse of the old consensus has caused educational historians to explore new questions, discard old assumptions, try new techniques, and attempt to meet more rigorous standards of evidence and argument.

4 Complementary methods

Many great social theorists, including Karl Marx, Max Weber, Emile Durkheim, Ferdinand Tönnies, and Talcott Parsons, wrote about history. Contemporary theorists from disciplines as diverse as sociology, linguistics, anthropology, philosophy, and statistics also do work that is relevant to historical study. Historians, however, differ in the amount of importance they give to theory, about whether they should attempt to test general theories with historical data, or about whether historians should get involved with theories at all.

There are several reasons why historians should read about theory and think about its relationship to their work. Because historical writing is selective and interpretative, it is necessarily guided by the individual historian's sense of what is important, where to find meaning, and how social change and human motivation work. The answers arise partly from the materials, of course. Although history is not *merely* inductive, it is *partly* inductive. The answers also lie, however, in an individual historian's temperament, convictions, hunches, and theories, whether explicit or implicit. By paying attention to the best theoretical work in related disciplines, historians can better identify their informal, personal theories. More important, they can shape their understanding of human experience by learning from other disciplines. Finally, historical work can reflect back in important ways on social theories, confirming, refuting, or modifying various theoretical statements. A historian need not, therefore, adopt an entire theoretical system in order to profit from theoretical work in other disciplines. Some excellent work has been done from rigorous and systematic theoretical viewpoints, but most historians use theory incidentally and selectively.

Theory has many implications for historical methodology, too numerous to cover in this entry. Theories may influence what sort of evidence we look for, what sort of evidence we will accept, and what sort of arguments we will make from the evidence. For example, if one accepts the Marxist theorem that an individual's relationship to the means of production is crucial to his experience, one will make a concerted effort to determine historical actors' class status and class consciousness, and one will make class a prominent part of the explanation of historical events. If one accepts anthropologist Clifford Geertz's theory that ritualistic or even apparently trivial everyday behavior can symbolize the deeper meaning of a culture, one will devote much attention to developing an interpretation that moves from observed behavior to cultural meaning. Whether a historian accepts a large theoretical system, uses theory incidentally, or resists the mixing of theory and historical writing, each should be conversant with major theoretical positions in related disciplines and self-conscious about their possible relevance for historical methodology.

5   Conclusion: pervasive methodological concerns

There are four key problems to watch for when assessing arguments about the history of education, problems that have been highlighted by recent work in the social history of education, but which are also pertinent to the intellectual history of education, the institutional history of education, and other approaches.

The first problem is the confusion of correlations and causes, a problem particularly salient in quantitative work, but certainly not unique to it. To demonstrate that two phenomena occur together systematically is not, of course, to prove that one causes the other, but historians as well as social scientists are constantly tempted into this kind of argument. For example, Irish families in nineteenth-century urban America sent their children to school less often and for fewer years, on the average, than many other groups. This does not, however, demonstrate that "Irishness" (whatever that is) caused low school attendance. First, it must as asked whether Irish immigrants also tended to be poor, because it might be poverty that caused low attendance. Then it would be necessary to control for family structure, religion, and other factors. If, in the end, after controlling for all other measurable factors, Irish status was independently associated with low school attendance, a causal relationship would still not have been established. It would be necessary to investigate, and speculate on, why and how being Irish affected school-going. Correlations are just concerned with proximate occurrence; causality is about how things work, and correlations do not indicate much about how things work. Because human motivation is often multiple and vague and because society is not very much like a clock, historians must exercise great caution in moving from systematic statistical associations to assertions of causality.

The second problem to which critical readers must give close attention is the problem of defining key terms. The problem of definition can be subdivided into two common pitfalls; vagueness and presentism. As an example of vagueness, the notion that industrialization caused educational reform is commonplace in educational history. However, the statement has almost no analytical value until the meanings of the umbrella terms "industrialization" and "educational reform" are specified. In contrast, consider the statement: "The expansion of wage labor in nineteenth-century communities or regions was followed by an expansion of annual school enrolment." This is much more precise, has important causal implications, and is amenable to empirical research.

By "presentism" is meant the danger of investing key terms from the past with their present connotations, or, conversely, applying to past developments present-day terms that did not exist or meant something else at the time. A classic example in American educational history involves the use of the word "public." In the eighteenth century a "public" educational institution was one in which children learned collectively, in contrast with private tutorial education, and it was one devoted to education for the public good, as opposed to mere selfish gain. Thus the colonial colleges, which were controlled by self-perpetuating trustees and financed mainly by tuition, were thoroughly "public" and were called so at the time, as in England. In today's terminology they would be called "private" in American, but calling them "private" in historical work greatly muddles understanding of eighteenth-century society. Avoiding presentism thus means paying close attention to the etymology of key terms, and it is a methodological imperative in good history.

A third problem that critical consumers of educational history should keep in mind is the distinction between ideas about how people should behave and how ordinary people in fact behaved. Too often evidence of the latter is lacking and evidence of the former is allowed to stand in its place; that is, it is assumed that people did as they were told. The methodological dilemma is posed by the following problem: if the legal and legislative bodies of a society constantly passed rules requiring school attendance, is it evidence that the society valued schooling highly, expressing this value in their legislation, or is it evidence of a society that did not value school-going very much, thus alarming its leaders into coercive efforts? To answer the question, something needs to be known about school attendance patterns by different groups. Here is a more specific example. There was widespread agreement among professional educators and physicians beginning in the late 1830s in the northeastern part of the United States that school attendance by very young children was unwise, even dangerous to their health, as well as being a nuisance to teachers. Parents were constantly urged to keep their children under 5 or 6 at home. This campaign continued throughout the 1840s and 1850s. To infer from this that children normally began school at 5 or 6 during these decades, however, would be incorrect. Parents resisted the conventional experience. As is now known from analysis of manuscript censuses and statistical school reports, they persisted in sending 3- and 4-year-old children to school, for reasons that can only be guessed at, until they were coerced to keep them home by local regulations on age of school entry in the 1850s and 1860s. Only then did the aggregate average age of entry rise substantially. Here, then, is an example of the lag between elite opinion and popular behavior, one which warns against equating literary sources with popular behavior. Child-rearing manuals may not cause or even reflect actual child-rearing practices; and exhortations about educational policies often fall on deaf ears.

The fourth and final problem has to do with the distinction between intent and consequences. No matter how wise educational leaders have been, their powers of foresight have rarely equaled the historians' powers of hindsight. It is an inherent advantage in historical analysis – and yet it is a problem too: historians know how things turned out. The problem lies in the danger of assuming that the historical actors could have (and should have) foreseen the full consequences of their ideas and of the institutions they shaped. It is undoubtedly true that many of the consequences of educational leadership have been precisely as the leaders intended; it does not follow, however, that intent can be inferred from consequences. The fact that large bureaucracies are effective instruments of racial discrimination does not necessarily mean that their creators had a racist intent. The fact that schooling has done an unimpressive job in reducing crime does not mean that school reformers who touted it for that purpose were hypocrites. Intent cannot be inferred from consequences. Direct evidence is needed of intent at the time an act occurred.

No historian can completely transcend or resolve these four problems, but each must recognize the problems and the associated methodological challenges when trying to make meaningful generalizations about the educational past. Historians have always been scavengers. Since history involves all human experience and thought, historians have constantly raided other disciplines for new techniques of analysis and for new insights into society and human nature. This helps explain why there is no single methodology in history, and why historians love their craft so much: because it is so complex and so all-encompassing.

Recent trends in the history of education – the effort to see education as broader than schooling, the effort to see school systems in the context of social and economic development, and the effort to study popular attitudes and behavior as well as the history of elite intentions and actions – have greatly accelerated the borrowing process in this historical subfield. Historians of education have reached out and become involved in the history of the family, of childhood, and of reform institutions, for example, in addition to deepening their traditional commitment to economic and political history as a context for educational development. They have also explored recent sociology, anthropology, psychology, and statistics for new ideas and techniques. Because this period of exploration and revision has resulted in a diverse, eclectic methodology, because no new methodological or ideological consensus has emerged – in short, because there is no successful paradigm in educational history today, it is all the more important that each reader of educational history be critically alert and independent.

See also: Educational Research, History of.

References

Bailyn, B. 1960 *Education in the Forming of American Society.* University of North Carolina Press, Chapel Hill, North Carolina.

Baker, D. N. and Harrigan, P. J. (eds.) 1980 *The Making of Frenchmen: Current Directions in the History of Education in France, 1679–1979.* Wilfred Laurier University Press, Waterloo, Ontario.

Butterfield, H. 1931 *The Whig Interpretation of History.* Bell, London.

Carnoy, M. 1974 *Education as Cultural Imperialism.* McKay, New York.

Craig, J. 1981 The expansion of education. In: Berliner D. (ed.) 1981 *Review of Research in Education.* American Educational Research Association, Washington, DC.

Cremin, L. A. 1970 *American Education: The Colonial Experience, 1607–1783.* Harper and Row, New York.

Cubberley, E. P. 1934 *Public Education in the United States: A Study and Interpretation of American Educational History.* Houghton-Mifflin, Boston, Massachusetts.

Dore, R. F. 1967 *Education in Tokugawa, Japan.* Routledge and Kegan Paul, London.

Johansson, E. 1973 *Literacy and Society in a Historical Perspective.* University Press, Umea.

Kaestle, C. F. and Vinovskis, M. A. 1980 *Education and Social Change in Nineteenth-century Massachusetts.* Cambridge University Press, New York.

Kaestle, C. F. 1992 Theory in comparative educational history: A middle ground. In: Goodenow R. and Marsden W. (eds.) 1992 *The City and Education in Four Nations.* Cambridge University Press, Cambridge.

Kaestle, C. F. 1992 Standards of evidence in educational research: How do we know when we know? *Hist. Educ. Q.* 32: 361–66.

Katz, M. B. 1968 *The Irony of Early School Reform: Educational Innovation in Mid-nineteenth Century Massachusetts.* Harvard University Press, Cambridge, Massachusetts.

Laqueur, T. W. 1976 *Religion and Respectability: Sunday Schools and Working-class Culture, 1780–1850.* Yale University Press, New Haven, Connecticut.

Maynes, M. J. 1979 The virtues of archaism: The political economy of schooling in Europe, 1750–1850. *Comp. Stud. Soc. Hist.* 21: 611–25.

Novick, P. 1988 *That Noble Dream: The "Objectivity Question" and the American Historical Profession.* Cambridge University Press, Cambridge.

Rury, J. 1993 Methods of historical research in education. In: Lancey D. *Research in Education.* Longman, New York.

Simon, B. 1960 *Studies in the History of Education, 1780–1870.* Lawrence and Wishart, London.

Spaull, A. 1981 The biographical tradition in the history of Australian education. *Aust. N.Z. Hist. Educ. Soc. J.* 10: 1–10.

Stone, L. 1969 Literacy and education in England, 1640–1900. *Past and Present* 42: 61–139.

Thaubault, R. 1971 *Education and Change in a Village Community, Mazières-en-Gâtine, 1848–1914.* Schocken, New York.

Tyack, D. B. 1974 *The One Best System: A History of American Urban Education.* Harvard University Press, Cambridge, Massachusetts.

12   Narrative Inquiry

F. M. Connelly and D. J. Clandinin

One of the dilemmas of educational studies is that often the more rigorous and scientific educational research becomes, the less it is connected to human experience. The objectivists sometimes call those who study experience "soft" and "subjective"; conversely experimentalists claim that the scientific study of education depersonalizes, dehumanizes, and objectifies people. Narrative and story-telling, two intimately related terms, are increasingly evident in the literature that swirls around these compelling scientific-humanistic modes of inquiry. They are terms representing ideas about the nature of human experience and about how experience may be studied and represented and about which they tread a middle course between the extremes. Narrativists believe that human experience is basically storied experience: that humans live out stories and are story-telling organisms. They further believe that one of the best ways to study human beings is to come to grips with the storied quality of human experience, to record stories of educational experience, and to write still other interpretative stories of educational experience. The complex written stories are called narratives. Properly done these stories are close to experience because they directly represent human experience; and they are close to theory because they give accounts that are educationally meaningful for participants and readers. The creation of these stories in research is based on particular experiential methods and criteria. This article outlines the theoretical origins of narrative inquiry; gives a brief description of narrative studies in education; describes appropriate methodologies; delineates distinctions between the field, field texts, and research texts; and outlines appropriate research criteria.

1   Theoretical context for narrative inquiry in education

Narrative has a long history in the study of fictional literature. Perhaps because it focuses on human experience, perhaps because story is a fundamental structure of human experience, and perhaps because it has an holistic quality, narrative is exploding into other disciplines. Narrative is a way of characterizing the phenomena of human experience and its study that is appropriate to many social science fields.

Literary theory is the principal intellectual resource. The fact that a story is inherently temporal means that history and the philosophy of history (Carr, 1986), which are essentially the study of time, have a special role to play in shaping narrative studies in the social sciences. Therapeutic fields are also making significant contributions. Psychology has only recently discovered narrative although Polkinghorne (1988) claimed that closely related inquiries were part of the field at the beginning of the twentieth century but disappeared after the Second World War when they were suffocated by physical science paradigms. Among the most fundamental and educationally suggestive works on the nature of narrative is Johnson's (1989) philosophical study of bodily knowledge and language. Because education is ultimately a moral and spiritual pursuit, MacIntyre's (1984) narrative ethical theory and Crites' (1986) theological writing on narrative are especially useful for educational purposes. (For a review of narrative in and out of education see Connelly and Clandinin (1990), and Clandinin and Connelly (1991).)

2   Related educational studies

Berk (1980) stated that autobiography was one of the first methodologies for educational study, though it essentially disappeared until recently (Pinar, 1988; Grumet, 1988). Autobiography is related to narrative (Connelly and Clandinin, 1987). The focus here is on an individual's psychology considered over a span of time.

Narrative inquiry may also be sociologically concerned with groups and the formation of community (Carr, 1986). To date in education, personal rather than social narrative inquiries have been more in evidence. In educational studies a social narrative inquiry emphasis has tended to be on teacher careers and professionalism. It is expected that social narrative will be increasingly emphasized in research.

Some closely related lines of inquiry focus specifically on story: oral history and folklore (Dorson, 1976), children's story-telling (Applebee, 1978), and the uses of story in preschool and school language experience (Sutton-Smith, 1986). Oral history suggests a range of phenomena for narrative inquiry, such as material culture, custom, arts, recollections, and myths. Myths are the storied structures that stand behind folklore and oral history. Van Maanen (1988) provided an introduction to the ethnography of story-telling, both as subject matter and as ethnographers' written form. The best known educational use of oral history in North America is the Foxfire Project (Wigginton, 1989). There have been curriculum proposals for organizing subject matter along story lines (Egan, 1986). In research on curriculum, teachers' narratives are seen as a metaphor for teaching–learning relationships. In understanding teachers and students educationally, it is necessary to develop an understanding of people with a narrative of life experience. Life's narratives are the context for making meaning of school situations.

Because of its focus on experience and the qualities of life and education, narrative is situated in a matrix of qualitative research. Eisner's (1988) review of the educational study of experience aligns narrative with qualitatively oriented educational researchers working with experiential philosophy, psychology, critical theory, curriculum studies, and anthropology. Elbaz (1988) focused on teacher thinking studies and showed how feminist studies and studies of the personal are related to narrative. She aligned narrative with many other educational studies which often use participant stories as raw data (e.g., case work research on expert teachers and naturalistic approaches to evaluation).

There is a large literature of teachers' stories and stories of teachers which is narrative in quality but which is not found in standard review documents. This literature refers to accounts of individual teachers, students, classrooms, and schools written by teachers and others.

In this overview of narrative inquiry it is desirable to locate narrative in a historical intellectual context. On the one hand, narrative inquiry may be traced to Aristotle's *Poetics* and St Augustine's *Confessions* (See Ricoeur's [1984] use of these two sources to link time and narrative) and may be seen to have various adaptations and applications in a diversity of disciplines including education. Dewey's (e.g. 1938) work on time, space, experience, and sociality is also central. On the other hand, there is a newness to narrative inquiry as it has developed in the social sciences, including education. The educational importance of this line of work is that it brings theoretical ideas about the nature of human life as lived to bear on educational experience as lived.

3 The process of narrative inquiry

The process of narrative research revolves around three matters: the field, texts on field experience, and research texts which incorporate the first two and which represent those issues of social significance that justify the research. Field, field text, research text, and the relations among them, name primary narrative inquiry decision foci. The relations between researcher and field range from the researcher being a neural observer to the researcher going native as an active participant. The relations between researcher and field text based on the field experience involve complex questions of the representation of experience, the interpretation and reconstruction of experience, and appropriate text forms. Constructing a research text involves the presence of the autobiographical researcher and the significance of this presence for the research text and for the field it represents. The main point about the transition from field text to research text is that the research text is written for an audience of other researchers and practitioners and must be written in such a way as to go beyond the particulars of experience captured in field texts.

3.1 *Working in the field: experiencing the experience*

The major issue confronting narrative researchers in the field is their relationship with participants. Traditional methodologies have taught that researchers should be objective and distant from participants, ensuring unbiased results. In narrative research, different degrees of closeness with participants are deliberately negotiated with the result that the experience of the researcher becomes intermingled with participants' field experience. The field is no longer being studied in a detached way. It is the field in relation to the researcher that is the object of study. This means that researchers need to pay close attention to their own experience and to the stories of them. They need to understand, document, and think through the consequences of establishing different degrees of closeness with participants.

The second major field concern for a narrative researcher is to look beyond the immediacy of any experience under study. For example, it is not enough to study the opening activities of a school day without understanding that those activities have a history for this teacher, for that class, for this school, and also for the larger history of schooling and culture. Narrative inquiry needs to establish the narrative, cultural history of the events under study for later interpretation in the creation of research texts.

3.2   From field to field texts

What are normally called data (e.g., field notes) are, in narrative research, better thought of as field texts. These are texts created by participants and researchers to represent aspects of field experience. They are called field texts rather than data because texts have a narrative quality. The common notion of data is that they are an objective recording of events. Field texts do not have that quality. They grow out of complex field experience involving relations among researchers and participants and they are selected, interpretative records of that experience. Researchers, relationship to participants' stories shape the field texts and establish their epistemological status. Narrative researchers need continually to monitor and record, the quality of these relationships and their influence on the status of the field texts. In the following section several methods for constructing field texts are outlined.

3.3   Oral history

One method for creating field texts is oral history. There are several strategies for obtaining an oral history, ranging from the use of a structured set of questions in which the researchers' intentions are uppermost, to asking a person to tell his or her own story in his or her own way in which the participant's intentions are uppermost. There is a tradition of oral history in the study of culture (e.g., Gluck and Patai, 1991).

3.4   Stories

A closely connected method is the telling or writing of stories. Stories are pervasive in human and social experience. Individuals have stories of their own experience, of school, and of their profession. Furthermore, institutions have a storied quality. For example, teachers, parents, students, and others tell stories about their school. There are also community and cultural stories about schooling generally, and about education and its place in society. Some of these stories take on the quality of myths and sacred stories (Crites, 1986).

3.5   Annals and chronicles

Annals are a simple dated history of significant moments or events for an individual or institution. Annals permit researchers to gain a historical context for the events under study. Chronicles are more thematic representations of the annals. Chronicles represent a thematic aspect of the field of interest (e.g., a chronicle of a school's administration).

3.6   Photographs, memory boxes, other personal/institutional artifacts

Physical artifacts are repositories of experience. The items that a person collects and a school's trophies and mementos can, with discussion with knowledgeable participants, reveal important depths of experience. These items, furthermore, are important triggers for memory.

3.7   Research interviews

Interviews can be made into field texts by verbatim transcription, note-taking, and the use of interview segments. Interview methodologies range from inquisitional questioning to informal conversation on mutually agreed upon topics to therapeutic methods that shift the focus of inquiry to the participant. Interviews are one of the clearest places for seeing the significant effect that different researcher–participant relationships have on the kind of data collected and field texts written.

3.8   Journals

Journals have been increasingly used for teaching purposes. It is sometimes overlooked that the same qualities that make them an influential teaching tool also make them a valid research tool. Journals provide both a descriptive and reflective record of events, and of personal responses to them. Journals tend to be written in solitude and in a participant's personal time. The energy to write them often flags unless the participant has strong personal reasons for continuing.

3.9   Autobiographical and biographical writing

Autobiography and biography are more comprehensive methods than the compilation of journals for interpreting life experience. Narrative researchers commonly think of a life as a story in which a person is the central character and author. Therefore, autobiographical or biographical field texts are interpretative retellings of a story already lived. This interpretative, in contrast to objective, quality applies to other kinds of field texts described in this section. Furthermore, "data" are commonly thought to be true or not. When it can be shown that they "could be otherwise,: their validity is undermined. But autobiographical or biographical field texts can always "be otherwise" as they are written for one or other purpose, thereby emphasizing one or other narrative theme. The fact that many autobiographical or biographical field texts may be written for any participant does not undermine the validity of the research provided its purposes are clear and its relationship to the field is established. This point of diversity applies to other field texts though it is most evident in autobiography and biography.

3.10   Letters

Letters, unlike journals, are written to another person with the expectation of a response. Both letters and journals are used in autobiographical and biographical methods. It is common to write intellectual biographies of key figures in the social and physical sciences (e.g., Charles Darwin), and to base these, in part, on letters. Letters reveal much about the intellectual and social conditions in a person's thought. This applies to the use of letters in narrative research whether or not the research is biographically oriented.

3.11   Conversations

Conversation covers many kinds of activities, including letter writing. Usually conversation refers to nonhierarchical oral exchanges among researchers and participants in collaborative inquiries. Because of the underlying trust in conversation, this methodology may end up probing more deeply than aggressive questioning techniques. Conversations tend to be open-ended and therefore require special attention to methods of recording and interpretation.

3.12   Field notes and other stories from the field

Field notes are the standard ethnographic method of data collection. Commonly thought to be drafted by researchers, field notes may, in collaborative studies, be written by participants. Field notes may take the form of descriptive records, theoretical memos, points of view, biases, and speculations. Researchers anxious to represent experience truthfully may replace field notes with tape or video recordings. While these time-consuming methods are sometimes warranted, researchers should only use them when verbatim verbal or physical acts are essential.

3.13   Document analysis

Documents are an easily overlooked source of field texts, particularly in the narrative study of groups and institutions. Documents have a special status because they are public records and often represent an official position. The narrative context in which documents were written and used is crucial to their interpretation and researchers need to collect information on dates, authors, personalities, contextual matters (e.g. board policies as context for a school document), climates of opinion, and so on.

4   From field texts to research texts

Converting field texts into research texts is a difficult phase of narrative research. Ordinarily the process consists of the construction of a series of increasingly interpretative writings. For instance, a narrative study of the influence of immigration on school opening and closing routines might involve any or all of the above methodologies to construct a second order historical field text. The text might be so compellingly interesting because of its factual and textual liveliness in the form of conversations and personal anecdote that the research might conclude prematurely. This frequently happens with autobiographical and biographical work, where the writing may be so interesting to the researchers that they neglect to consider the social significance of the text or why it might be of interest to others. Field texts tend to be close to experience, descriptive, and shaped around specific events. They have the quality of being a record. Research texts on the other hand tend to be at a distance from the field and from field texts. They are written in response to questions about meaning and significance. It is not enough to write a narrative; the author needs to understand the meanings of the narrative and its significance for others and for social issues. Research texts, therefore, tend to be patterned. Field texts are shaped into research texts by the underlying narrative threads and themes that constitute the driving force of the inquiry.

The intermingling of the researcher's outlooks and points of view which were so central in the field and in the creation of field texts play an equally important role in the writing of research texts. Relationships established in the field and reflected in field texts are also evident in the thematic reinterpretation of those field texts into research texts. Thus, throughout a narrative inquiry the *researcher's presence* needs to be acknowledged, understood, and written into the final research account. Discovering a researcher's presence in a research text has traditionally been sufficient justification to dismiss the text as inappropriately subjective. But the reverse applies in narrative inquiry: a text written as if the researcher had no autobiographical presence would constitute a deception about the epistemological status of the research. Such a study lacks validity.

Voice and signature are two terms helped in understanding autobiographical presence. Voice refers to a researcher's sense of having something to say. There is no voice in extreme forms of "objective" research because it is the reliability and validity of the method, and not of the researcher, that is the basis for judgment of the research. But voice creates personal risks for researchers because they must take stands on matters that are only partially supported by field texts. Taken to the extremes, voice is merely an excuse to vent the researcher's biases. Too strong a voice leads to an autocratic subjectivity; too little voice leads to technical objectivity. The dilemma for a researcher is to establish a voice that simultaneously represents participants' field experience while creating a research text that goes beyond the field and its field texts to speak to an audience. There are no formal rules for establishing voice and the matter can only be sorted out judicially study by study.

Signature refers to the writing style that makes it possible to identify a text as an author's work. Developing a signature is difficult, especially for novice narrative researchers. The traditional research signature is impersonal and marked by a well-known structure of problem, literature review, data, etc. But narrative research texts have a personal signature and may be written in seemingly endless literary, poetic, and scientific ways. A word of practical advice for novice narrative researchers is to model their writing on a researcher they admire, just as novice artists become apprenticed to a master painter. The adaptations of a master researcher's work will eventually yield a signature for the apprentice narrative researcher.

Voice and signature come together in the writing of a research text aimed at an audience. The audience redirects a researcher's attention from participant and research self to others and thereby complicates the problem of voice and signature which are more easily established in the field and in the writing of field texts. The researcher now needs to decide on a relationship with the audience. Chatman (1990) described four kinds of research texts which yield four kinds of relationships: descriptive, expositional, argumentative, and narrative. Providing descriptive information differs from explaining (exposition), convincing (argument), or inviting readers into storied meanings with the author (narrative). Each text form can be used in the service of others. For instance, a narrative study might yield a set of narrative field texts. But the author may wish to influence a policy, school practice, or research direction and decide to write an argumentative "if–then" research text for this purpose. Accordingly, a narrative inquiry may, but need not, be concluded with a narrative research text. Thus, the researcher's intended relationship to an audience complicates the matter of voice and signature since each of these four research text forms has its own qualities independent of the researcher.

5   Notes on criteria

Because narrative methods in education are so new, and because qualitative methods in general are new and not fully established, during the 1990s there was much writing on the criteria for judging narrative inquiry. The most important thing to note for this entry is that criteria have been under discussion. In general it may be said that reliability and validity have assumed less importance as matters such as apparentness and verisimilitude have been raised. The mainstay criteria of social science research are overrated and are being supplemented by numerous other considerations (Guba and Lincoln, 1989). Narrative researchers are concerned with the representation of experience, causality, temporality, and the difference between the experience of time and the telling of time, narrative form, integrity of the whole in a research document, the invitational quality of a research text, its authenticity, adequacy, and plausibility. Currently, in narrative inquiry, it is important for each researcher to set forth the criteria that govern the study and by which it may be judged. It is also the case that others may quite legitimately adopt other criteria in support of, or in criticism of, the work. The development of narrative inquiry within the social sciences is fascinating to follow as debates rage over narrative inquiry's challenges to traditional research forms.

See also: Biographical Research Methods.

References

Applebee, A. N. 1978 *The Child's Concept of Story: Ages Two to Seventeen.* University of Chicago Press, Chicago, Illinois.

Berk, L. 1980 Education in lives: Biographic narrative in the study of educational outcomes. *J. Curr. Theor.* 2(2): 88–153.

Carr, D. 1986 *Time, Narrative, and History.* Indiana University Press, Bloomington, Indiana.

Chatman, S. 1990 *Coming to Terms: The Rhetoric of Narrative in Fiction and Film.* Cornell University Press, Ithaca, New York.

Clandinin, D. J. and Connelly, F. M. 1991 Narrative and story in practice and research. In: Schön D. A. (ed.) 1991 *The Reflective Turn: Case Studies in and on Educational Practice.* Teachers College Press, New York.

Connelly, F. M. and Clandinin, D. J. 1987 On narrative method, biographical and narrative unities in the study of teaching. *Journal of Educational Thought* 21(3): 139–39.

Connelly, F. M. and Clandinin, D. J. 1990 Stories of experience and narrative inquiry. *Educ. Researcher* 19(5): 2–14.

Crites, S. 1986 Storytime: Recollecting the past and projecting the future. In: Sarbin T. R. (ed.) 1986 *The Stories Nature of Human Conduct.* Praeger, New York.

Dewey, J. 1938 *Experience and Education.* Macmillan, New York.

Dorson, R. M. 1976 *Folklore and Fakelore: Essays Toward a Discipline of Folk studies.* Harvard University Press, Cambridge, Massachusetts.

Egan, K. 1986 *Teaching as Story Telling: An Alternative Approach to Teaching and Curriculum in the Elementary School.* Althouse, London.

Eisner, E. W. 1988 The primacy of experience and the politics of method. *Educ. Researcher* 17(5): 15–20.

Elbaz, F. 1988 Knowledge and discourse: The evolution of research on teacher thinking. Paper given at the Conference of the International Study Association on Teacher Thinking. University of Nottingham, September 1988.

Gluck, S. B. and Patai, D. (eds.) 1991 *Women's Words: The Feminist Practice of Oral History.* Routledge, New York.

Grumet, M. R. 1988 *Bitter Milk: Women and Teaching.* University of Massachusetts Press, Amherst, Massachusetts.

Guba, E. G. and Lincoln, Y. S. 1989 *Fourth Generation Evaluation.* Sage, Newbury Park, California.

Johnson, M. 1989 Special series on personal practical knowledge: Embodied knowledge. *Curric. Inq.* 19(4): 361–77.

MacIntyre, A. 1981 *After Virtue: A Study in Moral Theory,* 2nd edn. University of Notre Dame Press, Notre Dame, Indiana.

Pinar, W. F. 1988 "Whole, bright, deep with understanding": Issues in qualitative research and autobiographical method. In: Pinar W. F. (ed.) 1988 *Contemporary Curriculum Discourses.* Gorsuch Scarisbrick, Scottsdale, Arizona.

Polkinghorne, D. E. 1968 *Narrative Knowing and the Human Sciences.* State University of New York Press, New York.

Ricoeur, P. 1984 *Time and Narrative,* Vol. 1 University of Chicago Press, Chicago, Illinois.

Sutton-Smith, B. 1986 Children's fiction making. In: Sarbin T. R. 1986 *Narrative Psychology: The Storied Nature of Human Conduct.* Praeger, New York.

Van Maanen, J. 1988 *Tales of the Field: On Writing Ethnography.* University of Chicago Press, Chicago, Illinois.

Wiggington, E. 1989 Foxfire grows up. *Harv. Educ. Rev.* 59(1): 24–49.

13 Naturalistic and Rationalistic Enquiry

E. G. Guba and Y. S. Lincoln

Persons concerned with disciplined enquiry have tended to use what is commonly called the scientific paradigm – that is, model or pattern – of enquiry. A second paradigm, also aimed at disciplined enquiry, is commonly known as the naturalistic paradigm, although it is often referred to (mistakenly) as the case study or qualitative paradigm. Its distinguishing features are not, however, its format or methods, or even, as its title might suggest, the fact that it is usually carried out in natural settings. What differentiates the naturalistic from the scientific (or, as it is sometimes referred to, the rationalistic paradigm) approach is, at bottom, the different interpretations placed on certain basic axioms or assumptions. In addition, the two approaches characteristically take different postures on certain issues which, while not as basic as axiomatic propositions, are nevertheless fundamental to an understanding of how the naturalistic enquirer operates.

1 Axiomatic differences between the naturalistic and rationalistic paradigms

Axioms may be defined as the set of undemonstrated (and undemonstrable) propositions accepted by convention or established by practice as the basic building blocks of some conceptual or theoretical structure or system. As such they are arbitrary and certainly not "self-evidently true". Different axiom systems have different utilities depending on the phenomenon to which they are applied; so, for example, Euclidean geometry as an axiomatic system has good fit to terrestrial phenomena but Lobachevskian geometry (a non-Euclidean form) has better fit to interstellar phenomena. A decision about which of several axiom systems to employ for a given purpose is a matter of the relative "fit" between the axiom sets and the characteristics of the application area. It is the general contention of naturalists that the axioms of naturalistic enquiry provide a better fit to most social/behavioral phenomena than do the rationalistic axioms.

1.1 Axiom 1: the nature of reality

Rationalists assume that there exists a single, tangible reality fragmentable into independent variables and processes, any of which can be studied independently of the others; enquiry can be caused to converge onto this single reality until, finally, it is explained. Naturalists assume that there exist multiple realities which are, in the main, constructions existing in the minds of people; they are therefore intangible and can be studied only in wholistic, and idiosyncratic, fashion. Enquiry into these multiple realities will inevitably diverge (the scope of the enquiry will enlarge) as more and more realities must be considered. Naturalists argue that while the rationalist assumptions undoubtedly have validity in the hard and life sciences, naturalist assumptions are more meaningful in studying human behavior. Naturalists do not deny the reality of the objects, events, or processes with which people interact, but suggest that it is the meanings given to or interpretations made of these objects, events, or processes that constitute the arena of interest to investigators of social/behavioral phenomena. Note that these constructions are not perceptions of the objects, events, or processes but of meaning and interpretation. The situation is very much approximated, the naturalist would say, by the ancient tale of the blind men and the elephant – provided it is conceded that there is no elephant.

1.2 Axiom 2: the enquirer–respondent relationship

The rationalist assumes that the enquirer is able to maintain a discrete and inviolable distance from the "object" of enquiry; but concedes that when the object is a human being, special methodological safeguards must be taken to prevent reactivity, that is, a reaction of the object to the conditions of the enquiry that will influence the outcome in undesirable ways. The naturalist assumes that the enquirer and the respondent in any human enquiry inevitably interact to influence one another. While safeguards need to be mounted in both directions, the interaction need not be eliminated (it is impossible to do that anyway) but should be exploited for the sake of the inquiry.

Naturalists point out that the proposition of subject–object independence is dubious even to areas like particle physics, as exemplified in the Heisenberg Uncertainty Principle. The effect is certainly more noticeable in dealing with people, they assert. Nor should it be supposed that the interpolation of a layer of apparently objective instrumentation (paper and pencil or brass) solves the problem. Enquirers react to the mental images they have of respondents in developing the instrumentation; respondents answer or act in terms of what they perceive to be expectations held for their behavior as they interpret the meaning of the items or tasks put before them; enquirers deal with responses in terms of their interpretation of response meaning and intent, and so on. Nor, say the naturalists, is interactivity a generally undesirable characteristic; indeed, if interactivity could be limited by some methodological tour de force, the trade off would not be worthwhile, because it is precisely the interactivity that makes it possible for the human instrument to achieve maximum responsiveness, adaptability, and insight.

1.3 Axiom 3: the nature of truth statements

Rationalists assert that the aim of inquiry is to develop a nomethic body of knowledge; this knowledge is best encapsulated in generalizations which are truth statements of enduring value that are context free. The stuff of which generalizations are made is the similarity among units; differences are set aside as intrinsically uninteresting. Naturalists assert that the aim of inquiry is to develop an idiographic body of knowledge; this knowledge is best encapsulated in a series of "working hypotheses" that describe the individual case. Generalizations are not possible since human behavior is never time or context free. Nevertheless, some transferability of working hypotheses from context to context may be possible depending on the similarity of the contexts (an empirical matter). Differences are as inherently important as (and at times more important than) the similarities. Naturalists well understand the utility of generalizations such as $f = ma$ or $e = mc^2$ in physics, although even in the hard or life sciences, as Cronbach (1975) has pointed out, generalizations are much like radioactive materials, in that they decay and have a halflife. Surely it is unreasonable to suppose that analogous tendencies do not exist in the social and behavioral sciences?

1.4 Axiom 4: causality

For the rationalist, the determination of cause–effect relationships is of prime importance; for each effect, it is assumed, there is a cause which can, given sufficiently sophisticated enquiry, be detected. The ultimate form for demonstrating cause–effect relationships is the experiment. The naturalist asserts that the determination of cause–effect is often a search for the Holy Grail. Human relationships are caught up in such an interacting web of factors, events, and processes that the hope that "the" cause–effect chain can be sorted out is vain; the best the enquirer can hope to establish are plausible patterns of influence. Naturalists point out that there have been a variety of cause–effect theories proposed since the simplistic "if–then" formulation was critiqued by Hume in the early eighteenth century, including Hume's own constant conjunctions or regularity theory, "law" theories, formulations about "necessary and sufficient" conditions, and more recently, various attributional and semantic theories of causation. All have flaws in the opinion of epistemologists; however, the attributional and semantic formulations provide some insight into the possibility that if the realities with which humans deal are constructed so, most likely, are their ideas of causation. If causality demonstrations are intended by rationalists to be compelling, naturalists feel the best they can do is to be persuasive. Causality can never be demonstrated in the "hard" sense; only patterns of plausible influence can be inferred.

1.5 Axiom 5: relation to values

Rationalists assume that enquiry is value free and can be guaranteed to be so by virtue of the "objective" methodology which the rationalist employs. The naturalist asserts that values impinge upon an enquiry in at least five ways, in terms of: the selection made by the investigator from among possible problems, theories, instruments, and data analysis modes; the assumptions underlying the substantive theory that guides the enquiry (for example, a theory of reading or an organizational theory); the assumptions underlying the methodological paradigm (as outlined in the preceding section on axioms); the values that characterize the respondents, the community, and the culture in which the enquiry is carried out (contextual values); and, finally, the possible interactions among any two or more of the preceding, which may be value consonant or value dissonant. Of particular interest is the possibility of resonance or dissonance between the substantive and methodological assumptions which can produce quite misleading results. Naturalists in particular take the position that many of the ambiguities and other irresolutions that tend to characterize social and behavioral research can be traced to such dissonances. So long as methodologies are assumed to be value free, naturalists assert, the problem of dissonance will not be recognized, since by definition it cannot exist. But once the role that values play in shaping enquiry is recognized, the problem becomes very real.

2   Postural differences between the naturalistic and rationalistic paradigms

Postures differ from axioms in that they are not logically necessary to the integrity of the paradigm nor are they important to assess in determining fit between a paradigm and the area proposed to be studied. Nevertheless they characterize the "style" of the two positions and are, for a variety of reasons, "congenial" or reinforcing to the practice of each. Some writers who have been anxious to compromise the two paradigms – what might be called an attempt at conceptual ecumenicism – have pointed out that these postures may be seen as complementary, and have urged that both rationalists and naturalists attempt a middle course. But despite good intentions, neither group seems to have been able to respond to this advice, which gives rise to the possibility that, unless one wishes to write off enquirers of both camps as obstinate or intransigent, there must be some more fundamental reason for the failure. That reason is simply that there exists a synergism among the postures as practiced by either camp that virtually precludes compromise. In fact, the arguments that might be made by naturalists, say, in defense of their choices depend in the case of every posture on the choices made among the other postures. And so with rationalists.

Consider first the postures themselves; six are of special importance:

2.1   Preferred methods

Rationalists tend to prefer quantitative methods probably because of their apparently greater precision and objectivity and because of the enormous advantage of being mathematically manipulable. Naturalists prefer qualitative methods, probably because they appear to promise the most wholistic products and they seem more appropriate to the use of a human as the prime data collection instrument. The distinction between quantitative and qualitative methods is often mistakenly taken to be the chief mark of distinction between the paradigms; in fact, the two dimensions are orthogonal. Either methodology is appropriate to either paradigm, even though in practice there is a high correlation between quantitative and rationalistic, on the one hand, and qualitative and naturalistic on the other.

2.2 Source of theory

Rationalists insist on *a priori* formulations of theory; indeed, they are likely to assert that enquiry without *a priori* theory to guide it is mindless. The naturalist believes that it is not theory but the enquiry problem itself that guides and bounds the enquiry; that *a priori* theory constrains the enquiry to those elements recognized by the investigator as important, and may introduce biases (believing is seeing). In all events, theory is more powerful when it arises from the data rather than being imposed on them. The naturalist does not, of course, insist on grounding theory afresh in each and every enquiry; what the naturalist does insist on is that the theory to be used shall have been grounded at some time in experience.

2.3 Knowledge types used

Rationalists constrain the type of knowledge admissible in an enquiry to propositional knowledge; that is, knowledge that can be stated in language form. In view of their commitment to *a priori* theory and their interest in shaping enquiry preordinately about particular questions and hypotheses, this is not surprising. The naturalist, often intent on the use of the human-as-instrument, also admits tacit knowledge – insights, intuitions, apprehensions that cannot be stated in language form but which are nevertheless "known" to the enquirer. Of course naturalists seek to recast their tacit knowledge into propositional form as quickly as possible. It is equally clear that rationalists depend upon tacit knowledge at least as much as do their naturalist counterparts; however, the reconstructed logic of rationalism militates against exposing this dependency publicly.

2.4 Instruments

The rationalist prefers nonhuman devices for data collection purposes, perhaps because they appear to be more cost efficient, have a patina of objectivity, and can be systematically aggregated. The naturalist prefers humans as instruments, for reasons such as their greater insightfulness, flexibility, and responsiveness, the fact that they are able to take a wholistic view, are able to utilize their tacit knowledge, and are able simultaneously to acquire and process information. Obviously both sets of advantages are meaningful.

2.5 Design

The rationalist insists on a preordinate design; indeed, it is sometimes asserted that a "good" design makes it possible for the enquirer to specify in dummy form the very tables he or she will produce. The naturalist, entering the field without *a priori* theory, hypotheses, or questions (mostly), is unable to specify a design (except in the broadest process sense) in advance. Instead, he or she anticipates that the design will emerge (unfold, roll, cascade) as the enquiry proceeds, with each step heavily dependent on all preceding steps. Clearly, the naturalist is well-advised to specify as much in advance as possible, while the rationalist should seek to keep as many options open as possible.

2.6 *Setting*

The rationalist prefers to conduct studies under laboratory conditions, probably because the laboratory represents the epitome of control. The naturalist prefers natural settings (it is this propensity that has lent its name to the paradigm), arguing that only in nature can it be discovered what does happen rather than what can happen. Moreover, studies in nature can be transferred to other, similar contexts, whereas laboratory studies can be generalized only to other laboratories. Clearly both kinds of studies have utility – it may be just as important to know what can happen as what does happen.

   While it might appear that compromise is indeed possible on these six postures, in fact the postures are bound together by a synergism such that each posture requires a counterpart position to be taken on all other postures. Consider rationalists, for example. Begin with a posture, say their preference for *a priori* theory. Rationalists do not exhibit this preference by accident, however. In part they prefer *a priori* theory because they deal in propositional language, and theory is the best means for formulating clarifying their propositional statements. The hypotheses or questions are propositional deductions from theory. Because of the precision of these hypotheses or questions, it is possible to imagine a design for testing them, and to devise appropriate instruments. Having such instruments makes it unnecessary to interpolate a "subjective" human between data and respondents. Moreover, these instruments can best be used in the highly controlled environment of the laboratory. And precise instruments yield data that can conveniently be expressed in quantitative form, a marked advantage since numbers can be easily manipulated statistically. Hence quantitative methods. And of course numbers can be aggregated and summarized, yielding apparent generalizations, expressions of causality, and so on. The sum exhibits a synergism such that each posture depends on every other one.

   Similar observations can be made about the naturalists' preference. Naturalists are forced into a natural setting because they cannot tell, having no *a priori* theory or hypotheses, what is important to control, or even to study. They could not set up a contrived experiment because they do not know what to contrive. If theory is to emerge from the data, the data must first be gathered. Since the nature of those data is unknown, an adaptive instrument is needed to locate and make sense of them – the "smart" human. Humans find certain data collection means more congenial than others; hence they tend toward the use of qualitative methods such as observation, interview, reading documents, and the like, which come "naturally" to the human. These methods result insights and information about the specific instance being studied but make it difficult to produce aggregations, generalizations, or cause–effect statements. Again, the naturalists' behavior demonstrates a kind of synergism among postures which is understandable and defensible only in terms of the totality of positions.

3   The trustworthiness of naturalistic enquiries

Because of its unusual axioms and the apparent "softness" of its postures, naturalistic enquiry is often attacked as untrustworthy, in contrast to rationalistic enquiry which has well-developed standards of trustworthiness.

Recently, serious efforts have been undertaken to develop standards which are parallels of those commonly used by rationalists, that is, counterparts to standards of internal and external validity, reliability, and objectivity. Analogous terms have been proposed, viz., (respectively) credibility, transferability, dependability, and confirmability.

Credibility is seen as a check on the isomorphism between the enquirer's data and interpretations and the multiple realities in the minds of informants. Transferability is the equivalent of generalizability to the extent that there are similarities between sending and receiving contexts. Dependability includes the instability factors typically indicated by the term "unreliability" but makes allowances for emergent designs, developing theory, and the like that also induce changes but which cannot be taken as "error". Confirmability shifts the emphasis from the certifiability of the enquirer to the confirmability of the data.

It is premature to expect that adherents of the naturalistic paradigm would have evolved as sophisticated a methodology for dealing with trustworthiness questions as have the rationalists, who have had centuries of experience to shape their standards. However, some suggestions have emerged for handling trustworthiness questions.

With respect to credibility it is proposed that the following techniques may be profitably used: (a) prolonged engagement at a site to overcome a variety of possible biases and misperceptions and to provide time to identify salient characteristics; (b) persistent observation, to understand salient characteristics as well as to appreciate atypical but meaningful features; (c) peer debriefing, to test growing insights and receive counsel about the evolving design, discharge personal feelings and anxieties, and leave an audit trail (see below); (d) triangulation, whereby a variety of data sources, different investigators, different perspectives (theories), and different methods are pitted against one another; (e) referential adequacy materials, whereby various documents, films, videotapes, audio recordings, pictures, and other "raw" or "slice-of-life" materials are collected during the study and archived for later use, for example, in member or auditor checks (see below); and (f) members checks, whereby data and interpretations are continuously checked with members of the various groups from which data were solicited, including an overall check at the end of the study.

With respect to transferability, it is proposed to use theoretical or purposive sampling to maximize the range of information which is collected and to provide the most stringent conditions for theory grounding; and thick description, furnishing enough information about a context to provide a vicarious experience of it, and to facilitate judgments about the extent to which working hypotheses from that context might be transferable to a second, similar context.

With respect to dependability, it is proposed to use overlap methods, one kind of triangulation which undergirds claims of dependability to the extent that the methods produce complementary results; stepwise replication, a kind of "split-halves" approach in which enquirers and data sources are divided into halves to pursue the enquirer independently, provided, however, that there is sufficient communication between the two teams to allow for the articulated development of the emergent design, and the dependability audit, a process modelled on the fiscal audit. A fiscal auditor has two responsibilities: first, to ascertain that the accounts were kept in one of the several modes that constitute "good practice," and second, to ascertain that every entry can be supported with appropriate documentation and that the totals are properly determined. The dependability audit services the first of these functions.

With respect to confirmability it is proposed to use triangulation (as above); to keep a reflexive journal that can be used to expose epistemological assumptions and to show why the study was defined and carried out in particular ways; and the confirmability audit, which carries out the second of the two auditor functions mentioned above.

It is generally understood that the use of even all of these techniques cannot guarantee the trustworthiness of a naturalistic study but can only contribute greatly to persuading a consumer of its meaningfulness.

4 Summary

Naturalistic enquiry is one of two paradigms currently being used by investigators within the framework of disciplined research. While this paradigm has distinguished antecedents in anthropology and ethnography, it is nevertheless relatively emergent and not as much is known about its properties as might be desired.

Naturalistic enquiry differs from rationalistic enquiry in terms of interpretations based on five basic axioms; reality, enquirer–object relationship, generalizability, causality, and value freedom. In addition, a number of salient postures also play important roles; methods, sources of theory, knowledge types used, instruments, design, and setting.

As a relatively new paradigm, naturalism suffers in not having yet devised as solid an approach to trustworthiness as has its rationalistic counterpart. Nevertheless important strides are being made. It seems likely that, given several decades in which to develop, the naturalistic paradigm will prove to be as useful as the rationalistic paradigm has been historically. The major decision to be made between the two paradigms revolve about the assessment of fit to the area under study, rather than to any intrinsic advantages or disadvantages of either.

See also: Ethnographic Research Methods; Hermeneutics; Narrative Inquiry.

Reference

Cronbach, L. J. 1975 Beyond the two disciplines of scientific psychology. *Am. Psychol.* 30: 116–27.

Further reading

Cook, T. D. and Campbell, D. T. 1979 *Quasi-experimentation: Design and Analysis Issues for Field Settings.* Rand McNally, Chicago, Illinois.

Cook, T. D. and Reichardt, C. S. 1979 *Qualitative and Quantitative Methods in Evaluation Research.* Sage, Beverly Hills, California.

Cronbach, L. J. and Suppes, P. (eds.) 1969 *Research for Tomorrow's Schools: Disciplined Inquiry for Education.* MacMillan, New York.

Filstead, W. J. (ed.) 1970 *Qualitative Methodology: Firsthand Involvement with the Social World.* Rand McNally, Chicago, Illinois.

Glaser, B. G. and Strauss, A. L. 1967 *The Discovery of Grounded Theory: Strategies for Qualitative Research.* Aldine, Chicago, Illinois.

Guba, E. G. 1978 *Toward a Methodology of Naturalistic Inquiry in Educational Evaluation.* Center for the Study of Evaluation, University of California, Los Angeles, California.

Guba, E. G. 1981 Criteria for assessing the trustworthiness of naturalistic inquiries. *Educ. Comm. Tech. J.* 29(2): 75–92.

Guba, E. G. and Lincoln, Y. S. 1982 *Effective Evaluation.* Jossey-Bass, San Francisco, California.

Kaplan, A. 1964 *The Conduct of Inquiry: Methodology for Behavioral Science.* Chandler, San Francisco, California.

Polani, M. 1966 *The Tacit Dimension.* Doubleday, Garden City, New York.

Scriven, M. 1971 Objectivity and subjectivity in educational research. In: Thomas, L. G. (ed.) 1971 *Philosophical Redirection of Educational Research.* University of Chicago Press, Chicago, Illinois.

14   Action Research

S. Kemmis

The lively debates about educational research methodology in the 1970s and 1980s raised fundamental questions about the connections between educational theory and educational practice, between the conduct of research and the improvement of educational practice, and between researchers and teachers and learners. Around the world, a number of theorists of educational research have fostered the development of action research as an approach that provides ways of making these connections. Action research aims to help practitioners investigate the connections between their own theories of education and their own day-to-day educational practices; it aims to integrate the research act into the educational setting so that research can play a direct and immediate role in the improvement of practice; and it aims to overcome the distance between researchers and practitioners by assisting practitioners to become researchers.

This article outlines a view of action research as a form of participatory and collaborative research aimed at improving educational understandings, practices, and settings, and at involving those affected in the research process. It describes a variety of international perspectives on educational action research, linking it to participatory action research for community development and ideas about critical social and educational science. Some of the contemporary contests about how action research is to be understood are described in terms of a debate between two main schools of thought about action research, one (more collaborative) based on the idea of a critical educational science and the other (more individualistic) based on ideas about practical reasoning and "the reflective practitioner".

1   Definition of action research

Kemmis and McTaggert (1988) defined action research as a form of *collective* self-reflective enquiry undertaken by participants in social situations in order to improve the productivity, rationality, and justice of their own social or educational practices, as well as their understanding of these practices and the situations in which the practices are carried out. Groups of participants can be teachers, students, principals, parents and other community members – any group with a shared concern. Kemmis and McTaggart stress that action research is *collaborative*, though it is important to realize that the action research of a group depends upon individual members critically examining their own actions. In education, action research has been employed in school-based curriculum development, professional development, school improvement programs, and systems planning and policy development (e.g., in relation to policy about classroom rules, school policies about noncompetitive assessment, regional project team policies about their consultancy roles, and state policies about the conduct of school improvement programs).

Based on the work of Kurt Lewin, frequently described as "the father of action research", Kemmis and McTaggart (1988) presented an introductory sketch of the process of action research, outlining a spiral of cycles of reconnaissance, planning action, enacting and observing the planned action, reflecting on the implementation of the plan in the light of evidence collected during implementation, then replanning (developing a changed or modified action plan), taking further action and making further observations, reflecting on the evidence from this new cycle, and so on. These steps are (of course) far too mechanical and procedural to be more than a starting point: they are best thought of as tips for beginners.

Kemmis and McTaggart also set out some possible questions to be asked by intending action researchers as they plan and conduct their enquiries, linking each stage of the process (reconnaissance, planning, enacting and observing, reflecting) to three interdependent domains of social and educational life: (a) language and discourse, (b) activities and practices, and (c) social relationships and forms of organization. The first of each of these pairs of terms relates to events and states of affairs in the lifeworld of a setting; the second to its more formal, institutional, systemic aspects (on the distinction and relationships between lifeworld and system, see Habermas, 1984, 1987). To address the complexity of the relationships within and between these pairs of terms requires reflective and critical judgment – a kind of judgment incompatible with a mechanical view of the action research process.

In action research, teachers (and others) are encouraged to treat their own educational ideas and theories, their own work practices, and their own work settings, as objects for analysis and critique. On the basis of careful reflection, it is argued, teachers may uncover theoretical ideas or assumptions that turn out to be unjustified and liable to lead them astray in their teaching (e.g., if they hold too rigid assumptions about the nature of students' innate abilities). Similarly, concerning their practices, teachers may find ways in which practices shaped by habit or tradition have become irrelevant or useless (e.g., finding that practices of classroom discipline, formerly seen as appropriate, may now be unacceptable or even counterproductive). Similarly, concerning the educational settings in which they practice, teachers may discover how the structure of the settings may place obstacles in the way of attaining educational goals (e.g., that the physical structure of the conventional classroom may hinder mixed ability grouping or the use of new technologies, or the management structure of a school may mitigate against new forms of curriculum organization).

The activities in this spiral of cycles aim at the *improvement* of practices, understandings, and situations, and at the *involvement* of as many as possible of those intimately affected by the action in all phases of the research process. Especially when they collaborate with other teachers in action research focused on their ideas, practices, and settings, teachers regularly find new ways of thinking, practicing, and structuring educational settings that will allow them to overcome obstacles and difficulties. In this way, action research contributes directly to the improvement of practice.

The involvement of teachers and others in the action research process – in data-gathering, analysis, and critique – creates an immediate sense of responsibility for the improvement of practice. Participation in action research is thus a form of professional development, linking the improvement of practitioners with the improvement of practices. It enhances the professional role of the teacher, even where beginning teacher–researchers are assisted by outside consultants or facilitators.

Many of the improvements that have flowed from teacher action research, in Australia and elsewhere, have escaped notice in the conventional educational research literature. Teachers have not generally been comfortable in contributing to educational research journals, nor are they frequent readers of such journals. Nevertheless, there is a growing body of action research work authored by teachers. It remains fugitive largely because its justification is the improvement of practitioners' own practices, and writing for others is seen as secondary to this purpose. Moreover, the action research "movement" has contributed to a subtle change in the educational research literature; as a consequence there are many more references to the research work and research problems of teachers in the "official" research literature, and there is a growing number of citations of work on the theory and practice of educational action research. A number of the journals of learned societies for educational research in Australia, Spain, the United Kingdom, and the United States of America, for example, have become more "teacher friendly," making particular efforts to carry reports of teachers' action research projects. Moreover, some specialist action research journals have sprung up (e.g., *Educational Action Research*), and some more conventional research journals have offered special issues on action research (e.g., the *Peabody Journal of Education*, which offered two special issues on action research in 1989). Nowadays, educational researchers outside schools also seem less likely to regard the teacher as "other" or "object" in their reporting of educational research, and are more likely to regard teachers as readers of and contributors to the improvement of education through research. This may be only a subtle effect, but it is an important one in the realignment of the relationship between educational research and educational practice.

2   Key points about action research

Kemmis and McTaggart (1988) outlined a number of key features of action research:

(a) Action research is an approach to improving education by changing it and learning from the consequences of changes.

(b) Action research develops through a self-reflective spiral of cycles of planning, acting (implementing plans), observing (systematically), reflecting, and then replanning, further implementation, observing, and reflecting. It is a systematic learning process in which people act deliberately, though remaining open to surprises and responsive to opportunities.

(c) Action research is participatory: it is research through which people work toward the improvement of their own practices.

(d) Action research is collaborative: it involves those responsible for action in improving it, widening the collaborating group from those most directly involved to as many as possible of those affected by the practices concerned. It establishes self-critical communities of people participating and collaborating in all phases of the research process.

(e) Action research involves people in theorizing about their practices – being inquisitive about circumstances, action, and consequences, and coming to understand the relationships between circumstance, action and consequence in their work and lives.

(f) Action research requires that people put their practices, ideas, and assumptions about institutions to the test by finding out whether there is compelling evidence that could convince them that their previous practices, ideas, and assumptions were false or incoherent (or both).

(g) Action research is open-minded about what counts as evidence (or data), but it always involves keeping records, and collecting and analyzing evidence about the contexts, commitments, conduct and consequences of the actions and interactions being investigated. It involves keeping a personal journal recording progress in, and reflections about, two parallel sets of learnings: learnings about the practices being studied, and learnings about the process of studying them (the action research process itself).

(h) Action research allows participants to build records of their improvements: (a) records of changes in activities and practices; (b) records of changes in the language and discourse in which practices are described, explained, and justified; (c) records of changes in the social relationships and forms of organization which characterize and constrain practices; and (d) records of change and development in the action research process itself. It thus allows participants to provide reasoned justifications of their educational work because it allows them to show how evidence and reflection have provided a basis for a developed, tested, and critically examined rationale for what is being done.

(i) Action research starts small. It normally begins with small changes which even a single person can try, and works toward more extensive changes; with small cycles of planning, acting, observing, and reflecting which can help to define issues, ideas, and assumptions more clearly so that those involved can define more powerful questions for themselves as their work progresses; and it begins with small groups of collaborators at the beginning, but widens the community of participatory action researchers so that it gradually includes more and more of those involved in and affected by the practices in question.

(j) Action research involves people (in making critical analyses of the situations (classrooms, schools, systems) in which they work – situations that are structured socially, historically, and institutionally. Critical analysis aim to recover how a situation has been socially and historically constructed, as a source of insight into ways in which people might be able to reconstruct it.

(k) Action research is a political process, because it involves making changes in the actions and interactions that constitute and structure social life (social practices); such changes typically have effects on the expectations and interests of others beyond the immediate participants in these actions and interactions.

3   International perspectives on action research

One view of educational action research is associated with the work of a group at Deakin University in Australia. The views of this group derive from the ideas of social psychologist Lewin (1846), the thinking of Stenhouse and his colleagues at the University of East Anglia in the United Kingdom (e.g., Stenhouse, 1975; Elliott, 1978), and the ideas of the Frankfurt School in critical social science (see Carr and Kemmis, 1986). This view of action research emphasizes the importance of collaboration, believing that some action research work of the past has been rather too individualistic, too little aware of the social construction of social reality, and too poorly attuned to the social processes and politics of change. It also understands action research to be a cultural process, in similar terms to Freire's (1970) notion of "cultural action for freedom". On this view, action researchers are understood as groups of people who participate systematically and deliberately in the processes of contestation and institutionalization which are always at work in social and educational life, aiming to help in the improvement of social or educational life by the reflective and self-reflective ways they participate in it.

This Australian view of action research is far from being the only extant view of action research, however. There are many other groups around the world with different views about the development of the theory and practice of action research; indeed, it has become something of a worldwide movement.

A great deal of action research work goes on in the United Kingdom, for example – much of it inspired by Stenhouse's (1975) notion of the teacher as researcher. The Ford Teaching Project of Elliott and Adelman (1973) broke new ground in action research in education in the 1970s, and their work has spawned a great diversity of action research work in schools and colleges around the United Kingdom – some of which can be accessed through publications and conferences of the Classroom Action Research Network based initially at the Cambridge Institute of Education and now at the University of East Anglia. British action research work ranges from the enquires of individual teachers into their own practice to shared work by groups of teachers (e.g., Hustler *et al.*,

1986, McKernan, 1991); from work focused on the analysis of contradictions in practitioners' own theories and practices (Whitehead 1989) to work more critically relating these to wider social, cultural, and political trends (Elliott, 1991); and from work informed by practical and interpretative views of social science and its possibilities for professional development (Nixon, 1981) to work more closely allied with reflexive sociology and critical theory (Winter, 1987, 1989). Despite Stenhouse's (1975) disquiet about "movements" and the possibility of a curriculum development movement based on the notion of teachers as researchers, there can be no doubt that there is an action research movement in the United Kingdom, nor can there be any doubt that it has provided an important source of professional inspiration for teachers and school administrators throughout the country.

There has also been a resurgence of interest in action research in the United States and Canada. Early United States views of action research in education were inspired by the work of Corey (1949); later it was influenced by Schwab's (1969) ideas about practical reasoning, by Schön's (1983) ideas about "the reflective practitioner", by concerns to recognize and develop teachers' craft knowledge, by the desire of university educational researchers to employ field methods that engage teachers in research for their own professional development (Oja and Smulyan, 1989), and by teacher educators committed to exploring action research in pre-service and in-service teacher education (Zeichner and Liston, 1987). In general, educational action research in the United States has been less responsive to the arguments of critical social and educational theory, but the themes of critical theory have been taken up by a number of American advocates of action research (Noffke and Brennan, 1988; Noffke, 1991). In addition to this critical work in education, there is a strong tradition of critical action research for community development in the United States, exemplified by the work of Horton, Gavena, and their colleagues at the Highlander Center in Tennessee (Gaventa, 1991; Horton and Freire, 1990).

In Canada, one strong current of educational action research is based in the phenomenological tradition (Van Manen, 1990), and there is also a strong movement in participatory action research in adult education and community development which shares the critical communitarian commitment of the participatory action research of Gaventa in the United States and of Freire and others in Central and South America.

By the beginning of the 1990s there were many European advocates of educational action research, for example in Germany (Klafki, 1988a, 1988b; Finger, 1988), Austria (Altrichter and Posch, 1990), and Asturias, Spain (Rozada et al., 1989, Cascante, 1991). Some of these theorists have been influenced by the ideas of Habermas (1972, 1974) about "sciences of social action" (now known as critical social science), though others have clearly been influenced by the British action research movement, and others by phenomenological approaches.

In Central and South America there has been a tradition of participatory action research work which has been strongly influenced by Freirean ideas, in Mexico, Colombia, Venezuela, Nicaragua, Brazil, and elsewhere. The social and political commitments of the participatory action research movement in these countries (see Fals Borda, 1990, Fals Borda and Rahman, 1991, Serra, 1988) have extended from community development to popular education and action research in education. The extent to which the forms and content of these community development efforts through action research are realizable in the reconstruction of institutionalized schooling in the developed industrial nations of the West is, of course, a matter for continuing exploration, but the communitarian ethic they embody provides a powerful model of ordinary people reconstructing the circumstances of their own lives.

The Central and South American tradition of participatory action research in community development has spread, through the work of Freire, to other parts of the world; for example, to Africa, India, Nepal, the Philippines, Sri Lanka, and Thailand. There is now a substantial tradition of action research in community development in India (Tandon 1988, Handay and Tandon, 1988), and in Southeast Asia (e.g., in Singapore, Malaysia, and Thailand). Some of this work is associated with nongovernment organizations, while other work is associated with official educational projects. In the Southeast Asian context, for example, there has been an exploration of action research for community development through adult education and the Freireian participatory action research movement, on the one hand, and a somewhat separate development of action research in institutional contexts of school improvement and evaluation on the other (a good example of the latter being a project in the initial and postinitial education of nurses; see Chuaprapaisilp, 1989). The latter trend seems more closely aligned with the kinds of interests in the educational profession that inspired the British action research movement in its early days.

As this brief review suggests, there is a wide diversity of motivations, forms, and contents of action research around the world. It would be mistaken, therefore, to regard educational action research as expressing a single school of thought or as embodying a coherent and unified point of view on social or educational research.

4   Contest over the term "action research"

Like any significant theoretical term, the ideas of "action research" is contested. Its meaning and significance cannot be fixed by any one person or group. It is the subject of continuing argument and debate within and outside the relevant traditions and professions.

There is an internal debate between two main contemporary "schools" of action research internationally, one adopting a critical social science view of action research, while the other draws more on the Schwabian tradition of practical reasoning and, more recently, on Schön's (1983) notion of "the reflective practitioner". The debate between these two schools of thought may have reached the point where they now relate to one another as "external" critics of each other's positions, rather than as "internal" critics who share broad agreements about the nature and conduct of action research, though they also keep these agreements under critical review. When there is uncertainty about whether participants in the field share a common system of beliefs, values, and commitments, it is uncertain whether they are members of and participants in a single tradition. As disagreements about fundamental issues in a field accumulate, it is pushed toward a division into two or more new and opposed traditions. Perhaps it is already true that debates previously regarded as "internal" debates within the field of action research – clarifying and continuously revitalizing a more or less coherent tradition – are now "external" debates between advocates of opposed traditions.

Since the early 1980s, the critical social science view of action research has been subjected to sharp criticism (e.g., Gibson, 1985; Elliott, 1991). This reaction was partly caused, no doubt, by the drawing of distinctions between "technical", "practical", and "emancipatory" (or critical) action research (Carr and Kemmis, 1986), and the insistence of advocates of "emancipatory" view that action research undertaken primarily by individual teacher–researchers was less significant than action research undertaken by collaborating groups in "self-critical communities." Reaction was further fanned by advocacies (like those of McTaggart and Garbutcheon-Singh, 1988, Kemmis and Di Chiro, 1989) of connections between action research groups and the critical efforts of activists in broader social movements. While at first such advocacies were treated as "utopian" and "idealistic", and as attempting to "capture" action research to a particular view of critical educational science and a particular understanding of the relationship between theory and practice (see, e.g., Gibson, 1985; Lewis, 1987), they have since been regarded by some as "dangerous" (Elliott, 1991). Arguably, some of these criticisms are based on a misunderstanding of critical social science and the possibility of a critical educational science.

A key element of the difference between the two main contemporary schools in educational action research lies in how the aspirations of action research are to be interpreted: whether (on the one hand) they are to be interpreted as a means of improving professional practice primarily at the local, classroom level, within the capacities of individuals and the constraints of educational institutions and organizations, or (on the other) whether they are to be interpreted as an approach to changing education and schooling in a broader sense. Like other choices of principle, this is a choice between different views of human nature and different views of the good for humankind. Like other such debates, it will be resolved not by argument alone, but by the judgment of history.

5   Shortcomings of some contemporary advocacies for action research

The critical social science view of action research emphasizes the connections between particular elements of action research in theory and practice, not the separations between them, regarding these elements as dialectically related, not as dichotomies. In particular, the critical view has sought to emphasize the connections between:

(a) the individual and the social (the social construction of social realities and practices) in the practice of action research and in the practice of education (see, e.g., Kemmis and McTaggart, 1988);
(b) the cognitive (practitioners' ideas) and the theoretical (formal discourses, whether employed by researchers or by others involved in education; see, e.g., Kemmis, 1990);
(c) theory and method in action research practice (the role of action research as a systematic social practice that provides a way of formulating and attacking educational research problems in an educational and social context; see, e.g., McTaggart and Garbutcheon-Singh, 1988).

When these terms are regarded as dichotomies, not as dialectically related, advocates and practitioners of action research may be led into fallacies of dualistic, black and white reasoning. Some of these fallacies arise when advocates and practitioners of action research believe, or appear to believe:

(a) that action research can involve the work of individuals without being, simultaneously, intrinsically social (rooted in the fundamental connections between individuals embodied in and shaped by the social media of language, work, and power, through social practices of communication, production, and organization);
(b) that action research can deal with practitioners' ideas without simultaneously recognizing that these ideas are theoretical (or at least pretheoretical and proto-theoretical), in the sense that they draw on public discourses which give meaning and significance to their work as educators or as researchers;
(c) that action research is a relatively "neutral" research technology which can be separated from particular intellectual traditions, involving particular notions and theories about society, education, and social and educational change (especially participatory views about social practices, education, democracy, and change).

When views of action research become structured by dichotomized thinking about these relationships, their advocates may fall into the trap of focusing too much on the individual action researcher and her or his development (e.g., as an individual professional) without also taking a critical view of the social context in which the individual works. They may focus too much on individuals' ideas and thinking without giving sufficient critical attention to the ordinary language and formal discourses that give form and content to individual thinking. Moreover, they may focus too much on action research as a method or procedure without giving critical attention to the social framework in which the procedure operates, and to the way the procedures of action research actively connect with and coordinate processes of change in history – which is to say, politically. Some contemporary action research literature seems to have fallen into these traps.

6 Conclusion

Understanding of action research has been, and will continue to be, reconstructed anew for changing times and circumstances. The idea of action research may be no more perfectible than the idea of the perfectibility of humankind, but over 50 years it has offered and demonstrated possibilities for linking social research and social action, and it has made worthwhile contributions to the improvement of education, science, and society. As Sanford (1970) argued, action research is a social practice that still contains possibilities that may prove useful in addressing the social, cultural, and educational problems of contemporary times.

The notion of action research is just that: it is a notion, not a thing. As a notion, it does no more than give form to a particular kind of democratic aspiration to engage in changing the world as well as interpreting it. It offers an embryonic, local form of connecting research with social, educational, and political action in complex practical circumstances. In this, it is similar to the aspiration sloganized by the environmental movement in the words "think globally, act locally", and, as such, it may be a social form that can help educators address the contradictions, constraints, and limitations of their theories and practices, of their words and our world.

See also: Research in Education: Epistemological Issues; Research Paradigms in Education; Scientific Methods in Educational Research

References

Altrichter, H. and Posch, P. 1990 *Lehrer Erforschen Ihren Unterricht. Eine Einführung in die Methoden der Aktionforschung.* Klinkhardt, Bad Heilbrunn.
Carr, W. and Kemmis, S. 1986 *Becoming Critical: Education Knowledge and Action Research.* Falmer, London.
Cascante Fernandez C. 1991 Los ámbitos de la practica educativa: Una experiencia de investigación en la acción. *Revista Interuniversitaria de Formación del Profesorado* 10: 265–74.
Chuaprapaisilp, A. 1989 Critical reflection in clinical experience: Action research in nurse education (Doctoral dissertation, University of New South Wales).
Corey, S. 1949 Action research, fundamental research and educational practices. *Teach. Coll. Rec.* 50: 509–14.
Elliott, J 1978 What is action-research in schools? *J. Curric. St.* 10(4): 355–57.
Elliott, J. 1991 *Action Research for Educational Change.* Open University Press, Milton Keynes.
Elliott, J. and Adelman, C. 1973 Reflecting where the action is: The design of the Ford Teaching Project. *Education for Teaching* 92: 8–20.
Fals Borda, O. 1990 Social movements and political power: Evolution in Latin America. *International Sociology* 5(2): 115–28.
Fals Borda, O. and Rahman, M. A. 1991 *Action and Knowledge: Breaking the Monopoly with Participatory Action-Research.* Apex, New York.
Finger, M. 1988 Heinz Moser's concept of action research. In: Kemmis S. and McTaggart R. (eds.) 1988
Freire, P. 1970 *Cultural Action for Freedom.* Center for the Study of Change, Cambridge, Massachusetts.
Gaventa, J. 1991 Toward a knowledge democracy: Viewpoints on participatory research in North America. In: Fals Borda, O. and Rahman, M. A. (eds.) 1991
Gibson, R. 1985 Critical times for action research. *Camb. J. Educ.* 15(1): 59–64.
Habermas, J. 1972 *Knowledge and Human Interests.* Heinemann, London.
Habermas, J. 1974 *Theory and Practice.* Heinemann, London.

Habermas, J. 1984 *The Theory of Communicative Action. Vol. 1: Reason and the Rationalization of Society.* Beacon, Boston, Massachusetts.

Habermas, J. 1987 *The Theory of Communicative Action. Vol. 2: Lifeworld and System: A Critique of Functionalist Reason.* Beacon, Boston, Massachusetts.

Handay, G. and Tandon, R. 1988 *Revolution through Reform with People's Wisdom.* (videotape) Society for Participatory Research in Asia, Khanpur, New Delhi.

Horton, M. and Freire, P. 1990 *We Make the Road by Walking: Conversations on Education and Social Change.* Temple University Press, Philadelphia, Pennsylvania.

Hustler, D. Cassidy, A. and Cuff, E. (eds.) 1986 *Action Research in Classrooms and Schools.* Allen and Unwin, London.,

Kemmis, S. 1990 Some Ambiguities of Stenhouse's Notion of "the Teacher as Researcher": Towards a New Resolution. 1989 Lawrence Stenhouse Memorial Lecture to the British Educational Research Association, School of Education, University of East Anglia, Norwich.

Kemmis, S. and Di Chiro, G. 1989 Emerging and evolving issues of action research praxis: An Australian perspective. *Peabody Journal of Education* 64 (3): 101–30.

Kemmis, S. and McTaggart, R. (eds.) 1988 *The Action Research Reader,* 3rd edn. Deakin University Press, Geelong.

Klafki, W. 1988a Decentralised curriculum development in the form of action research. In: Kemmis S. and McTaggart R. (eds.) 1988.

Klafki, W. 1988b Pedagogy; Theory of a practice. In: Kemmis S. and McTaggart R. (eds.) 1988.

Lewin, K. 1946 Action research and minority problems. *J. Soc. Issues* 2(4): 34–46.

Lewis, I. 1987 Encouraging reflective teacher research: A review article. *Br. J. Sociol. Educ.* 8(1): 95–105.

McKernan, J. 1991 *Curriculum Action Research: A Handbook of Methods and Resources for the Reflective Practitioner.* Kogan Page, London.

McTaggart, R. and Garbutcheon-Singh, M. 1988 A fourth generation of action research: Notes on the Deakin seminar. In: Kemmis, S. and McTaggart, R. (eds.) 1988.

Nixon, J. (ed.) 1981 *A Teacher's Guide to Action Research.* Grant McIntyre, London.

Noffke, S. E. 1991 Hearing the teacher's voice: Now what? *Curriculum Perspectives.*

Noffke, S. E. and Brennan, M. 1988 Action research and reflective student teaching at U W Madison: Issues and examples. Paper presented at the Annual Meeting of the Association of Teacher Educators, San Diego, California.

Oja, S. N. and Smulyan, L. 1989 *Collaborative Action Research: A Developmental Approach.* Falmer, London.

Rozada Martnez, J. Cascante Fernández, C. and Arrieta Gallastegui, J. 1989 *Desarrollo Curricular y Formación del Profesorado.* Cyan Gestión Editorial, Gijón.

Sanford, N. 1970 Whatever happened to action research? *J. Soc. Issues* 26(4): 3–23.

Schön, D. A. 1983 *The Reflective Practitioner: How Professionals Think in Action.* Temple Smith, London.

Schwab, J. J. 1969 The practical: A language for curriculum. *Sch. Rev.* 78: 1–24.

Serra, L. 1988 Participatory research and popular education. Paper presented to the North American Adult Education Association Research Conference, University of Calgary.

Stenhouse, L. A. 1975 *An Introduction to Curriculum Research and Development.* Heinemann, London.

Tandon, R. 1988 Social transformation and participatory research. *Convergence* 21(2,3): 5–18.

Van Manen, M. 1990 *Researching Livid Experience: Human Science for an Action-Sensitive Pedagogy.* State University of New York Press, Albany, New York.

Whitehead, J. 1989 Creating a living educational theory from questions of the kind, "How do I improve my practice?" *Camb. J. Educ.* 19(1): 41–52.

Winter, R. 1987 *Action-Research and the Nature of Social Inquiry.* Gower, Aldershot.

Winter, R. 1989 *Learning from Experience: Principles and Practice in Action-Research.* Falmer, London.

Zeichner, K. and Liston, D. P. 1987 Teaching student teachers to reflect. *Harv. Educ. Rev.* 57(1): 23–48.

15　Critical Discourse Analysis

A. Luke

Critical discourse analysis is a contemporary approach to the study of language and discourses in social institutions. Drawing on poststructuralist discourse theory and critical linguistics, it focuses on how social relations, identity, knowledge, and power are constructed through written and spoken texts in communities, schools, and classrooms. This article describes the historical contexts and theoretical precedents for sociological models for the study of language, discourse, and text in education. It then outlines key terms, assumptions, and practices of critical discourse analysis. It concludes by describing unresolved issues and challenges for discourse analysis and educational research.

1　Language and discourse in contemporary education

In a context of unprecedented educational expansion and population growth, postwar sociology of education focused urgently on issues around institutional structure, the production of skilled workers, and increased educational access and participation. By the 1960s, attempts to explain and redress educational inequality for minority and lower socioeconomic groups generated major debates in sociolinguistics with the ethnography of communication. Much of that work focused on language development and literacy acquisition as key factors in differential student achievement and the intergenerational reproduction of educational inequality. Debates over the role of social class-specific "speech codes", "linguistic deficits", the educational consequences of multilingualism, and the institutional status of nonstandard English are still not fully resolved.

Some 30 years later, educators face the challenges of "new times" (Hall, 1996); new cultural practices and media texts, hybrid cultural identities, emergent social formations and institutions, and changing structures of work and economy. In postindustrial and newly industrializing nation-states, the rapidity and depth of many of these changes have drawn anew many sociologists' attention to language, texts, and discourses. There is an increasing recognition that these now form the central media of community life, education, and work.

Large-scale immigration and the emergence of multicultural, multilingual nation states have marked the postwar era. In urban and suburban areas, schools and educators are facing new student bodies and rapidly changing community demographic profiles. These conditions have called into question the relevance and efficacy of longstanding administrative, curriculum, instruction, and evaluation practices, many of which were developed in early and mid-century secular school systems designed for monocultural, homogeneous nation-states. The recognition and enfranchisement of linguistic and cultural minority students has generated a host of practical issues around new dynamics of ethnic, cultural, and gender difference in communities, families, and institutional life, differential power in pedagogic relations in classrooms, and the knowledge and epistemological claims of historically disenfranchised groups over what should count as curriculum knowledge (see Apple, 1996).

At the same time, the commodification of Western popular culture and the multinational globalization of economies have changed the patterns and practices of work and leisure in many communities. In an emergent "post-Fordist" economic and sociological context, new industrial conditions and information technologies have begun to alter the requisites and parameters of what might count as educationally produced skilled labor. In service, information, and media sectors of the economy, the exchange of symbols, discourses, and texts have become key modes of value and exchange. Current definitions of educationally produced skills, competences, and knowledge appear to be in transition, with the emergent requisites of new technologies and recognized labor practices and markets making new demands on academic and vocational education. In response, research and theory in many areas of the social sciences and applied human services have shifted from a focus on traditional labor markets to an analysis of the economic and cultural consequences of new modes of information.

These conditions raise questions about the relevance and value of the structures and practices of early and mid-twentieth century schooling. These include questions about apparent disjunctions between community and school cultures; the appropriateness of curricular, instructional models for new student populations; and the practical requirements and challenges of new workplaces and civic spheres where these students live and work. However, many prevailing social and cultural theories of education and their affiliated practices are based on historical critiques of industrial-era schooling and work, and sociological analyses of the late nineteenth and early twentieth century monocultural monolingual nation-state. The move towards discourse analytic approaches to education thus begins from the assumption that many of these challenges can only be addressed by a focus on how language, discourse, and text figure in educational processes, practices, and outcomes (New London Group 1996).

2   Poststructuralist and postmodern discourse theory

The development of the "new" sociology of education in the early 1970s was a key moment in the application of Western social philosophy and sociology to educational theory and problems. Phenomenological, symbolic interactionist, and neo-Marxian approaches to the study of identity, knowledge, and institutional change in turn led to the development and application of various interpretative methods in educational research. These include action research, literary analysis, revisionist historiography, and critical ethnography. Yet these various approaches are often conflated, erroneously, with later poststructuralist and postmodern social theory under the general category of "critical theory".

The application of French discourse theory to educational research followed from the translation and dissemination of the work of Michel Foucault and Jacques Derrida in England and America during the 1970s and 1980s. What distinguishes French and Anglo-American poststructuralist theory is a recognition of the centrality of language and discourse. According to Foucault and Derrida, language and discourse are not transparent or neutral means for describing or analyzing the social and biological world. Rather they effectively construct, regulate, and control knowledge, social relations, and institutions, and indeed, such analytic and exegetic practices as scholarship and research. By this account, nothing is outside of or prior to its manifestation in discourse.

Foucault asks whether the natural and social worlds are indeed knowable, accessible, and analyzable without recourse to the constitutive forces of discourse. He does not limit his notion of discourse to language, but refers more generally to reiterated key words and statements that recur in local texts of all kinds. Such statements appear intertextually across texts and comprise familiar patterns of disciplinary and paradigmatic knowledge and practice. For instance, one might speak of discourses of "physics" or "politics", but also might specify more fine-grained categories of discourse, like "quantum mechanics" or "socialist politics", depending on the texts in question and the purposes of the analysis. Discourses have both disciplinary and, to use Foucault's term "disciplining" effects. They enable and delimit fields of knowledge and inquiry, and they govern what can be said, thought, and done within those fields.

Poststructuralist discourse theory examines how writing, texts, and discourses are constructive phenomena, shaping the identities and practices of human subjects. In his historical studies of asylums, governments, prisons, and schools, Foucault focused on how historical configurations of discourse constructed new kinds of human subjects. He argued that institutionalized discourses consist of categorical "grids of specification" that classify and regulate people's identities, bodies, domestic and civil spaces, and social practices in different relations of knowledge and power. These discourses, he goes on to argue, work in the local situations of social institutions in ways that cannot be explained by reference to any individual's or group's roles, intents, or motivations. Indeed, poststructuralist theory questions whether there are essential human subjects, individual agents, and social realities independent of their dynamic historical construction in social and cultural discourses.

By this account, social institutions such as schools and universities are comprised by and through discourses. Discourses make up a dense fabric of spoken, written, and symbolic texts of institutional bureaucracies (e.g., policies, curriculum documents, forms) and their ubiquitous face-to-face encounters (e.g., classroom interaction, informal talk). Within these institutions, human subjects are defined and constructed both in generic categories (e.g., as "children" and "teachers") and in more specialized and purposive historical categories (e.g., as "professionals", "adolescents", "linguistic deficit", "pre-operational"). These discourse constructions act both as institutional "technologies of power", implemented and enforced by official authorization, and they act as "technologies of the self" (Foucault, 1980), internalized means for the self-discipline of action, practice, and identity. According to Foucault, these technologies potentially have both productive and negative material, bodily and spatial consequences for human subjects and communities.

While Foucault's work shifts the attention to the regulatory nature of discourses, Derrida questioned whether any cultural texts can have intrinsic authority or canonical status as accounts of "truths" about the phenomenal world. That is, Derrida's approach to philosophic and literary "deconstruction" queries whether definitive or authoritative interpretations are possible in the first place. All texts comprise a dynamic play of "*differance*" which necessarily renders them polysemous: multiple and potentially quite idiosyncratic meanings can be generated by readers in particular social contexts. Each text's distinctive features and differences thus are reconstructed and reconstituted into distinctive "readings" in "local institutional sites" (Baker and Luke, 1991).

Poststructuralist work thus forms a critique of ontology and epistemology in empirical approaches to social science. It makes the case that: (a) all inquiry is by definition a form of discourse analysis; and (b) all research consists of a "reading" and "rewriting" of a series of texts from a particular historical and epistemological standpoint. In so doing, it provides a radically different perspective on students and teachers, policy and curriculum, schools and classrooms. If its premises are accepted then an appropriate focus on sociological studies would be on how the texts of schooling construct such taken for granted phenomena as individuals, skills, knowledge, and institutions. At the same time, it raises significant methodological questions about the status of data and the epistemological standpoint of the educational researcher. Given the primacy of discourse, the social facts studied by sociologists are constructed artefacts of researchers' own discourses and "naming", and any data collected in the field needs to be treated as a "readable" text, subject to interpretation.

This theoretical shift has the potential for destabilizing dominant paradigms and theories. Prevailing models of educational research and practice comprise what Lyotard (1984) has called "metanarratives": stories about human progress and scientific development that prescribe, rather than describe in any empirical sense, what will count as individual and institutional development. Consequentially, the very foundational theories that have been used to study the child, education, curriculum, and instruction may be viewed as discourses, taken-for-granted "truths" that "systematically form the object about which they speak" (Foucault, 1972, p. 39). Following a postmodern radical scepticism towards "metanarratives", no disciplinary or commonsense source of "truth claims" would be exempt.

Poststructuralist theory thereby encourages a counterontological critique of those broad theories of human development, social agency, and social structure that were used in the nineteenth century to analyze and develop educational interventions. In this way, it enables a self-reflexive critique of the modernist and industrial-era administrative and curricular models mentioned at the outset of this article. At the same time, it encourages the further development of experimental, interpretative modes of inquiry to examine new educational phenomena.

The insight of philosophic poststructuralism, then, is that there are no educational truths, practices, or phenomena that can be studied outside of discourse. By such an account, educational institutions could be seen as complex sites constructed by and through discourses expressed in various texts: from policy statements and textbooks to face-to-face talk in classrooms. These texts are seen as "heteroglossic" articulations of various historical, class, and cultural interests contending for social power and capital. The question of how to collect, read, and interpret these texts and how to analyze and situate their "symbolic power" is complex. It requires the study of the diverse "linguistic markets" and "social fields" where educationally acquired competence is used (Bourdieu, 1992, pp. 51–65). For while poststructuralism provides a wide-ranging epistemological critique of how discourse works, Foucault and Derrida assiduously avoided offering more than broad theoretical directions for the study of discourse in specific local institutions.

3   Educational applications of discourse analysis

As noted at the start of this article, the heralded "linguistic turn" in the social sciences had a significant impact on educational research in the postwar era. Discourse analysis describes an interdisciplinary family of methodologies and approaches to the study of language and text that draws variously upon linguistics, literary theory and cultural studies, philosophy of language, sociology, and psychology. Initially, the term was used in the 1950s to describe linguistic analysis of semantic structures above the level of the sentence. In the 1960s and 1970s, it was applied by English teachers to the systematic analyses of the error patterns of second language learners' spoken and written texts and by educational psychologists to the development of cognitive text processing models.

American and European psycholinguistics and sociolinguistics in the 1960s focused on the development of linguistic models that describe how people produce and use language. However, interactional sociolinguistics and its various subdisciplines (e.g., ethnography of communication, language planning) have tended to draw extensively from structural functionalist sand symbolic interactionist sociological theory (see Williams 1992). The principal focus of discourse analysis in education in the 1970s and 1980s was on instances of face-to-face talk between, for instance, care-givers and children as key moments in language socialization, and the development of literate competence and cultural identity (see Cazden, 1988). Application of ethnomethodological approaches to a study of classroom talk (see Mehan, 1979) and to educational texts (see Baker and Freebody, 1989) further showed how normative categories of gender, student disability, deficit, and disadvantage were constructed in the exchange structures and themes of classroom talk.

Sociolinguistics and ethnomethodological discourse analysis yielded detailed studies of language in classrooms, supplanting psychological "deficit" models with descriptions of cultural difference and the regulatory effects of schooling and classroom language. As sociological research, however, this work stops short of addressing larger questions about the unequal social production of "cultural capital", and about relationships of power among social actors and classes. In sum, this work provided a detailed description of everyday language use and textual practice but struggled to reconnect these systematically to larger ideological issues in what by the late 1980s appeared to be an increasingly conflict-ridden and heterogeneous social institutions of schooling.

At the same time, Foucault's work had begun to provide a framework for describing how educational texts construct children, teachers, students, and human subjects in different relations of power and knowledge. Henriques et al. (1984) began to meld poststructuralist and neo-Marxist educational analysis to describe the hegemonic power of educational discourses in the construction of gender, cultural identity, and child development. A range of studies described the broad development and intellectual history of particular paradigms and networks of ideas as "genealogical" discourses that build institutions of "governmentality" and moral order. These included historical studies of childhood, progressive education, and mental measurement as well as contemporary studies of educational policy and curriculum fields including mathematics, physical education, language, and literacy teaching (see Ball, 1990).

There is, additionally, a growing corpus of feminist and postcolonial work that, following Derrida and Foucault, attempts to write and hear historically marginalized speakers and voices. This includes significant work in educational autobiographies of women and members of indigenous, cultural, and ethnic minority groups. One of the shared tenets of poststructuralist feminist and postcolonial theory is the need to generate a public and intellectual "space" for the critique of dominant discourses and for the speaking and writing of the "unsaid", "subaltern" voices and stories that have been silenced historically. Within the fields of 'critical pedagogy" and "feminist pedagogy", this work is seen to serve education and emancipatory political projects (see Luke and Gore, 1993).

The developments of discourse analysis of educational texts thus mirrors some of the unresolved theoretical dilemmas in the sociology of education and in the emergence and application of cultural studies to education. While sociolinguistic work has stressed microanalyses of face-to-face language use in classrooms, textbooks, and student texts, genealogical studies of curriculum and policy have tended to provide broad interpretative analysis of the historical development of institutional and knowledge structures with less detailed textual analysis. By contrast, much feminist and postcolonial writing has focused on the production of situated accounts of experience and identity formation, marginality, and exclusion. The outstanding task for critical discourse analysis, then, is to provide detailed analysis of cultural voices and texts in local educational sites, while attempting to connect theoretically and empirically these with an understanding of power and ideology in broader social formations and configurations. In many ways, this is a restatement of an archetypal task of the sociology of education: to link specific educational processes with systemic sociological outcomes. But that task has been reframed by the challenge of poststructuralism: to theorize and describe the relationships between discourse change and social change, between the word and the material world.

4   Critical discourse analysis

Critical discourse analysis refers to the use of an ensemble of techniques for the study of textual practice and language use as social and cultural practices (Fairclough, 1992b). It builds from three broad theoretical orientations. First, it draws from poststructuralism the view that discourse operates laterally across local institutional sites, and that texts have a constructive function in forming up and shaping human identities and actions. Second, it draws from Bourdieu's sociology the assumption that actual textual practices and interactions with texts become "embodied" forms of "cultural capital" with exchange value in particular social fields. Third, it draws from neo-Marxist cultural theory the assumption that these discourses are produced and used within political economics, and that they thus produce and articulate broader ideological interests, social formations, and movements within those fields (see Hall, 1996).

   The practical techniques of critical discourse analysis are derived from various disciplinary fields. Work in pragmatics, narratology, and speech act theory argues that texts are forms of social action that occur in complex social contexts. Research and theory in systemic functional linguistics (Halliday, 1985) shows how linguistic forms can be systematically related to social and ideological functions. Critical discourse analysis uses analytic tools from these fields to address persistent questions about larger, systemic relations of class, gender, and culture. In educational research, this work has been turned to the examination of how knowledge and identity are constructed across a range of texts in the institutional "site" of the school.

   Critical discourse analysis begins from the assumption that systematic asymmetries of power and resources between speakers and listeners, readers, and writers can be linked to their unequal access to linguistic and social resources. In this way, the presupposition of critical discourse analysis is that institutions like schools act as gatekeepers of mastery of discourse resources: the discourses, texts, genres, lexical, and grammatical structures of everyday language use. What this suggests is a reframing of questions about educational equality in terms of how systematically distorted and ideological communication may set the conditions for differential institutional access to discursive resources, the very educational competences needed for social and economic relations in information-based economies.

Discourse and language in everyday life may function ideologically. They may be used to make asymmetrical relations of power and particular textual portrayals of social and biological worlds appear given, commonsensical, and "natural". Accordingly, the task of critical discourse analysis is both deconstructive and constructive. In its deconstructive moment it aims to disrupt and render problematic the themes and power relations of everyday talk and writing. In its constructive moment, it has been applied to the development of critical literacy curriculum that aims towards an expansion of students' capacities to critique and analyze discourse and social relations, and towards a more equitable distribution of discourse resources (Fairclough, 1992a).

The principal unit of analysis for critical discourse analysis is the text. Texts are taken to be social actions, meaningful and coherent instances of spoken and written language use. Yet their shape and reform is not random or arbitrary. Specific text types of "genres" serve conventional social uses and functions. That is, particular kinds of texts attempt to "do things" in social institutions with predictable ideational and material effects. These include functional written texts (e.g., business letters, forms, policies, textbooks), spoken face-to-face interactions (e.g., clinical exchanges, service exchanges, classroom lessons), and multimodal visual, electronic, and gestural texts (e.g., Internet home pages). Taken as historically and culturally specific social actions, genres are dynamic and continually subject to innovation and reinvention. They remain affiliated nonetheless with particular conventionalized discourses. For example, business letters are likely to feature discourses of finance and business; tabloid news reports would be sites for discourses of romance and sexuality. As conventional forms, then, genres and subgenres thus both constrain and enable meanings and social relations between speakers and listeners, writers, and readers.

All genres can be analyzed in terms of their sequences structures of propositions, their textual macrostructures. The structures of spoken and written narratives have identifiable segments, movements or "chunks". In the case of, for example, children's reading or science textbooks, the sequencing and montage of key actions, portrayals, and claims follows an identifiable order. The resultant text structures tend to operate as large-scale "grammars" of actions and events chained together, as expressions of a "cultural logic", and taken for granted assumptions about historical and human agency, social, and natural causality. The study of narrative structures has been used to study the representation of gender relations, cultures and cultural groups, wars, and other major historical events, and civic and political structures in textbooks (see Luke, 1995).

Studies of UK, US, and Australian classrooms have focused on how classroom talk can shape and reshape what will count as knowledge, subjectivity, legitimate social relations, and textual practices. Classroom talk is a primary medium through which teachers and students construct "readings" of textbooks, in effect reshaping text structures, features, and knowledge into authoritative interpretations. The turn-taking structure of classroom lessons and other spoken texts can be analyzed for its topic and propositional macrostructure, to document patterns of who can speak, when, about what topics, and with what officially recognized authority and force. As noted, ethnomethodological studies of classroom talk detail many of the typical discourse moves and techniques with which teachers regulate classroom knowledge. Studies of gender and cultural identity document how students' resistance can reshape school knowledge and social relations (see, for example, Gutierrez *et al.*, 1995).

Critical discourse analysis also focuses on sentence and word-level analysis, drawing analytic methods from systemic functional linguistics. Halliday (1985) argues that lexical and grammatical features of texts have identifiable functions: (a) they represent and portray the social and natural world ("field"); (b) they construct and effect social relations ("tenor"); and (c) they develop conventions as coherent, identifiable texts in particular media ("mode"). A range of other descriptions of language functions have been developed. According to Kress (1989), written and spoken texts represent particular selective views of the world or "subject positions" (i.e. field) and they set out social relations of "reading positions" (i.e., tenor). By establishing reading positions, texts can interpellate readers, situating and positioning them in identifiable relations of power and agency in relation to texts.

The study of subject positions of textbooks has focused on selective traditions of values, ideologies, "voices", and representations. In addition to describing the cultural assumptions expressed in the text macrostructure, analysis can describe particular lexical choices (e.g., "wordings", "namings") and the grammatical representation of agency and action (e.g. transitivity, mode, and modality). The use of an active or passive voice in a history textbook description of the "colonization" of the Americas, for example, may have the ideological effect of foregrounding or backgrounding Anglo/European agency. The lexical choice of "colonization" rather than "invasion", and the verbs and adjectives affiliated with indigenous people would represent a particular version of the historical event. Critical discourse analysis, thus, can document how the world is portrayed and how human, biological, and political actions are represented, sanctioned, and critiqued in the official texts of educational institutions (see for example, Muspratt *et al.*, 1997).

At the same time, texts can be analyzed in terms of how they structure and stipulate social relations between human subjects. As noted, teachers and students in classroom talk tend to reconstruct text features and knowledge, often in resistant and idiosyncratic ways. However, educational texts hail readers, and position them in ideological relations through various lexical and grammatical devices. Texts operate pragmatically through the use of pronominalization, modal auxiliaries, and the selection of speech acts such as questions and commands, orders, and injunctions. Consider, for example, how the aforementioned history textbook might define and position the reader through the use of "We" to refer to Anglo/European settlers. Or perhaps, like many other textbooks, it directs its readers' analyses and actions with questions and imperatives (e.g., "Answer these questions after reading"). These lexical and grammatical choices build differential relations of power and agency between readers and writers, between students and textbooks.

Critical discourse analysis thus employs interdisciplinary techniques of text analysis to look at how texts construct representations of the world, social, identities, and social relationships. This has already enabled the detailed study of policy texts, official curriculum documents, textbooks, teachers' guidebooks, and student writings. It has also been used to look at a range of formal and informal spoken texts, including classroom talk, administrators' public talk, staffroom talk, and parent–teacher interviews. Several studies of the social construction of school knowledge attempt to track different discourses across a range of texts within school systems (Corson, 1995). In her study of social science education in Australian secondary schools, Lee (1996) examined syllabus documents, textbook forms, teacher commentaries on students and student work, classroom talk, and students' written assignments. Operating from a poststructuralist feminist perspective, she documented the construction of gender and gendered textual practices. This research design, used by many Australian and UK researchers, involves a series of text analyses that use different analytic tools, but which are nested within an overall set of social theoretical frameworks and sociological questions.

In its constructive moment, critical discourse analysis is being used as the basis for the teaching of "critical language awareness" and "critical literacy" to students in Australia and the United Kingdom (Fairclough, 1992a). Critical deconstruction and social critique are key teleological principles of, respectively, poststructuralist discourse theory and Frankfurt School social analysis. The assumptions of such curricula are: (a) that students can be taught now to analyze critically the texts of the culture around them as part of literacy and social science education; and (b) that critical literacy is the "new basis" for postmodern conditions.

5 Conclusion

Discourses constitute what Wittgenstein called "forms of life", ubiquitous ways of knowing, valuing, and experiencing the world. They can be used for the assertion of power and knowledge and they can be used for purposes of resistance and critique. They are used in everyday local texts for building productive power and knowledge and for purposes of regulation and normalization, for the development of new knowledge and power relations, and for hegemony. If the poststructuralist view of primacy of discourse is accepted, then critical discourse analysis is necessary for describing and interpreting, analyzing, and critiquing social life.

Critical discourse analysis provides an interdisciplinary analytic approach and a flexible metalanguage for the sociological analysis of texts and discourses. The emergence of critical discourse analysis has at least three interrelated implications for educational studies and the sociology of education. First, it makes out a retheorization of educational practice. Educational theory and practice has relied historically on foundational metaphors of the unfolding child, the industrial machine, the individual rationalist mind, and, most recently, the digital computer. The metaphor offered by poststructuralism is that of the text as an interpretable phenomenon that is constitutive of all educational and intellectual endeavors.

Second, critical discourse analysis marks out a new set of methodological techniques and possibilities. The assumption shared by many quantitative and qualitative approaches to sociological research has been that observable realities, truths, and social facts have an essential existence prior to discourse. Critical discourse analysis begins from a recognition of language and discourse as nontransparent, opaque ways of studying and representing the world. It recasts all data and research artefacts as discourse. It raises and addresses the question of self-reflexivity by making researchers' own uses of discourse a key problematic in design and inquiry.

Third, critical discourse analysis marks out the grounds for rethinking pedagogical practices and outcomes as discourse. The assumption underlying many postwar curriculum development and instructional models is that the purpose of education is to produce behaviors, skills, and competences required for industrial-era workplaces and civic spheres. Critical discourse analysis suggests that mastery of discourse is the principal educational process and outcome, and that this mastery can be reshaped normatively to introduce teachers and students to critical analyses of text-based, postmodern cultures and economies.

This article began by describing the challenges posed by information-based multi-cultural economies and nation-states for the sociology of education. Critical discourse analysis provides a means for the sociology of education to examine new phenomena, including:

(a) New workplaces, communities, and civic spheres: shifting population demographics, new social geographies, multiculturalism, and new information technologies are altering social relations and how discourse is learned and used. There is a need for detailed study of new textual demands and practices in these institutions;

(b) New texts, genres, and discourses: these conditions are encouraging the articulation and commodification of new, unprecedented modes of expression. There is a need for the study and critique of hybrid written forms (e.g., newspaper formats that emulate TV "soundbites"), intercultural and "creolized" communications, new popular cultural forms of textual expression (e.g., rock videos, infomercials), electronic communications;

(c) New social identities: in these contexts, youth have access to unprecedented symbolic and material means for the construction of social values, beliefs, and identities. From the discourse analytic perspective presented here, youth identities and affiliated phenomena such as "class", "race" and "gender" cannot be viewed as having prior essential characteristics independent of their formation and representation in discourse. There is a need for study of how and to what end youth are using texts and discourses to construct and reconstruct new identities and communities.

The application of critical discourse analysis to educational research will require nothing less than the development of a new sociology of educational discourse. Critical discourse analysis enables modeling of how language, text, and discourse figure in the production and reproduction of educational outcomes. The focus of the sociology of education historically has been on the structures, processes, and consequences of educational institutions. A turn to the study of languages, discourses, and texts will be needed if indeed we are to understand how educational institutions might make a different in postmodern economies, nation-states, and cultures.

See also: Critical Theory and Education; Hermeneutics; Postmodernism.

References

Apple, M. W. 1996 *Cultural Politics in Education.* Teachers College Press, New York.

Baker, C. D. and Freebody, P 1989 *Children's First Schoolbooks.* Blackwell, Oxford.

Baker, C. D. and Luke, A. (eds.) 1991 *Towards a Critical Sociology of Reading Pedagogy.* Benjamins, Amsterdam.

Ball, S. (ed.) 1990 *Foucault and Education.* Routledge, New York.

Bourdieu, P. 1992 *Language and Symbolic Power.* Polity Press, Cambridge.

Cazden, C. 1988 *Classroom Discourse.* Heineman, Portsmouth, New Jersey.

Corson, D. (ed.) 1995 *Discourse and Power in Educational Organizations.* Hampton Press, Creskill, New Jersey.

Fairclough, N. (ed.) 1992a *Critical Language Awareness.* Longman, London.

Fairclough, N. 1992b *Discourse and Social Change.* Polity Press, Cambridge.

Foucault, M. 1972 *The Archaeology of Knowledge.* Harper and Row, New York.

Foucault, M. 1980 *Power/Knowledge.* Pantheon, New York.

Gutierrez, K. Larson, J. and Kreuter, B. 1995 Cultural tensions in the scripted classroom: The value of the subjugated perspective. *Urban Educ.* 29: 410–42.

Hall, S. 1996 The meaning of New Times. In: Morley, D. and Chen, K. (eds.) 1996 *Stuart Hall: Critical Dialogues in Cultural Studies.* Routledge and Kegan Paul, London.

Halliday, M. A. K. 1985 *An Introduction to Functional Grammar.* Edward Arnold, London.

Henriques, J. Hollway, W. Urwin, C. Venn,C. and Walkerdine, V. 1984 *Changing the Subject: Psychology, Social Regulation and Subjectivity.* Methuen, London.

Kress, G. 1989 *Linguistic Processes in Sociocultural Practice.* Oxford University Press, Oxford.

Lee, A. 1996 *Literacy, Gender and Curriculum.* Taylor & Francis, London.

Luke, A. 1995 Text and discourse analysis in education: An introduction to critical discourse analysis. *Rev. Res. Ed.* 21: 1–48.

Luke, C. and Gore, J. (eds.) 1992 *Feminism and Critical Pedagogy.* Routledge, New York.

Lyotard, J. F. 1984 *The Postmodern Condition: A Report on Knowledge.* University of Minnesota Press, Minneapolis, Minnesota.

Mehan, H. 1979 *Learning Lessons.* Harvard University Press, Cambridge, Massachusetts

Muspratt, S. Luke, A. and Freebody, P. (eds.) 1997 *Constructing Critical Literacies.* Hampton Press, Creskill, New Jersey.

New London Group 1996 A pedagogy of multiliteracies: Designing social futures. *Harv. Educ. Rev.* 66: 60–92.

Williams, G. 1992 *Sociolinguistics: A Sociological Critique.* Routledge and Kegan Paul, London.

Further reading

Fairclough, N. 1989 *Language and Power.* Longman, London.

Gee, J. P. 1995 *Social Linguistics and Literacies.* Taylor & Francis, London.

Harvey, D. 1989 *The Condition of Postmodernity.* Blackwell, Oxford.

Lash, S. 1990 *Sociology of Postmodernism.* Routledge and Kegan Paul, London.

Mey, J. L. 1985 *Whose Language? A Study in Linguistic Pragmatics.* John Benjamins, Amsterdam.

Poster, M. 1990 *The Mode of Information.* Polity Press, Cambridge.

16 Critical Theory and Education

G. Lakomski

Among the various theories competing for acceptance, if not dominance, in the field of education, critical theory is a vigorous and ambitious contender. It is the purpose of this article to ask just how serious a contender critical theory is by examining its validity as a theory and its usefulness as an approach to educational research.

As a relative newcomer to education theory, the critical theory of society – whether in its original, or later Habermasian, form – has already marshaled significant support and won over a dedicated group of educators. Its arrival in educational research was greeted enthusiastically by writers such as Bredo and Feinberg (1982), for example, who believe that critical theory is able to transcend the distance between the dominant positivist school and its challenger, the interpretivist paradigm. Both schools of educational research have come under attack. Positivist research has been challenged both from within analytic philosophy of science and from interpretivists who criticize its reductionism, while the implicit relativism of the interpretivist approach is said to make it an unsuitable successor to positivism. Critical theory, as seen by its advocates, promises to solve the problems of both schools in a higher order synthesis which allocates the empirical–analytical and the historical–hermeneutic sciences to their own, mutually exclusive, object domains, complete with their respective methodologies.

In addition to relegating the sciences to their respective spheres of influence and thus deflating any claims for the superiority of one or the other methodology, critical theory has a distinctive political orientation. It suggests that the dominance of science and the rise of technology and bureaucracy are developmental tendencies of late capitalism which increasingly encroach on the domain of social life (Habermas, 1976b). As a result of such imperialism which is accompanied by the decline and erosion of traditional institutions and legitimations, the legitimary vacuum thus created is filled by the new belief in science (Habermas, 1972c). What is obliterated in this process, according to Habermas, is the possibility of raising questions about social norms and values, and questions about "the good life" in the public domain. Where they are raised, they can only be perceived through the distorting lens of instrumental action, or the technical interest, which makes them appear solvable by the application of Weber's means–end scheme. Unmasking the illegitimate intrusion of science into the realm of social norms, Habermas believes, makes critical theory "critical" in the sense Marx understood the term, since science and technology have thus been shown to be ideological. The perspective which makes such insight possible is that of critical reflection which liberates or emancipates actors from false beliefs and subsequently leads to concrete proposals for overcoming oppression.

It is not difficult to see the attraction of critical theory for a number of educators who, critical of positivism, wary of the implicit relativism and conservatism of the interpretative school, and disenchanted with the so-called "economism" of Marxist education theory (e.g., Bowles and Gintis, 1976), have been searching for a more appropriate foundation for a socially just educational theory and practice. Critical theory, consequently, has found application in, for example, curriculum theory (Apple, 1982; Van Manen, 1977), educational administration (Foster, 1980, 1986; Bates, 1983; Giroux, 1983), action research (Carr and Kemmis, 1986), teacher education (Baldwin, 1987), educational policy analysis (Prunty, 1985) and planning (Weiler, 1984), educational theory (Young, 1989), and adult education (Mezirow, 1985). It has also been used to explain the crisis in formal schooling (Shapiro, 1984). (For a more comprehensive list see Ewert, 1991.)

Applying critical theory to curriculum making, Van Manen (1977, p. 209) notes that "Curriculum is approached as a nexus of behavioral modes which must be monitored, objectified, rationalized, and made accountable." Questions about the practical relevancy of, for example, teacher education programs, in Van Manen's view are then directly translatable into demands for increasing teacher competency and curriculum effectiveness.

In educational administration, writers such as Bates, Foster, and Giroux argue that the administration of schools, when carried out from within the scientific theory of administration (which they equate with positivism), merely emphasizes the technical–procedural aspects of their operations which are then taken as the only relevant and legitimate focuses of analysis. They contend that schools ought to be studied in all their interactional complexities. This is to be done by the method of "cultural analysis" with its emphasis on understanding and critical reflection. The rationale for cultural analysis is that, in Giroux's words, "the notion of culture . . . a political force . . . a powerful moment in the process of domination" (Giroux, 1983, p. 31).

The advantage of critical theory as seen by those who adopt its central concepts are, as Foster (1980, p. 499) notes, that "it is possible to have a social science which is neither purely empirical nor purely interpretative," on the assumption that critical theory thus escapes the criticisms leveled at positivism and interpretivist theory respectively. The stakes, then, are high, and the goal ambitious, for if critical theory could achieve what is claimed on its behalf, and what it claims for itself, then it would indeed be an outstanding candidate for a new, comprehensive social theory in general, and for education in particular.

The version of critical theory considered here is that presented in the work of Habermas, since it is his version which provides the source material for most educators interested in critical theory, Giroux's emphasis on the older school notwithstanding. The task is then not only to examine critical theory's central claims, but also to explicate briefly what it sets itself to achieve. This is important since critical theory is presented by its advocates as both theoretically superior to positivist social and educational theory and as practically and politically more desirable. While neither claim is considered justified, the first will be examined since the validity of any theory depends on the justification not only of its claims to knowledge, but also on the grounds on which these claims are made. If these are inadequate, then any claims derived from them, be they "practical" or "political", are equally unjustified. If critical theory turns out to be incoherent, so is any educational theory which seeks to derive its justification from it.

This entry examines two central doctrines of the theory: (a) the conception of interests, and (b) the notion of communicative competence which culminates in the "ideal speech situation". The first concept provides the justification of the theory as knowledge, and the second is Habermas's proposed solution to the "theory–practice" problem, that is, the proposal for overcoming domination.

1 Habermasian interests

Central to understanding Habermas's approach to social theory is what he takes to be the fundamental problem of contemporary social science: the relationship between theory and practice (Habermas 1974). He means by this that the connection between knowledge and social action has become an instrumentalist one, a relation which assumes the neutrality of science. Science is considered to be free of values and cannot, therefore, give people any guidance on how to conduct their lives. This development is the result of the victory of "scientism", or positivism, which, Habermas argues, presents itself as the only valid form of knowledge. As a consequence, it has become impossible, he suggests, to reflect critically on current forms of domination since even they appear as problems which are solvable by technical means. Habermas's aim is to restore to theory the dimension of reflection eclipsed by positivism and present a social theory which, as "ideology–critique", reunites theory with practice.

The quest for a comprehensive theory of social evolution as a theory of rationality leads Habermas to examine recent developments in the social sciences and in the analytic philosophy of science on the one hand (Habermas, 1985b), and investigations in the field of philosophy of language and theoretical linguistics on the other (Habermas, 1972a, 1972b, 1976a, 1979). In addition, he also re-examines the crisis potential of late capitalism (Haberman, 1976b, 1976c) and the foundations of the older school of critical theory (Habermas, 1982). These issues are outside the scope of this entry. For present purposes, the concept of "interests" (*Interessen*) is most important since it is the cornerstone of critical theory, aiming as it does at the re-examination of the connection between knowledge and human interests in general.

Interests, Habermas contends, are not like any other contingent empirical fact about human beings; neither are they rooted in an ahistorical subjectivity. Rather, they are grounded in the fundamental human conditions of work (following Marx) and interaction. What Habermas also calls a "cognitive" interest is consequently:

> a peculiar category, which conforms as little to the distinction between empirical and transcendental or factual and symbolic determinations as to that between motivation and cognition. For knowledge is neither a mere instrument of an organism's adaptation to a changing environment nor the act of a pure rational being removed from the context of life in contemplation. (1972a, p. 197)

Cognitive, or knowledge-constitutive, interests are hence ascribed a "quasi-transcendental" status, an ascription Habermas acknowledges as being problematic (1974, pp. 8 ff.). Critical theory claims three such interests: the technical, the practical, and the emancipatory. These three are asserted to correspond to the three types of sciences. The natural sciences, in Habermas's view, incorporate a technical interest; the historical–hermeneutic sciences the practical interest; and the critical sciences (such as sociology and Freudian psychoanalysis) the emancipatory. The technical interest guides work, the practical guides interaction, and the emancipatory guides power. Work, or purposive–rational action, is defined as:

> either instrumental action or rational choice or their conjunction. Instrumental action is governed by technical rules based on empirical knowledge. In every case they imply conventional predictions about observable events, physical or social. These predictions can prove correct or incorrect. The conduct of rationale choice is governed by strategies based on analytic knowledge. They imply deductions from preference rules (value systems) and decision procedures; these propositions are either correctly or incorrectly deduced. Purposive rational action realizes defined goals under given conditions. But while instrumental action organizes means that are appropriate or inappropriate according to criteria of an effective control of reality, strategic action depends only on the correct evaluation of possible alternative choices, which results from calculation supplemented by values and maxims. (Habermas, 1972c, pp. 91–92)

The second cognitive interest – the practical – enables the grasping of reality through understanding in different historical contexts (Habermas, 1972a, Chaps. 7, 8). It involves interaction patterns which provide a reliable foundation for communication. What Habermas terms "interaction" or "communicative action" is, like the technical interest, a distinct, nonreducible kind of action which demands specific categories of description, explanation, and understanding. It is this conception which provides the justification for the method of "cultural analysis" employed by some writers in education.

Habermas argues that just as human beings produce and reproduce themselves through work, so they shape and determine themselves through language and communication in the course of their historical development. While he emphasizes with Marx the historically determined forms of interaction, he nevertheless insists that symbolic interaction, together with cultural tradition, forms a "second synthesis" and is the "only basis on which power (*Herrschaft*) and ideology can be comprehended" (1972a, p. 42). Marx is accused of not understanding the importance of communicative action since it does not play a separate role in, and is subsumed under, the concept of social labor which Habermas claims fits his own notion of instrumental action. Nevertheless, undistorted communication which, in Habermas's view, is the goal of the practical interest inherent in the hermeneutic sciences, requires the existence of social institutions which are free from domination themselves. On Habermas's own admission, these do not yet exist. By adding the model of symbolic interaction, he wishes to expand epistemologically Marx's conception of labor.

Finally, the notion of the emancipatory cognitive interest leads one to the most fundamental, yet also derivative, interest. It must be understood in the context of the German idealist tradition whose underlying theme, Habermas asserts, is that reason, once properly understood, "means the will to reason. In self-reflection knowledge for the sake of knowledge attains congruence with the interest in autonomy and responsibility. The emancipatory cognitive interest aims at the pursuit of reflection as such" (1972a, p. 314). It is this interest which provides the epistemological basis for Habermas's notion of critique which is alleged to be the function of the critical social sciences. Consequently, this interest is of equal importance for educational theory which aims to be "interested" in just this way.

2   Interests and their epistemological status

Habermas's conception of interests was developed in critical response to positivism. The peculiar status of the interests resulted from his desire to avoid a naturalistic reduction of quasi-transcendental interests to empirical ones. Habermas wants to say, on the one hand, that humans have transformed nature, built social systems, and developed science in the course of their evolution, a process which is analogous to the evolution of claws and teeth in animals (1972a, p. 312). On the other hand, he is not content with such naturalism and claims that these achievements of human evolution are not merely accidental or contingent but have developed the way they have because of *a priori* knowledge–constitutive interests. These cognitive interests are described as being of "metalogical necessity . . . that we can neither prescribe nor represent, but with which we must instead come to terms" (p. 312). They are "innate" and "have emerged in man's natural history" (p. 312) and are located in "deeply rooted (invariant?) structures of action and experience – i.e., in the constituent elements of social systems" (p. 371). From the observation that humans have in fact transformed nature, built social systems, and created science, it does not follow that they have done so because of transcendental interests. In other words, there is no equivalence between asserting that the technical, practical, and emancipatory interests have emerged in human natural history, and asserting that they are true and provide the transcendental framework for all human knowledge. How could such a transcendental framework be justified?

Two alternatives are possible. Habermas can resort to another transcendental framework or, alternatively, concede that there is a framework which exists *a priori*. In the case of the first alternative, Habermas argues that cognitive interests are rooted in the depth structures of the human species. This is merely another transcendental, anthropological concept which is itself in need of justification. This solution leads to an infinite regress of transcendental frameworks since one can press the point of justification with each new framework. This means that in the end, no justification is provided. If this regress is to be avoided one would need to fall back on an *a priori* framework, a solution Habermas wants to avoid. It would seem that no matter which of these two alternatives is chosen, the status of interests which are neither amenable to empirical demonstration nor to be sought in the transcendental realm (being "*quasi*-transcendental" entities) remains unclear. If the epistemological status of the interests remains in such jeopardy, the consequences for critical theory are serious, since the interests were meant to provide the foundation for the claims made on behalf of the sciences. This means that Habermas's assertion of the existence of two categorically distinct forms of knowledge and inquiry lapses for want of adequate justification.

In the light of various criticisms of the epistemological status of the interests (e.g., McCarthy, 1981; Evers and Lakomski, 1991, in particular Chap. 7), Habermas felt compelled to note: "My view is today that the attempt to ground critical theory by way of the *theory of knowledge*, while it did not lead astray, was indeed a round-about way" (1982, p. 233). This assessment leads him to ground his theory in the theory of language instead (Habermas, 1979, 1985a).

3   Communicative competence and the ideal speech situation

The concept of communicative competence culminating in the ideal speech situation is the centerpiece of critical theory, since here the various strands of Habermas's investigations are drawn together. Parallel to Marx's critique of political economy, Habermas attempts to elucidate contemporary forms of alienation expressed in distorted communication. He wants to show that the potential for emancipation inheres in ordinary language which both presupposes and anticipates an ideal speech situation in which communication free from domination is possible. The full impact of Habermas's theory of communicative competence cannot be grasped adequately without taking recourse to its three underlying tenets which need further explication: (a) the notion of discourse and its relation to interaction, (b) the consensus theory of truth, and (c) the conception of an ideal speech situation.

Habermas argues that one can proceed from the fact that functioning language games, in which speech acts are exchanged, are based on an underlying consensus which is formed in the reciprocal recognition of at least four claims to validity. These claims comprise the "comprehensibility of an utterance, the truth of its propositional component, the correctness and appropriateness of its performatory component, and the authenticity of the speaking subject" (Habermas, 1974, p. 18, 1979, Chap. 1). Habermas contends that in normal communication these claims are accepted uncritically. Only when a background consensus is challenged can all claims be questioned. Their justification is subject to "theoretical discourse" which is an intersubjective enterprise within a community of inquirers. This concept is adapted from Habermas' interpretation of Peirce's model of empirical science (Habermas, 1972a, Chaps. 5, 6). Although theoretical discourse demands the "virtualization of constraints on action," it still remains implicitly presupposed in interaction because Habermas assumes that the subjects are in fact capable of justifying their beliefs discursively. Such a capability is characteristic of a functioning language game. Yet he is also aware of the fact that there is no complete symmetry of power among the partners of communication.

If one considers a consensus to be rational and discovers after further reflection and argumentation that it is not, how is one to decide what does constitute a rational consensus? Habermas claims that the only resource one has is to discourse itself. He is aware that this answer might lead into a vicious circle and contends that not every achieved agreement is a consensus, that is, can be considered a criterion for truth. If, for example, an agreement is reached on the basis of what Habermas calls (covert or open) "strategic" action, then than consensus is a "pseudo-consensus" (Habermas, 1982, p. 237). Strategic action is that which is undertaken primarily to safeguard an individual's personal success by means of conscious or unconscious deception. In the case of systematically distorted communication (i.e., unconscious deception), Habermas believes that "at least one of the participants is deceiving *himself* or *herself* regarding the fact that he or she is actually behaving strategically, while he or she has only apparently adopted an attitude orientated to reaching understanding" (p. 264). Even in this case, he contends, the actors themselves can know – even though only "vaguely and intuitively" – which of the two attitudes they were adopting. Both kinds are seen as "genuine types of interaction" and may be mixed up with each other in practice. As a result, Habermas asserts: ". . . it is often difficult for an observer to make a correct ascription" (p. 266). If one wants to reach a true (or "founded") consensus, he argues, one must admit as the only permissible compulsion the force of the argument, and consider as the only permissible motive the cooperative search for truth (1972a, p. 363).

An argument, then, qualifies as rational when it is cogent and motivates one in one's search for truth. Implicit in this thesis is Habermas's belief that there must be increased freedom for discourse to reach higher levels, that truth claims and claims to correctness of problematic statements and norms must be able to be assessed discursively, and in the course of assessment, also be able to be changed or rejected. The conditions under which such freedom can be attained are, in Habermas's view, given in the "ideal speech situation" because "the design of an ideal speech situation is necessarily implied with the structure of potential speech; for every speech, even that of intentional deception, is oriented towards the idea of truth" (1972b, p. 144). The ideal speech situation is attained when the requirements of symmetrical relations obtain which involve all speakers having equal chances of selecting and employing "speech acts" and their being able to assume interchangeable dialogue roles. Since practical discourse is generally distorted, according to Habermas, and since the ideal speech situation can only be anticipated, it is difficult to assess empirically whether or not, or to what extent, the conditions of an ideal speech situation actually obtain. This problem, Habermas contends, cannot be solved in any *a priori* way. There is no single decisive criterion by which one can judge whether a consensus reached is "founded," even under ideal conditions; one can only determine in retrospect whether the conditions for an ideal speech situation obtained. This difficulty resides in the fact that:

> the ideal speech situation is neither an empirical phenomenon nor simply a construct, but a reciprocal supposition or imputation (*Unterstellung*) unavoidable in discourse. This supposition can, but need not, be contra-factual; but even when contra-factual is a fiction which is operatively effective in communication. I would therefore prefer to speak of an anticipation of an ideal speech situation [·]. This anticipation alone is the warrant which permits us to join in an actually attained consensus the claim of a rational consensus. At the same time it is a critical standard against which every actually reached consensus can be called into question and checked. (Habermas in McCarthy, 1976, p. 486)

What, exactly, does this notion amount to? Stripped of its abstractions, one is left with a procedural model of negotiation which has the following characteristics in practice: (a) not everyone can participate in a given negotiation because of the existing power differential in society; (b) even when one reaches agreement practically, one is not sure whether it really is a consensus, nor does one have the means to check this (presuming that that is a worthwhile thing to do in the first place); and (c) the language one uses to reach consensus is itself a carrier of ideology. While Habermas emphasizes that his model is only an "anticipation" possessing the status of a "practical hypothesis" which does not refer to any historical society (Habermas, 1982, pp. 261–62), one is nevertheless entitled to press the point regarding its potential for realization in the here and now. Recall that the solution to this dilemma is that one can only determine with hindsight whether or not its conditions obtained. Recall further that these are the postulates of symmetrical relations in which all speakers have equal chances of "selecting and employing speech acts." This still does not solve the problem because one has to repeat the question of how one would ever know that these "equal chances" did obtain. Since all one has to go by are self-reports which may be consciously or unconsciously misleading, or even false, even a retrospective assessment would not avoid the skeptical regress.

Habermas calls his model a "constitutive illusion" and an "unavoidable supposition of discourse" which, however, is possibly always counterfactual. From this, McCarthy draws the conclusion that: "Nonetheless this does not itself render the ideal illegitimate, an ideal that can be more or less adequately approximated in reality, that can serve as a guide for the institutionalization of discourse and as a critical standard against which every actually achieved consensus can be measured" (1981, p. 309).

While this not an uncommon defence of the ideal speech situation, it is nevertheless invalid. This is so because the ideal speech situation is in principle unrealizable. It cannot be "more or less" adequately approximated in reality because the condition of retrospectivity does not get Habermas out of the problem of stopping an infinite skeptical regress, as was argued above. It follows that one cannot even achieve what self-reflection and the emancipatory interest promised; the liberation from dogmatic attitudes which is, in any case, only the formal precondition for practical, political theory in Habermas's scheme of things. For his theory to work, one must assume as already given, what, on his own account, does not yet exist but is supposed to come into existence as the result of the theory: namely, a world in which power and control are equalized. On the issue of social change then, this theory, which makes so much of its historical–materialist heritage, is silent. (For further critical comment on this aspect see Evers and Lakomski, 1991, Chap. 7).

4   Conclusion

It is perplexing that this model of rationality (i.e., rational persons discussing their differences in an ideal speech situation) has been hailed as at least potentially the solution to the so-called "theory/practice problem" which holds that traditional (positivist) theory is incapable of informing and guiding practice. If the preceding analysis is correct, it seems that critical theory is similarly incapable of doing so. While the reasons outlined above go a considerable way toward explaining the problems of the theory of communicative competence, and hence critical theory, it finally fails because truth-as-consensus is removed from direct confrontation with the "objects of possible experience." In other words, the consensus theory of truth rules out the possibility of making true statements about empirical reality. If one cannot, in principle, know whether or not there is, as Habermas asserts, distorted communication and oppression in contemporary society, then one is left with mere speculation. However intuitively convincing this may be, speculation comes a poor second to knowledge. These fundamental problems need to be resolved if the critical theory of society is to be relevant for this world.

See also: Action Research; Research Paradigms in Education.

References

Apple, M. W. 1982 *Education and Power.* Routledge and Kegan Paul, London.
Baldwin, E. E. 1987 Theory vs. ideology in the practice of teacher–education. *J. Teach. Educ.* 38(1): 16–19.
Bates, R. J. 1983 *Educational Administration and the Management of Knowledge.* Deakin University Press, Geelong.
Bowles, S. and Gintis, H. 1976 *Schooling in Capitalist America.* Basic Books, New York.
Bredo, E. and Feinberg, W. (eds.) 1982 *Knowledge and Values in Social and Educational Research.* Temple University Press, Philadelphia, Pennsylvania.
Carr, W. and Kemmis, S. 1986 *Becoming Critical: Education Knowledge and Action Research.* Falmer Press, London.
Evers, C. W. and Lakomski, G. 1991 *Knowing Educational Administration.* Pergamon Press, Oxford.

Ewert, G. D. 1991 Habermas and education: A comprehensive overview of the influence of Habermas in educational literature. *Rev. Educ. Res.* 61(3): 345–78.

Foster, W. P. 1980 Administration and the crisis of legitimacy: A review of Habermasian thought. *Harv. Educ. Rev.* 50(4): 496–505.

Foster, W. P. 1986 *Paradigms and Promises: New Approaches to Educational Administration.* Promethus, Buffalo, New York.

Giroux, H. 1983 *Critical Theory and Educational Practice.* Deakin University Press, Geelong.

Habermas, J. 1971 *Toward a Rational Society.* Heinemann, London.

Habermas, J. 1972a *Knowledge and Human Interests.* Heinemann, London.

Habermas, J. 1972b Towards a theory of communicative competence. In: Dreitzel H. P. (ed.) 1972 *Recent Sociology, No. 2: Patterns of Communicative Behavior.* Macmillan, New York.

Habermas, J. 1972c *Toward a Rational Society.* Heinemann, London.

Habermas, J. 1974 *Theory and Practice.* Heinemann, London.

Habermas, J. 1976a Systematically distorted communication. In: Connorton P. (ed.) 1976 *Critical Sociology.* Penguin, Harmondsworth.

Habermas, J. 1976b *Legitimation Crisis.* Heinemann, London.

Habermas, J. 1976c *Zur Rekonstruktion des historischen Materialismus,* 2nd edn. Suhrkamp, Frankfurt.

Habermas, J. 1979 *Communication and the Evolution of Society.* Beacon Press, Boston, Massachusetts.

Habermas, J. 1982 A reply to my critics. In: Thompson J. B. and Held D. (eds.) 1982 *Habermas: Critical Debates.* Macmillan, London.

Habermas, J. 1985a *The Theory of Communicative Action I: Reason and the Rationalization of Society.* Beacon Press, Boston, Massachusetts.

Habermas, J. 1985b *Zur Logik der Sozialwissenschaften.* Suhrkamp, Frankfurt.

McCarthy, T. A. 1976 A theory of communicative competence. In: Connerton P. (ed.) 1976 *Critical Sociology.* Penguin, Harmondsworth.

McCarthy, T. A. 1981 *The Critical Theory of Jürgen Habermas.* MIT Press, Cambridge, Massachusetts.

Mezirow, J. 1985 Concept and action in adult-education. *Adult Educ. Q.* 35(3): 142–51.

Prunty, J. J. 1985 Signposts for a critical educational policy analysis. *Aust J. Education* 29 (2): 133–40.

Shapiro, S. 1984 Crisis of legitimation: Schools, society and declining faith in education. *Interchange* 15(4): 26–39.

Van Manen, M. 1977 Linking ways of knowing with ways of being practical. *Curric. Inq.* 6(3): 205–28.

Weiler, H. N. 1984 The political economy of education and development. *Prospects* 14(4): 467–77.

Young, R. E. 1989 *A Critical Theory of Education: Habermas and Our Children's Future.* Harvester Wheatsheaf, New York.

Further reading

Carr, W. 1995 *For Education: Towards Critical Educational Inquiry.* Open University Press, Philadelphia, Pennsylvania.

Maddock, T. 1995 The light of redemption – Adorno and the task of critical reason. *Arena* 219–37.

17   Hermeneutics

P.-J. Ödman and D. Kerdeman

Until the nineteenth century, "hermeneutics" was commonly defined as "the art (or science) of interpretation (especially of the Bible)." As a consequence of contributions by Schleiermacher, Dilthey, and late existential philosophers such as Heidegger and Gadamer, the meaning of the term has changed. No longer does hermeneutics refer solely to methods of textual exegesis and interpretation. Hermeneutics also describes a philosophical position which regards understanding and interpretation as endemic to and a definitive mark of human existence and social life.

For this article hermeneutics will be defined as the theory and practice of interpretation and understanding (German, *Verstehen*) in different kinds of human contexts (religious as well as secular, scientific, and quotidian). Several different topics fall under the rubric of this definition. Hermeneutics embraces discussions about: (a) the methodological foundation of the human sciences (German, *Geisteswissenschaften*); (b) the phenomenology of existence and existential understanding; (c) systems of interpretation, used by people to reach the meaning behind myths, symbols, and actions (Palmer, 1969). To this list might be added debates concerning: (d) theories of the process of interpretation and the validity of interpretative claims; (e) empirically oriented schools of research that study people in social contexts. It should be noted, however, that many still define hermeneutics as the theory of biblical exegesis, general philological methodology, and the science of linguistic understanding (Palmer, 1969).

1   Differences in relation to other traditions of thought

Hermeneutics is not the only philosophical tradition that regards understanding and interpretation as central to social life. During the twentieth century, a number of other philosophies have come to embrace this position. While they and hermeneutics share many of the same assumptions, it is helpful to sketch some of the differences that make hermeneutics unique.

1.1 Phenomenology

Like hermeneutics, phenomenology is concerned with the structure of understanding. Phenomenology, however, construes understanding primarily in terms of cognitive constructs and functions. For hermeneutics, by contrast, understanding is not only a cognitive function: it is also the ontological condition of human existence. Moreover, while hermeneutics stresses the social nature of meaning, it is not altogether clear whether meaning for phenomenology is primarily subjective or social.

1.2 Wittgenstein's later philosophy

Both hermeneutics and the later philosophy of Ludwig Wittgenstein (1889–1951) posit that meaning resides in the conventions and practices of ordinary social life. Meaning, in other words, is not fixed by the rules of an ideal grammar or calculus but instead is negotiated, conditioned, practical, and fluid. Wittgenstein, however, believed that there is no structure common to all "language games" which philosophical analysis could uncover and use to mediate between different life-forms. Hermeneutics, by contrast, holds that mediation between different life-forms is possible. Indeed, articulating the conditions that make mediation or translation possible constitutes a central problem of hermeneutics. Additionally, hermeneutics looks upon language as the mode by which Being is revealed. No such concern for Being characterizes linguistic analysis.

1.3 Critical theory

Both hermeneutics and critical theory maintain that understanding and meaning are constitutive of social life. Hermeneutics, however, holds that since one's present situation is always involved in any process of understanding, it is impossible to grasp in any final or definitive form all of the meanings embedded in a tradition. Hermeneutics thus eschews the quest to ground understanding in a theoretical framework or method and concentrates instead on interpreting cultures from within given situations and contexts. Critical theory, by contrast, regards understanding as only one interest in the constitution of culture. It aims, therefore, to situate understanding within a broader or more universal explanatory framework, the purpose of which is to make transparent the ways in which ideology informs and conditions not only understanding but all of the interests and relations that constitute social life. (see *Critical Theory and Education*)

1.4 Marxism

Unlike Marxism, the underlying theory of hermeneutics is not primarily materialistic. Moreover, hermeneutics does not focus on the question of historical determinism. Rather, several branches of hermeneutics emphasize freedom in human action.

2   Purpose of hermeneutics

The purpose of hermeneutics is to increase understanding as regards other cultures, groups, individuals, conditions, and life-styles, present as well as past. The process must be mutual, implying an increase in self-understanding on the part of subject and interpreter alike. Moreover, hermeneutics aims to clarify its own working principles, to "understand understanding". This goal is realized not through the application of method but by bringing into focus the deep assumptions and meanings that inform everyday existence.

Hermeneutics can contribute much to both the practice of education and to educational research. A hermeneutically oriented educator would endeavour, for example, to interpret the meaning that educational practices and conventions hold for those who experience and participate in them. Such an educator might also try to understand various groups of pupils and their life-styles. Additionally, he or she would accentuate the significance of mutual understanding, such as that between teachers and pupils or between pupils of different backgrounds.

Insofar as research is concerned, hermeneutics can deepen the understanding of education by focusing on the meanings that underlie specific educational strategies and practices. A hermeneutic approach to inquiry would explore questions such as the following. How should certain administrative practices be understood? What are their hidden meanings? How might phenomena such as time-scheduling or the separation of learning into different subject-areas be interpreted in a broader cultural and historical context? By means of which educational and teaching strategies is cultural reproduction realized (Bourdieu and Passeron, 1970)? Answers to such questions are often given as interpretations through which understanding is promoted.

3   Understanding, preunderstanding, and interpretation

The concept of "understanding" can only be defined with the help of analogies and synonyms. The original literal meaning of the term may have been, "to stand close to or under something," or "to place something close to or under oneself." To stand close to something breeds a sense of familiarity. One knows well that to which one is close; one is understanding it. In other words, one is seeing it. The analogy with seeing is appropriate, because it coincides with linguistic practice. In many languages, "to see" connotes "to understand". Often, in fact, the two verbs are used interchangeably.

According to hermeneutics, the idea of familiarity is essential to the interpretative process. Insofar as familiarity obtains, a person to some extent already has understood that which he or she is trying to interpret. This preliminary understanding is known in the hermeneutic tradition as "preunderstanding".

To illustrate the notion of preunderstanding, it is helpful to think about how sense is made of problematic sections in texts. When a difficult passage or word in a narrative is encountered the reader tries to see how that particular part of the text fits within the pattern of the work as whole. Now, the reader may not completely understand the whole text.

Indeed, insofar as he or she finds certain passages opaque, understanding is precluded from being complete or absolutely clear. Nonetheless, on some level the reader already does understand the text, albeit in a preliminary way. For without at least a dim sense of familiarity with the work as a whole, there would be no context within which to make sense of or relate individual parts. In this respect, preunderstanding makes reflective understanding possible: it functions as a structure, a whole within the limits of which reflective understanding evolves.

If preunderstanding of an entire text makes it possible to grasp its parts, so the clearer the reader becomes with respect to its parts, and the more clearly the whole narrative will be understood. New dimensions of the text may be noticed. Thus in coming reflectively to understand the parts, the sense of the whole is revitalized.

In short, hermeneutic understanding begins with an inchoate sense of a text in its entirety. At the same time, it is only by probing and analyzing its parts that the whole of a text can be constituted. In this respect, preunderstanding and understanding mutually inform and refine each other. The dialectical relationship of preliminary and reflective understanding is known as the "hermeneutic circle". By means of the hermeneutic circle, texts are clarified or interpreted. According to contemporary hermeneutics, the circular process of preunderstanding, understanding, and interpretation describes more than a method of textual exegesis. Insofar as understanding is central to human existence, the hermeneutic circle captures how ordinary people experience and make sense of life.

4   Historical background

The word "hermeneutics" derives from Greek antiquity. The Greek verb *hermeneuein* (to interpret) and the noun *hermeneia* (interpretation) are the sources of the modern concept. Additionally, hermeneutics is associated with Hermes, who was both the messenger of and interpreter for the Greek gods. Hermes is also associated with the discovery of language and writing, the most important tools for grasping meaning and conveying it to others (Palmer, 1969).

4.1   Hermeneutics as biblical exegesis

Biblical exegesis has a very long tradition, dating back to the time of the Hebrew Bible. Indeed, canons for interpreting the Hebrew Bible already had been developed by the first century AD. By the Middle Ages, two main approaches to interpreting both the Hebrew and Christian Bibles had come into use. One approach endeavored to interpret the text literally, spelling out meanings that were already more or less explicit. Over time the literal approach to biblical exegesis became more directed towards reconstructing the historical meaning of biblical texts. The second approach was more concerned with symbolic content. Since the text was regarded as a message from God, it had to be interpreted allegorically. The purpose of allegorical interpretation was to reconstruct or uncover divine meanings not literally apparent.

With the Enlightenment, the scope of hermeneutics broadened. Entering the field of philological research, hermeneutics took a critical first step into the world of modern science. This move had important consequences for biblical exegesis. As an object of philological interpretation, the Bible became simply one among many objects of interpretation; classical and legal texts also were subjected to interpretative philological exegesis. In this respect, literal interpretation constituted an important bridge between interpretation as biblical exegesis and interpretation as a tool for scientific purposes.

4.2   Hermeneutics as "the art of understanding"

The German theologian and philosopher Friedrich Schleiermacher (1768–1834) was the first to formulate a new direction for hermeneutics. In Schleiermacher's view, understanding was not automatic: it was an achievement, a coming to grips with meaning which was opaque and problematic. Accordingly, Schleiermacher did not focus on hermeneutics as a body of practical rules: his aim, rather, was to examine the conditions that make understanding possible. How was it, Schleiermacher wondered, that understanding was accomplished? Answering this question, Schleiermacher hoped to established hermeneutics as the discipline of understanding.

For Schleiermacher, understanding consisted of two elements, one grammatical and one psychological. The relationship between these two elements is dialectical. In grammatical interpretation, the work is interpreted in terms of its linguistic principles, while psychological interpretation aims to interpret a text with regard to the thoughts and feelings of its author. The interpreter does this by identifying with the author's life and situation.

Schleiermacher's conception of understanding was rooted in the principle of the hermeneutic circle. In grammatical interpretation, a work is regarded as a context of meaning. Within this context, specific parts are elucidated, even as the explication of parts makes the entire context intelligible. For its part, psychological interpretation is founded on intuition. In the act of divining an author's intended meaning, the interpreter grasps an inchoate sense of the whole text which he or she will subsequently refine.

4.3   Hermeneutics as the theoretical foundation of the human sciences

The German philosopher Wilhelm Dilthey (1833–1911) extended the application of hermeneutics from the interpretation of texts to the whole field of human studies. His line of thought led in ontological as well as methodological directions. Dilthey's thinking can be summarized as an enormous widening of the hermeneutic circle. His central concepts were experience (*Erlebnis*), expression (*Ausdruck*), and understanding (*Verstehen*). Experience for Dilthey had a much broader connotation than it has today: "one may call each encompassing unity of parts of life bound together through a common meaning for the course of life an 'experience' – even when the several parts are separated from each other by interrupting events" (Palmer, 1969). Dilthey, in other words, held that people understand discrete life-experiences by assigning them a special place within an experiential whole. At the same time, one singular experience can change the way a person understands himself or herself and his or her life. The very experience of life, in short, is characterized by Dilthey as a continuous interaction between "wholes" and "parts".

The following example illustrates Dilthey's ideas. A teacher wishes to understand why a certain pupil is having difficulty. In order to make sense of the phenomenon, the teacher situates the problem within the context of his or her experience as an instructor. The teacher has previously seen that lack of interest on the part of parents greatly influences a child's progress in school. This understanding prompts the teacher to ask the child how he or she gets along at home; the teacher learns that relations between the child and the parents are very cold. By drawing on his or her experience to clarify the child's situation, the teacher achieves a better understanding of how to help the student. By the same token, understanding the situation of this particular student refines and enriches the teacher's entire instructional experience.

By "expression" Dilthey had in mind all the manifestations or "objectifications" of human experience, even those that are unintentional and nonverbal. Life-expressions, in other words, objectify or make concrete a person's understanding of life. Although expressions of meaning are personal, they are not created in a vacuum, Dilthey says. It is only by drawing on the common stock of meanings embedded in one's culture that an individual is able to express what experience means to him or her.

According to Dilthey, reflective understanding or "interpretation" consists in recovering the intimate connection between experience and expression. In explicating the meanings of a concrete expression, the interpreter brings to light not only the way a particular individual has understood his or her life-experience: because life-expressions are embedded in historical contexts, the interpreter illuminates a cultural milieu as well. As a consequence, an otherwise distant world comes alive in the present. The following example illustrates Dilthey's theory.

A Swedish educational historian seeks to interpret the meaning of some financial accounts which a gymnasium student in the seventeenth century gave to his headmaster. The accounts tell how much money the student collected during one of his wanderings. (Wanderings were common during this period and formed an important source of income for Scandinavian schools.) The interpreter's first task is to clarify the expressions; that is, the meaning of the symbols used in the student's accounts. Second, an attempt should be made to detect the personal experiences that these particular accounts express. Finally, the interpreter must reconstruct the context of forgotten meanings which characterized the practice of wandering and shaped the lives of Scandinavian students during the seventeenth century. In so doing, the interpreter unites the past (the student and his historical context) with the present world of contemporary readers and their pre-understandings.

In extending the hermeneutic circle to the domain of life experience, Dilthey at once both deepened and broadened the concept of "understanding." In particular, Dilthey's vision underscored the situational nature of the interpretative process. This insight profoundly influenced the development of existential hermeneutics in the twentieth century. No longer was understanding seen as the result of interpretation: with Dilthey, ordinary understanding was transformed into the existential ground from which reflective interpretation derives.

Dilthey hoped to demonstrate how the understanding that occurs in quotidian experience could ground a theory of human science. For Dilthey, however, the scientific study of social life posed an intractable dilemma. Ordinary understanding makes use of part–whole relations conditioned by particular historical contexts. Science, however, demands objectivity, the overcoming of situation. Can an interpretation be at once historically conditioned and also objectively valid? To avoid the threat of relativism, Dilthey felt he had to forgo the condition of historicity. In so doing, he gave up his most profound and influential insight.

5   Hermeneutics as a phenomenology of existence

With the German philosophers Martin Heidegger (1889–1976) and Hans-Georg Gadamer (1900–   ), the existential implications latent in Dilthey's thought became fully developed. According to Heidegger and Gadamer, understanding and interpretation denote how human beings define themselves as beings in the world. In understanding, self and world emerge together: they are fundamentally related.

Understanding is relational in another way as well. Understanding constantly refers to the future. At the same time, it is conditioned by a person's situation: it operates within a totality of already interpreted relations. This relational totality Heidegger called the "world". A teacher entering a classroom can serve as an example. The teacher's understanding of the situation is referenced towards the future: he or she anticipates, for instance, how the pupils will respond to instruction and fears that some of them may cause trouble. Understanding for the teacher is also conditioned by his or her former experience of this class, or by earlier experiences he or she had during the day. In this respect, the teacher's present understanding at once calls up the future and recalls the past.

The linguisticality of understanding is a point stressed by Gadamer (1975). According to Gadamer, language is like a storehouse of assumptions or "prejudices". In this respect, language forms a parameter or "horizon" of possible understandings. This does not mean that language confines individuals to the meanings of particular times and places. Indeed, by means of language, past and present understandings are mediated. Gadamer calls the mediation of past and present a "fusion of horizons".

For Gadamer, a "fusion of horizons" is an interpretative event which demands an attitude of openness on the part of the interpreter. This openness is similar to the kind of attitude with which a person confronts great art. In Gadamer's view, both the encounter with art and the interpretation of historical texts are marked by genuine questioning, founded on a sense of expectancy and a readiness to be changed or transformed by the meaning of a work.

An historian trying to understand a diary written by an elementary school teacher in the nineteenth century illustrates this principle. Based on the way the teacher describes himself in his diary, the historian initially concludes that the teacher was a nice man. As the historian reads further, however, she discovers that in some passages of the diary, the teacher discusses how he used corporal punishment to discipline his students. When confronted with this information, the historian experiences a clash between her "horizon" of understanding and the world of the teacher. The historian could react by shutting off further efforts to understand. Or, she could ask herself: "how is it possible to make sense of these actions when performed by such a nice person?" In order to reduce her conflict, the historian reads books about the role of corporal punishment in earlier eras of education. Gradually, she comes to see that the teacher in the past was only doing what other teachers and school authorities of his day thought best. The historian also learns that children in the late nineteenth century were not looked upon in the same was as they are in her time. Through a series of questions, then, for which there is a real need to know answers, the historian develops new understanding. In so doing, she extends the limits of her meaning–horizon and lays the groundwork for future understanding.

According to Gadamer, every hermeneutical endeavor proceeds from a stance of openness. In this respect, the interpreter does not "take possession" of the text that he or she interprets. Rather, the interpreter must let the text reveal its world.

6   The model of the text

The contribution of the French philosopher Paul Ricoeur to interpretative theory is all-encompassing. It can be described as an effort to synthesize the problems and insights of hermeneutics from Aristotle to the late twentieth century. In one of his definitions, Ricoeur calls hermeneutics "the theory of rules that governs an exegesis; that is to say, an interpretation of a particular text or collection of signs susceptible of being considered as a text" (Palmer, 1969, p. 43). For Ricoeur, the literal meaning of a text or system of symbols constitutes a closed world. This view parallels that of structural analysis, which studies language as a closed system of signs. A text also represents an open system, Ricoeur explained, because it refers to a world that exists outside of itself. In this respect, texts-as-discourse are similar to oral discourse, which is characterized by nonverbal signs and cues that direct the attention of the participants to circumstances and facts beyond the immediate discourse situation (Ricoeur, 1971). Unlike oral discourse, however, texts are not limited to particular contexts. This is because texts refer not to situations but to worlds.

Texts, therefore, can be regarded in two different ways. First a text can be viewed as representing a closed system of signs. From this perspective, the aim of interpretation is to clarify the meaning inherent in words. Ricoeur calls this the "archaeological" aspect of hermeneutics. Owing to the referential function of words, however, texts can also be viewed as pointing to an existential space. Thus, once the meaning of a text's words has been made evident, the interpreter can focus on the existential world to which the text points. Put differently, once the "what" of the text has been explicated, the "about what" of the text can be sought.

According to Ricoeur, the interpreter in this way moves from what the text says to what it is talking about. This movement, Ricoeur stressed, does not result in an identification with an unknown mentality through acts of empathy (as Schleiermacher thought). On the contrary, the interpreter confronts a world: the world about which the text is talking. Interpretation for Ricoeur is thus not a matter of detecting secrets behind a text. Rather, interpretation is a process of reading the references that constitute a text's existential space. This often entails confronting new perspectives on life through the life-styles of other existential worlds. As a consequence of interpretation and understanding, something heretofore alien becomes part of the interpreter's world, and the interpreter comes to understand himself or herself in a new way. The hermeneutic circle is moving between the interpreter's way of being and the being disclosed by the text.

In Ricoeur's view, all aspects of human communication and activity, including cultural products and artifacts, are analogous to texts. Accordingly, Ricoeur conceived his interpretative schema as pertaining not only to literature but also to the human sciences.

7   Hermeneutic social science

Since the late 1960s philosophers and practitioners alike have joined Ricoeur and Gadamer in exploring the implications of hermeneutics for the investigation of social life. A particularly influential contribution was advanced by Taylor (1971). Taylor's conception of human inquiry is anchored by a crucial premise of existential hermeneutics: meaning is not located in the minds of individuals. Rather, meaning consists in matrices or specific intersubjective agreements and understandings which are both constitutive of and expressed in social institutions and practices. Meaning, in short, is not private or subjective in Taylor's model: it is public, relational, and contextual.

This premise, Taylor argues, implies that the logic of hermeneutic inquiry is fundamentally different from the logic of positivistic science which has dominated social research since the nineteenth century. These differences become salient when one compares how hermeneutic and positivistic social science conceive the data of inquiry, the interpretation or explanation of data, and the justification and assessment of interpretative claims.

In the positivist model, physical behavior is distinguished from values, intentions, and goals. The former is observable and "brute identifiable"; the latter are hidden within the psyche, unavailable to sight. Positivist social science, Taylor said, strives to correlate public behaviors with subjective states of mind (Taylor, 1971, pp. 18–21). When a significant convergence obtains, events and phenomena are said to be explained.

Such a science is extremely limited, Taylor declares. Because the positivist model regards meaning as hidden and subjective, it vastly underestimates and often just misses the import of social events. Breakdowns in fundamental institutions and practices such as voting, negotiation, and work, for example, represent more than the "public eruption of private pathology." These breakdowns, Taylor says, signal deep crises which represent "a malady of society itself, a malaise which affects its constitutive meanings" (Taylor, 1971, p. 41). Like Ricoeur, Taylor argues that changes and crises of meaning *per se* are not grasped through acts of empathy. Nor can they be explained by subsuming observable sequences of "brute" behavior under general laws. Insofar as the data of social science express "a certain vision of the agent and his relation to others and to society" (Taylor, 1971, p. 26), such a science will be unavoidably hermeneutic, less an application of theory and law than a reading of social meaning.

According to the hermeneutic model of inquiry, the only way researchers can justify their interpretations is by pointing to other readings. Man "is a self-interpreting animal," Taylor writes. "He is necessarily so, for there is no such thing as the structure of meanings for him independent of his interpretation of them . . . already to be a living agent is to experience one's situation in terms of certain meanings" (Taylor, 1971, p. 16). For Taylor, in short, the justification and acceptance of interpretative claims – no less than their formulation – cannot appeal beyond the hermeneutic circle. Failure to grasp an interpretation is not due to an insufficiency of evidence or an inability to follow the logic of an argument. Inability to see instead derives from a fundamental inadequacy of self-definition which marks out the parameters of possible understanding. It follows, Taylor concludes, that in a hermeneutial science, "a certain measure of insight is indispensable" (Taylor, 1971, p. 46). Some interpretations, as a consequence, simply will be "nonarbitrable".

8   Hermeneutics and validity

The idea that interpretations may resist arbitration is disputed by a number of hermeneuticists. Betti (1967), for example, holds that without theoretical rules of verification, interpretation becomes anarchic. Betti tries to define a method that would allow interpretations to be passed with "relative objectivity". Since human expressions are objectifications of the human spirit, Betti reasons that it is possible for an interpreter to reconstruct the meaning an author intended. The principle of authorial intention is also propounded by Hirsch (1967). It stands in clear contradiction to the view of Ricoeur, who argues that the author's intention is of secondary interest. This is because texts, when completed, must be regarded as autonomous from their authors.

Whether or not one agrees with Hirsch and Betti, the problem with which they wrestle is crucial. As Heidegger and Gadamer have noted, interpretation is a function of situated engagement: without a context of already interpreted meanings, understanding is impossible. At the same time, emphasis on the situatedness and finitude of interpretative understanding raises the question of whether or not interpretations in principle are decidable (Connolly and Keutner, 1988). Is it possible for a hermeneutic philosophy to stay within a historically conditioned circle of understanding and at the same time posit rational principles as conditions for the possible validity or truth of particular claims to understanding (Hoy, 1978)? Unless such principles can be articulated, is it clear how competing or conflicting interpretations can be adjudicated, or how the specter of relativism can be avoided?

9 Criteria of interpretation

One important response to the above questions has been put forward by Ricoeur. In an essay on the relation between explanation and understanding, Ricoeur argues that the contradiction between the natural and human sciences to a great degree is an artifact (Ricoeur, 1986). Texts and other human products can be subjected to explanation in a way similar to that used by the natural sciences. In fact, understanding is impossible without explanation, and, of course, vice versa. Interpretation and understanding are thus promoted by means of logic and argumentation. Moreover, interpretation and under-standing often play important roles in the introductory and final stages of scientific research.

The question regarding situatedness and rationality therefore may be wrongly put. Because of its dependence on interpretation and understanding, physical science, no less than hermeneutic philosophy, is always situated within a particular time and place. As Gadamer has stated, there is no position outside our historicity. Humans, therefore, must make themselves aware of their historical situatedness and the preunderstandings that attend this condition (Gadamer, 1975). Canons of interpretation, Gadamer maintains, help to achieve this awareness. In Gadamer's view, interpretative processes employ the very rationality and reason that contributed to the birth of the natural sciences.

The main interpretative principle, of course, is that of the hermeneutic circle: the parts of a text and its whole must be checked against each other. By means of the hermeneutic circle, a text can be interpreted mainly in two ways. It can be interpreted literally; or an attempt can be made to reconstruct the world of the text. With respect to literal interpretation, the logic of sentences and actions is often rather strict. It is therefore possible to apply strict logic to check interpretations. One such logical canon holds that an interpretation of phenomena and actions cannot be accepted unless it explains all available relevant information (Trankell, 1972). If some important action or meaning in the text as a whole is excluded or only vaguely taken into consideration, the interpretation must be rejected. A second canon holds that an interpretation cannot be fully accepted unless it is the only one that explains the meaning of a research object. In many cases, this second criterion is difficult to satisfy. Even in those successful situations where only one interpretation remains after scrutiny in light of other competing interpretations, there is no guarantee that the interpretation will remain the correct one.

With respect to reconstructing the world to which a text or text-analog refers, the canon of the hermeneutical circle functions as a contextual criterion. According to this principle, every single interpretation must be checked against all available relevant facts, sources, and circumstances in connection with the interpreted object. If knowledge of those facts, sources, and circumstances contradicts the interpretation, it must be rejected or modified. By creating alternative interpretations of the same phenomena, cultural products, actions, or events from the very start, the interpretative process can be systematized. Concomitant with testing his or her main interpretation, then, the interpreter also can judge the validity of alternative interpretations. He or she thereby gradually refines his or her conceptions of the interpreted object.

10   The position of hermeneutics

The explosion of existential hermeneutics in the twentieth century has served to challenge a number of dualisms that are deeply rooted in modern epistemology and scientific method. Distinctions between facts and values, explanation and understanding, knowledge and self-knowledge, theory and practice were once regarded as inviolable; now these basic categories are being reconceptualized (Bernstein, 1978, Dallmayr and McCarthy, 1977). In the process, the relationship between hermeneutics and science with respect to the definition and determination of knowledge has been undergoing change. Some, such as Taylor (1971), have held that the logics driving hermeneutics and science are separate and incompatible. Others, such as Rorty (1979) and Gadamer (1975), have held a very different view. Overturning the old positivist position regarding the universality of science, Rorty and Gadamer have maintained that all knowledge is interpretative. There thus is no essential distinction between science and hermeneutics. Still others, such as Habermas (1973) and Apel (1973), have argued for the integrity of each domain but have posited a dialectical relationship between them.

Within the world of education, hermeneutics has flourished since around 1970, particularly with respect to educational research. The rise of so-called qualitative methods has broadened not only the scope and aim of educational research: it has also prompted investigators to reexamine the principles and aims of social inquiry (see, e.g. Erickson, 1986 and the *International Journal of Education Research*, 1991). A surge of interest in interpretative inquiry has prompted a number of important debates with the education community. Issues that have been discussed include the nature of the relationship between interpretative inquiry and more traditionally scientific designs; standards for adjudicating competing or conflicting interpretative claims; and the continued development of interpretative methods.

See also: Research in Education: Epistemological Issues

References

Apel, K. O. 1973 *Transformation der Philosphie.* Suhrkamp Verlag, Frankfurt.

Bernstein, R. J. 1978 *The Restructuring of Social and Political Theory.* University of Pennsylvania Press, Philadelphia, Pennsylvania.

Betti, E. 1967 *Allgemeine Auslegungslehre als Methodik der Geiteswissenschaften.* Mohr. Tübingen.

Bourdieu, P. and Passeron, J.-C. 1970 *La Reproduction: Éléments pour une Théorie du Système d'Enseignement.* Editions de Minuit, Paris.

Connolly, J. M. and Keutner, T. (eds.) 1988 *Hermeneutics versus Science? Three German Views.* University of Notre Dame Press, Notre Dame, Indiana.

Dallmayr, F. R. and McCarthy, T. A. (eds.) 1977 *Understanding and Social Inquiry.* University of Notre Dame Press, Notre Dame, Indiana.

Erickson, F. 1986 Qualitative methods in research on teaching. In: Wittrock M. C. (ed.) 1986 *Handbook of Research on Teaching,* 3rd edn. Macmillan Inc., New York.

Gadamer, H.-G. 1975 *Wahrheit und Methode: Grundzüge einer Philosophischen Hermeneutik,* 4th edn. Mohr, Tübingen.

Habermas, J. 1973 *Erkenntnis und Interesse,* 6th edn. Suhrkamp Verlag, Frankfurt.

Hirsch, E. D. 1967 *Validity in Interpretation.* Yale University Press, New Haven, Connecticut.

Hoy, D. C. 1978 *The Critical Circle: Literature, History and Philosophical Hermeneutics.* University of California Press, Berkeley, California.

International Journal of Educational Research 1991 15(6): (special issue).

Palmer, R. E. 1969 *Hermeneutics: Interpretation Theory in Schleiermacher, Dilthey, Heidegger and Gadamer.* Northwestern University Press, Evanston, Illinois.

Ricoeur, P. 1971 The model of the text: Meaningful action considered as a text. *Soc. Res.* 38(3): 529–62.

Ricoeur, P. 1986 Essais d'herméneutique, Vol. 2: *Du Texte à l'Action* Editions du Seuil, Paris.

Rorty, R. 1979 *Philosophy and the Mirror of Nature.* Princeton University Press, Princeton, New Jersey.

Taylor, C. 1971 Interpretation and the sciences of man. *Rev. Metaphysics* 25(1): 3–51.

Trankell, A. 1972 *Reliability of Evidence: Methods for Analyzing and Assessing Witness Statements.* Beckman, Stockholm.

Further reading

Baumann, Z. 1978 *Hermeneutics and Social Science.* Columbia University Press, New York.

Bernstein, R. J. 1988 *Beyond Objectivism and Relativism: Science, Hermeneutics, and Praxis.* University of Pennsylvania Press, Philadelphia, Pennsylvania.

Bleicher, J. 1980 *Contemporary Hermeneutics: Hermeneutics as Method, Philosophy and Critique.* Routledge, Chapman and Hall, New York.

Bubner, R. 1981 (trans. Matthews E.) *Modern German Philosophy.* Cambridge University Press, Cambridge.

Dilthey, W. 1976 (ed. and trans. Rickman H. P.) *Selected Writings.* Cambridge University Press, Cambridge.

Engdahl, H. *et al.* 1977 *Hermeneutik.* Rabén and Sjörgen, Stockholm.

Ermarth, M. 1981 The transformation of hermeneutics: Nineteenth century ancients and twentieth century moderns. *Monist* 64(2): 175–94.

Føllesdall, D. 1979 Hermeneutics and the hypothetico-deductive method. *Dialectica* 33(3–4): 319–36.

Habermas, J. 1981 *Theorie des Kommunikativen Handelns,* Vol. 1, *Handlungsrationalität und Gesellschaftliche Rationalisierung.* Suhrkamp Verlag, Frankfurt.

Habermas, J. 1981 *Theorie des Kommunikativen Handelns,* Vol. 2, *Zur Kritik der Funktionalistischen Vernunft,* 3rd edn. Suhrkamp Verlag, Frankfurt.

Heidegger, M. 1977 *Sein und Zeit.* Klostermann, Frankfurt.

Howard, R. J. 1982 *Three Faces of Hermeneutics: An Introduction to Current Theories of Understanding.* University of California Press, Berkeley, California.

Gadamer, H. G. 1977 (trans. and ed. Linge D. E.) *Philosophical Hermeneutics: Hans-Georg Gadamer.* University of California Press, Berkeley, California.

Mueller-Vollmer, K. (ed.) 1985 *The Hermeneutics Reader.* Continuum, New York.

Ödman, P.-J. 1979 *Tolkning, Förståelse, Velande: Hermeneutik i teori och praktik.* AWE/Gebers, Stockholm.

Ödman, P.-J. 1992 Interpreting the Past. *International Journal of Qualitative Studies in Education* 5(2): 167–84.

Ormiston, G. and Schrift, A. (eds.) 1990 *The Hermeneutic Tradition: From Ast to Ricoeur.* State University of New York Press, Albany, New York.

Rabinow, P. and Sullivan, W. (eds.) 1979 *Interpretative Social Science: A Reader.* University of California Press, Berkeley, California.

Ricoeur, P. 1965 *De l'Interpretation: Essai sur Freud.* Editions du Seuil, Paris.

Ricoeur, P. 1981 (trans. and ed. Thompson J.) *Hermeneutics and the Human Sciences.* Cambridge University Press, Cambridge.

Ricoeur, P. 1984–88 (trans. McLaughlin Pellauer D.) *Time and Narrative*, 3 vols. University of Chicago Press, Chicago, Illinois.

Taylor, C. 1985 *Human Agency and Language: Philosphical Papers,* Vol. 1. Cambridge University Press, Cambridge.

Taylor, C. 1985 *Philosophy and the Human Sciences: Philosphical Papers,* Vol. 2. Cambridge University Press, Cambridge.

Thompson, J. B. 1981 *Critical Hermeneutics: A Study in the Thought of Paul Ricoeur and Jürgen Habermas.* Cambridge University Press, Cambridge.

Wachterhauser, B. (ed.) 1986 *Hermeneutics and Modern Philosophy.* State University of New York Press, Albany, New York.

Part III

Issues

18 Research in Education: Nature, Needs, and Priorities

J. P. Keeves and P. A. McKenzie

The major issues for educational research at the end of the twentieth century are those of overcoming the crisis within many countries of the lack of leadership and support for educational research. It is necessary to identify needs and priorities, to publicize the findings of research, to promote and focus debate on the issues confronting policy and practice, and to foster the building of a coherent body of knowledge from current and past research. This article is concerned with the nature of the research process in education, the utilization of its findings in educational practice and policy-making, and the ways in which the needs and priorities across the whole field of educational research might be identified.

The expansion of teachers' colleges and schools of education in universities that took place in the industrialized countries in the 1950s and 1960s and which was essential to cater for the expanding student population, was followed by marked augmentation of support for educational research. Since then, however, with the decline in school enrollments and financial austerity in most highly developed countries, the expenditure for education had to be reduced, and support for research proved an easy field for a withdrawal of funds. The 1980s saw a crisis situation for educational research in many countries. However, staff and students in universities were often able to devise research activities that did not require heavy sources of funding. These investigators proceeded quietly with their scholarly work within the frameworks of their basic disciplines. Moreover, they often sought to publish the results of their research primarily in journals related to a discipline and not necessarily in ways that would influence educational policy or practice.

In the 1990s most educational research investigations have been conducted within universities by students undertaking studies for higher degrees and by staff who carry out studies to enhance their prospects for advancement, to inform their teaching, and to satisfy both a drive for recognition by their peers and for greater understanding of the field to which they are professionally committed. In addition, staff also supervise their students. Very few universities seek – other than in superficial ways – to publicize the research findings of their own staff and students. Theses and detailed reports of scholarly work commonly remain unpublished and largely inaccessible to all but the most diligent research workers.

The National Academy of Education (1991) report in the United States identified six leading concerns in the organization of educational research that applied in the early 1990s. These concerns are relevant not only to the United States but also to other highly industrialized countries, such as Australia and the United Kingdom.

1. Research on education lacks comprehensive, effective strategies to shape funding . . . . Today a powerful consensus is needed on a strategy of research and development to improve education.
2. Patterns of support for research on education are episodic, buffeted by changing demands, vacillating leadership, unstable commitments and institutional pressures.
3. Studies tend to be small-scale, short term, not interconnected, and rarely longitudinal.
4. Funding is not at a sufficient scale for centers of research to maintain momentum over periods of time long enough to communicate effectively with educational practitioners.
5. Most of the public funding . . . for education research goes into designated studies and research centers regulated more or less overtly by current but rapidly changing political and policy considerations.
6. Too little room is left for coordinating field-initiated ideas, for theory-building and conceptual work to shape new inquiries, and for the cumulative insights of long-term empirical investigations (National Academy of Education, 1991, p. 32).

1   Problems in educational research

The problems facing educational research are greater than those of merely identifying a list of priority area. Educational research as a whole has tended to become highly fragmented and conducted without coherent theory. There is a need to respond to new leads from basic research in allied disciplines, for intensive experimentation, and sustained collaboration with educational practitioners. In addition, there is a need to re-establish active educational research agencies both within large bureaucratic structures and as independent bodies. This demands new and stable sources of funding for educational research, and the identification of fields where the reformed agencies might concentrate their efforts. More research activity is required to support and inform the massive spending that takes place in the field of education than can be provided by the intermittent endeavors of university staff who are also heavily committed to teaching and administration.

2   Dangers of priority lists

It is necessary to acknowledge that the establishment of a list of priorities at a national level for the conduct of research in any field carries with it certain dangers. In a review of educational research in Australia in the early 1970s, Radford (1973) argued:

> I do not believe in the laying down of priorities by a central body, and the refusal to support with funds, or staff or interest anything outside that set of priorities. My reason is simple. Such a laying down of priorities to me implies an impossible omniscience, and lays up trouble for itself. But this is not to say that different centres, different units, different institutions, because of their interests, and their perception of priorities should not by their own determination of policy decide to concentrate their efforts rather than disperse them, decide to collaborate with others in an integrated program, and where feelings are strong enough to persuade others to join them. (Radford, 1973, p. 120).

The major problem associated with any attempt to establish priorities and to rationalize research effort, whether within a country, an institution, or a small unit comes at the point of making a decision to check the development of one project to the benefit of another, or to transfer support for a research and development enterprise from one institution to another. Snow (1969) has discussed in detail a critical incident that occurred in England in the years immediately prior to and during the Second World War. The incident involved a choice between two research centers at a time when resources were very limited: one was concerned with the development of radar, the other with long-range bombing programs. The issues arose from the different views and interpretations of the scientific evidence available, as well as from long-term personal differences between two individuals in key positions. Only by chance was disaster averted, triggered by a sudden and complete change in priorities. The lessons from this incident for the funding and support for research are clear. In an open society, where there are many avenues to be followed to obtain funding for research and many places to be found where the research might be pursued, if one course of action is closed, then it is always possible to turn elsewhere for support. It is apparent that if there is one individual or even one committee with sole power, the situation is potentially dangerous: error of judgment can easily occur. The solution must lie in the provision of alternatives in both sources of funding and in locations where research might be carried out. Without such alternatives there is no way in which errors of establishing priorities can be exposed. Other problems associated with the setting of priorities are both the possible ossification of research directions, and the risk of being unable to respond quickly to developments that were unknown at the time the priorities were initially set.

These remarks on the rationalization of research effort should not be taken to imply that the setting up of priorities and the need for rationalization from time to time are not important. What is essential is the rejection of a universal listing of priorities and a denial of alternative avenues that might be pursued for the funding and conduct of research. Furthermore, it is important that any groups concerned with the establishment of priorities should be credible bodies, broadly based, and with the authority to implement the results. Moreover, there should be mechanisms for regular reviews of the appropriateness of the priorities that have been laid down.

3   Nature of educational research

Superficially it may seem a relatively straightforward task to rationalize research effort in the field of education, to make statements of policy, and to establish a list of priorities. However, the fluctuations in the funding of educational research over the 30-year-period from the mid-1960s to the mid-1990s, and the widespread closure of educational research institutions and research units within bureaucratic organizations clearly indicate the complexity of the tasks involved and the divergent views that have existed. In part, these circumstances have arisen from a failure to reflect on the nature of educational research activity and misunderstanding about how the findings of educational research are applied. As a consequence too much has been expected by politicians and policymakers from educational research too soon after initial studies have been conducted. Moreover, the physical and medical sciences, eager for funds and able to point to the spectacular successes of some of their research efforts, have been all too ready to disparage research in the social and behavioral sciences without consideration of the unique character of such research activity.

3.1   Functions of research in education

It is well-established practice in the natural and technological sciences to make distinctions between basic or fundamental scientific research and applied research. Underlying this perspective is the view of a chain of activity starting with basic research, which leads on to applied research, and on again to technological development and the translation of research findings into practice. However, the writings of Conant (1947) and others have gradually influenced understanding of the interrelations between science, technology, and society and while the distinction between basic and applied research may be an administrative convenience in providing support for research in these fields, in practice the strategies and tactics employed in such research are rather more complex than a simple dichotomy would imply.

Coleman (1972) in a discussion of the nature of research in the social sciences distinguished between discipline research and policy research (see *Policy-Oriented Research*). While there is much to be said in support of Coleman's categorization (see Husén and Kogan, 1984), it is important to recognize that educational research cannot be viewed in terms of a single discipline, as an educational science, since educational research frequently draws on many fields from within the social and behavioral sciences as well as from the humanities. Cronbach and Suppes (1969), arguing from the point of view of behavioral scientists, have seen a distinction between conclusion-oriented and decision-oriented educational research as useful. Underlying their perspective is the long-standing view held by psychologists that the field of education is one where the basic findings of psychology may be directly applied. While psychology remains the strongest primary discipline within educational research, it no longer dominates the field to the extent it once did (see, e.g., McGaw *et al.*, 1992). Moreover, the drawing of conclusions in the study of education is enmeshed in a web of belief and the making of decisions is greatly influenced by political expediency. Thus the distinction between basic and applied research is questionable, and other dichotomies that have been proposed must also be challenged.

3.2 Outcomes of research in education

It can be argued that educational research and development generate outcomes that fall into three distinct categories. Rich (1977) initially distinguished between the instrumental and conceptual utilization of knowledge in the field of education. Likewise, Fullan (1980) suggested that there are two main ways in which knowledge is used in education. In the first usage, knowledge is applied to a particular problem, and that knowledge may be derived from a particular investigation or from a series of investigations. In the second usage, the knowledge available is cumulative knowledge and action is taken on the basis of cumulative knowledge. There is, however, a third and important form or outcome of educational research and development that involves the preparation of a tangible product for direct use in schools, classrooms, and homes and which incorporates the findings of educational research. In these three types of usage the emphasis is on the outcomes rather than the functions of research. Sometimes in the development of materials, the sequence of basic research, applied research, and materials development might be seen to apply, but this is only one type of usage. The situation is commonly more complex, since when action is taken implicitly or explicitly on the basis of accumulated knowledge, the applied research stage and the materials development stage are commonly not invoked.

3.3 Nature of social action

Giddens (1984) has argued that it is important to recognize that the research and development model that relates to research in the natural sciences has been largely discredited in the social and behavioral sciences. Human beings are agents who are responsible for their own ideas and actions. In the study of educational problems and societal processes, human beings as a group do not remain as passive subjects of inquiry. They understand the debate that occurs during the formulation of ideas in a research study, and they not only assimilate these ideas but they also accommodate to them and are changed. Moreover, the social world is unknowable without using the views and perceptions that are held by human beings. Thus the very foundations of behavioral and social science knowledge lack certainty and the situation arises in which generalizations are advanced from research, but their nature has been influenced by the theories held by the research workers.

Furthermore, universal schooling and widespread higher education have during recent decades greatly facilitated the dissemination of advances in social theory and new educational ideas, through paperback publication, review journal articles, and not the least through the mass media. Consequently, the new ideas arising in the fields of social and educational theory are now quickly fed back into the thinking and actions of human beings and the social and behavioral world is itself changed. As a consequence the social and educational processes that are the subject of investigation are also changed. This does not mean that social or educational inquiry has no utility. Indeed, new ideas and their interrelations, which are the direct products of research, are very powerful initiators of change. Clearly, the nature of social action is very different from the application of scientific knowledge directly through technological development.

3.4 Evaluation and prospective inquiry

Educational and social research must not only be concerned with what was, and what is, but also with what might be. Research must help to identify issues and problems before they have emerged. It should also illuminate, employing both theory and pilot programs, the new and alternative pathways that lead toward desired educational and social goals. It has the task of generating new ideas and new ways of doing things from inquiry that is prospective rather than retrospective in orientation. The task for those persons who specify priorities for research is that of identifying those fields where it is possible to generate new ideas and new findings and where it is possible to attain desired goals more satisfactorily than in the past. The danger with a list of priorities identified at a high level by consensus is that problems and issues may be specified at too late a stage, when immediate solutions are required. Time is not available for systematic investigation.

4   Toward a coherent body of knowledge about education

In educational research a tension exists between responding to the immediate needs of practitioners and the building of a cumulative body of knowledge about educational processes, with recognition that the educational processes themselves are not static and are in a state of change. On the one hand, Tyler (1980) contended that priority should be given to the problems that teachers consider important, and that teachers are, in general, skeptical of problems for research that have been identified by groups outside the schools. On the other hand, Sanders (1981) has argued that educational research has become excessively atheoretical and has not produced an accumulated body of systematic knowledge. There is a danger in viewing these two approaches as alternatives. Unless the attention of research workers in education is focused on problems confronting policymakers and teachers there is the danger that important questions for research will be ignored and that the goodwill of schools and administrators toward research and researchers will disappear. However, unless educational research can add to a cumulative body of knowledge about education, there is the danger that after massive research effort over a long period no progress is made and each new generation of research workers must start afresh.

In the attempts that must be made to build a body of knowledge about the educational process it is important to recognize several key characteristics of research in education.

4.1   Cross-disciplinary research

The stereotyped view is still held by many that the typical educational research worker has been trained in the discipline of psychology and that he or she prescribes for pedagogical practice the "dos" and "don'ts" that may be derived from the laws and generalizations of psychological theory. The audience for the counsel of the educational research worker and psychologist is seen to be the practicing classroom teacher who seeks to improve the effectiveness and efficiency of his or her daily work (Jackson and Kiesler, 1977). It is not surprising that this view should have become established at a time at the beginning of the twentieth century when psychology was developing as a science, and when schools of education were being created. However, a more appropriate perspective is to consider educational research as cross-disciplinary in nature, cutting across and transcending or working at the interfaces between a variety of disciplines in the social and behavioral sciences and the humanities.

It would seem to be unduly restrictive to advance the claim that educational research commands a discipline of its own forming a field of educational or pedagogical science. During the twentieth century most developments in educational research have taken place as a result of thinking about educational problems from the perspectives of the social sciences, the humanities, and the behavioral sciences. Each disciplinary field in these areas can contribute to an examination of educational questions. Furthermore, perhaps the most interesting advances occur at the interfaces between two or more disciplines. Moreover, the educational problems that warrant investigation and for which solutions must be sought are not simply those that occur in the classroom. Education takes place not only in the school, but also within the home and the peer group, and through the mass media, in libraries and museums, at work and at play. The multifaceted nature of education means that there is a very broad variety of groups to whom the findings of educational research are of concern. Those wishing to contribute to educational policy and practice must draw upon the cumulative body of knowledge from many disciplinary areas about many different facets that are relevant to education.

4.2   Variables of the educational process

The second key characteristic of educational research is that it must often deal with very complex relationships involving many variables operating simultaneously. It is rare that a high-quality investigation into an educational problem or research situation can be reduced to the examination of a relationship between only two variables. One of the strategies that is commonly employed to investigate the simultaneous action of many variables is to carry out an intensive case study of a situation in which many factors are at work and to report in detail the full complexity and context of the events observed.

A commonly used alternative strategy involves the use of high-speed computers to analyse considerable bodies of qualitative or quantitative data associated with many variables. Because of the capabilities of computers to undertake complex statistical control of specific factors in the analysis of data, it is no longer essential to design an experiment to remove the effects of many variables by random selection procedures. The educational research worker is as a rule not able to design and conduct a controlled experiment to test a specific hypothesis, because it would involve interfering with the lives or schooling of people. The alternative that has emerged is to develop a complex statistical model, to examine the structure of the model, and then to estimate the parameters of the model through the statistical control of variables rather than through random allocation. Nevertheless, it must be acknowledged that a truly experimental approach, if it were a practicable alternative, would provide more soundly based conclusions than could be obtained from a nonexperimental study in a natural situation.

4.3   Educational operations on many levels

Most educational activity takes place within a social setting where characteristics of the group have influences on the behavior and attitudes of the individual members of the group. For example, student learning and the development of attitudes may be influenced by factors associated with groups, namely: the home, the peer group, the class, the school, and the school system to which the individual student belongs. Moreover, many research problems in the field of education lead to the formulation of hypotheses about the effects of practices and policies implemented at the class, school, district, or national level, since the activities of these organizational units are generally more under the control of educational policymakers than are the practices of families and peer groups. As a consequence data collected in educational research studies associated with some key independent variables are obtained at the group level and others at the student level, while the outcomes of achievement and attitude are necessarily obtained solely at the individual student level. This multilevel nature of educational inquiry must be taken into consideration in the design of a study and the analysis of data. Only comparatively recently has it become possible to undertake the analysis of multilevel data, even where an experimental design is involved. Further developments must also be expected in this field in the future. The potential that now exists for the more effective analysis of multilevel data has important implications for the identification of priorities in educational research.

Failure to recognize the multidisciplinary, multivariate, and multilevel nature of educational problems, in contrast to those research problems commonly encountered in the physical and biological sciences, or those commonly studied in the health and behavioral sciences, can lead funding agencies and committees responsible for the allocation of research grants, especially those comprised of members drawn from noneducational fields, to be uncertain in their identification of priorities for educational research. Even within the field of educational research, an individual steeped in the perspectives of one disciplinary area only, may have restricted views about priorities which result from a failure to understand the nature of educational processes, and the complexity of the issues that must be addressed.

5   Factors influencing the directions of research

Some understanding of the factors that influence developments in educational research has emerged from the studies reported by Suppes (1978). Three factors can be identified, namely: (a) a response to critical issues; (b) the impact of technology and practice; and (c) new ideas and new perspectives that are derived from other disciplinary areas.

5.1   Research in response to critical issues

In the past, critical issues have from time to time emerged in education that have changed the direction of educational research while these problems were being investigated. Commonly, public concern for the issues has released funds for such work, but the public debate about the issues has also helped to generate ideas about the nature of the problems involved and to identify aspects that are amenable to research. Persons responsible for the identification of research priorities must attempt to anticipate such problems and to have work at least in progress at the time the issues become critical. As a consequence, in the coordination or rationalization of research in education, there is the danger that priorities are determined solely by what are widely seen to be critical issues at a time when it is too late to conduct systematic research, because immediate solutions are required. Educational research workers ought to become aware of the long-term needs of society, should seek to investigate research issues related to those needs, and should initiate the research activity. There is, however, the danger that some issues that purport to be educational matters are not appropriate or amenable to research in an educational context because the issues are in essence societal problems. If priorities were established solely by a select group who saw educational reform to be the agent of social reform, society would run the risk of being engineered by the select group with evident inherent dangers.

5.2   Impact of technology on research and practice

Since at least the early 1930s, much of the mathematical knowledge necessary for the examination of the interrelations between many predictor variables and many outcome variables has been available. Very little progress was made in developing these ideas for use in the analysis of educational data until the mid-1960s, when advances in technology made widely available increasingly powerful electronic computers. As a consequence of these new procedures for the analysis of large bodies of data, both the types of problems that could be investigated and the ways of thinking about these problems changed. This rapidly led to the development of statistical and mathematical models for the examination of educational questions. However, these developments also contributed to a relatively widespread rejection of what was seen to be a positivist approach, and a turning to the use of alternative methods for the investigation of educational problems (see *Action Research; Case Study Methods*).

Thus advances in technology have had an impact on both how problematic situations in the field of education are conceptualized and on how research is conducted. Moreover, this impact involves not only the use of computers for multivariate analysis, but also a search for other strategies to investigate problems, in which many causal factors may be involved, and which are more exploratory and descriptive and do not demand the use of the computer.

Other advances in educational research may also be traced back to technological development, such as the use of mark-sensed answer sheets which make feasible large-scale cross-national surveys, such as those conducted by the International Association for the Evaluation of Educational Achievement (IEA). A further example is the introduction of the calculator into the classroom which at all levels of schooling makes more time available in the sciences and mathematics for new curricular content and an emphasis on the development of cognitive rather than computational skills, and thus opens up new fields of research, particularly those concerned with the development of cognitive skills and problem-solving.

5.3 Cross-disciplinary contribution

There is little doubt that new approaches and strategies for educational research will continue to evolve from fertilization across disciplines, as developments in the contributory disciplines are seen to be relevant to educational problems. In identifying priorities for educational research, it is essential that the interdisciplinary nature of research into educational problems should be recognized. There is the danger that certain problems are seen to be not amenable to effective investigation when viewed from the perspective of a single discipline. However, appropriate conceptual theory and methodological approaches can commonly be found if a bridge can be built across several disciplinary areas.

The determination of priorities solely through reference to the magnitude and consequences of the issue involved is unwise. Sometimes it would be of greater benefit to consider the researchability of a problem and whether the development of new technology, or the availability of new methodology or new conceptual frameworks from other disciplines would make the problem more amenable to investigation than it was previously.

6 Determining priorities for research

Priorities for research must be identified at many levels. First, there is the individual research worker in a university who must decide what issues should be chosen as worthy of investigation and the devotion of a substantial segment of working time. Second, there is the department or unit in an institution which involves collections of individuals working in collaboration, who must recognize the advantages of working as a team and focusing the efforts of the group on a particular problem, with different individuals investigating separately or jointly different aspects of the problem. Third, there is the research institution or center which must develop priorities for research and study and submit and argue the case for those priorities to an advisory or governing board. Fourth, there is the foundation that has trust funds to administer, whose priorities for research must be publicly stated as the basis for submissions for funding and support. Finally, there is the research council or board that is provided with substantial sums of public moneys which are to be allocated to research studies either as commissioned investigations, or on the basis of submissions received from research workers seeking support for studies they have chosen to undertake. Since the council must be publicly accountable for the allocation of moneys entrusted to it, there is commonly a need to identify its priorities and make them public both to those seeking funding and to those who provide the moneys.

At each of these levels priorities must be identified. Subsequently, there is the difficult task of making choices between applicants and projects in the light of the quality of the submissions received, the competence of the research workers making the submissions, the assessments of "peers" who have reviewed the research proposals submitted, and the judgments of the panel responsible for advising on the allocation of grants.

6.1   Criteria for setting priorities

An Australian Panel for a Strategic Review of Research in Education (McGaw *et al.*, 1992, pp. 72–75) has identified six criteria for setting priorities in a national educational research agenda. However, these six criteria also apply at all levels outlined above.

6.1.1   Social and economic needs

Research into educational problems is conducted within a changing social and economic context and this context must be taken into consideration in identifying problems that warrant investigation. Of particular importance are studies that anticipate changes in the social and economic context. Such research contributes to the capacity of the educational community to think systematically about the effects of change on educational policy and practice.

6.1.2   Enquiry and social justice

It is important that educational research should contribute to the promotion of social justice and equity in society. The capacity of research to assist in the identification of sources of educational disadvantage, and strategies to overcome barriers to effective participation in society by all social groups are major criteria for advancing priorities for research.

6.1.3   Needs of professional practice

The findings of educational research must help to meet the needs of professional practice both of those undertaking the research and those who study the findings of research. These contributions may not be immediately obvious, but a long-term influence on human and societal development, including the processes of learning and teaching at all age levels, must be sought.

6.1.4   Existing research strengths

The field of educational activity is so large and so complex that not all areas can be addressed, by an individual, a department, an institution, or even within a country. As a consequence it is desirable to identify existing strengths and to build on such strengths in the hope that significant advances will be made. Research in all fields commonly proceeds by the establishment of a group of scholars and students around an individual or small groups of individuals who have a proven capacity to identify key issues for research, and to deliver useful results from a program of inquiry. However, such centers of excellence are constantly shifting.

6.1.5   Advances in the research field

In the previous section the three main factors seen to influence advances in a field of research were identified and discussed. These three factors either separately or together can be employed to identify priorities.

6.1.6   Important gaps

A major function of identifying priorities is to fill important gaps in existing research programs. By focusing attention on the deficiencies that exist in research programs a more complete view of problem situations is obtained which provides evidence for solving those problems.

7   Statement of priorities

Statements of priorities for research in education can be made at many levels, including cross-national, national, institutional, and individual research worker levels. In this entry three statements of national research priorities, which were prepared in the early 1990s are briefly presented. These summary statements, however, give some indication of the issues that were seen at that time to be of importance in three different countries in different parts of the world.

The Review Panel for the Strategic Review of Research in Education in Australia in 1992 proposed nine priority areas that it considered should stand for a minimum period of three years before being reviewed (McGaw et al., 1992, pp. 78–81). These may be considered as three groups.

The first group comprises research in areas of continuing importance to education and the improvement of professional practice, in particular: (a) the teaching of thinking skills; (b) learning in the preschool and adult years; and (c) assessment of student learning.

The second group concerns research on the organization and management of educational structures, programs and personnel, and the interrelationship between education and the wider society, in particular: (a) leadership and management in devolved education systems; (b) education, training and work; and (c) teachers' work.

The third group involves research directed towards the revision and improvement of specific areas of the curriculum, in particular: (a) mathematics education; (b) science education; and (c) language and literacy education.

The Institute for Educational Research in The Netherlands in 1991 issued a statement on a research program for the three-year period 1992 to 1995 under the title *Problem-oriented Research: An Agenda for the Future*. It identified seven areas for investigation: (a) vocational qualifications; (b) preparation for participation in society; (c) individual development; (d) the quality of education; (e) evaluation of innovation and developments in education; (f) research as a direct service; and (g) fundamental educational research which included three subprograms; (i) motivation and self-regulation as determinants of achievement; (ii) mother tongue instruction and foreign language learning; and (iii) pupils' school careers. This research program must be viewed in the context of the integration of Europe, where greater mobility is available to those with qualifications and language skills (SVO, 1991).

The Report from the National Academy of Education in the United States identified five priority areas in a national research agenda: (a) active learning over the lifespan; (b) assessment; (c) bolstering achievement of historically underserved, "minority" and impoverished groups; (d) school organization; and (e) connection to teachers and teaching. The report argues that the current "research basis is under-funded, limited in focus, and lacks connection to what happens in the classroom" (National Academy of Education, 1991).

8   Conclusion

While it is neither possible nor desirable to attempt to develop universal research needs and priorities, there is some commonality between the themes chosen in these three countries from different zones of the developed world. It can be seen that support is advocated for studies that investigate issues that are not only associated with societal problems, but also have a likelihood of contributing successfully to new conceptual knowledge, new policy or practice, or new products for use in educational work. It is, however, important to recognize as Levin (1978) has pointed out after examining certain persistent educational dilemmas, educational research cannot and should not be expected to solve problems that are basically political or social questions.

See also: Policy-Oriented Research.

References

Coleman, J. S. 1972 *Policy Research in the Social Sciences.* General Learning Press, Morristown, New Jersey.

Conant, J. B. 1947 *On Understanding Science: An Historical Approach.* Yale University Press, New Haven, Connecticut.

Cronbach, L. J. and Suppes, P. C. (eds.) 1969 *Research for Tomorrow's Schools: Disciplined Inquiry for Education: Report.* Macmillan Inc., New York.

Fullan, M. 1980 An R & D prospectus for educational reform. In: Mack, D. P. and Ellis, W. E. (eds.) 1980 *Interorganizational Arrangements for Collaborative Efforts: Commissioned Papers.* Northwest Regional Educational Laboratory, Portland, Oregon.

Giddens, A. 1984 *The Constitution of Society: Outline of the Theory of Structuration.* Polity Press, Oxford.

Husén, T. and Kogan, M. 1984 *Educational Research and Policy: How Do They Relate?* Pergamon Press, Oxford.

Jackson, P. W. and Kiesler, S. B. 1977 Fundamental research and education. *Educ. Res.* 6(8): 13–18.

Levin, H. M. 1978 Why isn't educational research more useful? *Prospects Q. Rev. Educ.* 8(2): 157–66.

McGaw, B. *et al.* 1992 *Educational Research in Australia.* National Board of Employment, Education and Training, Canberra.

National Academy of Education 1991 *Research and the Renewal of Education: A Report from the National Academy of Education.* National Academy of Education, Stanford, California.

Radford, W. C. 1973 *Research into Education in Australia: 1972* Australian Government Publishing Service, Canberra.

Rich, R. F. 1977 Use of social science information by federal bureaucrats: Knowledge for action versus knowledge for understanding. In: Weiss C. H. (ed.) 1977 *Using Social Research in Public Policy Making.* Heath, Lexington, Massachusetts.

Sanders, D. P. 1981 Educational inquiry as developmental research. *Educ. Res.* 10(3): 8–13.

Suppes, C. P. (ed.) 1978 *Impact of Research on Education: Some Case Studies: Summaries.* National Academy of Education, Washington, DC.

SVO (Institute for Educational Research in the Netherlands) 1991 *Problem-oriented Research: An Agenda for the Future.* Institute for Educational Research, The Hague (mimeo).

Tyler, R. W. 1980 Integrating research, developments, dissemination and practice in science education. Position paper. *Journal Announcement: RIE* July 1991.

19   Equality of Educational Opportunity: Philosophical Issues

K. R. Howe

The principle of equality of educational opportunity is employed to evaluate the moral defensibility of systems of public education with respect to social justice, particularly within the Western liberal tradition. The following article characterizes the principle, compares competing interpretations, and discusses prominent controversies.

1   The principle of equality of educational opportunity

The principle of equality of educational opportunity is an offshoot of the general principle of equality of opportunity. The latter serves as a criterion in liberal political theory for determining whether given social arrangements are just: it stipulates that so long as individuals are afforded equal opportunities to obtain social goods, inequalities in the distribution of such goods are morally permissible. The principle of equality of educational opportunity focuses this reasoning specifically on education: it stipulates that so long as individuals are afforded equal opportunities to obtain an education, inequalities in educational results are morally permissible. On the assumption that educational attainment is an important determinant of the range of opportunities that individuals enjoy for other social goods, satisfying the principle of equality of educational opportunity is instrumental to satisfying the more general principle.

2   Two interpretations of equality of educational opportunity

The preceding characterization of equality of educational opportunity is open to two basic interpretations: "negative" and "positive" (Nagel, 1991). These may be distinguished in terms of the degree to which they call for governmental intervention in the course of social life.

2.1   The negative interpretation

The negative interpretation is noninterventionist: it identifies equality of educational opportunity with the absence of formal (especially legal) barriers to access to public

215

education that discriminate against individuals and groups on the basis of morally irrelevant criteria such as race, gender, and language.

Although the negative interpretation is progressive when compared with overt and legally sanctioned discrimination, it nonetheless may be criticized for falling far short of what equality of educational opportunity demands. For it is insensitive to the nonformal but powerful effects that factors such as race, gender, and language have on opportunities even when formal barriers are absent. For example, providing children with equal access to books and instruction in a language they do not understand fails to provide equality of educational opportunity in any but the most meaningless of senses. Thus, the negative interpretation can be quite hollow for those who lack the resources – cultural, linguistic, political, and economic – to take advantage of the formal opportunities it makes available.

2.2   *The positive interpretation*

The positive interpretation is interventionist: it requires public education to go beyond mere formal equality and to take positive steps to eliminate differences in the circumstances of schoolchildren that result in persistent inequality, particularly differences associated with disadvantaging social factors. Positive interpretations vary according to the degree of intervention required and, closely associated with this, with what factors are considered to be morally permissible sources of inequality.

To illustrate the range of interpretations, consider race, natural endowment, and effort as three possible sources of unequal educational opportunities (Nagel, 1991). From among these, race is the factor most widely judged as a morally impermissible source of inequality because the untoward effects of race on opportunity are so clearly objectionable. Adding natural endowment to the list is controversial because the intuition that natural talent is a morally permissible source of differential educational opportunities – in placement decisions, for instance – is entrenched. Finally, adding effort is even more controversial because if effort (which involves a large element of personal choice) is not a morally permissible criterion for differential opportunities, then it appears that nothing can be.

As the preceding characterizations suggest, the kind of criticisms to which a positive interpretation is open depends on the degree of intervention to which it is committed. At one end of the spectrum, the more factors that an interpretation judges to be morally permissible sources of inequality, the closer it is to the negative interpretation and the more likely it will be charged with being hollow. At the other end of the spectrum, the fewer factors that an interpretation judges to be morally permissible sources of inequality, the more likely it will be charged with posing a threat to liberty and encouraging heavy-handed social engineering. Interpretations that exclude even personal choice as a morally permissible source of inequality may be charged with destroying the distinction between equality of educational *opportunity* and equality of educational *results* (Burbules *et al.*, 1982).

3 Opportunity and liberal theories of justice

How political and educational theorists respond to the anomalies associated with different interpretations turns importantly on the broader perspectives on social justice to which they are committed. Within the natural home of the principle of equality of educational opportunity – i.e., the liberal tradition – three theories of social justice predominate: libertarianism, utilitarianism, and liberal egalitarianism.

3.1 Libertarianism

Libertarianism places a premium on individual liberty and, consistent with this, contends that states should be "minimalist" in their exercise of power (Nozick 1974). Chief among the things that a state should not do is redistribute resources in order to achieve equality among its citizens.

Libertarianism is most congenial to the negative interpretation of equality of educational opportunity. Positive interpretations are precluded on the grounds that they entail unwanted and objectionable state interference in private educational choices. Indeed, given libertarians' hostility toward state mandated and regulated public education *per se* – particularly the redistributive tax schemes that support it and its unavoidable tendency to purvey what the state deems educationally important – even a negative interpretation might go too far for libertarians.

Insofar as libertarians endorse the negative interpretation of equality of educational opportunity, they are liable to the charge that the kind of opportunities provided are hollow. Furthermore, such an interpretation implicitly holds children responsible for decisions that others – parents, teachers, and counselors, for instance – make on their behalf. Insofar as libertarians reject equality of educational opportunity, even under its negative interpretation, they are liable to the charge that children's educational fate is made even more precarious. If children's educational opportunities need not be equal in even a negative sense (or, indeed, if education need not even be publicly supported), it becomes solely a matter of private parental responsibility to pursue various avenues for educating their children. Children are made totally dependent on their parents' power, wealth, ambition, knowledge, and sense of parental obligation.

3.2 Utilitarianism

Utilitarianism is the form of liberal theory that has predominated through much of the nineteenth and twentieth centuries. Formally, it is an amazingly simple theory: the rightness of an action or policy is judged in terms of whether it satisfies the principle of maximizing the total good. More specific principles are judged by reference to this single overarching one.

In utilitarian theory, the principle of equality of educational opportunity is justified on the grounds that it contributes to maximizing the total good. Utilitarianism has no difficulty embracing a positive interpretation of equality of educational opportunity. For example, so long as they maximize the good, interventionist educational programs that target talented disadvantaged children for extra resources in order to develop their talents are justified on utilitarian grounds, as are the redistributivist policies that are necessary to support them.

Libertarians are quite hostile to utilitarianism. From their perspective, it goes much too far in the name of equality of educational opportunity because it requires a large bureaucracy to devise policies, to evaluate them, to calculate which will maximize the good, and to distribute resources accordingly. Even if such bureaucracies were not notoriously poor at delivering on their promises, they are objectionable for being paternalistic and undemocratic.

Liberal egalitarians are less hostile to utilitarians than libertarians and advance a very different kind of criticism. From their perspective, utilitarianism fails to go far enough in the name of equality of educational opportunity because it renders the principle too vulnerable to contingency. For example, if educational programs for the disadvantaged prove to be less effective means of maximizing the good than programs for the academically talented, then the justification for such programs is lost and, along with it, so is the justification for equalizing educational opportunity. But, according to liberal egalitarians, the principle of equality of educational opportunity – and principles of justice in general – should not be held hostage to maximizing the good.

3.3   Liberal egalitarianism

Liberal egalitarianism lays heavy stress on the principle of equality. However, it may be distinguished from strict egalitarianism in virtue of the fact that, like all liberal theories, it does not claim that inequality must always be eliminated. It claims instead that inequality is *prima facie* objectionable and therefore must be justified.

Dworkin (1979) distinguishes "equal treatment" from "treatment as an equal". "Equal treatment" is the interpretation of equality implicit in utilitarianism, in which everyone's interests are given equal weight. The problem with this interpretation is that it cannot protect essential interests, which should outweigh those that are not essential. As already observed, because equality of opportunity (like any other principle) is subordinate to maximizing the good, it is vulnerable to contingency within a utilitarian framework. An example is the flurry of government support for social programs in general, and educational programs in particular, following the riots in the United States inner cities in the late 1960s. Programs such as Head Start, children's educational television, and free school lunches were often justified on the utilitarian grounds that they would lead to a reduction of violence, an increased quality of life for all, the identification and development of talent that would otherwise be wasted, and so forth. Support for such programs has since drastically declined, and the problem for utilitarian thinking is that it has been an accomplice in this decline. Many United States citizens as well as policymakers have since perceived that such programs do not maximize benefit and therefore should be abandoned.

Liberal egalitarians are willing to accept – indeed, they insist on – foregoing maximizing the good in order to respect equality. In contrast to the "equal treatment" interpretation of equality, the "treatment is an equal" interpretation is sensitive to the relative legitimacy of different interests and is closely tied to the concept of "equal respect". This observation leads to Rawl's (1972) conception of the principle of equality of opportunity.

Rawls avoids a weak and contingent commitment to the principle of equality of opportunity because his theory exempts the requirements of social justice, of which the principle forms an important part, from utilitarian calculations. For him, equality of opportunity is required for individuals to have a fair chance to enjoy a reasonable amount of society's goods; for example, employment, income, healthcare, self-respect, and education. He contends that people are not responsible for disadvantages over which they have no control – who their parents are, how talented they are, whether they are handicapped, and so forth. Justice therefore requires social institutions, including education, to mitigate these disadvantaging contingencies to the greatest degree possible prior to, and sometimes in opposition to, maximizing the good.

The liberal egalitarian complaint against libertarianism is straightforward. Liberal egalitarians hold that liberty is hollow unless it is grounded in equality (Dworkin, 1977). They therefore eschew a negative interpretation of equality of educational opportunity in favor of the kind of positive interpretation described above, in which governmental intervention is required in order to mitigate disadvantaging social and personal circumstances to the greatest degree possible.

Libertarians and utilitarians rejoin liberal egalitarians in ways that are indicative of their particular perspectives. Libertarians claims (just as they claim against utilitarianism) that because liberal egalitarianism embraces a positive interpretation of equality of educational opportunity, it exacts too great a cost in liberty in order to advance equality. Utilitarians claim that because liberal egalitarianism has no overarching first principle, it is "intuitionist" (Hare, 1981). Whereas utilitarians may appeal to the principle of maximizing the good to set educational policy, liberal egalitarians must balance competing principles, including the principle of maximizing the good. They are criticized by utilitarians for having no principled (versus intuitive) way of doing this.

4   External critiques

The criticisms discussed so far are all internal to liberal theory, which is to say that they assume the overall viability of the liberal tradition. The principle of equality of educational opportunity is also the target of more fundamental criticisms advanced from other theoretical perspectives. Leftists have historically criticized liberal conceptions of justice for being insensitive to sources of inequality that are found in the underlying economic structures, particularly as they relate to social class (Bowles and Gintis, 1976). Critics from this perspective contend that underlying economic structures must be the focus of change if equality is to be realized, and that focusing on the meliorism associated with equalizing educational opportunity diverts attention from the real problem. In the process, it in fact serves to legitimate vast inequality.

In the 1980s liberal conceptions of justice came under increasing criticism (if only implicitly) for also being insensitive to the effects of race and gender, in addition to the effects of class (Weiss, 1988). From this perspective, the principle of equality of educational opportunity requires females and racial minorities to accept a "fair application" of rules governing the institution of schooling that have been rigged by the historical operation of patriarchy and racism to be to the advantage of White males. Thus, as with class, ignoring the deeper problems associated with gender and race also serves to legitimate vast inequality.

Notwithstanding their radical critics, liberal theorists deny that these kinds of difficulties are fatal either to liberal theory in general or to its conception of equality in particular. Kymlicka (1989), for instance, contended that liberalism's requirement of self-respect (central to Rawls's theory), permits – indeed, requires – liberalism to be revised as necessary to avoid the charge that it is insensitive to the influence of race, class, and gender. The basic idea is that fostering self-respect requires liberal institutions to be designed – or, more precisely, redesigned – so as to ensure that historically dominated groups are given an effective and equal voice in political decision-making.

5   Conclusion

The preponderance of current thinking is united in the view that in order to achieve just educational systems, something more substantive is required than the negative interpretation of equality of educational opportunity. Beyond this, however, it remains hotly contested as to how much intervention a positive interpretation may legitimately require; or, indeed, whether the principle of equality of educational opportunity ought to be abandoned altogether as irremediably inegalitarian.

References

Bowles, S. and Gintis, H. 1976 *Schooling in Capitalist America.* Basic Books, New York.
Burbules, N., Lord, B. and Sherman, A. 1982 Equity, equal opportunity and education. *Educ. Eval. Policy Anal.* 4(2): 169–87.
Dworkin, R. 1977 *Taking Rights Seriously.* Duckworth, London.
Hare, R. M. 1981 *Moral Thinking: Its Levels, Method, and Point.* Clarendon Press, Oxford.
Kymlicka, W. 1989 *Liberalism, Community, and Culture.* Clarendon Press, Oxford.
Nagel, T. 1991 *Equality and Partiality.* Oxford University Press, New York.
Nozick, R. 1974 *Anarchy, State and Utopia.* Blackwell, Oxford.
Rawls, J. 1972 *A Theory of Justice.* Clarendon Press, Oxford.
Weis, L. (ed.) 1988 *Class, Race and Gender in American Education.* State University of New York Press, New York.

Further reading

Coleman, J. 1968 The concept of educational opportunity. *Harv. Educ. Rev.* 38(1): 7–22.

Freire, P. 1970 *Pedagogy of the Oppressed.* Continuum, New York.

Gutman, A. 1987 *Democratic Education.* Princeton University Press, Princeton, New Jersey.

Husén, T. 1972 *Social Background and Educational Career.* CERI/OECD, Paris.

Liston, D. 1988 *Capitalist Schools: Explanation and Ethics in Radical Studies of Schooling.* Routledge, London.

Noddings, N. 1984 *Caring: A Feminine Approach to Ethics and Moral Education.* University of California Press, Berkeley, California.

Okin, S. M. 1989 *Justice, Gender and the Family.* Basic Books, New York.

Sterba, J. P. (ed.) *Justice: Alternative Political Perspectives,* 2nd edn. Wadsworth Publishing, Belmont, California.

Strike, K. 1984 *Educational Policy and the Just Society.* University of Illinois Press, Chicago, Illinois.

Wilson, J. 1991 Education and equality: Some conceptual questions. *Oxford Rev. Educ.* 17(2): 223–30.

20 Feminist Research Methodology

B. D. Haig

Since the 1960s feminist scholars have made significant contributions to educational and social science research methodology. These contributions are varied in nature and wide-ranging in scope. This article describes and evaluates some of the central developments in feminist methodology that are relevant to educational research. These include: (a) the feminist critique of standard empiricist research; (b) a consideration of methods used by feminist researchers; (c) the three major feminist epistemologies and their methodological implications; and (d) the relevance of pragmatist thought for the further development of feminist methodology.

1   Is there a distinctive feminist methodology?

A number of feminist researchers have debated the issue of whether there is a distinctive feminist methodology. Interestingly, few feminists have claimed that there is, or could be, though Reinharz (1983) has developed a communal approach to research called "experiential analysis," contending that it is distinctively feminist in character. However, most feminists appear to accept the view that it is a mistake to portray feminist methodology as distinctive. Clegg (1985) contends that there is no unified feminist methodology and that attempts to suggest otherwise run the risk of missing the real value of feminist contributions. Peplau and Conrad (1989) evaluate a number of proposals for distinctively feminist methods and conclude that any method can be misused in sexist ways. Similarly, Harding (1989) argues that attempts to identify a distinctively feminist method are misguided. She contends that feminist researchers use a variety of existing research methods, adapted to their own purposes, and that the arguments against a specifically feminist methodology are largely beside the point.

2   Common features of feminist methodology

Although feminist methodology comprises a diversity of offerings, a number of common themes have been identified in presentations of feminist methodology (e.g., Cook and

Fonow, 1986; Mies, 1983). The following features are often included in these presentations:

2.1 The rejection of positivism

Despite their many disagreements, feminist methodologists appear united in their opposition to the many positivist strands of orthodox educational and social science research.

This opposition ranges from efforts to improve on standard empiricism's positivist image by the development of a feminist empiricism, through the endorsement of extant postempiricist methodologies such as the "new" social psychology of Harré and Secord (Wilkinson, 1986), to the extreme postpositivism of skeptical postmodernism (Rosenau, 1992). The common features of feminist methodology mentioned immediately below are a part of its postpositivist commitments.

2.2 The pervasive influence of gender relations

Probably the most central feature of feminist methodology is its ubiquitous concern with gender. It is because of differences in the social position and power of women and men that gender relations are held to pervade social life. For this reason feminist researchers are committed to describing, explaining, and otherwise interpreting the female world. From these considerations feminist methodology has urged researchers to acknowledge and portray women's experiences, to identify the patriarchal bias of orthodox research and, relatedly, to assess the ways in which gender relations impact on the conduct of research (Cook and Fonow, 1986).

2.3 The value-ladenness of science

The persistent positivist myth that science is value-free has never been true to science and has been repeatedly challenged by feminist scholars. From their belief that science is a human social endeavor, feminists maintain that such inquiry takes on the values of the people who do the research as well as the values of the institutions that sustain it. Positivist empiricist research has been undertaken to produce secure factual knowledge bereft of explanatory power, which has served to maintain the *status quo* in respect of women's oppression. In stressing the value-ladenness of research, feminist methodologists have also been concerned to articulate a feminist ethic (Cook and Fonow, 1986) that is concerned with the way gender-biased language subordinates women, the fairness of practices which prevent the publication of feminist research and stifle career opportunities, and problems of researcher intervention into participatory research relationships.

2.4 The adoption of liberatory methodology

The feminist movement characterizes itself as being primarily concerned with the emancipation of women from oppression. In consequence, it is often claimed that research-based knowledge should be employed to help liberate women from their oppression. Mies (1983) forcefully expresses this view by claiming that, in order to change the *status quo*, feminists must integrate their research with an active participation in the struggle against women's oppression. Consistent with this, Mies claims further that the worth of a theory is to be judged, not through the application of methodological principles, but on its ability to assist the emancipatory process.

Liberatory methodologists are often critical of the use of attitude surveys in gathering knowledge about women on the grounds that they tell us little about women's true consciousness. In formulating a liberatory methodology, feminists have sometimes insisted that the research process must become a process of "conscientization" in Freire's (1972) sense (Mies, 1983; Lather, 1988). This process involves "learning to perceive social, political, and economic contradictions, and to take action against the oppressive elements of reality": (Freire, 1972, p. 15). As a problem-solving methodology, conscientization involves the study of oppressive reality by the subjects of oppression, where the social science researchers give their research resources to the oppressed so that they can formulate and come to understand their own problems. In these ways feminist liberatory methodology is seen to issue in action research.

2.5   *The pursuit of nonhierarchical research relationships*

A fifth common feature of feminist methodology is its strong endorsement of a nonhierarchical relationship between the researcher and the researched. This contrasts with positivist empiricism's penchant for assigning the researcher a position of epistemic privilege. In particular, feminist methodology seeks to replace the epistemic privilege of the professional researcher by democratic participatory inquiry where the researcher and researched enter into a social relationship of reciprocity in which there is a complementary recognition of their equal agency. The establishment of a relationship of nonhierarchy also requires the replacement of a spectator view of knowledge with "conscious partiality" (Mies, 1983) which the researcher achieves by partially identifying with the researched. Because the identification is not complete, the mutual correction of distortions remains possible.

3   Research methods

The conclusion that there are no distinctively feminist research methods is borne out by the widespread use of a variety of existing research methods by feminist researchers. However, feminist researchers tend to view these methods critically and deploy them in the light of their particular value commitments.

3.1   *Experimentation*

Feminists have criticized the use of experimental methods in the social sciences, both for assigning power and privilege to experimenters in their relationships with subjects, and for the artificiality of the laboratory experiment with its simplification of context (e.g., Parlee 1979). For these reasons, feminist methodologists have tended to favor nonexperimental methods in natural settings. However, it should be noted that a plausible case has been advanced by Greenwood (1989) for the constructive use of role-playing experiments in social psychological contexts in a way that can avoid the artificiality of altered social relations in laboratory experiments.

3.2   Meta-analysis

The extended history of research on gender differences has entered its latest phase with the adoption of meta-analytic procedures to summarize the disparate findings of numerous empirical studies in this controversial area. Meta-analysis is a recently developed approach to research integration that involves the statistical analysis of the results of data analyses from many individual studies in a given domain in order to synthesize those findings. Some (e.g., Hyde, 1990) see meta-analysis making a significant contribution to feminist research by providing strong quantitative conclusions about the extent and magnitude of gender differences. However, the empiricist basis of its most popular form should temper the widespread view that meta-analysis is a powerful method of research synthesis.

3.3   Ethnography

With the tendency of feminist methodologists to recommend qualitative methods over quantitative alternatives, ethnographic methods have frequently been used by feminist researchers. Such methods are attractive because they acknowledge the importance of the research context, focus on the experiential reports of women, and seek collaborative relationships between the researcher and researched. Glaser and Strauss's grounded theory perspective on ethnography (e.g., Strauss, 1987) has been used by a number of feminist social science researchers. Their approach to qualitative research breaks from the prevalent hypothetico-deductive practice of testing existing theories and encourages researchers to generate their own theories inductively to explain patterns in systematically obtained data. However, while acknowledging the methodological advantages that accrue to such ethnographic perspectives on the research process, some feminists worry about the possibilities of serious exploitation, betrayal, and abandonment of the research subject by the researcher in their collaborative relationship (e.g., Stacey, 1988).

4   Methodology and epistemology

In the early 1980s feminism seemed more willing to spell out its methodology than develop its theory of knowledge. However, since then developments in feminist methodology have proceeded more slowly than advances in feminist epistemology. Indeed, much of the content in feminist methodological writings has come to focus on general epistemological issues implicated in the feminist critiques of positivist research and the proposed alternatives. A consideration of feminist methodology, therefore, requires one to attend to the relevant epistemological literature. Harding (1986) distinguished three major alternative feminist epistemologies: feminist empiricism, feminist standpoint epistemology, and feminist postmodernism. A good deal of debate in feminist methodology in the early 1990s involved the ongoing elaboration and evaluation of these positions.

4.1   Feminist empiricism

Although some feminist scholars have criticized the positivist features of traditional science and sought to replace postpositivist science with a feminist successor, others have looked to reshape traditional science in the belief that it can serve feminist ends. "Feminist empiricism", as the modified account has been called, contends that the sexism and androcentrism evident in much research are social biases that result from doing bad science, but that they can be overcome, or minimized, by following the methodological norms of good orthodox science.

The attainment of these norms has been sought by the construction of guidelines for the conduct of gender-fair research (e.g., Eichler, 1988), and by efforts to identify and guard against gender differences in the sex composition of research participants as well as assessment of treatment conditions for gender neutrality.

Feminist research has sanctioned the continued use of many standard experimental, quasiexperimental, and observational methods, as well as a variety of qualitative methods, but with a heightened appreciation of the importance of bias in the deployment of these methods. New methods have also been enthusiastically accepted as improvements on the acknowledged limitations of older methods. For example, meta-analytic review procedures have been employed as a more effective gauge of gender differences than traditional tests of statistical significance (Hyde, 1990).

Although research from a feminist empiricist perspective helps to include women in science and can contribute to the improvement of conventional science, it has been criticized for improving the "masculinist conception of objectivity" (Heckman, 1990, p. 129) and for ignoring the important connection between science and politics.

4.2   Feminist standpoint epistemology

Feminist standpoint epistemologies are seen by their adherents to undergird a successor science that overcomes the inadequacies of both traditional empiricist science and its feminist improvement. In contrast to feminist empiricism, feminist standpoint theorists contend that the characteristics of researchers are crucial determinants of their understanding of reality. Drawing from Marxist, and/or psychoanalytic theorizing about gender, feminist standpoint epistemologies regard the subjugated social position of women as a privileged vantage point from which to view social reality. One explanation for women's epistemic privilege draws from object relations theory within psychoanalysis and claims that the formation of a distinctively female identity in infancy leads to a distinctive and superior form of knowing than that of men. However, the idea that women have a superior ability to reflect on and comprehend reality has been criticized by feminists and nonfeminists alike. For example, object relations theory has been judged to have weak evidential support, while the general claim of women as better knowers has been criticized as an untenable endorsement of cognitive privilege (Chandler, 1990).

4.3 Feminist postmodernism

Feminist postmodernism rejects the epistemological assumptions of modernist, Enlightenment thought. Thus, it stands opposed to the foundationalist grounding of knowledge, the universalizing claims for the scope of knowledge, and the employment of dualistic categories of thought. By contrast, postmodern feminism is an epistemology that is non-foundationalist, contextualist, and nondualist, or multiplist, in its commitments.

Feminist postmodernists sometimes maintain that language cannot really be used to refer, predicate, identify, and individuate an extralinguistic reality. This view of language underwrites an approach to discourse analysis research which substitutes the study of texts for the broader study of social reality.

Critics of postmodern feminism (e.g., Hawkesworth, 1989) argue that this flight to the text is inconsistent with its radical political aspirations. To shift the focus from the study of oppression suffered by women to the interpretation of texts is to abandon the real world for a relativist world of ideas. It is maintained that such a retreat can only serve to reinforce the *status quo*.

5 A pragmatist turn

Harding (1986) believes that because of the unstable nature of the categories they use, feminists should accommodate the tensions between these alternative epistemologies for now. However, Nelson (1990) has combined important insights from Quine's influential philosophy of science with feminist criticisms of science, to formulate an enriched feminist empiricism that she believes has the ability to resolve the differences amongst these epistemologies. With Quine, Nelson rejects foundationalist thinking and maintains that science should justify its claims in accordance with a coherence theory of evidence. While foundationalism maintains that theories are justified by being appropriately related to some privileged source, such as observation statements, coherentism maintains that knowledge claims are justified in virtue of their coherence with other accepted beliefs.

Relatedly, Nelson's neo-Quinean perspective regards knowledge as a seamless web with no boundaries between science, metaphysics, methodology, and epistemology. Thus, philosophy does not lie outside science, but is instead contained in, and is interdependent with, other parts of science. From this perspective it can be appreciated that epistemologies and methodologies do not function in isolation, but actually make metaphysical commitments. Traditional empiricist methodology, for example, regards the knower as an abstract and autonomous individual. However, Nelson breaks with Quine at this point and, by joining science and politics, she insists that it is communities rather than individuals who know; that it is the standards of a community that determines what counts as evidence for a knowledge claim.

Feminist scholars have been criticized for seeking distinctively feminist conceptions of science. Lakomski (1989), for example, has criticized Harding for pursuing such a project and suggests that progress in feminist theorizing will come from a consideration of mainstream epistemology and philosophy of science. Indeed, Nelson's radical feminist empiricism may be viewed in part as an advancement of the feminist understanding of science by exploiting Quinean epistemology.

6   Pragmatist realist methodology

Seigfried (1991) has lamented the fact that United States feminists have not appropriated their own country's philosophy of pragmatism, a philosophy that has resources suitable for the development of feminist theory. Of importance, however, is the fact that a number of writers in a pragmatist realist tradition have made significant contributions to methodology that are suitable for appropriation by feminist and other postpositivist researchers. This section of the chapter outlines some of these developments and briefly links them to feminist concerns about methodology.

6.1   Research problems

In her forceful plea for overcoming the uncritical employment of method, Daly (1973) suggests that the common practice of having the research problem determined by the method should be reversed so that the method is chosen to fit the problem. However, this reasonable suggestion fails to depict research adequately as a problem-solving enterprise.

Nickles (1981) has developed a constraint inclusion theory of problems which assigns to scientific problems a positive methodological role. On this account a problem is taken to comprise all the constraints on the solution (plus the demand that the solution be found). With this theory the constraints do not lie outside the problem, but are constitutive of the problem itself; they actually serve to characterize the problem and give it structure. This constraint inclusion account of problems stresses the fact that, in good scientific research, problems typically evolve from an ill-structured state and eventually attain a degree of well-formedness, such that their solution becomes possible. Incorporating such an account of problems into research method itself allows the problem to guide inquiry and explain how it is possible.

6.2   Generative methodology

Most traditional philosophies of science have insisted on drawing a strong distinction between the context of discovery and the context of justification. The context of discovery is concerned with the origin of scientific hypotheses and is thought to be a psychological, but not a methodological, affair. The context of justification is concerned with the validation of hypotheses and is the domain to which methodology properly belongs. Some feminist methodologists such as Harding (1989), for example, have argued that understanding the origin of scientific hypotheses requires one to admit that methodology can rightly operate in the context of discovery. Other advocates of discovery have argued for the same conclusion. This traditional methodological distinction, combined with the dominance of the hypothetico-deductive method, has resulted in a half methodology whereby researchers evaluate knowledge claims solely in terms of their consequences.

However, a methodology adequate to the full range of scientific reasoning must supplement consequentialism with a conception of methodology that is also generative in nature. In contrast to consequentialist thinking, generative methodologies reason to, and accept, the knowledge claims in question from warranted premises (Nickles, 1987). The widely used procedure of exploratory factor analysis serves as an example of a method that facilitates generative reasoning by helping to reason forward from correlational data to the plausible factorial theories that they occasion. The endorsement of generative methodologies will be an essential part of feminist methodologists' resolve to acknowledge and scrutinize the entire research process.

6.3 Heuristics

Feminists have frequently criticized positivist empiricism for its rather idealized portrayal of the researcher as a computationally adept being whose behavior is strongly guided by rules. However, this unrealistic picture has been rejected by pragmatist methodologists in favor of a more modest conception of themselves as knowers. A view of the researcher as a "satisficer" has been influential in this regard. The rational behavior of the satisficer is bounded by temporal, computational, and memorial constraints and, as a result, involves the frequent use of heuristic procedures. Heuristic procedures are "rules of thumb" which have the following characteristics (Wimsatt, 1981): (a) the correct use of heuristics does not guarantee a correct solution, nor even that a solution will be found: (b) heuristics are cost-effective procedures, making considerably fewer demands on time, effort, and computation than equivalent algorithmic procedures; (c) errors made in using heuristic procedures are systematically biased. Glaser and Strauss's grounded theory perspective on ethnographic methodology, which has been endorsed and used by a number of feminist methodologists, makes considerable use of heuristic procedures.

6.4 Coherence justification

Feminist scholars have frequently attacked positivist empiricism for justifying its knowledge claims by appealing to a privileged base of observational data. However, foundational theories of justification have been widely rejected in contemporary philosophy, and coherentist approaches to justification are being presented as an attractive option. As noted above, Nelson's (1990) neo-Quinean framework for feminist science explicitly adopts a coherence perspective on justification. Also, coherence justification has begun to receive consideration within educational research methodology (Lakomski, 19910. And in an important contribution to scientific methodology, Thagard (1989) has developed a new theory of explanatory coherence that is capable of evaluating competing hypotheses in science as well as in everyday affairs. Based on principles that establish the local coherence between a hypothesis and other propositions, Thagard's approach is able to integrate considerations of explanatory breadth, simplicity, and analogy into an overall gauge of explanatory coherence. Thagard's view of theory appraisal as explanatory coherence is a significant postpositivist contribution to a neglected aspect of research methodology that can be implemented widely in areas of research that boast competing explanatory theories.

These are just some of the features of a contemporary pragmatic realist methodology. A comprehensive formulation of such a methodology has been outlined by Nickles (1987) and is exemplified in Wamsatt's (1981) study of reductionism in biology. With its rejection of the methodologies of positivist empiricism, naive realism, and strong versions of social constructivism, pragmatic realism recommends itself as an attractive option. The feminist research enterprise strands to strengthen its hand by taking the pragmatic realist turn in methodology. For its part, pragmatic realism would be enriched by assimilating the gains made by feminist methodology since the late 1970s.

7   Conclusion

Feminist social science research in the 1970s operated largely from the confines of positivist empiricist methodology, but since that time virtually all developments in feminist methodology have been critical of positivism. The feminist methodology of the early 1990s is postpositivist in a number of ways. Although some feminists sought to develop a distinctively feminist approach to methodology, most adapted existing research methods to their own purposes. Feminist methodology broadened to include discussion of the three epistemologies of feminist empiricism, feminist standpoint epistemology, and feminist postmodernism. In the light of criticisms of these theories of knowledge, a pragmatic realistic perspective on science recommends itself with a methodology that is appropriate for advancing feminist inquiry and social science research generally.

See also: Research in Education: Epistemological Issues; Positivism, Anti-positivism and Empiricism; Postmodernism.

References

Chandler, J. 1990 Feminism and epistemology. *Metaphilosophy* 21(4): 367–81.
Clegg, S. 1985 Feminist methodology: Fact or fiction? *Quality and Quantity* 19(1): 83–97.
Cook, J. and Fonow, M. 1986 Knowledge and women's interests: issues of epistemology and methodology in feminist sociological research. *Sociological Inquiry* 56(1): 2–29.

Daly, M. 1973 *Beyond God the Father: Toward a Philosophy of Women's Liberation.* Beacon Press, Boston, Massachusetts.

Eichler, M. 1988 *Nonsexist Research Methods.* Allen and Unwin, Boston, Massachusetts.

Freire, P. 1972 *Pedagogy of the Oppressed.* Penguin, Harmondsworth.

Greenwood, J. 1989 *Explanation and Experiment in Social Psychological Science.* Springer-Verlag, New York.

Harding, S. 1986 *The Science Question in Feminism.* Cornell University Press, Ithaca, New York.

Harding, S. 1989 Is there a feminist method? In: Tuana N. (ed.) 1989 *Feminism and Science.* Indiana University Press, Bloomington, Indiana.

Hawkesworth, M. 1989 Knowers, knowing, known: Feminist theory and claims of truth. *Signs* 14(3): 533–57.

Heckman, S. 1990 *Gender and Knowledge: Elements of a Postmodern Feminism.* Polity Press, Cambridge.

Hyde, J. E. 1990 Meta-analysis and the psychology of gender differences. *Signs* 16(1): 55–73.

Lakomski, G. 1989 Against feminist science: Harding and the science question in feminism. *Educ. Phil. Theor.* 21(2): 1–11.

Lakomski, G. (ed.) 1991 Beyond paradigms: Coherentism and holism in educational research. *Int. J. Educ. Res.* 15(6): 499–597.

Lather, P. 1988 Feminist perspectives on empowering research methodologies. *Women's Studies International Forum* 11(6): 569–81.

Mies, M. 1983 Towards a methodology for feminist research. In: Bowles G. and Klein R. D. (eds.) 1983 *Theories of Women's Studies.* Routledge and Kegan Paul, London.

Nelson, L. 1990 *Who Knows: From Quine to a Feminist Empiricism.* Temple University Press, Philadelphia, Pennsylvania.

Nickles, T. 1981 What is a problem that we might solve it? *Synthese* 47(1): 85–118.

Nickles, T. 1987 Methodology, heuristics and rationality. In: Pitt J. and Pera M. (eds.) 1987 *Rational Changes in Science.* Reidel, Dordrecht.

Parlee, M. 1979 Psychology and women. *Signs* 5(1): 121–33.

Peplau, L and Conrad, E. 1989 Beyond nonsexist research: The perils of feminist methods in psychology. *Psychol. Women Q.* 13(4): 379–400.

Reinharz, S. 1983 Experiential analysis: A contribution to feminist research. In: Bowles G. and Klein R. D. (eds.) 1983 *Theories of Women's Studies.* Routledge and Kegan Paul, London.

Rosenau, P. 1992 *Postmodernism and the Social Sciences.* Princeton University Press, Princeton, New Jersey.

Seigfried, C. 1991 Where are all the pragmatist feminists? *Hypatia* 6(2): 1–20.

Stacey, J. 1988 Can there be a feminist ethnography? *Women's Studies International Forum* 11(2): 21–27.

Strauss, A. 1987 *Qualitative Analysis for Social Scientists.* Cambridge University Press, Cambridge.

Thagard, P. 1989 Explanatory coherence. *Behavioral and Brain Sciences* 12(3): 435–67.

Wilkinson, S. 1986 Sighting possibilities: Diversity and commonality in feminist research. In: Wilkinson S. (ed.) 1986 *Feminist Social Psychology.* Open University Press, Milton Keynes.

Wimsatt, W. 1981 Robustness, reliability and overdetermination. In: Brewer M. and Collins B. (eds.) 1981 *Scientific Inquiry and the Social Sciences.* Jossey-Bass, San Francisco, California.

Further reading

Fonow, M. and Cook, J. (eds.) 1991 *Beyond Methodology.* Indiana University Press, Bloomington, Indiana.

Jayaratne, T. E. 1983 The value of quantitative methodology for feminist research. In: Bowles G. and Duelli Kline R. (eds.) 1983 *Theories of Women's Studies.* Routledge and Kegan Paul, London.

Lather, P. 1991 *Getting Smart: Feminist Research and Pedagogy with/in the Postmodern.* Routledge, New York.

Reinharz, S. 1992 *Feminist Methods in Social Research.* Oxford University Press, New York.

Stanley, L. and Wise, S. 1983 *Breaking Out: Feminist Consciousness and Feminist Research.* Routledge and Kegan Paul, London.

Tomm, W. (ed.) 1989 *The Effects of Feminist Approaches on Research Methodologies.* Wilfred Laurier University Press, Waterloo.

21 Measurement in Educational Research

J. P. Keeves

Education is concerned with teaching and learning, but learning outcomes cannot be examined effectively unless the human characteristics, that are changed by learning, can be measured with sufficient accuracy to enable the factors influencing learning to be investigated. Marked developments have occurred in the theory of educational measurement over the past 40 years. However, it is only with the advent of computers, and widespread access to them, that it becomes possible for research workers in education to take advantage of the changes that have occurred in the theory of educational measurement. Both developments in theory and rapid calculation are changing the nature of the research that can be carried out, particularly in the field of learning, but also in many other areas of educational research.

Today, in the late 1990s, powerful computers are now so readily accessible on the office desk or at home, which have the capacity to store large amounts of data, and to carry out complex statistical analyses very rapidly, that the limitations in the conduct of research lie in the effective use of computers in research, rather than in an inability to tackle complex problem situations. Moreover, it is important to recognize that today computers not only facilitate the storage and analysis of data, but also the collection of data both efficiently and accurately through the use of data recording procedures that check the accuracy of the information as it is recorded. Unfortunately, however, the ubiquity of computers and the complex skills required to be mastered for their effective use have led to a polarization of the approaches employed in the conduct of research in education, in particular, into quantitative and qualitative methods. It is necessary from the outset in this article to challenge this artificial and spurious dichotomy, before addressing the issues involved in measurement.

1 Removing the quantitative and qualititative divide

In a discussion of the bifurcation of research methods into the quantitative and the qualitative, four aspects of the issue need to be addressed. First, there is the question of the difference between quantities and qualities. Secondly, there are the distinctions between data that are categorical, categorized and continuous. Thirdly, there are the little considered questions that relate to the analysis of categorical or qualitative data. Finally, there are considerations concerned with the role of measurement in research that are addressed in Section 2.

1.1 Quantities and qualities

It is frequently claimed that there are two different modes of inquiry in education which lead to the quantitative and qualitative approaches to research. However, this simple dichotomy involves a serious failure to understand the nature of both quantities and qualities. Kaplan (see *Scientific Methods in Educational Research*) argues that it is necessary to emphasize that measurement is not an end in itself, it merely performs an instrumental function of inquiry. He also argues that there is a danger of assuming that measures have an inherent value, without regard for the nature of the object being measured, and the intrusion of the observer into the measurement process. Furthermore, there is a tendency to disregard how the number assigned in measurement should be used in analysis. The treatment of measurement as if it had intrinsic scientific value is referred to by Kaplan (1964) as the "mystique of quantity". There is, however, a more persuasive "mystique of quality", which considers that any attempt which is made to measure in educational research is a gross distortion or obfuscation of both objects and events. Those who adhere to this perspective regard qualitative methods as the only meaningful way to investigate an educational problem.

   If these two views are considered as alternatives or even as opposites that are complementary, then a serious misunderstanding of the nature of both quantities and qualities has occurred. Kaplan (1964, p. 207) has clarified the point at issue in the following terms:

> Quantities are *of* qualities, and a measured quality *has* just the magnitude expressed in its measure.

Every measurement demands some degree of abstraction. The assigning of a number to an observable characteristic or relationship requires the refinement of that characteristic or relation before measurements can be made. This is not an assumption of measurement; it is a *requirement* that the characteristic or relation should be accurately specified and should be unidimensional before measurement is attempted.

1.2 Categorical, categorized and continuous data

When the characteristics of individuals and groups are examined, prior to the making of observations and the collecting of data, it is necessary to consider the nature of each particular characteristic and the observations that can be made. For some characteristics of an individual, such as the sex of a student, there are two distinct categories occurring in nature, and the data must be considered to be categorical. However, if observations are to be made and data are to be collected on the influence of educational attainment, or the number of years of education completed, the underlying characteristic involves a continuous variable, but the data are for convenience categorized in terms of years of education completed. Alternatively, if observations are to be made on a student's age, then the data collected involve a continuous measure that can be expressed readily in terms of years and months or possibly further refined to days. These distinctions between categorical, categorized and continuous data are of considerable importance at the stage of data analysis. Moreover, the analytical procedures to be used influence the manner in which data are collected and as a consequence the way in which the research study is conducted and the methods of investigation employed.

It is indeed fortunate that many human characteristics result from the operation of a large number of subordinate factors which give rise to an underlying normal distribution of the characteristic in the population. Likewise, when the characteristics of individuals are aggregated to form the observable characteristic of a group, then the aggregation and averaging of observations at the group level, generally yields a measure that has an underlying normal distribution. While some analytical procedures have to be used with great care if the assumptions of normality and of an underlying interval scale are violated, the problems encountered are being overcome through new approaches to measurement and to the analysis of categorical data. It is here that important developments have occurred in Europe that have not received widespread recognition in North America.

1.3   New methods for the examination of categorical data

In Continental Europe it is widely accepted that much data which are obtained in educational investigations are categorical in nature, and as a consequence analytical procedures have been developed for the examination of categorical data as distinct from categorized or continuous data. Where in the analysis of data associated with a continuous variable, the variance is partitioned into components and analysed systematically, the newly developed analytical techniques seek to analyse and partition the chi-square statistic or preferably the likelihood-ratio statistic into its components. This has led to the development of a family of procedures for statistical analysis which include: (a) CHAID (Kass, 1980; Magidson, 1989) which involves a sample splitting technique; (b) Log-linear modeling (Kennedy, Hak Ping Tam, 1997) which involves the hierarchical analysis of contingency table data; (c) configural frequency analysis (Kristof, 1997; von Eye, 1990; Krauth, 1993) which is a procedure for the identification of types and antitypes in the analysis of cross-classifications; and (d) correspondence analysis (Everitt and Dunn, 1991; Henry, 1997) which involves a procedure for the extraction of principal components from a body of categorical data. There are further analytical procedures for analyzing the hierarchical structure of categorical data which have also been developed in Europe: (a) Galois lattices (Ander, Joó, Mérö, 1997) which involves a graphical method for representing hierarchical structures; and (b) partial order scalogram analysis (Shye, 1997) which is a procedure for analyzing order relations among non-metric data.

2   Advances in measurement

Greater attention is now being paid in the field of educational research to the use of new approaches to measurement, so that more efficient and more powerful procedures for the statistical analysis of data can be employed. Studies in the past have been severely restricted by the inability to measure important predictor and criterion variables with sufficient consistency, other than for performance on multiple choice achievement tests, to achieve strong levels of prediction and explanation. However, advances have been made, through the use of item response theory (Stocking, 1997) and, in particular, the Rasch model (Allerup, 1997; Andrich, 1977) to obtain measures on an interval scale from ratings, attitude scales, and checklists. These developments are largely unknown outside the field of achievement testing where they are now being used in situations where there are groups of research workers with expertise in educational and psychological measurement. In arguing a case for improved measurement in the field of education several issues must be addressed, namely: (a) the advantage of using measurement; (b) single or multiple observations; (c) bandwidth and fidelity; (d) precision in measurement; and (e) Rasch scaling.

2.1   The advantage of using measures

The great advantage of using numbers to specify the degree or extent of a characteristic or relationship is that mathematics has provided the rules and procedures for working with numbers and matrices in order to examine relationships. In addition, statistics has provided the rules and procedures for examining the probabilities with which results might be observed, as well as the levels of magnitude and importance of such results. These mathematical and statistical procedures are necessary, not only because the interrelations between variables in educational research are complex, but also because measurements made in educational research often involve considerable error and require large samples of observations or persons for a hypothesized relationship to be detected. The rules and procedures provided by mathematics and statistics permit both the hypothesizing of relationships between measured variables and the subsequent testing of these hypothesized relationships, together with the estimation of the magnitude of the effects.

2.2   Single or multiple measurements

A general distinction must be drawn between measurements that are made through a single observation or judgment and measurements that are made by combining in an appropriate way multiple observations or judgments. Errors of measurement arise from three distinct sources: (a) variability in the making of the observation or judgment by the observer; (b) variability in the making of the observation or judgment due to the instrument being employed; and (c) variability in the characteristic being measured. Errors arising from the third source demand the making of multiple measurements by the sampling of behaviors or observable phenomena associated with the characteristic or relationship under survey. It is, however, not uncommon to make multiple observations in order to estimate and allow for observer errors and instrumental errors. Such procedures necessarily lead to the combining of the multiple observations in an appropriate way.

Consequently reliance on a single observation or judgment is relatively rare in measurement in both research and practice, and the use of multiple observations is widespread. Substantial problems arise because the multiple observations must be combined. Cronbach (1960), using an analogy with the recording of music, draws attention to the distinction made between *bandwidth* and *fidelity*. Thus in measurement with multiple observations it is necessary that the range of observations employed is sufficiently wide to provide a meaningful indicator of the variability in the characteristic or relationship under investigation. The range of observations is associated with the bandwidth of the recording. However, it is also necessary with multiple observations to ensure that the range of observations employed is sufficiently narrow to provide a high degree of fidelity. Only thus is it possible to ensure that the measurements are unidimensional and that it is meaningful to combine observations. This balance between bandwidth and fidelity becomes increasingly important as advances occur in educational measurement where multiple observations are made.

2.3   Bandwidth and fidelity

The terms, bandwidth and fidelity, have some overlap in meaning with the more technical terms of validity and reliability, but they are not synonymous, with these more familiar terms. Moreover, they are increasingly being used in situations where validity and reliability do not suffice, since they are more directly related to the combining of observations and judgments in the making of measurements.

Fidelity demands that not only should a characteristic or relationship be accurately defined, but the measurements should satisfy the requirement of *unidimensionality*. The development of procedures for confirmatory factor analysis (Spearritt, 1997) provides a rigorous test of unidimensionality, that is based on the variability in the items and in the sample employed. Bejar (1983, p. 31) has, however, drawn attention to the fact that unidimensionality as tested under these conditions does not imply that only a single characteristic is involved in responding or that a single process operates. If several characteristics or processes were to operate in unison, then unidimensionality would also hold. However, if the characteristics or processes did not operate together then it would not be meaningful to assign numbers to any combination of the items employed, unless another operation such as that of prediction, were to provide the rule for combination. If a set of measurements lacked this necessary fidelity, and if several identifiable dimensions were involved, then each dimension would need to be considered separately and a profile of measures recorded.

The idea of *bandwidth* is employed to ensure that there is a sufficient range of manifestations of the characteristic being measured for meaningful representation of that characteristic. If variability exists in the characteristic, a range of instances is required to represent adequately that characteristic. Consequently under some circumstances particular observations can be said to supply redundant information and serve no useful purpose and must be rejected. Observations can also supply information that can be shown not to relate to the specified characteristic and they must also be rejected. Thus, decisions need to be made prior to the undertaking of measurement on the bandwidth of acceptable observations when variability exists in the characteristic being measured.

The power of measurement is that once a characteristic or relationship has been specified in detail and in a meaningful way with sufficient bandwidth and fidelity, then the quantities that are obtained as measures of two objects or events can be compared. Where measurement is made through a single observation, the issues of bandwidth and fidelity do not apply. Consequently, there is a heavy burden placed on the single observation.

The same issues must be considered when multiple observations are made because of random variability due to the observer, or because of the random variability that arises from the instrument employed. Thus, most observations involve error. However, the word "error" implies not a mistake, but like the "knights errant" of old, a wandering around a central position. Where random error is associated with measurement, then statistical procedures can be employed which, according to established conventions, enable greater precision of measurement to be obtained. It is, however, the issues of bandwidth and fidelity that must be tackled in the improvement of measurement in educational research.

2.4   Precision

In educational research it is common to make measurements in the form of graded responses or ratings. It is also common in the use of rating scales to assign numbers to response categories that assume equal spacing, and to assume that the error involved in rating is the same across response categories. It is also generally assumed that greater precision is obtained through the use of a greater number of response categories that have each been carefully specified. In more advanced treatments of measurement in education (Andrich, 1995) it is assumed that categories do not have equal spacing, that errors of assignment to response categories cannot be ignored, and that the response categories employed are meaningful and have been carefully specified. In general, the larger the number of response categories the more precise the measurement. However, there may be a limit to the number of response categories that can be employed effectively in measurement by the observers making the measurement or by respondents to a rating scale.

2.5   Conjoint measurement

One of the major problems in measurement in education is that there is an interaction between the person being measured and the instrument involved in measurement at the time measurements are made. As a consequence the performance of a person is not independent of the measuring instrument employed. This uncertainty or confounding that arises between the person and the instrument is to some degree removed by the procedures of conjoint measurement proposed by Ferguson (see Lawley, 1943) and developed by Rasch (1960). In conjoint measurement it is always the performance of a person relative to a particular task that is being considered in terms of probabilities. Thus, a person's performance level is set at the same level as the difficulty of a task if that person has a specified probability, commonly 50 percent, of responding correctly to the task.

Furthermore, clear benefits would be gained in measurement if the persons measured by an instrument and the tasks in that instrument were located on a common scale. In this way performance with respect to particular tasks could be measured. Specific levels or standards of performance on a scale of this type could also be stated and shown in terms of either the characteristics of the tasks or the characteristics of the persons or alternatively by a defined level on the scale. The logistic transformation of the response odds enables the task and person parameters and their estimated values to be expressed as separate components on the conjoint scale. Conditional probabilities are then used to separate the person parameters from the task calibration, and the task parameters from the estimation of the person parameters. The requirement for this estimation procedure to provide meaningful results would be that both the tasks and the persons must fit a unidimensional model and behave in a consistent way across different samples.

It should be noted that the Rasch scale is not only an interval scale, but also has its own natural metric, with the scale unit referred to as a logit. All that is requires is that a fixed point should be specified in order to determine the location of the scale. In addition, the errors involved in the estimation of both the task difficulty parameters and the person performance parameters are obtained for each individual task and person, rather than for the instrument as a whole, provided conditions of independence of observation of tasks and persons are maintained. This scaling procedure eliminates the dependence of the task parameters on the sample of persons used in calibration, and the dependence of the person parameters on the sample of tasks used. Under these circumstances, the scale so formed has some properties of an absolute scale, but fails to have an absolute zero, being an interval, but not a ratio scale. Such a scale has substantial advantages in educational measurement, with the only requirement that the tasks and the persons used in the calibration of the scale must satisfy the conditions of unidimensionality.

2.6   The advantages of Rasch measurement

Some of the immediately obvious advantages of Rasch scaling in educational and sociological measurement can be listed. First, different instruments measuring the same underlying dimension can be readily equated through common tasks or common persons. Secondly, bias associated with specific tasks can be readily identified. Thirdly, persons with inconsistent behavior can also be easily identified since a particular person might be expected to respond correctly to those tasks whose difficulty levels are below that person's level of performance and to respond incorrectly to those tasks at a higher level of performance.

Furthermore, these scaling procedures can be employed for the rating of a set of tasks where there is: (a) a dichotomous rating of "can perform the task" or "cannot perform the task" (using the simple Rasch model) (Allerup, 1997); (b) a polychotomous rating associated with frequency of performance or degree of success in performance, without necessarily equal spacing on the scale between response categories (using the rating scale model (Andrich, 1997); (c) a polychotomous rating scheme with different numbers of ratings for different tasks (using the partial credit model) (Masters, 1997); (d) discontinuities in levels of performance (using the saltus model) (Wilson, 1997); (e) differences between different raters or judges (using the facet model) (Linacre, 1997); and (f) in situations where more than one dimension is involved (using a multidimensional model) (Swaminathan, 1997). The necessary requirement is that the tasks that are employed to form a particular scale must satisfy tests of unidimensionality. Under certain circumstances it may be necessary to eliminate persons and tasks from the calibration of a scale. However, it is commonly possible to estimate the level of performance of persons who perform correctly all tasks, or alternatively none of the tasks, or omit specific tasks.

It should also be noted that these procedures can be applied to the scaling of attitudes and values as well as to ratings of performance, or views towards a specific object or the climate of an institution, provided that the components forming the scale satisfy the conditions for unidimensionality. The benefits of the use of these scaling procedures are those of measurement on an interval scale, and a generality of measurement that extends beyond the particular tasks considered and the particular sample of persons under investigation.

The strengths of the Rasch model lie in the simplicity of the algebra involved as well as in the extension of the model to cover a range of situations. No longer is unidimensionality a restriction, provided a limited number of dimensions has been hypothesized, and the items and persons are constrained to these dimensions. There is no place for noise or for items and persons that do not conform to the dimensions specified in a model. If the necessary requirements of the model are satisfied, the benefits are substantial and involve the shift from deterministic approaches to measurement in education to probabilistic and stochastic models in order to advance the accuracy of measurement. There remain some limitations associated with a ceiling or floor for a particular instrument when respondents answer correctly all items or no items respectively. However, the ceilings or floors are false in so far as the use of further items that conform to the unidimensional scale involved would permit the accurate estimation of performance. Thus, unlike classical test theory, where the test or instrument is the scale, in Rasch scaling the scale is independent of the items in the test and the sample employed in calibration.

3   Conclusion

It must be recognized that problems are encountered if a latent trait under consideration does not remain invariant over the population being investigated. However, the capability exists to develop a scale that has the property of invariance, as well as to construct multidimensional scales. Insufficient work has been carried out in the field of education into the use of such scale sot determine the limitations imposed on the research questions that can be meaningfully investigated. In addition, further research is required into the robustness of scales measuring general educational characteristics and behavior in contrast to tightly defined cognitive abilities and educational achievement as well as the validity of the results obtained under different circumstances. Nevertheless, the potential exists for research in this area because computer programs for the necessary analyses are now readily available. Particular benefits are likely to arise from the repeated measurement of performance over time with scales that make allowance for the learning that might occur. From such measurements over more than two occasions, stability and change in human characteristics can be more effectively investigated.

References

Allerup, P. 1997 Rasch measurement theory. In: J. P. Keeves (ed.) *Educational Research, Methodology and Measurement. An International Handbook,* 2nd edn. Elsevier, Oxford.

Ander, C., Joó, A and Mérö, L. 1997 Galois Lattices. In: J. P. Keeves (ed.) *Educational Research, Methodology and Measurement. An International Handbook,* 2nd edn. Elsevier, Oxford.

Andrich, D. 1995 Models for measurement, precision and the non-dichotomization of graded responses. *Psychometrika,* 60, 7–26. Further remarks on the non-dichotomization of graded responses. *Psychometrika,* 60, 37–46.

Andrich, D. 1997 Rating scale analysis. In: J. P. Keeves (ed.) *Educational Research, Methodology, and Measurement. An International Handbook,* 2nd edn. Elsevier, Oxford.

Bejar, I. I. 1983 *Achievement Testing: Recent Advances.* Sage, Beverly Hills, California and London.

Cronbach, L. J. 1960 *Essentials of Psychological Testing.* Harper and Rowe, New York.

Everitt, B. S. and Dunn, G. 1992 *Applied Multivariate Data Analysis.* Edward Arnold, London.

Henry, G. 1997 Correspondence analyses of qualitative data. In: J. P. Keeves (ed.) *Educational Research, Methodology and Measurement. An International Handbook,* 2nd edn. Elsevier, Oxford.

Kaplan, A. 1964 *The Conduct of Inquiry.* Chandler, San Francisco.

Kass, G. 1980 An exploratory technique for investigating large quantities of categorical data. *Applied Statistics,* 9, 119–127.

Kennedy, J. J. and Hak Ping, Tam 1997 Log-linear models. In: J. P. Keeves (ed.) *Educational Research, Methodology and Measurement. An International Handbook,* 2nd edn. Elsevier, Oxford.

Krauth, J. 1993 *Einführing in die Konfigurations – Frequenz Analyse (KFA).* Beltz, München.

Kristof, W. 1997 Configural frequency analysis of categorical data. In: J. P. Keeves (ed.) *Educational Research, Methodology and Measurement. An International Handbook,* 2nd edn. Elsevier, Oxford.

Lawley, D. N. 1943 On problems connected with item selection and test construction. *Proc. Royal Soc. Edcn.* 61: 273–87.

Linacre, M. J. 1997 Judgments, measurement of. In: J. P. Keeves (ed.) *Educational Research, Methodology and Measurement. An International Handbook,* 2nd edn. Elsevier, Oxford.

Magidson, J. 1989 *Statistical Package in Social Science/PC + CHAID.* SPSS, Chicago, Illinois.

Masters, G. N. 1997 Partial credit model. In: J. P. Keeves (ed.) *Educational Research, Methodology and Measurement. An International Handbook,* 2nd edn. Elsevier, Oxford.

Rasch, G. 1960 *Probabilistic Models for Some Intelligence and Attainment Tests* (reprinted 1980). University of Chicago Press, Chicago, Illinois.

Shye, S. 1997 Partial order scalogram analyses of non-metric data. In: J. P. Keeves (ed.) *Educational Research, Methodology and Measurement. An International Handbook,* 2nd edn. Elsevier, Oxford.

Spearritt, D. 1997 Factor analysis. In: J. P. Keeves (ed.) *Educational Research, Methodology and Measurement. An International Handbook*, 2nd edn. Elsevier, Oxford.

Stocking, M. L. 1997 Item response theory. In: J. P. Keeves (ed.) *Educational Research, Methodology and Measurement. An International Handbook,* 2nd edn. Elsevier, Oxford.

Swaminathan, H. 1997 Latent trait measurement models. In: J. P. Keeves (ed.) *Educational Research, Methodology and Measurement. An International Handbook,* 2nd edn. Elsevier, Oxford.

von Eye, A. 1990 *Introduction to Configural Frequency Analysis.* Cambridge University Press, Cambridge.

Wilson, M. 1997 Developmental levels, measurement of. In: J. P. Keeves (ed.) *Educational Research, Methodology and Measurement. An International Handbook,* 2nd edn. Elsevier, Oxford.

22 Postmodernism

J. Marshall and M. Peters

"Postmodernism" is an increasingly used term to describe certain intellectual and cultural tendencies. Its use remains somewhat controversial. In this article the ideas of three postmodernist thinkers are introduced, and the direct implications of their works for education identified. There are also implicit implications, for they discuss knowledge and its legitimation (which is relevant for thinking about the nature of the school curriculum), and there are discussions which bring into question liberal notions of freedom through rational autonomy.

1 Defining the postmodern

The term "postmodernism" surfaced in the 1930s and 1940s mainly in relation to the arts, including architecture and history (Rose, 1991). However, to talk of modernism and postmodernism as periods or epochs implies by itself a modernist stance, namely, that it is possible to delineate the characteristics of a period and, thereby, to be beyond that period. It may be better to see postmodernism as a complex intellectual map of late-twentieth-century thought and practice rather than any clear-cut philosophic, political and/or aesthetic movement.

Is the distinction between the modern and the postmodern a polemical or a philosophical distinction? If it is the latter, and a "Kuhnian"-style paradigm shift is occurring in philosophy (see *Research Paradigms in Education: Research in Education: Epistemological Issues; Phenomenology and Existentialism*), then some philosophers may be "left behind". The paradigm shift question has been formulated and debated by, among others, Lyotard and Habermas. Whereas Lyotard rejoices in the shift away from post-Enlightenment thought and the philosophical "certainty" of meta-narratives, Habermas wishes to preserve what was important in the Enlightenment's view of reason. Jameson begins his foreword to Lyotard (1984) by saying: "[postmodernism] involves a radical break, both with dominant culture and aesthetic, and with a rather different moment of socio-economic organization against which its structural novelties and innovations are measured: a new social or economic moment (or even system)." Lyotard's (1984) well-known definition is that "postmodern" is an "incredulity towards meta-narratives" (a meta-narrative being a theoretical or justificatory discussion about narratives or "lower level" discourse or practices). It is this sense of the term which will be followed below.

2   Postmodernists

Whilst three French thinkers are identified as representatives of postmodernism, it should not be assumed either that they are exclusively representatives of postmodernism, or that they share anything in common other than this label (which itself is a modern "object").

2.1   Lyotard and the postmodern condition

Lyotard's (1984) major hypothesis maintains that the status of knowledge is altered as societies enter what is known as the postindustrial age and cultures enter what is called the postmodern age. He uses the term "post modern" to describe the condition of knowledge in the most developed societies. He follows sociologists and critics who have used the term to designate the state of Western culture "following the transformations which, since the end of the nineteenth century, have altered the game rules for science, literature and the arts" (1984, p. 3). Lyotard places these transformations within the context of the crisis of narratives, especially those Enlightenment meta-narratives concerning meaning and emancipation which have been used to legitimate both the rules of knowledge of the sciences and the foundations of institutions.

By "transformations", Lyotard is referring principally to the effects of the new technologies since the 1950s and their combined impact on the two functions of knowledge – research and the transmission of learning. Significantly, the leading sciences and technologies have all been based on language-related developments – theories of linguistics, cybernetics, informatics, computer languages, telematics, theories of algebra – and their miniaturization and commercialization. In this changed context the status of knowledge is permanently altered: its availability as an international commodity becomes the basis for national, commercial, and military competitive advantage and security. Knowledge has become the principal force of production, changing the composition of the workforce in developed countries. The commercialization of knowledge will further widen the gap between nation-states and the information-rich multinationals, thereby raising new legal, ethical, political, and educational problems.

2.2   The legitimation of knowledge

As knowledge becomes a question of government, the problem of legitimation necessarily arises: who decides what is "true" or "scientific"? The post-modernist maintains that knowledge and power are simply two sides of the same question. The problem of legitimation is highlighted with a recognition of the crises of narratives and specifically the inability of the sciences to legitimate themselves by reference to the grand narrative of philosophy. Postmodernism is characterized by an incredulity towards meta-narratives – a distrust of stories which purport to justify certain practices or institutions by grounding them upon a set of transcendental, ahistorical, or universal principles. The postmodern concept of knowledge begins with skepticism about the rules of consensus: that the truth value of a statement between the sender and addressee is acceptable if there is unanimity between rational minds. The crisis of narratives is symbolized in the postmodern dispersal of language elements. There is no universal meta-language, for there are many languages – a multiplicity of language games with each specific pragmatic valencies. Lyotard's reading of Wittgenstein emphasizes the pluralistic and incommensurable nature of language games, each with its body of rules defining its properties and uses (Lyotard 1988). There is an agonistics of language in which utterances are understood not as the transmission of information or messages, but rather as an unstable exchange between communicational adversaries. The rules do not have a bedrock justification; they are the object of a contract between players. If there are no rules, there is no game. Every utterance is a "move" in the game where to speak is to fight (in the sense of playing). Progress in knowledge is conceived of in two ways: the first is construed as a new move within the established rules; the second is construed as the invention of new rules, that is, the development of a new game.

This basic conflict model of language, then, challenges the rules of consensus – not only as it underlies the Enlightenment narrative of the hero of knowledge working towards good ethico-political ends, but also contemporary accounts of the fully transparent communicational society as advanced by Habermas, on the basis of the ideal speech community, where validity claims are said to be discursively redeemable at the level of discourse. The conflict model is ultimately unused for understanding the nature of the social bond: everyone lives at the intersection of many games.

The interpretation of language games as heteronomous (untranslatable) and paralogous (undermining rules) shatters the grand legitimating meta-narrative of science as the supreme voice of reason. Science is not only incapable of legitimating other language games but is incapable of legitimating itself, and metaphysical philosophy is forced to relinquish its role as legitimizer in face of the proliferation and splintering of language games. The idea of modernity, of science as the exemplification of rationality, is revealed as just one narrative among others – the grand narrative, but one which has broken apart and splintered into many different forms.

In the postmodern age, however, decision makers still proceed on the assumption that there is commensurability and that the whole is determinable. The legitimation of knowledge is formulated in terms of performativity. Increasingly, science has fallen under the sway of another game, technology, whose goal is not truth, but optimal performance, and whose criteria are minimizing input and maximizing output, rather than truth or justice. Research and progress in knowledge are relegitimated in terms of the performative or efficiency criterion.

2.3   Michel Foucault

Foucault attempts to avoid the trap of thinking in terms of epochs by viewing Enlightenment (following Kant) as an attitude. While he did not care much for the term, "modernity", which for him refers to a form of "post-Enlightenment slumber" whereby Kant's notion of modernity as an attitude has been reified into a certain view of humankind – the version of human nature to be found in the social sciences – and also into a certain view of rationality (post Descartes, Rousseau, and Kant). On these issues, and in his associated treatment of governmentality, Foucault (1979b) presents a dark face of the Enlightenment and the path it has taken.

Foucualt (1984) believed that by following Kant's attitude and critically interrogating the present, there is a way out. He does not accept the Enlightenment view of the improvement of human beings through the advancement of reason, for he rejects the form that reason has taken. In his first major book (1961), he launches an attack upon Western reason – and on Descartes in particular, arguing that by excluding madness in the *Meditations* Descartes has attempted to confine reason, thereby limiting the potential of the imagination (see also Foucault 1986c), and limiting creativity and freedom.

Nevertheless, Foucault maintains that there is no universal form that reason must take. Rather, there are multiplicities of reason, and multiplicities of theories in relation to specific local issues. If there are no meta-narratives, in this sense, then the role of intellectuals must be local and specific (see 1972a). Yet, Foucault believes, Kant was correct in urging that theory must be critical. Slumber was caused by a failure to continually respond to socio-historical conditions and failure to question the development of responses to human dilemmas through the critical questioning of the application of universal reason. Hence a source of his objections to Marxism and Sartre, for example.

Rather than reason unfolding, Foucault the archeologist would say (1972b), arbitrary formations of discourse – especially those which he designates as the human sciences – have frozen Kant's notion of an unfolding freedom and everyone has become embroiled in a senseless dynamic of power (modern power or bio-power) which continues to dominate and subjugate them as human beings (1979b). These arbitrary discourses are the result of the breakdown of the notion of language as representation (1970) and its dispersion and fragmentation. To be modern is to attempt to control this dispersion and fragmentation. Yet Foucault takes no general stand (1970, p. 307).

The human being, as the knowing subject and the object of knowledge of the human sciences, was, according to Foucault, permitted to emerge by the decline of the classical regime (at the end of the eighteenth century). Foucault believes that the modern individual has in part been "constructed" by techniques of examination, measurement, and categorization in disciplinary blocs by professionals in the human sciences; so individuals are normalized, that is, they become beings who lead useful, docile, and practical lives because they are politically dominated or subjugated (1979a).

Modern individuals also construct themselves through care of the self (Foucault 1980, 1986a, 1986b). The way out is to reject the "truths" of the human sciences in care of the self, thereby promoting forms of freedom different from the morally autonomous person of Kant and modern pedagogy. This is an aesthetic attitude towards personal identity. Foucault is not rejecting modernity *simpliciter*, but only those practices and discourses within the Enlightenment tradition that he calls "humanism" (as against Habermas's [1981] interpretation of a total rejection).

Foucault has been criticized for not providing norms for distinguishing between dominating and nondominating forms of power/discourse. On Foucault's grounds, it is only possible to distinguish intensity of domination and, lacking some normative stance, it is unclear when resistance is the proper ethical or political path to adopt. Furthermore, with no normative stance, it is not clear how one can engage the complex problems of modern societies. If, indeed, one can resist oppressive forms of power, this is not to give insight into the ways in which the problems and issues which resulted in such exercises of power can be resolved.

2.4 Derrida and deconstructionism

Deconstruction begins by questioning the almost received assumption that "philosophy" is a superior kind of truth, especially in relation to literature. This claim can be traced to Plato and his attack upon poetry as a form of irrational seizure (Norris, 1983, p. 1). It denies that philosophy has a privileged access to truth which literature does not, or which literature can only pervert or destroy. It is not, however, a mere traditional defense as mounted, for example, by Shelley, for these also are undermined by deconstructionism.

Hermeneutics (see *Hermeneutics*) goes beyond the foundationalism of Kantian epistemology (especially the privileged position of speaker and/or author) to claim that understanding involves an interpretation. Deconstruction claims that any system of thought is itself based upon contradictions. "Any reading" must therefore be capable of multiple and contradictory readings. Thus, texts do not just say "something" but many different things, some of which may be contrary to the writer's intentions. Texts do not have meanings which can be "read off"; for the traditional relationship between text and meaning is severed, and Derrida's deconstruction shows that the text can tell a different, new story.

Derrida stressed how different his position was from hermeneutics and used the term "grammatology" to capture this difference. His critical readings of texts – and of philosophy in general (1982 – were designed to bring out the underlying contradictions that undermine the apparent coherence of texts and philosophical systems. Following Nietzsche, he rejected binary logic (the principles of identity and noncontradiction) and read philosophy as a history of certain oppositions privileging one side of the binary opposition and establishing a "violent hierarchy" and "order of subordination". This hierarchy must be overturned, he felt, but not in a simple valorization of the opposing pole.

Derrida's starting points (1981) are basic words which have different and opposed meanings and syntactic contexts in which one of the meanings is not unequivocally eliminated. Because "the" meaning cannot be determined from the context, this opens up a play of possibilities of different and contrary readings of the text. Thereby texts are deconstructed. Foucault (1983) criticized Derrida for ignoring social practices that texts employ and reflect.

Derrida, along with Foucault and Lyotard, sees the traditional metaphysic of Western philosophy as being at an end. It is not so clear that he sees philosophy *per se* as being ended, but he certainly concentrates on the periphery of traditional philosophy (1982), on metaphor and rhetoric, rather than the central logical and epistemological concerns within the tradition. Along with Foucault, he attacks the humanistic notion of humankind central to phenomenology, existentialism, and some versions of Marxism.

3 Educational implications

Foucault's critique of the human sciences directs the attention toward how education shapes individual subjects, normalizing them through the exercise of power/knowledge in disciplinary blocs. There are strong implications here for issues related to gender and education. Foucualt provides a sharp critique of the notion of the morally autonomous person and of the roles of educational professionals in shaping identities. He directs attention at the use of power in education, rather than taking the traditional liberal approach to notions of social control and control of knowledge through discussions of authority (see Ball 1990). He provides a basis for analyzing the relations between truth and power in educational discourse and discursive practices (see 1983).

Lyotard's critique also covers the natural sciences. His account of knowledge and its changed form of legitimation has implications for education, for it will change the ways in which learning is acquired, stored, assessed, and classified. Learning, no longer entirely falling within the purview of the state, will be geared toward the production of knowledge to be sold. Knowledge is exteriorized with respect to the "knower," and the status of the learner and teacher is transformed into a commodity relationship of "supplier" and "consumer". Knowledge ceases to be an end in itself. On the basis of Lyotard's critiques, theorists would want to identify the main meta-narratives in education and the ways in which they have excluded local knowledge.

Derrida poses questions about the curriculum – and curriculum priorities – with his emphases on literature, rhetoric, and metaphor, rather than logic, mathematics, and the priority of the senses for knowledge and understanding.

All three writers emphasize the plurality of reason, the demise of grand totalizing theory, and the march of modern power and technocratic rationality.

An effect of the march of technocratic rationality has been a crisis of value. Conservatives have attempted to reassert traditional values in education, as elsewhere, blaming postmodernist tendencies for this crisis. Postmodernism, however, would merely assert that values cannot be legitimated by meta-narratives, nor that there are no values to be held.

References

Ball, S. (ed.) 1990 *Foucault and Education: Disciplines and Knowledge*. Routledge, London.
Derrida, J. 1981b *Dissemination*. Athlone Press, London.
Derrida, J. 1981a (trans. Bass A.) *Positions*. Chicago University Press, Chicago, Illinois.
Foucault, M. 1961 *Folie et Deraison: l'Histoire de la Folie a l'Age Classique*. Plon, Paris.
Foucault, M. 1970 *The Order of Things*. Tavistock Publications, London.
Foucault, M. 1972a Intellectuals and Power. In: Foucault M. and Bouchard D. (eds.) 1977 *Language, Counter-Memory, Practice*. Cornell University Press, Ithaca, New York.
Foucault, M. 1972b *The Archaeology of Knowledge*. Tavistock, London.
Foucault, M. 1979b On governmentality. *Ideology and Consciousness* 6: 5–26.
Foucault, M. 1980 *The History of Sexuality*, Vol. 1, Vintage, New York.
Foucault, M. 1983 Afterward: The subject and power. In: Dreyfus H. L. and Rabinow P. (eds.) 1983 *Michel Foucault: Beyond Structuralism and Hermeneutics*. University of Chicago Press, Chicago, Illinois.
Foucualt, M. 1984 What is enlightenment? In: Rabinow P. (ed.) 1984 *The Foucault Reader*. Pantheon, New York.
Foucualt, M. 1986a *The Use of Pleasure*. Penguin, Harmondsworth.
Foucualt, M. 1986b *The Care of the Self*. Penguin, Harmondsworth.
Foucault, M. 1986c Introduction to Binswanger Ludwig 1986 *Dream and Existence. Review of Existential Psychology and Psychiatry*.
Habermas, J. 1981 Modernity versus postmodernity. *New German Critique* 22: 3–14.
Lyotard, J.-F. 1934 *The Post Modern Condition: A Report of Knowledge*. University of Minnesota Press, Minneapolis, Minnesota.
Lyotard, J.-F. 1988 *The Differend*. Manchester University Press, Manchester.
Norris, C. 1983 *The Deconstructive Turn: Essays in the Rhetoric of Philosophy*. Methuen, London.
Rose, M. A. 1991 *The Post Modern and the Post Industrial*. Cambridge University Press, Cambridge.

Further reading

Derrida, J. 1963 Cogito and the history of madness. In: Derrida J. (ed.) 1978 *Writing and Difference*. University of Chicago Press, Chicago, Illinois.
Derrida, J. 1977 *Of Grammatology*. Johns Hopkins University Press, Baltimore, Maryland.
Eribon, D. 1991 *Michel Foucault*. Harvard University Press, Cambridge, Massachusetts.
Foucault, M. 1971 *The Discourse on Language*. In: Foucault 1972b.
Foucault, M. 1979a *Discipline and Punishment: The Birth of the Prison*. Penguin Books, Harmondsworth.
Hoy, D. C. (ed.) 1986 *Foucault: A Critical Reader*. Basil Blackwell, Oxford.
McLaren, P. (ed.) 1991 Post-modernism, post-colonialism and pedagogy. *Education and Society* 9(2): special issue, parts I and II.
Nicholson, L. (ed.) 1990 *Post-Modernism/Feminism*. Routledge, London.
Peters, M. and Marshall, J. 1992 Beyond the philosophy of the subject: Liberalism, education and the critique of individualism. *Educ. Phil. Theor.* 25(1): 19–39.

23 Positivism, Antipositivism, and Empiricism

D. C. Phillips

During the closing decades of the twentieth century, members of the international educational research community have displayed a growing interest in the philosophical underpinnings of their work – especially of the methodological aspects. One line of evidence for this is readily available in the pages of the *Educational Researcher*, the "house journal" of the American Educational Research Association, where since the mid-1970s a large number of articles on philosophical and methodological matters have appeared, many written by nonphilosophers; another indication is the special issue of the *International Journal of Educational Research*, which, in 1991, was given over entirely to philosophical issues in research (Lakomski, 1991). Special symposia have even been held to allow researchers to discuss these matters (see Guba, 1990). Amongst the topics most frequently referred to has been the "demise of positivism" (see, for example, Phillips, 1983; Miller and Fredericks, 1991; Schrag, 1992); in much of this literature, however, there has been confusion about the relationships between positivism, logical positivism, and empiricism, and also about how these positions relate to realism and relativism. This article will focus upon the former group of topics, while the latter are the subject of separate discussion.

1 Empiricism

Empiricism is one of the two major, classic positions in epistemology – the other being rationalism, which crudely put, holds that the main underpinning of human knowledge is the "light of reason". (Descartes is a quintessential figure in the history of rationalism; as is well-known, he searched through his ideas to find one which was clear and distinct to the light of reason, and which could not be doubted. Thus he arrived at his famous "cogito ergo sum", which become the ultimate foundation for his knowledge.) Both classic positions are complex, in the sense that within each there are many subschools of thought.

Empiricism, according to one authority, may be characterized as "Any of a variety of views to the effect that either our concepts or our knowledge are, wholly or partly, based on experience through the senses and introspection. The basing may refer to psychological origin or, more usually, philosophical justification" (Lacey, 1976, p. 55).

Thus, one form of empiricism holds that human knowledge originates from sense experience; a representative figure here is the British philosopher of the seventeenth century, John Locke, who held that at birth the mind of the individual was a "tabula rasa" (blank tablet) – and that the origin of every simple idea could be traced to sense experience or to introspection (inner experience). Locke had a view that later followers came to call "mental chemistry", for he envisioned simple ideas being combined in various ways to form more and more complex ideas; but there was no idea whose genealogy could not be traced back down the descending path from complex to simple to eventual origin in sense experience. A person who had never experienced the color lilac could not have the idea of lilac (although the person might know the word "lilac" from having heard or read it).

Thus, for Locke, the sequence of knowledge – growth was as follows: a newborn baby, devoid of ideas but with a cognitive mechanism that was potentially able to manipulate and work with ideas (a crucial point), might experience coldness, loudness, redness, and roundness (from the surrounding environment, a toy hanging over the crib, and so forth), and these would give rise to the corresponding simple ideas; gradually complex ideas like "red ball" would be built up – but only if the requisite simple ideas had been formed. Introspection, or reflection, or inner experience, would similarly produce simple ideas like "pain" or "anger". As should be evident, Locke was a strong opponent of the view that there could be innate ideas.

As the quotation from Lacey indicates, however, there are other forms of empiricism. A person might be more interested in the question of justification than of origin. Consider the claim that unadulterated water, at normal pressure, boils at 100°C. A narrow Lockean might want to emphasize the fact that the concepts here – "water", "boils", "pressure", and so on – must all have had their ultimate origin in sense experience; but others (and, for that matter, a Lockean as well) might want to know what justifies or warrants this particular claim – why is pure water believed to boil at 100°C rather than at 90°C? Empiricists would want to say that this claim is justified by experience, or by the empirical evidence that is available.

At first sight, this justificatory version of empiricism has a lot going for it – for it is hard to see how any philosopher could advocate a position that did not in some way allow for the fact that knowledge of the world must be constrained in some fashion by the way the world is, or appears to be. (Even so strong a contemporary critic of simplistic empiricism as Paul Feyerabend admits that he is prepared to march in company with empiricism at least this far; see Feyerabend, 1980.) In the second half of the twentieth century, however, some severe problems have come to the fore, especially as philosophers have pursued issues of justification with respect to the theoretical knowledge of the advanced sciences.

2   Challenges to empiricism

Perhaps the most important challenge to empiricism has been the realization that the items constituting knowledge – theories, hypotheses, and so on – are always undetermined by the evidence that is available. In other words, knowledge always goes beyond the evidence; or, to turn the point around, the evidence at hand is always compatible with a variety of theories or hypotheses. So it cannot be claimed that the belief in theory T1 is justified by a particular body of empirical evidence, because theories T2, T3, and so on, are also justified or warranted by this same evidence. To take an oversimple example, one might claim to know what there is a golf ball lying on the table, and by way of justification one offers the fact that one experiences seeing the ball there. However, another person may claim that it is not a golf ball, but a hologram; and another might offer the opinion that it is one of those light plastic replicas that are sometimes used to play practical jokes on golfers. The point is, the evidence that warrants one's own claim can also be used to warrant the other people's. If new evidence is collected, these alternative theories may be ruled out, but others might be dreamt up that are still compatible with the finite body of evidence that is available. These rival theories might be ruled out on the grounds that they are unreasonable or improbable, given the situation in which the observations are being made, but then it is evident that the knowledge that this is indeed a golf ball is based on more than the empirical evidence that is available – for some additional principle or principles have also been drawn on (in this example, concerning what is reasonable or probable under the circumstances). (For an important discussion of the limitations of the argument concerning underdetermination, see Laudan, 1990.)

Another problem concerns the status of theoretical entitles; such things as quarks, or subnuclear forces, are not directly observable, and to claim that they are "indirectly" observable is also to oversimplify the chains of reasoning involved. How, then, can it be claimed that knowledge of these things "originates" in experience, or is "justified" by experience? Locke's successor Hume (1711–76) raised a similar issue about knowledge of causation in nature: Causes are not actually observed at work, rather what is seen is mere "constant conjunction" (event A seems always to be followed by event B). As a consequence of all this, there is an antirealist tendency for empiricism to lead to the view that the only realities are the empirically observable phenomena, and that the entitles postulated within theoretical physics are "convenient fictions." (Empiricists differ over this, and other, matters.)

A further difficulty for empiricisms of both types outlined above is the fact that observation, or the gathering of empirical evidence, is not the pristine process that is presupposed by such philosophies. The varieties of empiricism discussed above make the assumption that sense experience is unadulatered, in that it is completely uncontaminated by theory; after all, experience can hardly be the origin of knowledge, or the justificatory "court" to which one appeals when one is asked to warrant knowledge claims, if prior beliefs or theories or knowledge can be shown to have influenced it. This is precisely what has been shown (by Wittgenstein, Popper, Hanson, Kuhn, and others; see Phillips, 1987 for further discussion) – observation is theory-laden, and is not theory-neutral. What is seen (or felt or heard or tasted or smelled), and how it is seen (or felt . . .), is influenced by knowledge the experiencer already possesses.

Finally, given the centrality of the notion of "experience," it has been crucial for empiricists to grapple with the issue of what is actually experienced during experience. Different answers have been forthcoming: only sense data are experienced (such things as "red patch here now," although the precise formulation is a matter of learned debate); actual objects are directly experienced; objects and the relations between them are experienced.

As a result of these and other problems (see Morrick 1980), an epistemological position known as non-foundationalism or nonjustificationism has been developed by (Popper and others), according to which knowledge is not to be regarded as being based upon some indubitable and neutral foundation such as experience or the light of reason; rather, those theories or hypotheses that have been adequately tested are tentatively accepted as knowledge – with the caveat that no knowledge is ever absolutely established. Knowledge, in short, is inherently hypothetical (which is not to say that people do not usually have substantial reasons for believing the things that they do) (see *Research in Education; Epistemological Issues*).

3   Positivism

Positivism – itself a complex of several subpositions – is merely one form of empiricism, despite the fact that critics of positivism in educational research tend to identify it as being coextensive with empiricism. In other words, while all forms of positivism are forms of empiricism, it is a mistake to infer back that all empiricisms are forms of positivism. As a consequence, not all problems facing positivism necessarily face other forms of empiricism.

The term "positivist" is used very loosely in the contemporary educational research literature to which reference was made at the outset: it has become a more or less generalized and vague term of abuse. A positivist is likely to be identified, *inter alia*, as someone who is an empiricist, a realist, a believer in the value of objectivity in research, a believer that truth is a sustainable ideal for research, an adherent of the experimental method, a supporter of quantitative/statistical methods, and a skeptic about qualitative methodologies. That such identifications are fantasies, and in some cases are directly the opposite of the true state of affairs, generally escapes notice. Certainly positivists believe a few of the things here attributed to them, but so do many others – so once again it is invalid to argue backwards and infer that anyone who holds one of these particular positions must be a positivist. Furthermore it is hard to follow the logic that leads to the conclusion that a positivist must be a lover of statistical methods and an opponent of qualitative/observational studies.

Classic positivism can be traced back to the writings of the Frenchman Comte (1798–1857), who in a multivolume work developed a position with three important prongs. First, that human knowledge has developed through three stages marked in each case by the distinctive way knowledge was established – the theological or fictitious stage, the metaphysical or abstract stage, and the scientific or positive stage (Comte, 1970, p. 1). Clearly, in Comte's view, the third stage is the one which is epistemologically most adequate.

Second, that the "positive sciences" can be classified in a manner which displays their mutual dependence (and which also relates to the order in which they have been developed) – mathematics, astronomy, physics, chemistry, physiology, and social physics (sociology) (Comte, 1970, pp. 46–52).

Third, that scientific knowledge "gives up the search after the origin and hidden causes of the universe and a knowledge of the final causes of phenomena" (Comte, 1970, p. 2). Instead, science focuses upon observation, and what can be gleaned by reasoning about observed phenomena. (This was his "positive" method.) Here it is clear that Comte was trying – unsuccessfully – to avoid the problem of classic empiricism concerning the status of inferred theoretical entities; by eschewing the search for hidden causes in nature, he worked himself into the same corner as Locke and Hume. Comte may have allowed scientists to reason, but he did not encourage their thoughts to wander too far from the realm of the observable. (For further discussion, see Phillips, 1992, Chap. 7.)

Comte's work had a marked impact on late-nineteenth- and early-twentieth-century thought about the nature of the sciences (and especially about the social sciences).

4 Logical positivism

It is clear that Comte's ideas were strongly empiricist, and that they had an antimetaphysical thrust – as indicated by his refusal to condone the search for "hidden causes" or "final causes". These interrelated elements were taken even further by an interdisciplinary group that formed in the 1920s around Mortiz Schlick in Vienna – a group that became known as the Vienna Circle. Schlick came from physics, Carnap and Waissman from mathematics and philosophy, Neurath from sociology, Godel and Hahn from mathematics, Kraft from history, Frank from physics. Later Reichenbach, Hempel, and Ayer, among others, became associated with the group; Karl Popper was resident in Vienna then, but was a strong critic of their ideas (this is significant, for anti-positivists in the educational literature sometimes include Popper among the logical positivists). The early work of Wittgenstein was a great stimulus to the group, especially his "picture theory" of language, according to which the logical structure of meaningful statements must be directly isomorphic with the elements in reality (Wittgenstein 1961).

The group flourished into the 1930s, when the rise of Hitler and the murder of Schlick by a deranged student (who was not prosecuted by the authorities) led to its disbandment; many members took refuge in the English-speaking world. Their ideas became very influential, especially in North America where they shaped the image of the nature of science for several decades: the young Skinner met logical positivism (or logical empiricism, as it was sometimes called) while a graduate student, and his behaviorism clearly bears its stamp (Skinner, 1953). The physicist Bridgman also succumbed, and developed his operationism; as a result of his work, the need for researchers to clarify their concepts by means of operational definitions (i.e., by precise specification of the procedures to be used in measuring them) became an item of faith.

Like Comte before them, the logical positivists were strongly antimetaphysical; and to expunge all traces of metaphysical from science they hit upon the stratagem of defining metaphysical claims as being meaningless – literally, "non-sensical". To this end they devised the well-known logical positivist verifiability criterion of meaning. This criterion started out being quite simple, but over the years it was complexified as various problems with it were recognized. Its pristine version was as follows: "A statement is held to be literally meaningful if and only if it is either analytic [i.e., a definition or a logico-mathematical truth] or empirically verifiable" (Ayer, 1960, p. 9). Colloquially this can be stated even more directly: "If it can't be seen or measured, it is not meaningful to talk about." The impact of this doctrine was colorfully described by Scriven:

> The Vienna Circle or *Wiener Kreis* was a band of cutthroats that went after the fact burghers of Continental metaphysics who had become intolerably inbred and pompously verbose. The *Kris* is a Malaysian knife, and the *Wiener Kreis* employed a kind of Occam's razor called the verifiability principle. It performed a tracheotomy that made it possible for philosophy to breathe again. (Scriven, 1969, p. 195)

As already mentioned, behaviorism and operationism are related forms of this "cutthroat" doctrine in educational research.

Finally, the logical positivists, and fellow travelers such as operationists, needed to give an account of what an acceptable "verification or measurement procedure" was; and although there was much debate over details, the agreed-upon theme – reminiscent of classic Lockeanism – was that verification must be via reduction to basic "sense data".

5   Difficulties of logical positivism, and antipositivism

It should be evident that the logical positivists faced the same kinds of problems that confronted all classic empiricists, only they faced these in particularly virulent forms. One additional issue concerns the status of the "verifiability criterion of meaning" itself, for it cannot be shown to be meaningful in the way that it prescribes itself; furthermore, the notion of meaningfulness embodied in this principle seems a truncated and unnecessarily narrow one. Clearly the chief embarrassment for the logical positivists was that their philosophy – which was devised to strength science, and to make scientific method more rigorous – actually threatened the existence of key elements of theoretical science. Laws of nature, for example, cannot be verified in terms of sense experience, for such experience can show at best only that a regularity holds in specific observed cases –

experience cannot show that the purported laws hold at all times and in all places (for all times and all places can never be observed). A parallel problem exists with respect to theoretical entities: the sciences have developed theories about realms that are unobservable (the realms of quarks, the conditions inside black holes, the events in the microseconds following the big bang, and so on). It is one thing to say that one does not accept some of these theories as true; but it seems shocking to say that one regards such speculation or theorizing as literally meaningless.

To overcome such problems, many logical positivists were led in antirealist directions; they argued that such theoretical entities as subatomic particles and subnuclear fundamental forces are not to be thought of as real – they have the status of "logical constructions", or "instruments" for making calculations or predictions. Thus, for many positivists, truth and reality were restricted to the domain of the phenomenal, to the realm of sense-experience. And yet the erroneous belief persists among many educational researchers that logical positivists are, quintessentially, realists who believe in "Truth". To cite one example, a well-known contributor to the *Educational Researcher* wrote (in a passage that displays several common misapprehensions): "philosophers of the positivist school, Carl Hempel and Karl Popper particularly, have posited that propositional statements of lawful relationship are the closest approximations of Truth – whether we are talking about physical matter or human" (Stake, 1978, p. 6). (For further examples drawn from the educational literature, see Phillips, 1983, and Phillips, 1987, Chaps. 4, 8.)

Indeed, it can be argued that many vocal antipositivists are closer than they realize to the spirit of the logical positivists (although, of course, there are significant differences as well) – what unites them is their mutual antirealism.

References

Ayer, A. J. 1966 *Language, Truth and Logic.* Gollancz, London.
Bridgman, P. W. 1927 *The Logic of Modern Physics.* Macmillan, New York.
Comte, A. 1970 (ed. Ferre F.) *Introduction to Positive Philosophy.* Bobbs-Merrill, Indianapolis, Indiana.
Feyerabend, P. 1969 How to be a good empiricist. In: Morick H. (ed.) 1980
Guba, E. (ed.) 1990 *The Paradigm Dialog: Options for Inquiry in the Social Sciences.* Sage, London.
Lacey, A. R. 1976 *A Dictionary of Philosophy.* Routledge & Kegan Paul, London.
Lakomski, G. 1991 (ed.) *Int. J. Educ. Res.* 15(6): whole issue.
Laudan, L. 1990 Demystifying underdetermination. In: Savage C. W. (ed.) 1990 *Scientific Theories,* Minnesota Studies in the Philosophy of Science. XIV. University of Minnesota Press, Minneapolis, Minnesota.
Miller, S. and Fredericks, M. 1991 Postpositivist assumptions and educational research. Another view. *Educ. Researcher* 20(4): 2–8.
Morick, H. (ed.) 1980 *Challenges to Empiricism.* Hackett, Indianapolis, Indiana.
Phillips, D. C. 1983 After the wake: Postpositivistic educational thought. *Educ. Researcher* 12(5): 4–12.
Phillips, D. C. 1987 *Philosophy, Science, and Social Inquiry.* Pergamon Press, Oxford.
Phillips, D. C. 1992 *The Social Scientist's Bestiary.* Pergamon Press, Oxford.
Schrag, F. 1992 In defense of positivist research paradigms. *Educ. Researcher* 21(5): 5–8.
Scriven, M. 1969 Logical positivism and the behavioral sciences. In: Achinstein P and Barker F. (eds.) 1969.
Skinner, B. F. 1953 *Science and Human Behavior.* Free Press, New York.
Stake, R. 1978 The case study method in social inquiry. *Educ. Researcher* 7(2): 5–8.
Wittgenstein, L. 1961 *Tractatus Logico-Philosophicus.* Routledge and Kegan Paul, London.

24 Phenomenology and Existentialism

R. Small

This article provides a brief survey of the philosophical traditions of phenomenology and existentialism, and a discussion of their relevance to educational thought. Although Jean-Paul Sartre is better known to the general public, it is Martin Heidegger who figures centrally in this discussion.

1 Phenomenology

Often associated with each other, phenomenology and existentialism are nevertheless distinct tendencies. Phenomenology is a philosophical methodology, arising from the work of Edmund Husserl (1859–1938).

Franz Bretano (1838–1917) had revived the scholastic concept of "intentionality" (*esse intentionale*) as the defining feature of physical phenomena (Brentano, 1973). On this view, mental acts are always directed towards an object, though not necessarily an existing thing. In classifying representation, judgment, and feeling as differing modes of intentionality, Brentano considered he had made a genuinely scientific psychology possible for the first time.

Husserl applied Brentano's concept of intentionality to a broader philosophical program, a radical empiricism characterized by his slogan: "To the things themselves!" ("*Zu den Sachen selbst!*"). He used the term "phenomenology" for a science of ideal meanings, based on a direct intuition achieved through successive "reductions" of given experience. By setting aside (or "backeting") the reality of the objects of experience, the investigator could isolate mental phenomena in their purity. A further "transcendental reduction", bracketing the reality of mental acts themselves, revealed that the world and its meanings are constituted in transcendental subjectivity. Transcendental phenomenology could thus provide the basis of all other sciences, in accordance with the traditional ideal of philosophy.

In his 1911 manifesto "Philosophy as Rigorous Science" Husserl reaffirmed this systematic program, repudiating "profundity" in favor of scientific clarity, and claiming that only phenomenology could answer the challenges of relativism and naturalism (Husserl 1981). In works such as *Ideas Towards a Pure Phenomenology* (1982) and

Cartesian Meditations (1960), as well as many unpublished writings, he continued to extend and apply his ideas. The 1935 Vienna lecture "Philosophy and the Crisis of European Humanity" announced the themes of his important final work, *The Crisis of European Sciences and Transcendental Phenomenology* (Husserl, 1970). In addressing the historical situation of European culture, Husserl introduces the idea of the pre-given, taken-for-granted "life-world", within which both philosophy and science arise as human activities. The modern crisis of rationality, he argues, is due to its estrangement from this basis. The sciences have become abstract and formal sets of ideas, irrelevant to human life and its meaning. Meanwhile, philosophy is misled by "naturalistic objectivism" into assuming the status of the world, without inquiring into its origins in subjectivity. Only transcendental phenomenology, Husserl concludes, can restore philosophy, and the European culture that depends on it, to their true path (Husserl, 1970).

Phenomenology has had a wide influence in philosophy and related disciplines such as psychology and sociology, due to the work of Alfred Schutz. However, the term "phenomenology" is often used loosely: Ivan Illich's claim to offer a "phenomenology of school" in his *Deschooling Society* is a case in point. Phenomenology has been used to explore educational issues by a group of American philosophers, amongst whom Maxine Greene, Leroy Troutner, and Donald Vandenberg are prominent. Here the existential version of phenomenology is a main influence. The contributions of European writers are not readily available in English, but Vandenberg (1971) provides a useful guide to their ideas.

2 Existentialism

"Existentialism" is a misleading word if it suggests either a unified school or a clearly definable set of beliefs shared by its members. Who counts as an existentialist depends on who is making up the list. Certainly it would be necessary to include literary figures, such as Dostoyevsky and Kafka, as well as philosophers; and Nietzsche is often included, if only because he cannot easily be put in any other category. Some philosophers are clearly central to the existential tradition: in the nineteenth century, Søren Kierkegaard (1813–55); and in the twentieth, Karl Jaspers (1883–1969), Martin Heidegger (1889–1976), and Jean-Paul Sartre (1905–80).

There are sharp differences between these thinkers: for instance, Kierkegaard and Jaspers were Christians, Sartre a militant atheist. In politics, Sartre was a left-wing activist, while Heidegger's tragic misjudgment in aligning himself with the Nazi regime is still a topic of heated controversy. There are common preoccupations, however. Individuality, subjectivity, and freedom are key themes in existential thought. This is why existentialists are sharply opposed to any kind of naturalism, which diminishes or eliminates the distinction between the human beings and other things.

While predecessors such as Blaise Pascal or J. G. Hamann can be found, the initiator of modern existentialism is Kierkegaard. His thinking can be seen as one revolt against the domination of philosophy by the systemic rationalism of Hegel. Marx rejected absolute idealism as a mystification of social life in its material reality; Kierkegaard thought it had left out the irreducible individuality of the thinking subject. The system in its totality took no account of this finite, imperfect, and temporal individual. Kierkegaard does not deny an absolute and eternal truth: on the contrary, it is precisely the tension between this truth and humans' finite being that constitutes the human predicament. He writes: "Two ways, in general, are open for an existing individual: *Either* he can do his utmost to forget that he is an existing individual, by which he becomes a comic figure, since existence has the remarkable trait of compelling an existing individual to exist whether he wills it or not . . . *Or* he can concentrate his entire energy on the fact that he is an existing individual" (Kierkegaard, 1941, p. 109). To do this is to become "subjective", "choosing and committing oneself to what must remain an objective uncertainty, and so grasping truth as a passionate appropriation.

Kierkegaard's philosophical writing differs considerably from that of conventional treatises. His continual use of humor and irony, his dramatic devices and highly personal tone, are all deliberately adopted in order to create a discourse appropriate to what he wants to communicate. Existential reality, Kierkegaard states, is incommunicable (Kierkegaard, 1941, p. 320). There he is referring to just one mode of communication: the direct sort appropriate to objective thinking, but not to a truth of inwardness and appropriation. For that Kierkegaard proposes instead another, *indirect* mode of communication. As he explains, "A communication in the form of a possibility compels the recipient to face the problem of existing in it" (Kierkegaard, 1941, p. 320). It is up to the recipient to recognize such a communication as pointing to a possibility of his or her own existence.

The existential influence has flourished in religious thought, with the Jewish thinkers Martin Buber and Franz Rosenzweig, and the Protestant Paul Tillich. The twentieth-century philosopher who stands closest to Kierkegaard is Karl Jaspers, whose sensitive treatment of what he terms the "boundary situations" of human existence – death, suffering, struggle, and guilt – is of particular value (Jaspers 1969–71). His "elucidation" of human existence makes no attempt to eliminate ambiguity and paradox. Not surprisingly, Jaspers rejected the existential phenomenology of Heidegger as a misguided exercise. He wrote: "Heidegger's thought is presented in objective terms, as a doctrine, and as a result it commits us no more than the traditional systems. What we have, then, is a noncommittal, phenomenological knowledge, and by the same token, a learnable, usable knowledge that is a perversion of philosophy: (Jaspers and Bultmann, 1958, p. 8).

3   Existential phenomenology

The confluence of phenomenology with existentialist thought began with Martin Heidegger's *Being and Time*, first published in 1927. The stated aim of the work is to open up what Heidegger called "the question of Being" (Heidegger, 1962). The "ontological difference" between Being and beings (or entities) is crucial here. Because most thinking is direct towards beings, Heidegger begins with an interpretation (or "hermeneutic") of a particular kind of Being: our own.

Heidegger calls the human mode of Being *Dasein*. The German word, usually left untranslated, means "Being-there". In the course of an analysis whose richness of detail can only be hinted at here, he elaborates this into a concept of "Being-in-the-world". People are always already in the world, not in the sense of simple location, but of living there, dwelling alongside and caring about things and other people. Heidegger's method is phenomenological; what he means by "phenomena" are not the usual objects of experience, however, but rather the hidden background which is usually overlooked, or apprehended only in exceptional moods, such as joy or anxiety. In uncovering the inconspicuous structures of everyday life, Heidegger shows how *Dasein* is absorbed into an anonymous public world. This is its "inauthentic" mode of Being, which nevertheless points out an alternative. The temporarity of human existence is not that of the world of objects, the time measured by clocks; *Dasein* always runs ahead of itself into the future, and retrieves its past possibilities. Above all, its temporality differs from objective time in being finite. On the one hand, one is thrown into the world, delivered over to one's situation; on the other, one faces the indefinite yet inevitable prospect of one's death. Authenticity (*Eigentlichkeit*) means taking over one's own existence as uniquely one's own, in a resolute appropriation of past and future possibilities.

Jean-Paul Sartre's *Being and Nothingness*, first published in 1943, takes up themes from Hegel, Husserl, and Heidegger; its dominant concern is Sartre's own preoccupation with freedom and responsibility. Sartre's literary flair is seen in his vivid treatment of inauthenticity, which he renames "bad faith". In one well-known passage, he describes the cafe waiter who is a little too attentive and assiduous in performing his tasks; Sartre explains that this person is "playing at being a waiter in a café" (Sartre, 1957, p. 59). After all, his being a waiter is always in question, never a settled fact. So why does he act as if it were? Social pressure may be a factor: the public needs to be reassured that the waiter is "only" a waiter. There is a deeper reason, though: the realization of one's own freedom is alarming and uncomfortable. Since one's existence precedes one's essence, one is continually creating oneself anew, with no higher authority to validate one's choices. The anguish of this freedom is just the human condition: Sartre insists that one face one's absolute responsibility without the comforts of self-deception.

The popular success of the French school of Sartre, Albert Camus, and Simone de Beauvoir, all literary figures as well as philosophers, made "existentialism" a household word in the postwar period. In a popular lecture, Sartre claimed existentialism as a form of humanism (Sartre, 1948). Heidegger was provoked into repudiating both "existentialism" and humanism" as misleading labels (Heidegger, 1977). By then, his own work had taken a different turn, still pursuing "the question of Being", but through a "deconstruction" of the Western traditions of thought, extending to an abandonment of terms such as "phenomenology" and even "philosophy" (in favor of "thinking"). This later work of Heidegger remains a powerful influence in the current postmodern and deconstructionist movements.

4 Problem areas in education

While existential phenomenology is relevant to many aspects of education, three particular areas in which it raises significant issues can be noted.

4.1 Childhood as a mode of existence

Where education has to do with children, it must take into account the nature of childhood. A biological model, in which learning is one aspect of growth, comes to mind readily. An alternative is to identify childhood as a social category, contrasting its forms in different societies. These still leave open the question: what *is* the child, as an individual person?

No existentialist writer has shown a greater awareness of the fragility of individual identity than Franz Kafka. His observations on education are of particular interest in identifying the family as the greatest threat to the separate identity of the child. He writes:

> The love that parents have for their children is animal, mindless, and always prone to confuse the child with their own selves. But the educator has respect for the child; and for the purposes of education that is incomparably more, even if there is no love involved. I repeat: for the purposes of education. For when I call parental love mindless and animal, that is not to denigrate it. It is as much an inscrutable mystery as the intelligent creative love of the educator. Only for the purposes of education we cannot denigrate it enough. (Kafka, 1977, p. 296).

Kafka insists on respect for the child both as an individual and as a child, and sees the educator as uniquely placed to protest and enhance both aspects. Other existential writers on education have explored the character of childhood as a mode of existence, to be grasped in terms of its own possibilities (Denton, 1978).

4.2 The school as a social institution

Education is seen as part of the everyday world. Schools are public institutions, more or less bureaucratic in character; teaching and learning are routine activities, plausibly characterized as social "roles". Existential thought is sharply critical of the "one-dimensionality" of modern societies. As happens in other professions, a teacher may be absorbed within every day functions, often reinforced by an administrative policy which minimizes individual autonomy. Can authenticity be achieved in such a setting? It seems unlikely. Yet Kierkegaard describes the "knight of faith", an individual whose deep spirituality requires no external expression, so that to the observer he or she is indistinguishable from a conventional member of society. Introduced to this individual, Kierkegaard says, one murmurs to oneself: "Good Lord, is this the man? Is it really he? Why, he looks like a tax-collector!" (Kierkegaard, 1941, p. 53). Authenticity is not something to be addressed by empirical research; it is an issue for the existing individual alone. It cannot be directly linked with particular social or political arrangements, or with one model of schooling.

4.3   Teaching and learning as interpersonal relations

Whatever its setting may be, education eventually comes down to the relation between teacher and learner. Given its radically individualistic character, can existential thinking assist people in grasping the interpersonal character of education? Heidegger's analysis of "Being-with-others" is mainly concerned with its inauthentic mode. When it comes to an authentic mode of communication, for example, he suggests that reticence and even silence are preferable to "idle talk". One's aim must be to free others for their own possibilities, rather than taking them over by open or hidden domination. The problem of domination is prominent in Sartre's *Being and Nothingness* (1957), where an elaborate construction of interpersonal relations is offered – but no solution. Sartre's play *No Exit* includes a memorable line: "Hell is other people".

In place of these discouraging ideas, existential writers on education often invoke the concept of dialogue. Any suggestion of a Socratic pedagogy needs care, however. Frank Rosenzweig contrasts the thinking of past philosophy, seemingly autonomous and timeless, with a thinking which is bound to speech and to life with others in a common world. A comparison between the Gospels and the Socratic dialogues, Rosenzweig suggests, brings out the point: since Socrates already knows what is to be thought, his conversation is merely a concession to the limitations of communication: nothing actually happens in it. In contrast, genuine dialogue is open to the unforeseen: "I do not know in advance what the other person will say to me, because I do not even know what I myself am going to say. I do not even know whether I am going to say anything at all" (Glazer, 1961, p. 199).

One writer who has emphasized "dialogical education" is Paulo Freire, whose *Pedagogy of the Oppressed*, mixing themes from existentialism, Marxism, and Christianity, appealed to a wide audience (Freire, 1972). Criticizing "a mechanistic, static, naturalistic, spatialized view of consciousness," he appealed to the Husserlian notion of intentionality (as interpreted by Sartre) for an alternative. Freire is both eclectic and selective: yet for all his passionate attack on oppression, he is a positive thinker, treating problems as soluble through action; so many existential themes find no place in his thinking. Just as important for him is Marx's third thesis on Feuerbach, with its warning that "the educator must himself be educated" and recommendation of a "revolutionary praxis" which transforms both the agent and the world. Freire denounces a "banking concept" of education, which treats knowledge as a ready-made product, to be transferred into the empty mind of a passive learner; he argues for a pedagogy of dialogue between equals, aiming primarily at social and political liberation.

The overlap between these ideas and the existential thought can be gauged from one lecture of Heidegger in which his own pedagogy is outlined with exemplary clarity. Teaching is an offering and giving, Heidegger explains, but learning it not just a taking:

> If the student only takes over something which is offered, he does not learn. He comes to learn only when he experiences what he takes as something he himself already has. True learning only occurs where the talking of what one already has is a self-giving and is experienced as such. Teaching, therefore, does not mean anything else than to let the others learn, i.e., to bring one another to learning. Learning is more difficult than teaching; for only he who can truly learn – and only as long as he can do it – can truly teach. The genuine teacher differs from the pupil only in that he can learn better and that he more genuinely wants to learn. In all teaching, the teacher learns the most. (Heidegger, 1968, p. 73).

See also: Hermeneutics; Research Paradigms in Education

References

Brentano, F. 1973 *Psychology from an Empirical Standpoint.* Routledge and Kegan Paul, London.
Denton, D. E. (ed.) 1978 *Existentialism and Phenomenology in Education: Collected Essays.* Teachers College Press, New York.
Freire, P. 1972 *Pedagogy of the Oppressed.* Penguin Books, Harmondsworth.
Glazer, N. N. (ed.) 1961 *Franz Rosenzweig: His Life and Thought,* 2nd rev. edn. Schocken Books, New York.
Heidegger, M. 1962 *Being and Time.* SCM Press, London.
Heidegger, M. 1968 *What is a Thing?* Henry Regnery, Chicago, Illinois.
Heidegger, M. 1977 (ed. Krell D. F.) *Basic Writings.* Harper and Row, New York.
Husserl, E. 1960 (1st edn. 1929) *Cartesian Meditations.* Martinus Nijhoff, The Hague.
Husserl, E. 1970 *The Crisis of European Sciences and Transcendental Phenomenology: An Introduction to Phenomenological Philosophy.* Northwestern University Press, Evanston, Illinois.
Husserl, E. 1981 Philosophy as rigorous science. In: McCormick P. and Elliston F. A. (eds.) 1981 *Shorter Works.* Harvester Press, Brighton.
Husserl, E. 1982 (1st edn. 1913) *Ideas Pertaining to a Pure Phenomenology and to a Phenomenological Philosophy,* First Book. Martinus Nijhoff, The Hague.
Jaspers, K. and Bultmann, R. 1958 *Myth and Christianity: An Inquiry into the Possibility of Religion without Myth.* Noonday Press, New York.
Jaspers, K. 1969–71 *Philosophy,* 3 vols. University of Chicago Press, Chicago, Illinois.
Kafka, F. 1977 *Letters to Friends, Family, and Editors.* Schocken Books, New York.
Kierkegaard, S. 1941 *Concluding Unscientific Postscript.* Princeton University Press, Princeton, New Jersey.
Kierkegaard, S. 1941 *Fear and Trembling.* Princeton University Press, Princeton, New Jersey.
Sartre, J.-P. 1948 *Being and Nothingness.* Methuen, London.
Vandenberg, D. 1971 *Being and Education: An Essay in Existential Phenomenology.* Prentice-Hall, Englewood Cliffs, New Jersey.

Further reading

Bollnow, O. F. 1959 *Existenzphilosophie und Pädagogik: Versuch über Unsteitige Formen der Erziehung.* W. Kohlhammer Verlag, Stuttgart.

Cooper, D. E. 1983 *Authenticity and Learning: Nietzsche's Educational Philosophy.* Routledge and Kegan Paul, London.

Greene, M. 1973 *Teacher as Stranger: Educational Philosophy for the Modern Age.* Wadsworth, Belmont, California.

Manheimer, R. J. 1978 *Kierkegaard as Educator.* University of California Press, Berkeley, California.

Morris, V. C. 1966 *Existentialism in Education: What it Means.* Harper and Row, New York.

Murphy, T. F. 1984 *Nietzsche as Educator.* University Press of America, Lanham, Maryland.

25 From Foundations to Coherence in Educational Research

C. W. Evers

The development of research methodologies is a way of formulating and making explicit sound procedures for inquiry – procedures that determine the nature of acceptable evidence, the kinds of inferences that may be drawn and, as exemplified in the praxis tradition, the kind of action that is appropriate. Construed this way, methodologies are influenced primarily by epistemological assumptions, particularly by assumptions about whether and how knowledge is justified. In prescribing canons concerning the nature and limits of justification, epistemologies exercise a normative function, directly over methodology, and indirectly over the structure and content of substantive theories purportedly sustained by research.

In the article that follows, three main stages in educational research methodology that have been associated with major epistemological positions, are explored. It is argued that all three stages reflect characteristic limitations associated with foundationalist assumptions in knowledge justification. As an alternative, a coherentist model of knowledge justification is outlined, and its incorporation into educational research methodology recommended. The coherentist model to be outlined is a species of naturalistic epistemology, that is, one informed by natural science accounts of how humans acquire knowledge and process information. One consequence of this approach is a blurring of the so-called quantitative/qualitative distinction. Another is a blurring of the alleged distinction between natural science and social science. The main result will be an approach to inquiry that is somewhat more inclusive in what it counts as knowledge, but also more discriminating in discerning what should be left out.

1 Stages of educational research methodology

It is convenient to categorize mainstream educational research methodology into three broad stages.

264

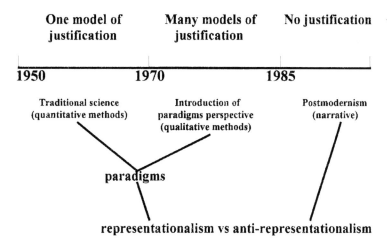

Figure 1 Three stages of educational research methodology.

Although in this very general characterization these stages are partly chronological, growing out of successive attempts to theorize inquiry, they all flourish today, with a view of methodology as comprising a range of paradigms still being the dominant perspective in the field. A more detailed account of each, together with an account of their key interrelationships follows.

1.1 Traditional science of educational research

Traditional quantitative scientific approaches to educational research, once seen as the only proper way to conduct inquiry, but now mostly regarded as just another paradigm, may be distinguished, as shown in Figure 2, by three structural features that reflect their background logical empiricist epistemological assumptions.

On the question of justification, a partition on knowledge claims is posited which demarcates an epistemically privileged subset from all the rest. This subset, usually observation reports, plays a foundational role in justification, with justification proceeding by way of testability, which has two components. Thus, non-privileged claims within a theory are thought to imply privileged ones. If these obtain, the theory is confirmed, and is said to be supported by evidence. If contrary observations obtain, the theory is said to be disconfirmed and in need of revision. A theory is more justified than its rivals if it has amassed more confirmations and fewer or no disconfirmations (for a standard account, see McMillan and Schumacher, 1993, pp. 78–90).

Because of the demands of testability, theories need to exhibit a **hypothetico-deductive structure** (Kerlinger, 1986, pp. 15–25). Since implication for testability runs from claims that are more general to claims that are less general, this structure will be a hierarchy of statements, with unrestricted law-like generalizations at the top, descending to singular

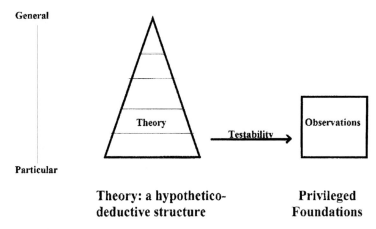

Theory: a hypothetico-deductive structure **Privileged Foundations**

Figure 2 Traditional science of educational research.

claims at the bottom. Educational theorizing, because it is context specific, is located in the intermediate layers of generality, such theories sometimes being called "theories of the middle range". They are justified in the usual way, by the deduction of claims that belong to the privileged subset for subsequent testing, but can also be justified if they follow from networks of warranted claims located further up the theoretical hierarchy. For this reason, some branches of educational studies (e.g. Educational Administration, Educational Psychology) appear to be influenced more by a generic parent discipline (e.g. Management, Psychology) than by Education.

The third structural feature of traditional science approaches to research is quite technical, residing in the background as an assumption of more rigorous formulations of logical empiricism. It concerns the language in which theories are to be formulated. Owing to the influence of Vienna Circle logical positivists of the 1920s and 1930s, scientific theories were thought to be best formulated in an austere logical language which had precise syntactical rules for forming valid symbol combinations and a precise semantics which displayed in unambiguous fashion the meaning of each sentence. The logical notation for which this had easily been achieved by the 1950s was the predicate calculus, developed at the turn of the century by Russell and Whitehead.

In understanding the implications of logical empiricist driven methodologies for the social sciences it is important to know that the predicate calculus, if used as an ideal language for theory construction, is **referentially transparent**, or **extensional** (Linsky, 1971). What this means can be illustrated by the following example:

Consider the argument
(1) 7 is less than 9
(2) 9 = the number of planets
(3) 7 is less than the number of planets.

Provided premise (2) is true, we can correctly deduce the truth of (3) from the truth of (1) and (2). Now consider a corresponding argument.

(4) Jones knows that (7 is less than 9)
(5) $9 =$ the number of planets
(6) Jones knows that (7 is less than the number of planets).

This argument for (6) is invalid even given the truth of (4) and (5).

There is a crucial difference between the two arguments. The first is valid regardless of how the number nine is referred to. Provided the different expressions "9", or "number of planets", or "number of my second cousins" or "number of coins in my pocket" all refer to the same object, in this case the number nine, any of these expressions can be substituted into the argument without affecting its validity. In the predicate calculus, all expressions that refer to the same thing can be exchanged without affecting the truth of the sentence which contains them. That is, this ideal language is referentially transparent. However, the second argument contains sentences that are referentially opaque. What Jones can be said to know depends importantly on how it is referred to. And this is the case not just for Jones's knowledge, but also for Jones's beliefs, desires, hopes, wants, imaginings, and all the rest of what are called the propositional attitudes. To restrict the damage referential opacity does to the job of constructing a human science, some way must be found for limiting the range of semantically valid descriptions of human conduct. The usual way has been to insist on giving operational definitions for any propositional attitudes that turn up in research. The effect is to restrict referring expressions to unambiguously specified, observable, measurable behaviors.

Whatever the merits of logical empiricist based accounts of research in natural science, they constitute an exceptionally severe restriction on the data of social science. Empiricist theory of evidence rules out familiar appeals to human subjectivity – including such matters as the individual construction of meaning and the interpreted significance of events – and also the relevance of ethics as an integral constraint on inquiry. The hypothetico-deductive model of theories, while useful for dealing with deductive relations among context invariant generalizations of the sort that can be found in theoretical physics, becomes rather brittle and implausible as a model for the highly context dependent social phenomena of education where there may be no true, non-trivial, law-like, generalizations. And finally, the background demand for an extensional ideal theoretical language rules out much of the vocabulary that is used to characterize human activity and conduct, filtering intentional, meaningful, action down to a set of intersubjectively measurable behaviors.

So restrictive are the methodological demands of traditional quantitative research approaches that they have seemed to many to be inapplicable beyond natural science, prompting belief in a fundamental methodological bifurcation between the natural and the social world. Indeed, this bifurcation has been virtually institutionalized by the widespread adoption of a paradigms view of research.

1.2   Paradigms of research

The abandonment of logical empiricism in philosophy was occasioned not so much by its inability to account for social science as its obvious deficiencies in accounting for theory choice among competing theories in natural science. Work in the 1950s by philosophers such as Quine, Hanson, Feyerabend, and Kuhn, raised three major difficulties for traditional empiricist accounts of knowledge justification in science.

First, there is no such thing as so-called "hard data". All observation reports in any epistemically favoured set of claims involve some interpretation, and are described in some theoretical vocabulary, even for the articulation of measurement procedures used in operational definitions. Experience itself is filtered by theory, and so too is the identification of epistemic privilege, (Petri, 1972). Second, many different theories can imply the same finite set of observations, thus making problematical the question of which competing theory is actually being confirmed. Finally, where a conjunction of many hypotheses is required to deduce an observation report, it is not always clear precisely which hypothesis or group of hypotheses a disconfirming observation is falsifying. Empirical test situations are always complex.

The influential conclusion drawn by Kuhn (1970) was that empirical evidence is always insufficient for rational theory adjudication. Assuming that empirical evidence is all the evidence there is for theory choice, and knowing that choices have been made in the ongoing development of science, he concluded that other, non-rational factors, were involved. Indeed, for Kuhn, the whole notion of some principle of rational choice extending beyond the influence of the comprehensive theoretical perspectives he called paradigms, was suspect.

Translated into an account of research, this means that questions about the relations between theory and evidence, and what counts as justification, are taken to be internal to comprehensive methodological perspectives. That is, there is no external methodological framework to which appeal can be made beyond particular paradigms of research, to rule on the appropriateness of paradigmatic differences. There are just different and distinct paradigms of research. With multiple models of justification in the offing, the matter of theory structure also fragments along paradigmatic fault lines, since theory of justification is a major determinant of the structure and content of substantive educational theories.

Hypothetico-deductive structures need function as a constraint only on theories in natural science, while the demands of understanding, or empathy, or insight, or the quest for meaning, can impose their own distinct demands. Semantical constraints on the language of theory formulations vary with paradigms too. For example, the theoretical motivation in logical empiricism for an austere referential semantics assumes no access to the lush domain of meaning that is part and parcel of our everyday communicative practices. Yet even to mount a case for austerity assumes a certain amount of the antecedent lushness that is unquestioned or perhaps celebrated in other paradigms.

More than any other stage of research, the paradigms view has been responsible for a vast opening up of knowledge in educational studies. Much of the diversity that is now commonplace in the field owes its existence to the anti-empiricist assumptions that underwrite multi-perspectivism. Indeed, it is hard to imagine today's flourishing of varieties of subjectivism, interpretivism, critical theory, and cultural studies, to name just a few of the current options, without a corresponding attack on traditional science and its purported methods (see *Research Paradigms in Education*).

Interestingly, while all this diversity might be thought dramatically to reduce the amount of screening performed by the paradigms research filter, the claim that the different paradigms are distinct, orthogonal, or better, totally independent, has a curiously opposite effect. For just as stage one methodology discounted the value of any research done outside traditional science methods, many of the paradigms return the compliment by discounting, or filtering out, natural science. The effect is odd. Consider, for example, what is required to interpret a measurable, intersubjectively observable sequence of behaviours in context, such as a person teaching a class. Either appeals to interpretations, and interpretation of others' interpretations, the analysis of shared meanings, and a grasp of understandings are regarded as part of a methodologically complete and autonomous level of explanation or they are not. If yes, then it needs to be noted that all the physical accompaniments of teaching, such as gesturing, speaking, organizing, or writing, are accomplished by a physical body enmeshed in a causal field, presumably explicable by some other level of explanation that makes use of talk of nerve pathways, the firing of neurons, and the activity of arm muscles. The puzzle is that if the autonomy of paradigm-relative explanation is true, it is something of a miracle for the body to gesture, or move appropriate speaking muscles, at precisely the time that a person intends to teach some matter. The point generalizes, rendering the link between thought and action entirely mysterious. On the other hand, if paradigms do not function to filter out alternative perspectives and some coherent interlevel meshing is required to avoid the miraculous coincidence problem, then the distinctiveness of paradigms is compromised in a major way. To date, these issues have not been squarely addressed in the methodology literature (for a philosophical treatment, see Cussins, 1992).

1.3   Research as narrative

Epistemological attacks on logical empiricism that gave rise to the acceptance of paradigms in research raised serious doubts about the adequacy of appeals to empirical foundations to justify knowledge. The upshot has been a shift towards relativism and a diversity of ways of forming and defending theoretical representations of educational reality. Since the mid-1980s, however, a third stage of research has developed drawing rather more skeptical conclusions from the arguments against foundationalism.

Under the influence of postmodernism, three doctrines have gained prominence. The first is anti-foundationalism: there are no foundations to knowledge, and hence the justificationalist problematic should be abandoned altogether. The second is anti-essentialism: concepts have no essential defining features, or things no corresponding essence. The third is anti-representationalism: theories, and the contents of our mind, do not mirror the world, or represent the way the world is. They fail to do so because there is no such thing as accurate representation (Evers and Lakomski, 1996, pp. 262–270; Constas, 1998).

For methodology framed within these doctrines, matters of truth and evidence drop out, along with the fiction/non-fiction distinction. Research ceases to be a quest for truth, or an attempt to build up a warranted representation of the world, but becomes rather an exercise in story-telling, in producing a narrative, and in giving voice to different viewpoints. Recorded data are more like texts whose meaning at first reflects the understandings the researcher has of the experiences of others, and then reflects the understandings of the reader. Outside of the justificationist problematic, the structure of theory is dictated by the requirements of narrative, with theory formulation characteristically being symbolic expressions of language (Connelly and Clandinin, 1990; Clandinin and Connelly, 1996) (see also *Narrative Enquiry*).

This transition from representational to non-representational conceptions of knowledge and research has consequences for research as social practice. For example, within the praxis tradition, the notion of integrating normatively directed change with inquiry still presupposes theories that in some way represent the world, even if that representation reflects only one of many different possible perspectives. That is, the theorizing of change itself is in terms of a dynamical representation of researchers and their material contexts. But for theories developed in a praxis tradition detached from the idea of representation, the conceptualization of change is weakened, being limited mostly to theoretical claims about voice. However, since these theoretical claims in turn are not usually thought of as being subject to a representationalist normative ideal of truth, the virtues of voicing non-representational research are not easily formulated, least of all within the language of change consequences. Non-representational theories of voice, value, politics, and social change, are particularly problematical as frameworks for the analysis of research as (non-representational) narrative. There are numerous reasons for this, but a basic one is the inability of postmodernist research approaches in general to function in an importantly discriminating way about certain features of human experience.

If human behaviour were totally random, no language would be possible, nor interpretation, nor understanding. For creatures inhabiting an environment in which there are limited resources, there are advantages in forming trajectories which lead to the solution of problems at better than chance. Driving a car, crossing a busy road safely, leaving a room through the door, making a cup of coffee, and performing a thousand other mundane physical and social acts is possible only against a background of sustained patterned, non-random, activity. The challenge to act on experience in a way that is more epistemically progressive than tossing a coin, is the challenge to solve what we might call the navigation problem. It is the task of devising non-arbitrary strategies for meeting needs, achieving goals, solving problems, and in general, getting around in the world while avoiding coming to grief sooner rather than later.

Part of the cognitive apparatus required to solve the navigation problem, to the extent that it is solved, is possession of a reliable map. Less metaphorically, navigating a successful trajectory is a matter of having a causally efficacious representational structure that contains epistemically useful information. Thus when a dog succeeds in uncovering the bone it buried, or when a bat utilizes acoustical evidence to fly between the bars of a cage, or when an infant negotiates its way around obstacles to obtain a favoured toy, or when an adult plans to make an organization more effective, giving a complete explanation of successful outcomes of these actions will involve reference to the adequacy of the organism's capacity to represent salient features of its environment to itself. A methodology which does not permit one to formulate the notion of filtering out failures from successes in this modest, piecemeal, sense will have little of value to contribute to the sciences – natural, social, or human.

2   Naturalistic coherentism

Any proposal to address the weaknesses canvassed in the three mainstream stages of educational research methodology will meet a number of conditions. First, to perform useful work as a discriminating filter at all, a plausible distinction between justified and unjustified knowledge claims need to be defended against the known difficulties with foundationalism. Second, some inclusive account of the structure of substantial theories needs to be given, especially one able to deal in a less brittle way with the graded, limited, and context dependent nature of social science generalizations. And finally, since much research in education concerns **practices**, some way of formulating practical knowledge needs to be found. It is claimed here that an approach to knowledge and its representation that incorporates elements of both naturalism and coherentism can provide an adequate framework for the development of more suitable research methodologies in educational studies (Evers, 1991).

2.1   The paradox of inquiry

One important test for any approach to research methodology is its capacity to deal with what is known as the "paradox of inquiry". Formulated by Plato in the *Meno*, it runs roughly as follows: either we know what it is that we are inquiring after, in which case inquiry is unnecessary, or we do not and so would not recognize it if we found it, making inquiry pointless; therefore inquiry is either unnecessary or pointless. Of the many possible responses to this paradox, it is useful to begin with one of the criticisms of traditional forms of empiricism, namely that observational foundations have a theoretical dimension. There is an analogue of this that also applies to inquiry which, we can say, is always theoretically motivated. Consider, for example, the task of opening a door by first unlocking it. Inquiry by means of trying out successive keys on a large key ring is necessary because the door is locked, and has point because the inquiry strategy will terminate successfully when a key is found that opens the door.

The general point is that like a lock, all objects of inquiry come with some theoretical structure. If this structure is sufficiently rich to determine what is to count as a solution, or a successful end to inquiry, Plato's paradox can be resolved in an epistemically progressive way. Some problems, or research issues, exhibit a very high degree of solution specificity, so the degree of fit (or coherence) among the elements of theorized issue, methodology, and theory-laden observational evidence is quite compelling. However, the point does not lapse for want of well structured problems. Epistemic progress can occur in more incremental ways, where the degree of fit may be defined over less ambitious elements, such as better formulations of a research problem, or ways of partitioning the problem into more manageable components.

A less abstract way of stating matters is in terms of a constraint satisfaction view of inquiry. We appeal to the theoretical structure presumed in any particular inquiry to specify constraints on what counts as an answer to a research question, or problem. Although, as Haig (1987, p. 30) notes . . .

> . . . our significant research problems will not be fully structured and, therefore, will not constitute complete descriptions of their solutions . . . yet we articulate our problems in terms of their constituent constraints, and these constraints do serve to direct us towards their problems' respective solutions.

Moreover, this process is iterative, involving over time the successive application of satisfying multiple soft constraints in as coherent a manner as possible and feeding back proposed solutions into the theoretical machinery of further research issue and problem specification.

2.2   *Coherentist justification*

While constraint satisfaction accounts of research are well known in the literature (e.g., Nickles, 1980; Haig, 1987; Robinson, 1993, 1998), there is a need to draw links between situated and specific contexts of successful constraint satisfaction implicit in the usual attempts to meet Plato's paradox, and the broader enterprise of attempting to articulate a post-empiricist account of knowledge and its justification, given the success of criticisms of epistemic foundationalism. This can be done by specifying more fully the epistemic notion of coherence that lies behind the normative adjudication of fit among the elements of inquiry.

To illustrate how coherence can operate, consider again the quest for foundations to knowledge. This was always theoretically motivated, assuming some view of the powers of the mind and how knowledge might be acquired. Mostly, these views were thought to be obvious commonsense, embodying folk-theoretical assumptions about the operation of sensory organs and the processing of sensory information. However, where these assumptions are less warranted than the foundations they demarcate are supposed to be, the point of foundational patterns of justification lapses. In building an epistemology it is more reasonable to make use of our most sophisticated scientific theories of how people acquire and process knowledge. But these theories occur fairly late in the build-up of knowledge, and certainly well after any of the usual candidates for privileged empirical foundations.

The lesson to draw from conceding the relevance of such disciplines as psychology, physiology, neuroscience and cognitive science to epistemology, is to abandon the demarcation task altogether and settle for developing the most coherent account of what we claim to know. Given that empirical evidence is never sufficient for theory choice, but that epistemically progressive choices are made all the time as we navigate our way through the environment, it would be more fruitful to attempt to discern how these choices are actually made.

Within any proposed framework for improving knowledge and enhancing inquiry, for doing better than chance or coin tossing, the following broad epistemic constraints are arguably central (see Quine and Ullian, 1978; Evers and Lakomski, 1991, pp. 37–45).

(a) *Empirical Adequacy:* There is a premium on theory driven empirical expectations being met, on predictions being fulfilled. This is just basic for navigating successful trajectories through the multiplicity of options presented by experience. Theories are therefore to be preferred over rivals to the extent that they achieve empirical adequacy.

(b) *Consistency:* As networks of claims that contain an inconsistency formally permit the deduction of any claim whatsoever, theory identity requires consistency. Without consistency, it is not possible to say where one theory ends and another begins. Nor is it possible to identify descriptions of particular states of affairs as being implied by the theory, thus compromising the nature of evidence for empirical adequacy.

(c) *Comprehensiveness:* Where explanation is seen as an advantage, theories that have the resources to explain more things rather than fewer are to be preferred.

(d) *Simplicity:* Theories that can explain the same phenomena while invoking fewer unexplained assumptions are to be preferred. This requirement penalizes recourse to *ad hoc* explanation, which is the practice of turning the inexplicable into a primitive additional assumption, or axiom, of current theory.

(e) *Learnability:* As a constraint on good theory development, learnability is aimed at ensuring that the account given of known phenomena leaves the phenomena plausibly knowable. Thus, if an attempt is made to explain human ethical judgment in terms of an abstract realm of ethical properties known only by intuition, and then fails to provide any account of the workings of this intuition, there is an offence against fulfilling the learnability requirement. It is a demand designed to ensure that accounts given of things that are known do not entail that they are unknowable.

(f) *Explanatory Unity:* This is really the result of combining both simplicity and comprehensiveness, in order to emphasize the advantages of being able to account for the most phenomena using the least theoretical resources.

Collectively, these criteria of theory choice are known as coherence criteria. It is claimed here that they constitute a set of soft constraints useful for guiding the development, or growth, of knowledge. Three sorts of arguments are relevant to defining their usefulness in providing a plausible distinction between justified and unjustified knowledge. First, arguments for various epistemological positions, whether foundational, paradigms views, skepticism, or postmodernist alternatives, in order to be persuasive characteristically employ strategies that conform to the theoretical virtues of coherence, especially if the observational requirement of empirical adequacy is omitted and the learnability requirement is ignored. To this extent, coherence conditions, or a more limited subset, function as touchstone, or common theory, across otherwise divergent theoretical perspectives. Those who wish to argue against this finding will still end up attempting to conform to coherentist conditions.

Now if the observational requirement is added, in as theoretical a sense as would satisfy any critic of traditional empiricism, with an eye to meeting the demands of successful navigation, then secondly, it is possible to defend representationalism by the following consideration due to BonJour (1985, p. 171).

> If a system of beliefs remains coherent (and stable) over the long run while continuing to satisfy the Observation Requirement, then it is highly likely that there is some explanation (other than mere chance) for this fact . . . [the best explanation for this fact] . . . is that: (a) the . . . beliefs which are claimed within the system, to be reliable are systematically caused by the sorts of situations which are depicted by their content; and (b) the entire system of beliefs corresponds, within a reasonable degree of approximation, to the independent reality which it purports to describe . . .

In the earlier discussion of the orthogonal paradigms of multi-perspectivism, it was noted that the perspectives adopted concerning some phenomenon will, after all, need to articulate at some point if they are isomorphic with respect to the background of causal structure embedded in that phenomenon. That is, because narrative accounts of teacher conduct (for example) will be isomorphic in causally significant ways to physiological and behavioural accounts, positing the existence of some shared basis for theoretical articulation has more antecedent plausibility than positing a miraculous coincidence. Now the same point can be made in relation to BonJour's consideration. The reason it is not a miracle that a coherent empirically adequate theory can satisfy the observation requirement over the long run is because the theory in some important sense can be said to **represent** features of the world that give rise to what is observed.

Third, the study of natural learning systems, creatures with nervous systems that learn from their environment, suggests that learning accomplished by massively parallel neuronal architectures operates in terms of a network relaxing into the coherent satisfaction of multiple soft constraints (Rumelhart and McClelland, 1986). It is a reasonable part of the naturalist's research agenda to expect an adequate characterization of coherent constraint satisfaction in neural networks (and their biologically realistic artificial models) to provide insights into the physical detail behind the operation of coherence criteria of theory choice defined over symbolic theory formulations (see Thagard, 1989). The methodological point to be made is that use should be made of the sheer ubiquity of successful, piecemeal, epistemic practice that occurs throughout the natural world as a starting point for constructing guidelines for epistemic practices. It is more advantageous to assume that across the phylo-genetic continuum, nature has regularly produced creatures that do better than chance in solving their navigation problems, and learn from those solutions.

2.3   *The structure of educational theories*

Just as logical empiricism's testability criteria of justification have consequences for structuring theories; namely, by favouring hypothetico-deductive hierarchical statement structures as illustrated in Figure 2, so coherentism's criteria, and a resulting concern to preserve natural representation, also have consequences. The general idea is to see inquiry from the perspective of an "epistemic engine", namely, something that builds up an internal representation of patterns extracted from experience subject to the constraint of coherently meeting the observation requirement over the long run. Figure 3 captures this dynamical process schematically.

The important question concerns the kind of knowledge structure that develops in what has been labelled the "Web of Belief". For **sentential** representations of knowledge, Quine's elaboration of the metaphor is appropriate. It is a body of sentences, variously associated, with those more central to the organization of ideas and concepts in the web located at the centre, and those more directly in contact with sensory experience at the periphery. It is helpful to see these web structures in terms of the revisability of statements in the light of experience. At the centre of the web would be areas of knowledge such as logic, mathematics, and some branches of science, such as theoretical physics, where singular items of experience will have least impact because the intellectual costs of revision are so great and ramify across the web so extensively. Revisions at this level would need to be driven by invoking consideration of additional virtues of coherence. Statements at the periphery, however, singular observation reports, for example, can be revised quite readily in light of contrary experience, with no systematic consequences (Quine, 1951; Quine and Ullian, 1978). Note that, methodologically, even statements at the periphery can be rendered immune from revision if drastic adjustments are made elsewhere in the web (Quine, 1951, pp. 40–43). In this respect, coherence criteria function as multiple soft constraints.

One consequence of this more relaxed approach to theory structure is a blurring of the distinction between natural and social science. This point can be made more strikingly by invoking naturalistic information-theoretic ideas to describe theories (for an introductory account see Chaitin, 1975; Dennett, 1991; Evers and Lakomski, 1996, pp. 134–136). Consider a set of data points, individuated under some suitable schema for description. Call the total set of descriptions a bit map of the data set. Then it is possible to regard the data set as patterned, or non-random, if there exists a description of it that requires fewer bits of information than the bit map. Figure 3 presents a map for justification as epislemically progressive learning. Non-random data will therefore be **compressible**. For the relatively context invariant data set of physics, or the level at which there is interest in phenomena conforming to the laws of arithmetic, extremely high levels of compression can be achieved, as is evident in the very simple equations that can be used to compress arbitrarily large bit map accounts of empirical data. But where context matters, compression grades off, not suddenly, but on a continuum. However, while the mainly linguistic theory formulations characteristic of the social sciences are clearly not as compressed as some physical science theories, they obviously comprehend significant regularities within contexts that are of great use in social navigation.

From this perspective not only are natural and social science on the same representational continuum, but in terms of coherentist justification they are also on the same methodological continuum. The so called qualitative/quantitative distinction is more an artifact of disputes concerning foundation epistemologies and their models of theory structure.

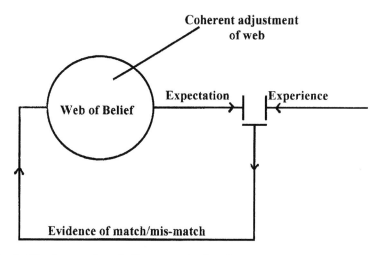

Figure 3   Justification as epistemically progressive learning.

3 Representing practical knowledge

The models of theory formulation that have so far been considered have been linguistic, or quasi-linguistic structures. This is hardly surprising since theorizing is a social activity and language is the prime mode of communication. The requirements of public communication should not, however, be translated uncritically into constraints on ways of representing the inner dynamics of knowledge and cognition. To do so is to end up seeing thought as a language-like, rule based, process of manipulating symbolic structures.

Unfortunately, very little of the vast bulk of human cognitive activity can be captured, or formulated in this fashion. Most human cognitive activity is manifested in the form of skilled performance involving finely graded judgments influenced by multiple shifting constraints. Linguistically expressed compression algorithms come nowhere near to representing an agent's practical knowledge, or to providing sound clues as to how such knowledge is acquired. The result is a familiar, but regrettable, filtering out of knowledge of practice from research, and the virtual institutionalizing of a methodological theory/ practice divide. From an information-theoretic perspective, however, the actual coding of knowledge is not a basic issue. Earlier conclusions about representation, justification and the dynamics of knowledge acquisition can be expected to hold up across divergent codings.

Recently, some very powerful research tools, drawn from neural network modeling, have been developed which hold promise of providing a valuable approach to this problem. Although the technicalities are complex, the main ideas can be given in outline (See e.g. Hassoun, 1995, for the technicalities, and Evers, 1997, 1998, for applications to education). Essentially, artificial neural networks are learning devices which, for the most common varieties in use, attempt to build up a sub-symbolic representation of the statistical structure of data sets through a process of trial and error, subject to a constraint of minimizing error which is defined as the difference between the network's output and some target output. The resulting sub-symbolic representational compression algorithm is an array of numbers that, roughly speaking, constitutes the connection strengths, or weights, between layers of artificial neurons comprising the net. Knowledge of patterns in data extracted by the net thus resides in the structure and value of its array of weights.

There are two key results that are of interest to researchers on practical, non-symbolic knowledge. First, once learning has been completed to the desired level of precision possible, the net's internal representation of the statistical features of its input environment can be examined and displayed. One such display, which illustrates a form of cluster analysis, is known as a dendogram and it measures the degree of similarity (on a plausible metric) between elements of the data set (see Plunkett and Elman, 1997, for an example of both the software and a workbook of applications).The second, rather stunning result, is that dendograms are mostly stable across different network architectures, drawing their properties primarily from the data (Churchland, 1998). This means that limited, artificial models, of brain cognitive processes have a greater likelihood of capturing significant features of the structure of human practical knowledge that has been built up from experience.

4 Conclusion

Inquiry, construed both broadly and modestly, as that repertoire of theorized strategies, techniques, and procedures which enables human beings to act in the world with a realistic expectation of doing better than chance, can be informed by a range of sources. It is one of the strengths of coherentism that it acknowledges the successes of the many natural and commonplace forms of inquiry all around and seeks to explain how they are possible, being willing to posit a wider variety of factors that make for that epistemic success. To the extent that coherentism is able to draw on the resources of natural science to account for that success, particularly recent developments in cognitive science, is indicative of one of its own epistemic virtues, namely, that accounts of inquiry should be able to profit from their own recursive application.

References

BonJour, L. 1985 *The Structure of Empirical Knowledge*, Harvard University Press, Cambridge, MA.

Chaitin, G. 1975 Randomness and mathematical proof. *Scientific American* 232(5), 47–52.

Churchland, P. M. 1998 Conceptual similarity across sensory and neural diversity: the Fodor/Lepore challenge answered. *Journal of Philosophy* 95(1), 5–32.

Connelly, F. M. and Clandinin, D. J. 1990 Stories of experience and narrative in enquiry, *Educational Researcher* 19(5), 2–14.

Clandinin, D. J. and Connelly, F. M. 1996 Teachers' professional knowledge landscapes: Teacher stories – stories of teachers – school stories – stories of schools, *Educational Researcher,* 25(3) 24–30.

Constas, M. The changing nature of educational research and a critique of postmodernism, *Educational Researcher*, 27(2) 26–33.

Cussins, A. 1992 The limitations of pluralism. In: D. Charles and K. Lennon (eds) *Reduction, Explanation, and Realism*, pp. 179–223. Clarendon Press, Oxford.

Dennett, D. 1991 Real patterns, *Journal of Philosophy*, 88(1), 27–51.

Evers, C. W. 1979 Philosophy of education: a naturalistic perspective. In: D. N. Aspin (ed.) *Logical Empiricism and Post-Empiricism in Educational Discourse*, pp. 167–181. Heinemann, Durban.

Evers, C. W. 1998 Decision-making, models of mind and the new cognitive science, *Journal of School Leadership*, 8(2), 94–108.

Evers, C. W. 1991 Towards a coherenterist theory of validity. *International Journal of Educational Research*, 15(6), 521–535.

Evers, C. W. and Lakomski, G. 1991 *Knowing Educational Administration*. Pergamon Press, Oxford.

Evers, C. W. and Lakomski, G. 1996 *Exploring Educational Administration*. Pergamon Press, Oxford.

Haig, B. D. 1987 Scientific problems and the conduct of research. *Educational Philosophy and Theory,* 19(2), 22–32.

Hassoun, M. H. 1995 *Fundamentals of Artificial Neural Networks*, MIT Press, Cambridge, MA.

Kerlinger, F. N. 1986 *Foundations of Behavioral Research*, 3rd edn. Harcourt Brace, New York.

Kuhn, T. 1970 *The Structure of Scientific Revolutions* (2nd edn). University of Chicago Press, Chicago.

Linsky, B. (ed.) 1971 *Reference and Modality*. Oxford University Press, London.

McMillan, J. H. and Schumacher, S. 1993 *Research in Education: A Conceptual Introduction* (3rd edn). Harper Collins, New York.

Nickles, T. 1980 Scientific problems: three empiricist models. In: R. Giere and P. Asquith (eds) *Philosophy of Science Association 1980*, Vol. 1, pp. 3–19. Philosophy of Science Association, East Lansing.

Petrie, H. 1972 Theories are tested by observing the facts: or are they? In: L. G. Thomas (ed.) *Philosophical Redirection of Educational Research*, 71st NSSE Yearbook, pp. 47–73. University of Chicago Press, Illinois.

Plunkett, K. and Elman, J. L. 1997 *Exercises in Rethinking Innateness: A Handbook for Connectionist Simulations*. MIT Press, Cambridge, MA.

Quine, W. V. 1951 Two dogmas of empiricism, *Philosophical Review*, 60, 20–43.

Quine, W. V. and Ullian, J. S. 1978 *The Web of Belief* (2nd edn). Random House, New York.

Robinson, V. M. J. 1993 *Problem-Based Methodology*. Pergamon Press, Oxford.

Robinson, V. M. J. 1998 Methodology and the research-practice gap. *Educational Researcher*, 27(1), 17–26.

Rumelhart, D. E. and McClelland, J. L. (eds), 1986, *Parallel Distributed Processing*, Volume 1, MIT Press, Cambridge, MA.

Thagard, P. 1989 Explanatory coherence. *Behavioral and Brain Sciences*, 12, 435–467.

26 Symbol Processing, Situated Action, and Social Cognition: Implications for Educational Research and Methodology

G. Lakomski

The discussion offered in this concluding article continues earlier work in naturalistic coherentist research methodology (Lakomski, 1991; Evers, 1991; Evers and Lakomski, 1991). It reinforces a number of critical points made by Evers (see *From Foundations to Coherence in Educational Research*) in his account of the development of research methodology from foundations to coherentism, and it expands upon the main theme raised by Keeves in the introduction to this volume which supports the unity of educational research.

The division of the field of educational research methodology into qualitative and quantitative paradigms, as was argued by Evers and Lakomski (1991, ch. 10), is unhelpful because the empiricist epistemological assumptions involved commit educational research to a narrow view of human cognition and learning as symbol processing. Unlike empiricism, naturalistic coherentism requires that its claims cohere with science rather than ignore or contradict its resources to defend its claims. It is an alternative to the paradigms view which it considers false and argues, *inter alia*, that modern cognitive science offers a more comprehensive view of cognition which considers symbol processing as but a part of human cognitive activity. Coherentism's more inclusive account of cognition, based on modern neural net accounts of brain functioning, enables the resolution of the central problem of educational research, its split between theory and practice, and its concomitant inability to explain practice. On the standard account, practice is tacit and cannot be formalized. Good teaching is thus caught rather than taught, and good practitioners learn their craft through long experience. How to create good practice, or what makes a practitioner effective, are issues which have resisted resolution. Thus, practice, that most important aspect of the educational enterprise, has remained shrouded in mystery.

The idea that the sum total of human cognition and intelligence resides in the ability to process symbols in our heads has recently come under attack from two quite different but intersecting fields. Situated action which is an umbrella description for a number of approaches, derives mainly from cultural anthropology, ethnomethodology, discourse analysis, and interpretative social science generally. The other prong of this new attack originates in recent developments in cognitive science, and especially modern connectionism.

Given its social anthropological and cultural roots, situated action stresses the importance of the construction of human cognition in the everyday cognitive practices of humans and rejects the view of cognition as uniquely symbol processing. The most important contribution of this perspective is its insistence on the cultural and contextual features as integral parts of cognition, demonstrated in various empirical studies including the learning of school mathematics. This perspective has recently become prominent in the educational research literature and can be considered the most prominent challenge, coming from education, to the symbol processing or cognitivist view.

Recent developments in connectionism, that is, neural net accounts of brain functioning, provide the currently best models of how the physical brain works. Although there is ongoing argument regarding the proximity of these models to the workings of the actual brain, their features have been very successful in modeling behaviors below the symbolic/conceptual level. This means they have been able to simulate practice, that part of cognitive human activity which operates at the non-sentential, performance level. Furthermore, connectionists have begun to explore cognition beyond the individual skull, and to consider cognition as distributed between other knowers and their material contexts. Hence, the interactive and reciprocal relationships between cognition and culture have become a prominent and new avenue for cognitive science research. In so far as situated action remains largely agnostic about the fine-grained detail of the causal mechanisms of cognition, and in so far as connectionism does combine a causal account with situated action's cultural perspective and includes symbol processing, it extends human knowledge of cognition into areas yet unexplored. It promises to provide a far more comprehensive framework for the explanation of human thought and action, in education as elsewhere.

In order to assess the substance and scope of these debates, the following sections discuss the main claims and features of situated action over against the classical definition of symbol processing, Newell and Simon's *Physical Symbol System Hypothesis*. In particular, since the proponents of either perspective engage one another directly in two separate debates, in the cognitive science and education literature respectively, a brief account of these is given to focus on their differences as well as agreements. Finally, some preliminary conclusions are drawn for the nature and conduct of educational research and methodology in light of the expanded view of cognitive activity proposed here.

1   Cognition as situated action

Situated Action is a perspective which covers a range of views and terminologies under headings such as "situated activity"; "situated social practice"; "situated learning", "situated" or "distributed cognition". The collections of essays in Rogoff and Lave, 1984, and Resnick, Levine and Teasley, 1991 provide good examples of these different views. It is not possible here to do justice to the complexity and diversity of situated action approaches which range from social psychological, anthropological, ethnomethodological and discourse analysis perspectives to those embedded in cognitive psychology and cognitive science. Attempts to identify claims as central to such a perspective need to be mindful of the theoretical contexts in which the claims figure.

However, there is at least one point of agreement in this diversity in virtue of which situated action qualifies as a distinct position. It is opposed to the central claim of the physical symbol system hypothesis that symbol processing is at the core of human intelligence and cognition. While most situated action theorists do not deny that symbol processing has a role to play in human cognitive activity, different positions are taken about what precisely this role is presumed to be. The importance and function of symbol processing in human cognition is an extraordinarily difficult and complex issue which is as yet not well understood. In the present context, some very recent developments in the artificial neural net connectionist literature are sketched to provide a glimpse of work in progress.

To begin the discussion of situated action, Lave's description of situated social practice, or where appropriate situated learning, provides a good starting point since she is one of situated action's most frequently cited and discussed theorists (Rogoff and Lave, 1984; Lave, 1988, 1991; Lave and Wenger, 1991; Chaiklin and Lave, 1993). Her broad description is characteristic of the social–cultural flavor of situated action. Describing her project as a social anthropology of cognition, Lave is concerned to emphasize the fluid boundary between intra- and extra-cranial human experience, that is a boundary more characterized by "reciprocal, recursive, and transformational partial incorporations of person and world in each other within a complex field of relations between them." (Lave, 1988, p. 1). "The point" she says,

> . . . is not so much that arrangements of knowledge in the head correspond in a complicated way to the social world outside the head, but that they are socially organized in such a fashion as to be indivisible. "Cognition" observed in everyday practice is distributed – sketched over, not divided among – mind, body, activity and culturally organized settings (which include other actors).

This view (see also Chaiklin and Lave, 1993, p. 17) not only maintains that cognition is distributed, but that the correct focal point for the study of human cognition is "out there" in the cognitive performance of people's everyday routines. Such a perspective is opposed to studying cognition in laboratory or other experimental settings which specify and test only certain kinds of specialized cognitive tasks. Among her early examples are empirical studies of arithmetic as cognitive practice, the Adult Math Project (AMP), conducted in such everyday contexts as supermarket shopping, and beginning a dieting program, with the goal of establishing how well formally taught school arithmetic transfers to practical everyday contexts. Lave finds that mathematical skills taught in the school context appear not to be used in everyday reasoning contexts.

According to Lave's position, acquiring knowledge and skill, and becoming a master practitioner, is a matter of ongoing practice in communities of practice, exemplified in, for example, some forms of apprenticeships which do not rely on formal teaching. The danger of the traditionally held cognitivist view is that it dis-embeds knowledge/cognition from the routine contexts of its use: "extraction of knowledge from the particulars of experience, of activity from its context, is the condition for making knowledge available for general application in all situations" (Lave, 1988, p. 8). In her view formal schooling epitomizes this disembedding. Hence, she concludes, learning in schools "is most likely to fail" (Lave, 1991, p. 80). The continuity of learning over different settings is, in cognitive psychology, attributable to the explanatory concept of transfer of learning whose cognitivist definition Lave rejects. Situated action, on her account, provides a better explanation of the internalization of knowledge, and of transfer than that offered by cognitive psychology.

While Lave's approach is more colored by critical social ethnography and anthropology, writers such as Greeno and Moore (1993, 1997), and Clancey (1993) can perhaps be located more directly in the cognitive science tradition. For Greeno and Moore (1993, pp. 49–50), for example, situated action or situativity theory claims

> ... that cognitive activities should be understood primarily as interactions between agents and physical systems and with other people. Symbols are often important parts of the situation the people interact with, and understanding how symbols are used and constructed in activities is one of the major problems of cognitive theory.

Greeno (1977, p. 15) believes that situated action is more useful in building a more comprehensive theory of human cognition than the physical symbol system hypothesis in that it "considers processes of interaction as basic and explains individual cognitions and other behaviors in terms of their contributions to interactive systems." Methodologically this implies studying the activities of groups to detect the properties of these social practices which provide the main explanatory concepts of situated action (for examples, see Hastie and Pennington, 1991; Scribner, 1984; Hutchins, 1991; Levine and Moreland, 1991). A useful summary of the main claims of situated action is offered by Clancey (1993, pp. 90–93) who, unlike his social anthropology colleagues attempts to give a comprehensive rather than oppositional picture of both symbol processing and situated action in neuropsychological terms. Situated action research, Clancey (1993, p. 92) states, is " . . . Not merely about an agent 'located in the environment', 'strongly interactive', or 'real time' . . . rather [it is] a claim about the internal mechanism that coordinates sensory and motor systems." His formulation makes it clear that he wishes to integrate symbol processing into a kind of neuropsychological version of situated action.

In introducing the debate between the two sides in the 1993 Special Issue of *Cognitive Science*, the editor (Norman, 1993, p. 5) formulated the core issue like this: "Is symbolic cognition a special case of cognitive activity (the position Greeno and Moore hold), or is situated action a special case of symbolic cognitive ability (the position that Vera and Simon hold)?". Drawing on both the 1993 *Cognitive Science* debate and the subsequent publication of another critical exchange between Simon and colleagues and Greeno and colleagues in the 1996 and 1997 issues of *Educational Researcher*, the nature of the disagreements between these two approaches come to light even more clearly; for a parallel critical discussion regarding teaching see Packer and Winne, 1994. For Greeno (1997, p. 5), the issue is fundamentally about which "framework offers the better prospect for developing a unified scientific account of activity considered from both social and individual points of view, and which framework supports research that will inform discussions of educational practice more productively."

Of particular interest in the present discussion are the contributions by Vera and Simon (1993a) and Anderson, Reder and Simon (1996) which, as critics of situated action, in turn provide the foil for critique by Clancey (1993), Greeno and Moore (1993) and Greeno (1997). Given the above statements, the positions advocated and defended are not considered amenable to compromise with the possible exception of Clancey. Vera and Simon (1993a) argue that advocates of situated action have nothing new to contribute. Thus, they do not threaten the symbol processing view which is able to contain the claims and arguments of the opposition. Greeno and colleagues, for their part, contest their argument believing their approach to be superior in that they can accommodate symbol processing in their broader account. Before it is possible to consider what a preliminary resolution of this issue might look like, it is necessary to understand better the nature and issues of disagreement. In order to do so it is helpful to take a closer look at what is meant by the physical symbol system hypothesis which is at the heart of classical artificial intelligence and which until very recently has defined how to understand human cognition, reason, and intelligence.

2   Cognition as symbol processing

Put in its simplest form, the physical symbol system hypothesis maintains that human knowledge and rationality consist in the ability to manipulate (linguistic and quasi-linguistic) symbols in the head. The emphasis is on the internal processing structures of the brain and the symbolic representations of mind. Discussed and defended extensively (Newell and Simon, 1972; Newell and Simon, 1976; Simon, 1979; Anderson, 1983), it is worthwhile to quote Simon (1990, p. 3) in full. The physical symbol system hypothesis

> states that a system will be capable of intelligent behavior if and only if it is a physical
> symbol system. ... [it] is a system capable of inputting, outputting, storing, and

modifying symbol structures, and of carrying out some of these actions in response to the symbols themselves. "Symbols" are any kinds of patterns on which these operations can be performed, where some of the patterns denote actions (that is, serve as commands or instructions). . . . Information processing psychology claims that intelligence is achievable by physical symbol systems and only such systems. From that claim follow two empirically testable hypotheses: 1. that computers can be programmed to think; and 2 that the human brain is (at least) a physical symbol system. These vioews are developed further by Vera and Simon (1993a, pp. 8–11; 1993b).

In order to test these hypotheses, a computer is programmed to perform the same tasks used to judge how well humans think, and to demonstrate that the computer uses the same processes humans employ in performing the tasks. Simon and his colleagues use "thinking-aloud protocols, records of eye movements, reaction times, and many other kinds of data as evidence" (Simon, 1990, p. 3).

In computers, symbols are typically patterns of electromagnetism but their physical nature differs depending on the kind of computer. In any case, Simon does not believe that their physical nature matters: what matters is their role in behavior. He observes that humans do not actually know how symbols are represented in the brain other than that they are likely to be patterns of some kinds of neuronal arrangements (Vera and Simon, 1993a, p. 9). Another important feature of patterns as symbols is their ability to designate or denote, either other symbols, patterns of sensory stimuli or motor actions: "Perceptual and motor processes connect the symbol system with its environment, providing it with its semantics, the operational definitions of its symbols" (Vera and Simon, 1993a, p. 9). While the social environment is considered to some extent, the explanation of how and in what form new knowledge is stored in memory, how learning occurs, can be studied "primarily in terms of its internal mechanisms . . . taking the input (e.g., material from a textbook) as given, and seeking to model how that input changes the internal contents of memory so that the system will subsequently possess the desired skill or the desired knowledge" (Vera and Simon, 1993a, p. 43). Simon insists that symbols, and hence symbolic processing, must not be identified as exclusively verbal or linguistic processing. Rather symbols may "designate words, mental pictures, or diagrams, as well as other representations of information" (Vera and Simon, 1993a, p. 10).

Although the physical symbol system hypothesis has been highly successful in that it "has been tested so extensively over the past 30 years that it can now be regarded as fully established, although over less than the whole gamut of activities that are called 'thinking'" (Simon, 1990, p. 3), Simon concedes a number of unresolved issues. One of the most important is how the brain's symbol processing capacities are realized physiologically. He notes that while information processing psychology says much about the "software of thinking", it has little to say about its "hardware" or "wetware", a gap which needs to be filled (Simon, 1995, p. 5; see also Newell, Rosenbloom, and Laird, 1996).

It is also acknowledged that there are computational limits in information processing in terms of both speed and organization of a system's computations and sizes of its memories. The example of playing a perfect game of chess is instructive here. Such a feat would require examining more chess positions than there are molecules in the universe. Simon draws the following conclusion, "If the game of chess, limited to its 64 squares and six kind of pieces, is beyond exact computation, then we may expect the same of almost any real-world problem, including almost any problem of everyday life." (Simon, 1990, p.6). On the basis of this observation he concludes that ". . . *intelligent systems must use approximate methods to handle most tasks. Their rationality is bounded*" (Simon, 1990, p. 6; emphases in original). The doctrine of bounded rationality is arguably the most influential feature of mainstream organization and (educational) administration theory, which, as a theory of rationality, has determined all the major features of organizational functioning.

Finally, in their assessment of the success of the perspective that they have been instrumental in shaping, Newell, Rosenbloom and Laird (1996, p. 127) single out some items as yet unknown regarding their effects on cognitive architecture. These are the issues (1) of "acquiring capabilities through development, of living autonomously in a social community, and of exhibiting self-awareness and a sense of self . . ."; (2) how to square their cognitive architecture with biological evaluation which puts a premium on perceptual and motor systems; and (3) how to integrate emotion, feeling and affect into cognitive architecture. These comments show clearly the boundary drawn between cognitive architecture and the world although the exact drawing of it is accepted as problematic.

3 Situated action verses symbol processing

The difficulty of presenting the arguments of both perspectives is that either side believes that its view can accommodate the perspective of the opponent when suitably redescribed. Vera and Simon (1993a, p. 46) conclude their account of situated action "without finding reasons why such action cannot be accommodated within the physical symbol–system hypothesis: and that "SA [situated action] is not a new approach to cognition, much less a new school of cognitive psychology". Greeno and Moore (1993, p. 55) in turn deny the centrality of the physical symbol system hypothesis for human intelligence, but agree that "cognition includes symbolic processing, but they are not coextensive". In addition, each side accuses the other of misrepresenting at least some aspects of their position, resulting in continual adjustments, redefinitions, and misunderstandings. It is clear that their differing theoretical backgrounds and philosophical assumptions account largely for the language in which the arguments are couched. An attempt is made in the following pages to present both sides to demonstrate where they differ from each other and also point to possible agreements.

In their critical review of situated action, Anderson *et al.* (1996, p. 5) assert that the following four claims are central:

(1) action is grounded in the concrete situation in which it occurs;
(2) knowledge does not transfer between tasks;
(3) training by abstraction is of little use; and
(4) instruction must be done in complex, social environments.

The authors agree with the weak versions of claim (1) in that much of what is learnt is specific to the situation but they reject the strong version that all knowledge is situation – specific. The latter version gives rise to the claim (2) that more general knowledge cannot transfer to other contexts, such as arithmetic formally learnt in school contexts. They take Lave's (1988) position to be an example of the strong version. However, whether one assumes the weak or strong versions of lack of transfer between contexts, there is a large amount of empirical evidence in the psychological literature which shows that degrees of transfer – from large to modest to none to negative – is a function of "representation and degree of practice; of the experimental situation and the relation of the material originally learned to the transfer material, and on "where attention is directed during learning or at transfer" (Anderson *et al.*, 1996, pp. 7–8).

A corollary of claim (2), claim (3), if interpreted in its strong version, undercuts the legitimacy of school learning in that it leads to a demand for apprenticeship training in real-world contexts on the assumption that what is learnt in school contexts is too abstract for the job at hand. A weak version could consist in training by modeling, a more traditional pedagogical device. Anderson *et al.* (1996) provide further empirical studies which qualify the claim that abstract instruction is of little help. The literature of modern information processing appears to suggest that a combination of abstract instruction and concrete task execution is best for learning to take place. As for claim (4) that learning is inherently a social activity and should be done in complex social situations, the authors point out that while social aspects of jobs are important, skills can well be taught independently of the social context. Part training is often more effective where the part is practically independent of the larger task. This does not deny that it is useful and necessary in some situations to practice skills in their complex contexts, such as playing the violin in an orchestra. Anderson *et al.* (1996, p. 10) conclude their critical examination of the four claims attributed to situated action by noting that

> [I]n general, situated learning focuses on some well-documented phenomena in cognitive psychology and ignores many others: while cognition is partly context-dependent, it is also partly context-independent; while there are dramatic failures of transfer, there are also dramatic successes; while concrete instruction helps, abstract instruction also helps; while some performances benefit from training in a social context, others do not.

Greeno's (1997) reply exemplifies the different discourses from within which learning and cognition are addressed. He notes that the differences between the two perspectives are really differences between explanatory frameworks. He does not accept the claims Anderson and his colleagues describe as characteristic of situated action, and he attributes their formulation to the different framing assumptions of the cognitivist perspective. While the latter begins on the assumption of a theory of individual cognition, supplemented by further analyses of additional components which serve as contexts, situated action begins from the assumption of a theory of social and ecological interaction which leads it towards a more comprehensive theory of analyses of information structures in the contents of people's interactions. These basic assumptions clearly show in the answers Greeno gives to the criticisms raised.

Situated action starts with interactive systems, including people and other material and representational systems. Where the physical symbol system hypothesis advocates the acquisition of knowledge in form of abstract representations and procedures for application in many contexts, situated action emphasizes learning to participate in interactions in ways that succeed over a broad range of situations. The implications for theory are that the physical symbol system hypothesis is wrongly committed to a "factoring assumption" in that properties of individual mental processes can be analyzed and that the properties of other systems can be taken as contexts in which these processes and structures function (Greeno, 1997, p. 7). As such, Greeno also admits that the cognitive perspective has been very successful. It is however "unacceptably incomplete" in that it is not possible in the cognitive view to specify the contribution other systems have made in an individual's construction of knowledge in interaction with the environment. For situated action, more effective participation in groups across a wide range of situations is the relevant criterion for learning having taken place. This is juxtaposed to the formal testing of knowledge retention, attributed to the cognitive view.

Replying to Anderson and his colleagues' claim (4), Greeno comments that the issue is not one of the acquisition of skills but of the appropriate arrangement of the social conditions of learning. Learning always happens in complex social environments, such as the social arrangement which produced both textbook and computer. The educational implications of either position are that for the cognitive perspective it becomes central how to arrange for the collection of skills and understandings to be acquired most efficiently. For situated action, alternative arrangements for learning need to consider "the values of having students learn to participate in the practices of learning that those arrangements afford" (Greeno, 1997, p. 10). This might mean beginning with relatively more complicated arrangements since learning sequences are considered "trajectories of participation" rather than sequences of knowledge and skill acquisition of increasing complexity.

Regarding claim (2) in Anderson and his colleagues' critique, Greeno rejects the assertion that transfer of learning is antithetical to situated action. Rather, the issue is one of appropriately framing the question of generality and transfer, not one of discussing whether or not transfer occurs. In Greeno's conception, a test for transfer "involves transforming the situation in which an activity was learned. To succeed in the transfer test, the activity – that is, the interaction of the learner with the other systems in the situation – has to be transformed in a way that depends on how the situation is transformed"

(Greeno, 1997, p. 12). The question of generality of learning is very important because it relates directly to the school curriculum which is designed on the assumption that school-based knowledge is inherently general because it is abstract. Here Greeno refers to Lave's empirical work on school-learnt algorithms which were not used in reasoning away from school. However, he warns that the conclusion drawn by cognitive writers overshoots the mark when they allege that situated action claims that school-based learning cannot be used in non-school settings. What situated action does maintain is that a school learning situation has its own practices and characteristics of performance which differ from those of other non-school settings. Hence, he points out "We cannot safely assume that, by learning the procedures of symbol manipulation which they have traditionally been taught in school mathematics, students' participation in other kinds of interactions will be strongly influenced (Greeno, 1997, p. 12).

In discussing the issue of abstraction, claim (3) of Anderson and his colleagues' critique, Greeno notes that as far as situated action is concerned, the concept of abstraction is part of that of representation. Here, as before, it is obvious that fundamental theoretical formulations, rather than empirical data, are the main bone of contention. If considered as part of representation, then it involves "the portability of symbolic or iconic representations that can be interpreted apart from their referents" (Greeno, 1997, p. 13). For students to learn these properly, for example, the representational systems of mathematics and science, they also need to learn the standard conventions used to interpret them. Such representational systems have a role to play in situated action as an aspect of social practice provided their meanings are understood. Only then do they contribute to learning as understood in situated action, and is sharply differentiated from learning a set of mechanical rules. Greeno (1997, p. 13) observes that more needs to be known about the role of abstract representation in activity.

In their final word on the present exchange, Anderson and his colleagues confirm that there are some agreements between the perspectives, but continue to insist that situated action does not possess the "right theoretical or experimental tools for understanding social cognition. Such understanding can only be achieved through serious attention to what goes on in the human mind, and not simply through external observation of social interaction" (Anderson et al., 1997, p. 20). The differences between the two approaches are sharply in focus in the cognitive perspective's appraisal of the social which it attempts to understand "through its residence in the mind of the individual". The strength of the information-processing approach "comes not just from its decision to focus on the individual but from its decision to analyze the knowledge possessed by the individual and how it is, and can be, acquired" (Anderson et al., 1997, p. 21).

The two perspective, as has been amply documented, come from different disciplines and research traditions, and begin from diverse starting points. Yet despite such ostensive differences and outright disagreements both approaches deliver valuable insights into human cognition and its function in the world. Weaving these into a coherent account of cognition, however, requires a closer look at symbol processing in light of the challenge posed by the connectionist artificial neural networks account. Ironically, it is through work done in this branch of connectionist neuroscience that it is possible to foreshadow a productive integration of both symbol processing and the demands of situated action that cognition be considered a cultural phenomenon, created through reciprocal interaction with the environment, including symbol systems.

4   Symbols in the head?

The cognitive perspective, based on symbol processing as the central characteristic of human cognition and intelligence, is a rule-based approach to cognition. Simply put, the classical cognitive perspective assumes that a computer is able to simulate human cognition and information processing when it is programmed with human like rules. For a machine to be able to learn, according to this perspective, it can be fed rules for modifying or adding rules. It was not believed that the architecture of the physical brain was of fundamental significance since the higher cognitive processes of importance for the physical symbol system hypothesis – information processing, problem solving, and planning – are at some remove from and at a higher level of abstraction than basic neuronal processes. An excellent source book of the foundations of cognitive science is Posner, 1996; see also Lycan, 1990 for various philosophical implications of cognitive science and connectionism.

Despite considerable success, there are remaining difficulties which appear resistant to resolution within the symbolic perspective, as pointed out earlier. What in Simon's (1990) terminology is the problem of explaining "rationality without optimization", i.e. how such everyday accomplishments as devising university or factory schedules, for example, are possible since they go beyond the practical bounds of computation by even the fastest super computer, is believed to be more than a temporary glitch in the program. Rather, it is indicative of what Tienson (1990) calls the "Kuhnian crisis" of GOFAI ("good old-fashioned artificial intelligence", as Haugeland 1985, phrased it). This crisis is underscored by a range of cognitive phenomena which are either inadequately explained or ignored by the physical symbol system hypothesis. Examples identified by Clancey (1993, pp. 97–98) include the following situations.

- Regularities develop in human behavior without requiring awareness of the patterns, that is, without first person representations . . .
- People speak idiomatically, in ways grammars indicate would be nonsensical.
- We experience interest, a sense of similarity, and value before we create representations to rationalize what we see and feel . . .
- Know-how is at first inarticulate and disrupted by reflection . . .
- Immediate behavior is adapted, not merely selected from prepared possibilities . . .

In addition, it seems difficult for human beings to carry out chains of reasoning in their heads or to number-crunch, feats easily accomplished by the computer. On the other hand, people are extremely good at recognizing and completing patterns and retrieving memory, capabilities which pose enormous problems for rule-based systems. Since such capabilities appear to be more in keeping with evolutionary and biological developments, it is more plausible to believe that since nature solves complex tasks by drawing on overlapping systems ("swarming", see Bereiter, 1991) that the brain would do likewise. Distributed cognition appears to be the better choice to cope with complex environments and tasks than the neat and orderly process adopted by the physical symbol system hypothesis.

A further worry relates to the top-down nature of rule-based systems which seem to be incompatible with either learning or evolution. As Bereiter (1991, p. 11) notes, "If a system is already operating according to a given set of rules, there does not seem to be any way that those rules could generate a higher level rule that controlled them." Neither evolution nor learning appear to have a place in this conception. These observations have been complemented by a growing body of psychological research (e.g. Johnson-Laird, 1983). The importance of this combined research serves to indicate that human cognition is not much like the account given by the physical symbol system hypothesis, since it does not resemble our natural intelligence which, after all, it was supposed to simulate. Cognition seems much "messier" and more haphazard than believed by the advocates of the physical symbol system hypothesis.

The additional difficulties, expressed as those of real time and graceful degradation add to the physical symbol system hypothesis's problems, as well as two further, and more potentially threatening, sets of concerns. The real time issue refers to the fact that most artificial intelligence programs require many more than 100 steps to carry out a basic cognitive task in contrast to human problem solving. Although neurons are slow, operating in times measured in milliseconds and being thus much slower than computers, they accomplish their task within about 100 steps (the "100-step rule", see Bechtel, 1990, p. 259). Similarly, graceful degradation refers to the fact that the performance of natural systems runs down gradually. Persons who suffer a stroke, for example, lose some but not all mental functions, the nervous system being "relatively fault tolerant". A von Neumann machine, on the other hand, which is the material basis for the physical symbol system hypothesis, "is rigid and fault intolerant, and a breakdown of one tiny component disrupts the machine's performance" (Churchland and Sejnowski, 1990, p. 233).

But the more severe problem for the physical symbol system hypothesis is that it has not been possible to construct the kinds of rules that it requires, a difficulty already hinted at in Simon's chess example above. This difficulty arises in relation to two clusters of problems: (1) multiple simultaneous soft constraints; and (2) any piece of commonsense knowledge might turn out to be relevant to any task or any other piece of knowledge; the latter cluster includes the frame and the folding problem (Tienson, 1990, pp. 328 *et seq.*).

The first problem is nicely illustrated by Shulman in his description of an exceptional teacher, Nancy, who was like a symphony conductor, posing questions, probing for alternative views, drawing out the shy while tempering the boisterous. Not much happened in the classroom that did not pass through Nancy, whose pacing and ordering, structuring and expanding, controlled the rhythm of classroom life ... [Her] pattern of instruction, her style of teaching, is not uniform or predictable in some simple sense. She flexibly responds to the difficulty and character of the subject matter, the capacities of the students ... and her educational purposes. She can not only conduct her orchestra from the podium, she can sit back and watch it play with virtuosity by itself. (Shulman, 1987, pp. 2–3)

It is computationally impossible to write rules for a computer which could model such skilled performance since an enormous number of factors come into play which are unpredictable. And yet good practitioners/teachers seem to be able to combine such a vast range which produces what can be recognized as exceptional practice. Constraints are soft in the sense that any constraint can be violated, needing immediate responses and adjustments, without thus jeopardizing overall performance.

The second cluster has to do with commonsense understanding. In dealing with a cognitive task, it is necessary to judge what information is relevant and to find relevant information in all the knowledge already possessed. In other words, it is necessary for an individual to be able to "fold" knowledge together which has been acquired under different circumstances and while solving unrelated problems. Humans manage to mix-and-match effortlessly, but computers are far less capable of such feats. At the other end of the spectrum, according to Tienson (1990, p. 385) is the frame problem which is the problem of determining how much of the new information would either change, or leave unchanged, an existing set of beliefs. This implies that it is first necessary to determine which old beliefs are in any way relevant to the new information. These kinds of inferences are drawn naturally, but a computer would need to search every piece of old information to assess relevance, which is highly inefficient. The magnitude of this problem for a computer is such that even if it did have access to all of a human being's knowledge, it would need to specify rules in advance for what each piece of new information would or would not change in any given situation.

Humans never know which bit of information might be useful for the solving of what problem, but they are very good at retrieving or finding the relevant information when they need it, and also note failures. In order to do this it is necessary first to see information as relevant and then retrieve it and do so all at once. Human memory appears to be based on content, or is content addressable. This poses a problem for the physical symbol system hypothesis since in computer architecture, information is retrieved from where it is stored, from its address.

What the above discussion shows is that humans are routinely capable of cognitive feats which appear to surpass the capabilities of von Neuman machines to simulate them. Although advocates of the physical symbol system hypothesis have made some progress and developed more sophisticated programs which manage to overcome some of the biological constraints of serial processing, computers were not able to overcome (e.g.

Anderson's ACT and Newell's SOAR), whether such fine-tuning of the physical symbol system hypothesis is more helpful in understanding human cognition, does in the end depend on the architecture of the physical brain. And insights into its workings cannot ultimately be established by behavioral data alone.

In so far as artificial neural nets attempt to model real brain functioning characterized by massive interconnectivity and parallel distributed processing, and in so far as nets can program themselves without the benefit of rules (Rumelhart and McClelland, 1986; Churchland and Sejnowski, 1994), artificial neural nets can be said to provide a more productive framework for understanding human cognition. The "ancient paradox" (Smolensky) between those who place "the essence of intelligent behavior in the hardness of mental competence . . ." and those who place "it in the subtle softness of human performance" (Smolensky, 1988, p. 199) can indeed be solved.

Information and knowledge in connectionist systems is actively represented in the weights between the nodes which make up a pattern of activation. Learning in such a system consists of having the weights changed. For more detail regarding neural net architecture and its implications for education see Evers and Lakomski (1996, ch. 9). Activation of a representation may be brought about by a sufficient number of its nodes, but not necessarily all of them. This means that the same representation may be brought about by the activity of different nodes on different occasions (Tienson, 1990, p. 391). It is also a feature of connectionist systems that weights are set so that representations can complete themselves when only a few of their nodes are active. Patterns of activation are not stored in the manner of data structures. When the information is not actively in use there is no pattern in the system; the role of symbol in a connectionist system is played by a pattern of activation. Hence, connectionism can also be described as the sub symbolic paradigm (Smolensky, 1988). Pattern recognition, carried out with ease by neural nets, is a central cognitive function and more fundamental than the rule-based processing presumed to be the pinnacle of cognitive work.

Other important features of artificial neural nets are that they do not contain a central processor which determines how the system functions as a whole since connections between nodes are local. There is no one place in the system which knows what the system is doing as a whole, and what goes on in one part is independent from other parts. A neural net nevertheless does represent content across the system when it is in a particular state, and it can be said to have stored knowledge in the connection weights between its nodes. Networks are thus capable of internal representations, only such representations are not symbolic, they are certain patterns of activation. Hence, the cornerstone of connectionism can be expressed as "The intuitive processor is a sub conceptual connectionist dynamical system that does not admit a complete, formal, and precise conceptual-level description" (Smolensky, 1988, p. 160).

But this does not imply that connectionists eschew symbolic representation, although its significance is still being debated. Formalized knowledge in linguistic structures as the most prominent example of symbol processing indeed serves important functions: (1) it is publicly accessible; (2) different people can check its validity thereby attesting to its reliability or otherwise; and (3) its formal character, logical rules of inference, means that it is universally applicable and that people need not necessarily have to have experience in the actual domain to which it applies (Smolensky, 1988, p. 153). Knowledge formalization at the cultural level, however, differs significantly from that of the individual in that it is neither publicly available nor completely reliable; it is also dependent on ample experience. In the section to follow, consideration is given to how embodied and environmentally embedded cognition attempts to solve the problem.

5   Embodied and embedded cognition

While modern connectionism is concerned to model in ever finer detail how the physical brain works, there is also another direction in which the new connectionism has been developing. This research is directed outwards to the cultural contexts in which humans exist and in which they enact their cognitive activity. In order to get a better understanding of the importance of this shift, it is first necessary to ask what led symbols to be placed in the head at all? What kinds of assumptions have made it possible for the physical symbol system hypothesis to edit culture out in its attempt to define human cognition?

The task of this section is to explore how the insights of situated action and symbol processing might be rendered coherent in the light of recent developments in connectionism. This attempt at synthesis provides a first step at simultaneously naturalizing culture and context and enculturating cognition (see the work of Hutchins, 1991, 1996 and Clark, 1997). Such a move implies a conception of culture quite different from the traditional in that it is not considered as a collection of artefacts external to the mind, but as a process.

The origins of the idea that symbols are in the head are to be found in the Cartesian idea of what it is to be a thinking thing (Fetzer, 1996). Dreyfuss's summary, reported in Hutchins (1996, p. 357), provides as succinct an account of the origins as one might have wished for:

> GOFAI is based on the Cartesian idea that all understanding consists in forming and using appropriate symbolic representations. For Descartes, these representations were complex descriptions built up of primitive ideas or elements. Kant added the important idea that all concepts are rules for relating such elements, and Frege showed that the rules could be formalized so that they could be manipulated without intuition or inter-pretation.

Thus, entities thought to be inside the head are modeled on a class of entities external to it, symbolic representations. Symbolic logic in turn was essential to early computation, and it was an easy step to conceive of computers as somehow representing a person's reasoning processes, and to see a person as resembling a machine in some sense. If the brain could be considered as a digital machine, then such a machine – the Turing universal machine – could compute any function provided it was explicitly specified, and it could be programmed to do so.

What has happened according to Hutchins' (1996) alternative history of cognitive science is that the actual person, such as Turing, the inventor of the universal machine, dropped out of the picture. After all, it was originally he who physically manipulated those symbols in interacting with the world whose cognitive properties while doing the manipulation were not the same as the properties of the symbol systems which were manipulated (see also Clark, 1997, ch. 3). The manipulation of the system by the cognitive properties of the human produces a computation but it does not follow that this computation is happening in the person's head.

Hutchins' navigation example makes this point well. This system is in large part characterized by the execution of many formal operations, but not all the formal operations used to process the computational properties of this system are in the heads of the quartermasters. Quite a few are in the material environment which is shared and produced by them in their mutual interactions. The fact that this could be bleached out of the history of cognitive science is due to the central assumption that the formal manipulation of abstract symbols is both a necessary and sufficient condition for modeling human cognition. What has really been modeled here according to Hutchins is the operation of a sociocultural system from which the human actor has been deleted since what does the work in this model is the interaction of abstract symbol systems and not any one person. The computer then was hardly made in the image of a human being; it was made in the image of the formal manipulations of abstract symbols. It is in this way that symbols have found their way into human heads, by stipulating an isomorphism between symbol structures and neuronal activity patterns where the latter are said to bear 'a one-to-one relation to the symbol structure of Category 4 in the corresponding program [Category 4 = data stored in the computer]" (Vera and Simon, 1993c, pp. 120–121).

As a result, there is a vast gulf between internal cognition and the outside world of experience of people perceiving and moving about in their changing environments, as is recognized and misidentified as a left-over problem for the physical symbol system hypothesis. It was thus entirely logical that the testing of cognition happened in the laboratory, and that the tasks to which subjects were subjected were at the unusual end of the spectrum of human cognitive activity, such as puzzle solving or playing chess. These are cultural activities which do not belong to the humdrum cognitive activities of everyday life, and studying these yielded results which are not typical or representative of ordinary human cognition.

Given this analysis, it can be concluded that the empirical success the physical symbol system hypothesis has apparently enjoyed is rather a case of confirmation of an abstract model of symbol manipulation embedded in larger cultural production than confirmation of the symbol processing nature of a single human being.

What emerges from the preceding is an indication of how cognition is spread or distributed in the world. In one sense this has been known. Organizations, including schools, are examples of such successful distribution of human cognitive activity since no one individual can carry out all the cognitive functions conducted under the roof of one school or factory. Many computational tasks are too complex for one individual mind (Clark, 1997) and, as a consequence, the mind/brain off loads some important problem-solving tasks onto external structures. Such external structures in turn exhibit their own dynamics which react back onto and shape individual cognition in reciprocal interaction. An example is living in a democracy with its established rules and freedoms as opposed to living in an authoritarian society in which freedom of speech and freedom of association may be curtailed. These structural, legal, and social conditions shape how the citizens behave and exercise whatever rights they possess, including the freedom to learn. Since humans have limited cognitive capacities, the contracting out of cognitive tasks, or the cognitive division of labor, has been essential in order for people to become the kinds of advanced knowers that they are by some kind of cognitive bootstrapping. It is in this sense that external structures are extensions of the mind. This is rarely considered explicitly, and yet it is deeply embedded in everyday life. Patients who suffer from advanced Alzheimer's disease (Clark's example) depend on external structures to find the way around in their world. Without markers on doors, shopping-lists stuck to the refrigerator, a favorite chair in the right place, or the milk bottle by the back-door, these people lose their place in the world. Shifting objects, or altering anything in the environment serves to destabilize them and quite literally to rob them of their minds. Mind and world are indeed indivisible, as Lave had argued earlier.

Translated into larger social contexts, it can be seen that organizations serve a similar purpose as having a favorite chair in its normal position. By means of their structures, practices and norms they provide external resources which define the contexts for people being in them. This applies also to linguistic structures such as policies and regulations which help reshape some cognitive tasks into formats which are better suited to human basic computational capacities. The role and function of language goes far beyond that of communication. It is reasonable to see it as presenting a kind of trade-off between "culturally achieved representations and what would otherwise be . . . time-intensive and labor-intensive internal computation." (Clark, 1997, p. 200). This includes the off loading of memory by way of written texts; the devising of labels which serve as a kind of cognitive shorthand in navigating the environment successfully; language which allows people to coordinate their actions with those of others; and it also allows people to manipulate their own attention by inner rehearsal of speech.

Given these various functions, it may be concluded with Churchland, (1995, p. 270) that "language makes it possible, at any time, for human cognition to be *collective*." Language as the cultural externalization of individual thought transcends the cognitive system of the individual, and any single individual's life span, and conjoins it with that of others. The result is a far more powerful system with vastly increased cognitive resources to solve shared problems. The full import of this can only be appreciated on the background of human learning capacity, which seems to be characterized by extreme path dependence (Elman, 1994). This means that neural net learning, given the specific learning algorithm, the back propagation of error, is dependent on the sequence in which training cases are presented. Extrapolating this to human learning, some ideas have to be in place before others can be learnt, and given that a net's knowledge is located in its connection weights, any new learning is similarly constrained by those weights in so far as they serve as the original parameters for new learning. It is thus easy to see that neural net learning cannot jump around (Clarke, 1977) to any place it pleases. If this is so, the role of public language, in allowing the packaging and migration of ideas between individuals (Clark, 1997, p. 205), truly collectivizes human cognition and in so doing makes available immensely powerful cognitive resources way beyond individual capacity.

6   Implications for educational research and methodology

In light of this account of cognitive history with its emphasis on studying cognition in the confines of the laboratory, it is clearly important to support situated action in its conduct of ethnographic field studies as a first descriptive step to understand ordinary cognitive activity in its specificity. The contribution situated action makes is in terms of displaying the minutiae of everyday life, fine-grained descriptions whose frameworks are informed by such ethnographic concepts as "normal routines of collaborative work, distributions of accountability and authority, mutual availability of and attention to information sources, mutual understanding in conversation, and other characteristics of interaction that are relevant to the functional success of the participants' activities" (Greeno, 1997, p. 7). This approach enables researchers to focus on how human actors actually display their cognition in interaction with others and with material-structural systems which in turn shape and change their cognitive behavior. In doing so, this direction is not only compatible with evolution and biology in so far as it allows for human perception and locomotion, it does so within the context of socially and culturally created systems. It thus coheres much better than the physical symbol system hypothesis with what is known about human origins, biological, physiological, social and historical.

What it seems to lack, on the other hand, is a causal account of the actual mechanisms by means of which actors accomplish what they do. While cognition is social in the sense of being accomplished within broader cultural frameworks, it is nevertheless also in some sense the accomplishment of an individual mind/brain in interaction with other minds/ brains. While the symbol processing view located all cognition inside the head and treated the environment as a mere extension of memory, situated action appears to locate it all outside in the interactions between people and social structures. Yet short of attributing causal powers to structures which would leave open the question as to how such powers came about, it is humans who interpret and make sense of the structures and their interactions with them and with one another. However, situated action remains agnostic about the fine-grained physiological detail of how humans do can what they do so well, including the creation of human history and culture. In addition, it clearly is the case that humans do manipulate symbols successfully, and that linguistic structures have a role to play in the human cognitive economy, a facet not explained by situated action although acknowledged.

What results can be derived from such a seemingly abstract and difficult discussion for educational research and methodology? Looking back at the debates between situated action theorists and physical symbol system hypothesis advocates from a naturalistic coherentist point of view, the obvious first conclusion is that both groups appear correct in certain ways and incorrect in others. The difficulty of the present argument is to identify and specify in as much as is possible why this is so, given what has been learnt from recent developments in connectionist neural net research. One major difficulty resides in the fact that it is necessary to use ordinary language in order to explain what goes on at the sub symbolic/sub conceptual level of neuronal activity. Another is to dislodge the commonsense understandings about language and learning and to replace them with unfamiliar and technical redescriptions derived from cognitive science.

If for the present paradigmatic and other theoretical differences are discounted between situated action and the physical symbol system hypothesis as frameworks, and the primary issue of symbol processing is considered, then what has been gained is a redefinition of the relationship between educational theory and practice. This is so given the account of learning provided by neural net modeling which repositions symbol processing within the overall cognitive economy of human beings. Not only is symbol processing repositioned, connectionism is also beginning to explain what its functions may be in such a fully integrated view of cognition as embodied and distributed in social space. Linguistic constructs serve not only as a necessary relief function for a computationally limited brain, but also as facilitators of collective thought and action. It is presumably for this reason, if modern connectionists are half right, that schools have been as successful as they have in enabling learning, Lave's earlier comments notwithstanding.

Furthermore, in having extended the focus of learning beyond the individual skull, modern connectionism has begun to provide some explanatory framework for why culture has emerged at all, which is a continuation of the social evolution argument at the level of neuronal activity.

It also provides some explanation for why culture and context are indeed as important as stressed by those social science disciplines which have made it their starting point of analysis but which do not concern themselves with the biological and physiological processes which drive it. This result has the methodological consequence of supporting naturalistic field work and the kind of detailed studies of everyday human cognitive activity conducted in the situated action perspective since these varied local contexts are extensions of the mind/brain whose specific interactions with the agent and other agents and structures together form the object of analysis. This means at the very least that educational research directed at for example, the reading skills of students, needs to theorize the specificity of the context of its analyses from the outset. In this sense, situated action theorists are right in emphasizing instruction as taking place in complex social situations.

The most important outcome of this discussion, however, is a better understanding of the nature of practice and how humans are able to become skilled practitioners in their specific social and cultural contexts. If external structures are the scaffolds of the human mind, as Clark expresses it, then studying the reciprocal interactions of the scaffolds with the individual, and groups of individuals, becomes a central issue for research. The structural arrangement of classrooms and schools and the social conditions of learning are thus integral to the understanding of how children learn.

A further educational implication is that the notion of human cognition has been much broadened to include the vast amount of sub-symbolic cognitive activity in which humans engage. This should lead to a reformulation of what human intelligence is considered to be, and subsequently, to changes in how to teach, and how to assess the performance of children. The teaching–learning nexus itself has to be seen as far more interactive and reciprocal than standard views of intention-based learning have claimed (Evers and Lakomski, 1991). Educational research should be able to account for all of human cognitive potential, not just the most symbolically specified and specifiable.

In addition, if the extreme path dependence characteristic of neural net learning does apply to humans, then this might explain why learning does and does not transfer. Since new neural net learning is dependent upon its already established connection weights (its prior knowledge), and since the environment as discussed above has a specific role to play in knowledge acquisition, learning acquired in situation A, represented in its specific weight space, may just be too much out of kilter with the ensemble of situation–specific interactions encountered in situation B. Given the degree of discrepancy between the situations, for example Lave's case studies of school arithmetic and arithmetic employed in the supermarket, the net may or may not learn the new knowledge, or may do so after a considerable time and much effort. General as this interpretation is, it might indicate the direction of a possible explanation at the sub-symbolic level for what is termed transfer of learning. Further empirical research needs to be done to test this suggestion.

7 Conclusion

It is fitting that this volume should end with a large canvas view of a new coherentist framework which simultaneously broadens as well as specifies both the nature of educational research and methodology and points to directions of future development. Much of what has been stated in the previous section will ring familiar. In practical terms, research in education will continue to rely on many of the methods and techniques discussed in this volume. There has, however, been a substantive shift in terms of redirecting the whole enterprise. Understanding the broad spectrum of human cognitive activity from the bottom up, from the fine-grained neuronal activity inside and outside our skulls, has immeasurably expanded both the potential and the difficulties of educational research. The net gain of a naturalistic account is an explanation of human thought and action which coheres with what is known about humans as biological beings who negotiate their complexly structured environments largely successfully. While we do not yet possess a language appropriate for representing our skilled performance, we at least begin to understand how it is possible that a child learns to ride a bicycle, and what makes Nancy the skilled practitioner she is. Many more avenues need to be explored about how our minds/brains work, but in the face of such complexity we can take heart from Clarke's (1997, p. 175) delightful (although borrowed) phrase that ". . . if *the brain* were so simple that a single approach could unlock its secrets, *we* would be so simple that we couldn't do the job!"

References

Anderson, J. R. 1983 *The Architecture of Complexity*. Harvard University Press, Cambridge, MA.

Anderson, J. R., Reder, L. M. and Simon, H. A. 1997 Situative versus cognitive perspectives: Form versus substance. *Educational Researcher* 26(1), 18–21.

Anderson, J. R., Reder, L. M. and Simon, H. A. 1996 Situated learning and education, *Educational Researcher*, 25(4), 5–11.

Bechtel, W. 1990 Connectionism and the philosophy of mind: An overview. In: W. G. Lycan (ed.) *Mind and Cognition – A Reader*. Basil Blackwell, Oxford.

Bereiter, C. 1991 Implications of connectionism for thinking about rules, *Educational Researcher*, 20(3), 10–16.

Chaiklin, S. and Lave, J. (eds.) 1993 *Understanding Practice – Perspectives on Activity and Context*. Cambridge University Press, Cambridge.

Churchland, P. M. 1995 *The Engine of Reason, The Seat of the Soul*. The M.I.T. Press, Cambridge, MA.

Churchland, P. S. and Sejnowski, T. J. 1994 *The Computational Brain*. The M.I.T. Press, Cambridge, MA.

Churchland, P. S. and Sejnowski, T. J. 1990 Neural representation and neural computation. In: W. G. Lycan (ed.) *Mind and Cognition – A Reader*. Basil Blackwell, Oxford.

Clancey, W. J. 1993 Situated action: A neuropsychological interpretation, response to Vera and Simon, *Cognitive Science*, 17, 87–116.

Clark, A. 1997 *Being There: Putting Brain, Body, and World Together Again*. The M.I.T. Press, Cambridge, MA.

Elman, J. 1994 Learning and development in neural networks: The importance of starting small. *Cognition*, 48, 71–99.

Evers, C. W. 1991 Towards a coherentist theory of validity. In: G. Lakomski (ed.) *Beyond Paradigms: Coherentism and Holism in Educational Research, International Journal of Educational Research*, Special Issue, 15(6), 521–535.

Evers, C. W. and Lakomski, G. 1996 *Exploring Educational Administration*. Elsevier, Oxford.

Evers, C. W. and Lakomski, G. 1991 *Knowing Educational Administration*. Elsevier, Oxford.

Fetzer, J. H. 1996 *Philosophy and Cognitive Science*. Paragon House, New York.

Greeno, J. G. 1997 On claims that answer the wrong questions, *Educational Researcher*, 26(1), 5–17.

Greeno, J. G. and Moore, J. L. 1993 Situativity and symbols: Response to Vera and Simon, *Cognitive Science*, 17, 49–59.

Haugeland, J. 1985 *Artificial Intelligence: The Very Idea*. The M.I.T. Press, Cambridge, MA.

Hastie, R. and Pennington, N. 1991 Cognitive and social processes in decision making. In: L. B. Resnick, J. L. Levine and S. D. Teasley (eds.) *Perspectives on Socially Shared Cognition*. American Psychological Association, Washington, DC.

Hutchins, E. 1996 *Cognition in the Wild*. The M.I.T. Press, Cambridge, MA.

Hutchins, E. 1991 The social organization of distributed cognition. In: L. B. Resnick, J. L. Levine and S. D. Teasley (eds.) *Perspectives on Socially Shared Cognition*. American Psychological Association, Washington, DC.

Johnson-Laird, P. N. 1983 *Mental Models*. Harvard University Press, Cambridge, MA.

Lakomski, G. (ed.) 1991 *Beyond Paradigms: Coherentism and Holism in Educational Research, International Journal of Educational Research*, Special Issue, 15(6), 499–597.

Lave, J. 1988 *Cognition in Practice*. Cambridge University Press, Cambridge.

Lave, J. and Wenger, E. 1991 *Situated Learning*. Cambridge University Press, Cambridge.

Lave, J. 1991 Situating learning in communities of practice. In: L. B. Resnick, J. L. Levine and S. D. Teasley (eds.) *Perspectives on Socially Shared Cognition*. American Psychological Association, Washington, DC.

Levine, J. M. and Moreland, R. L. 1991 Culture and socialization in work groups. In: L. B. Resnick, J. L. Levine and S. D. Teasley (eds.) *Perspectives on Socially Shared Cognition*. American Psychological Association, Washington, DC.

Lycan, W. G. (ed.) 1990 *Mind and Cognition, A Reader*. Blackwell, Oxford.

Newell, A. and Simon, H. A. 1976 Computer science as empirical enquiry: symbols and search. In: M. A. Boden (ed.) 1990 *The Philosophy of Artificial Intelligence*. Oxford University Press, Oxford.

Newell, A. and Simon, H. A. 1972 *Human Problem Solving*. Prentice-Hall, Englewood Cliffs, N.J.

Newell, A., Rosenbloom, P. S. and Laird, J. E. 1996 Symbolic architectures for cognition. In: M. I. Posner (ed.) *Foundations of Cognitive Science*. The M.I.T. Press, Cambridge, MA.

Norman, D. A. 1993 Cognition in the head and in the world: an introduction to the special issue on situated action. *Cognitive Science*, 17, 1–6.

Packer, M. J. and Winne, P. H. 1994 The place of cognition in explanations of teaching: A dialog of interpretative and cognitive approaches, *Teaching and Teacher Education*, 1–21.

Posner, M. I. (ed.) 1996 *Foundations of Cognitive Science*. The M.I.T. Press, Cambridge, MA.

Resnick, L. B., Levine, J. M. and Teasley, S. D. (eds) 1991 *Perspectives on Socially Shared Cognition*. American Psychological Association, Washington, DC.

Rogoff, B. and Lave, J. (eds.) 1984 *Everyday Cognition: Its Development in Social Context*. Harvard University Press, Cambridge, MA.

Rumelhart, D. E. and McClelland, J. L. (eds.) 1986 *Parallel Distributed Processing*. Volumes I & II. The M.I.T. Press, Cambridge, MA.

Scribner, S. 1984 Studying working intelligence. In: B. Rogoff and J. Lave (eds.) *Everyday Cognition: Its Development in Social Context*. Harvard University Press, Cambridge, MA.

Shulman, L. S. 1987 Knowledge and teaching: Foundations of the new reform, *Harvard Educational Review* 57(1), 1–22.

Simon, H. A. 1990 Invariants of human behavior, *Annual Review of Psychology*, 41, 1–19.

Simon, H. A. 1979 *The Sciences of the Artificial*. The M.I.T. Press, Cambridge, MA, 2nd edition.

Smolensky, P. 1988 On the proper treatment of connectionism. In: D. J. Cole *et al.* (eds.) *Philosophy, Mind, and Cognitive Inquiry*. Kluwer, Netherlands.

Tienson, J. L. 1990 An introduction to connectionism. In: J. L. Garfield (ed.) *Foundations of Cognitive Science: The Essential Readings*. Paragon House, New York.

Vera, A.H. and Simon, H. A. 1993a Situated action: a symbolic interpretation. *Cognitive Science*, 17, 7–48.

Vera, A. H. and Simon, H. A. 1993b Situated action: Reply to William Clancey, *Cognitive Science*, 17, 117–133.

Vera, A. H. and Simon, H. A. 1993c Situated action: Reply to Reviewers, *Cognitive Science*, 17, 77–86.

Name index

The Name Index has been compiled so that the reader can proceed directly to the page where an author's work is cited, or to the reference itself in the bibliography. For each name, the page numbers for the bibliographic section are given first, followed by the page number(s) in parentheses where that reference is cited in text. Where a name is referred to only in text, and not in the bibliography, the page number appears only in parentheses.

Subject index